American Film and Society since 1945

American Film and Society since 1945

Fifth Edition

LEONARD QUART
and
ALBERT AUSTER

 PRAEGER™

An Imprint of ABC-CLIO, LLC
Santa Barbara, California • Denver, Colorado

Library of Congress Cataloging-in-Publication Data

Names: Quart, Leonard, author. | Auster, Albert, author.
Title: American film and society since 1945 / Leonard Quart and Albert Auster.
Description: Fifth edition. | Santa Barbara, California : Praeger, an imprint of
    ABC-CLIO, LLC, [2018] | Includes bibliographical references and index
Identifiers: LCCN 2018000836 (print) | LCCN 2018007934 (ebook) |
    ISBN 9781440859458 (pbk.) | ISBN 9781440833212 (alk. paper) |
    ISBN 9781440833229 (ebook)
Subjects: LCSH: Motion pictures—Social aspects—United States. | Motion
    pictures—United States—History—20th century.
Classification: LCC PN1995.9.S6 (ebook) | LCC PN1995.9.S6 Q37 2018 (print) |
    DDC 302.23/43/0973—dc23
LC record available at https://lccn.loc.gov/2018000836

ISBN: 978-1-4408-3321-2 (print)
       978-1-4408-5945-8 (pbk.)
       978-1-4408-3322-9 (ebook)

22   21   20   19   18   1   2   3   4   5

This book is also available as an eBook.

Praeger
An Imprint of ABC-CLIO, LLC

ABC-CLIO, LLC
130 Cremona Drive, P.O. Box 1911
Santa Barbara, California 93116–1911
www.abc-clio.com

This book is printed on acid-free paper ∞

Manufactured in the United States of America

To my late parents
Meyer and Luba Quart
and to my wife Barbara

To my late parents
Lazar and Mollie Auster
and to my wife
Susan Hamovitch

CONTENTS

PREFACE TO THE FIFTH EDITION

Our aim in writing a fifth edition of *American Film and Society since 1945* was to expand and update the original and the previous editions, which were published in 1984, 1991, 2002, and 2011. The fifth edition adheres to the structure and critical premises of the other four.

The most significant change was the updating of the book to include a lengthy chapter on film in the second decade of the 21st century. The book will encompass among other subjects: an analysis of Obama, the man and his policies; Hillary Clinton's stunning defeat by Donald J. Trump; the state of the economy slowly recovering from 2008's devastating recession; and the rise and fall of the Arab Spring and the growth of Islamist terrorism. In addition, we explore the state of the film industry, including its facing competition from cable television's high-quality series, and the continuing development of technologies like Netflix and Hulu that stream films making it harder to attract film audiences. Most importantly, we place a great deal of emphasis on one problem that has haunted Hollywood for decades—the issue of diversity.

In order to do this, much of the chapter analyzes films dealing with Afro-American history and life like *12 Years a Slave* and *Moonlight*, with LGBTQ life like *The Kids Are All Right*, films like *Wonder Woman* depicting the comic book heroine who becomes a superhero, and others that assert the capacity and power of ordinary women like *Joy*. However, we also analyze brilliant political films like *Lincoln*, controversial Iraq films like *American Sniper*, and a film dealing with the roots of the 2008 recession, *The Big Short*.

We conclude the chapter with two films, *The Social Network* and *Steve Jobs* dealing with two titans of the revolution in communication and information—Mark Zuckerberg and Steve Jobs. That revolution—the transformation in digital technology and one of its major sectors, social media—is one of the most dynamic sources of change in the lives of people on a day-to-day basis in this century.

Ultimately, we see this book as providing students, teachers, and the general public an accessible, cogent, critically incisive, and synthetic approach to American film. We hope it succeeds.

ACKNOWLEDGMENTS

Though we often consider the act of writing a solitary one, there are people whose help has been invaluable in completing this edition of the book. Al Auster wishes to acknowledge the love, support, and creative inspiration of his wife Susan Hamovitch. Leonard Quart wishes to acknowledge his wife Barbara, whose love has always sustained him as a writer, helping make him a better one than he ever thought he could be. Finally, a special note of thanks to Chris Brookeman, who helped launch the first edition of this book many years ago.

1

INTRODUCTION

From shadows and symbols into the truth.
—John Henry, Cardinal Newman

In 1981, John Huston's almost legendary World War II documentary about psychologically crippled veterans, *Let There Be Light* (1945), received its first commercial public showing, 35 years after it was produced. Originally suppressed by the U.S. Defense Department, which feared its possible pacifistic influence, interest in it was kept alive by film critics—most notably James Agee, who even included it on his best films list of 1946. Unfortunately, time had not dealt too well with *Let There Be Light*, and most contemporary film critics found it ingenuous and naive to the point of simplemindedness.[1]

Despite the fact that *Let There Be Light* failed to live up to its critical reputation, it succeeded on another level. In fact, the showing of the film might be compared to lifting the lid on a time capsule—one that provided a clear insight into an era's cultural and social perspective and mood. By contemporary standards, a film that adheres to *Let There Be Light*'s magical faith in the healing power of psychiatrists and Freudianism would be seen as innocent and overly sanguine. It's a vision of the human condition that would hardly be emulated by today's more cynical (albeit no more sophisticated) films. *Let There Be Light* may have left modern critics unimpressed with its moving portrayal of the plight of shell-shocked soldiers, but it does serve as a useful conduit to help understand the intellectual assumptions of the postwar period.

It is hardly an original point, though it bears repeating, that films have the ability to evoke the mood and tone of a society in a particular era. However, there was a time when a number of historians and social scientists were hesitant about accepting this truism. By films, one means not merely documentaries, which obviously directly capture something of the reality of people's lives and feelings, but also mainstream Hollywood commercial films. It is not only that these films sometimes convey and imitate the surfaces of day-to-day life, the way people talk, dress, and consume—though social realism is clearly not an aesthetic that Hollywood usually embraces or has seen as commercially viable. But, more important, fictional films reveal something of the dreams, desires, displacements, and, in some cases, the social and political issues that confront American society.

Undeniably, films are a powerful and significant art form. As art historian and critic Erwin Panofsky has suggested, their absence from our lives would probably constitute a "social catastrophe."[2] He wrote, "If all the serious lyric poets, composers, painters and sculptors were forced by law to stop their activities, a rather small fraction of the general public would seriously regret it. If the same thing were to happen with the movies the social consequences would be catastrophic."[3] That sentiment obviously is somewhat hyperbolic, but films shown in theaters, on television, and on DVDs are clearly one of the prime forms of entertainment for the general public and one of the most democratic and accessible elements in the cultural fabric.

That films give a great deal of pleasure to a great many people does not necessarily connote that they are a significant form of cultural and historical evidence. But the fact that they reach a mass audience signifies that films do connect with some part of the conscious or unconscious experience of the general public or, at least, a large proportion of it. However, the attempt to define the specific relation of Hollywood film to popular consciousness is a difficult one. One problem is that the writers and directors of films—be they assembly-line products like *Risky Business* (1983) or works expressing a complex individual sensibility like Martin Scorsese's *Taxi Driver* (1976)—have no mystical access to the zeitgeist. There are no straight, clear lines to be drawn between the film industry and the popular mind—neither is it a mirror of public feelings and habits, nor can one make the vulgar, mechanistic connection that implies that the industry is some evil empire conspiratorially shaping the social values and political opinions of a supine public. However, there is no question that Hollywood's genius for manufacturing and publicizing seductive images like John Wayne's World War II heroes—icons who had a profound effect on the lives of countless young Vietnam enlistees—should not be minimized, the images often becoming a substitute for reality for their audiences.

The popular mind itself is no monolith. It is divided by age, social class, gender, region, ethnicity, and race and often fickle and changeable in its response to films. In a matter of four or five years, during the late 1960s and early 1970s, the movie audience shifted from the sympathy to social outlawry of *Bonnie and Clyde* (1967) to the law and order vigilantism of *Dirty Harry* (1971), and it's doubtful that that shift corresponded with some radical transformation of popular feeling. Still, it's possible that during that period, both responses toward crime coexisted in American society and that the films tapped different audiences. It's also hard to be certain why a film achieves popular success. For example, was the success of *Rambo* based on its political significance—its voicing populist, patriotic, and anticommunist sentiments—or because of Stallone's muscle-headed charisma and the film's nonstop action and violence? The answer is that it is probably a combination of all these elements that helped garner a large audience for the films. And it's truly difficult to distinguish which aspects of the film were the basis of its audience appeal.

All one can say with certainty is that American directors, like Altman, Coppola, and Gus Van Sant, most of whose films express powerful personal visions and styles, share some of the same dreams and cultural tensions and influences other Americans do. Consequently, films like *Nashville* (1975) and *Godfather I* and *II* (1972 and 1974) cannot help but convey some of the cultural and social strains the directors hold in common with their audience. And for the rest of Hollywood's output—films that are much less personal in nature—the movie industry spends a great deal of time and money trying to divine popular values and trends, often succeeding in attracting an audience by knowing just how to package those concerns. For example, some of the biggest commercial hits of the summer of 1989 were films like *Field of Dreams*, which constructed a mythic American past by nostalgically conjuring up the Chicago Black Sox of 1919 playing on a pristine and bucolic baseball diamond, and the well-crafted sitcom *Parenthood*, which views the family as the foundation of American life and consecrates the act of having babies as if family planning never existed. Both of these films lure audiences by shutting out much of the larger social world and being awash with nostalgia for an earlier America. Clearly, film images rarely determine our values, but they are both suggestive signs of and reinforcers of popular feelings.

During the past 30 years, a number of historians and culture critics have begun to give films their due as important social and cultural evidence. Among the noteworthy ones are *History/American Film* edited by Jackson and O'Connor, *Movie-Made America* by Robert Sklar, *We're in the Money* by Andrew Bergman, *Film: The Democratic Art* by Garth Jowett, *America in the Movies* by Michael Wood, *From Reverence to Rape* by Molly Haskell, *A Certain*

Tendency of the Hollywood Cinema, 1930–1980 by Robert B. Ray, *Camera Politica* by Michael Ryan and Douglas Kellner, and *Pictures at a Revolution: Five Movies and the Birth of the New Hollywood* by Mark Harris. In fact, the pendulum may have swung so far that, for a number of historians, films have come to be one of the most important clues to understanding the state of the American mind. As Arthur Schlesinger Jr. has said, albeit in an inflated manner,

> Strike the American contribution from drama, painting, music, sculpture and even dance, and possibly poetry and the novel and the world's achievement is only marginally diminished. But the film without American contribution is unimaginable. The fact that film has been the most potent vehicle for the American imagination suggests all the more strongly that movies have something to tell us not just about the surfaces but the mysteries of American life.[4]

Of course, stating this is much easier than defining precisely how we can penetrate those surfaces and reveal those mysteries. Obviously, the political and social significance of explicitly political films, ranging from Polonsky's Marxist, film noir *Force of Evil* (1948) to Kubrick's sardonic and apocalyptic *Dr. Strangelove* (1964) through Oliver Stone's mixture of social realism and Manichaean melodrama in *Platoon* (1986), can easily be gleaned, though, again, the relation of the political and social perspectives of even these films to the public's social and cultural beliefs is never a seamless one.

All films, however, can be considered political, for films as varied as *On the Town* (1949) and *Avatar* (2009) convey a point of view, an implicit ideological perspective, on the nature of American reality. Of course, it is more difficult to discover cultural and social meaning in ostensibly nonpolitical and apolitical films like Tourneur's *Out of the Past* (1947) and Spielberg's *E.T.* (1982). These two works, like the great majority of American films, rarely attempt to consciously illuminate cultural and social patterns. They usually stylize, mythologize, and at times trivialize the social world—primarily aiming to provide glamour, escape, thrills, or a sense of emotional security to a mass audience. That these films, both the explicitly political and the nonpolitical, were and are often bound by institutional forces like the power of the studios or producers to make final cuts, genre conventions, collective screenwriting and rewriting, censorship, and the star system, provides one more difficulty in gleaning the social and cultural perspective of the films, the film's original intent being blurred by the number of people and industry controls that go into shaping the final product, inadvertently creating conflicted texts in some films. Given all these variables, the effort to explore the link between these films and the basic premises, values, and problems of American society must be by its very nature tentative and touched with ambiguity. There are no absolutes or certainties that underlie this relationship, and there are few films whose social meaning is not open to contesting and contradictory interpretations.

In the act, however, of either displacing or stylizing social reality, Hollywood was able to create vital and reverberating images, characters, and dialogue that granted a great deal of insight into the culture. It succeeded in helping to shape the consciousness of its audience by creating mythic landscapes and urbanscapes—the transcendental West of John Ford's Monument Valley and the magical, neon-lit Broadway of countless musicals—and archetypal figures like the gangster, private eye, and femme fatale. The link between Hollywood and its audience, as stated previously, is a reciprocal one. Frank Capra's humane, harmonious small towns and the New York apartments and nightclubs of 1930s screwball comedies like *Holiday* (1938) and *The Awful Truth* (1937) were distinctive Hollywood creations that had resonance for audiences because they reinforced existing public fantasies and feelings.

The nature of cinematic archetypes and landscapes has changed through the years, but most Hollywood films still follow a set of narrative and stylistic conventions, though in the past three or four decades, a number of major directors have played with and veered from them. The classic Hollywood film was committed to a linear narrative, temporal and spatial coherence, and closure, usually centering around a protagonist the audience could emotionally identify with and through whose actions the narrative would be resolved. Implicitly, this narrative tradition, with its emphasis on the patterned and predictable, usually reinforced the social status quo. The films were also built around either individual heroism or at least the centrality of the individual—a value that Hollywood has embraced since its beginnings. In fact, most American social and political films from *The Best Years of Our Lives* (1946) to *Platoon* of the 1980s define political events in terms of an individual's fate and consciousness. The ideological and political context of Vietnam, for example, is left untouched by *Platoon*, the war being basically conceived as a murderous rite of passage and existential drama that one individual soldier goes through.

Hollywood films have also been firm believers in the American success ethic, almost never questioning the viability and virtue of the country's social and economic system. As a result, films have usually promoted the notion, in a wide variety of genres, that most white males have the ability and opportunity to succeed in America. In recent years, in films like *Working Girl* (1988), some women have been added to the host of Hollywood characters who easily overcome the obstacles of class, ethnicity, gender, and even race (at least for stars like Eddie Murphy and Morgan Freeman) and are able to achieve the American Dream.

Socially subversive and anarchic elements obviously exist in popular American films—like the psychopathic gangster and the detective who breaks all the institutional rules. However, despite their deviant behavior, characters like Cagney's psycho gangster in *White Heat* (1949) or Eastwood's vigilante cop Harry Callahan in *Dirty Harry* don't ultimately disrupt the social status quo. Still, despite the fact that classical Hollywood has usually restored the traditional order of things at the film's conclusion, a great many of its films contain camera setups, snatches of dialogue, elements in the mise-en-scène, and performances that counter the thrust of the narrative and call the conventional world and its values into question. Even amid the familial sweetness of a film like *Meet Me in St. Louis* (1944), there are dark and uneasy images that, for a scene or two, subvert the film's serene vision.

Hollywood, however, has made films that break ideologically from the status quo. In the 1930s, King Vidor's low-budget *Our Daily Bread* (1934) envisioned a collective farm where unemployed people would work communally as an alternative to the harshness of depression poverty and capitalism. But American films that proffer alternative political and social visions are very rare. Films, however, that see the world as dark and murderous—without political or social alternatives—and provide no concluding image of hope or reconciliation are far more common. However, for every film like Stanley Kubrick's *Full Metal Jacket* (1987), a black comic, profoundly pessimistic and genuinely critical vision of the American military and the human condition, there are innumerable *To Live and Die in L.A.*s (1985) with their pop nihilism and gratuitous violence—conventional films that seemingly have merely inverted the classical Hollywood idea of closure and made the bleak, bloody climax their parallel to the happy ending.

Nevertheless, American films can be clearly politically radical and liberal or conservative, nihilistic, ambiguous, confused, and conflicted ideologically, and the analysis of the relationship between them and the society still remains problematic. For example, can one really link *E.T.*'s affirmation of innocence and distrust of adult authority to the nostalgia-drenched, anti–big-government pieties of the early Reagan years? And what does the audience really perceive that film's ideological intent or, more important, a film like Spike Lee's *Do the Right Thing* (1989) to be? However, despite our wariness about coming up with facile generalizations about the connection between film and society, it is as important to explore that relationship as to study the nature of directorial sensibility and style, the range of Hollywood genres, star biographies, and the history of the studios—not that any of these elements are mutually exclusive.

Clearly, any cultural and social analysis of Hollywood films would have to take into account a variety of theoretical and critical approaches. The auteurist critics' origins go back to French critics cum directors like Truffaut, Godard, Rivette, and Chabrol, who wrote for *Cahiers du Cinema* about neglected commercial directors—mostly American—who needed to be explored in depth. They promoted the notion that the basic starting point of film is the personal sensibility, style, and especially the motifs of the director, which give him a "signature"—a coherent worldview—and that the best films are those that most clearly bear the "signature" of their creator.

Though clearly more interested in defending, even glorifying, the aesthetic value of the Hollywood studio films than in exploring their social and political meaning, American auteurist critics like Andrew Sarris (writing in *Film Culture* and *The Village Voice*), who took their lead from the French, did chart how John Ford's vision of family and community had remained constant through such diverse films as *The Grapes of Wrath* (1940), *They Were Expendable* (1945), and *She Wore a Yellow Ribbon* (1949). Auteur critics were, however, in their unsystematic, polemical (in their homages to individual auteurs they overrated their mediocre work and almost never mentioned how powerful a role the studios played in producing these films),[5] sometimes defensive manner, interested primarily in demonstrating how a film's visual style was redolent with meaning. They loved to demonstrate just how the mise-en-scène of a Budd Boetticher B western had much greater aesthetic and even intellectual value than the liberal pieties pervading a Stanley Kramer or Richards Brooks social-problem film. As a result, they were able to redeem and sometimes create the critical reputations of directors such as Howard Hawks, Nicholas Ray, Douglas Sirk, and other much less deserving figures.

In doing that, the auteur critics granted added luster and cultural importance to commercial Hollywood genres like the western, thriller, screwball comedy, and woman's picture. These genres themselves were subject to a body of criticism that explored their themes, structures, and iconography. Genre criticism often traced the shifts in the form's conventions and themes (e.g., the changes in the western from Tom Mix through John Ford to Sam Peckinpah) or examined the relation of the genre to its audience. Most genre critics were more interested in analyzing the films as self-contained forms, dissecting the iconography of the musical rather than evoking its cultural and social significance. However, there were critics such as Robert Warshow and Leo Braudy who sought to analyze the relationship between a genre's popularity and the attitudes and needs that audiences bring to it. For example, Warshow's essay on the gangster film asserting that the vicious, avaricious behavior of the protagonist in films like *Little Caesar* (1930) appealed to that part of the American psyche that rejects official American culture.[6]

There have also been film critics who have directly sought to unravel by using a psychoanalytic interpretation, the hidden social and psychological meaning of a film. A theorist like Siegfried Kracauer believed that films are never merely the product of an individual artist but also a collaborative expression of mass feelings.[7] For instance, his landmark work, *From Caligari to Hitler*, although marred by too heady a faith in German films' ability to reveal the secrets of the collective mind as well as predict the rise of Nazism, still yields interesting insight into film as a means of illuminating the "deepest psychological dispositions"[8] of a society. This, coupled with the Freudian notion that films, like dreams, have a latent and manifest content, has proved of some value in wringing social meaning from even the most escapist of films.

Nonetheless, these perceptions are weakened by the fact that they make the meaning of a film dependent on some kind of unconscious activity. It is impossible to demonstrate how the Jungian "collective unconscious" (even if we accept its existence) or the latent content of Freudianism manifests itself in the narrative and imagery of the film. A critic must maintain an almost mystical faith that it does or, more commonly, see it as mere speculation and feel it unnecessary to prove its existence. But in writing about notions such as the mass unconscious, there is a tendency to graft elaborate meanings onto the most common of films. As a result, the work of art becomes something secondary, even insignificant; what becomes all-important is the analysis and interpretation, or else, as in the words of Paddy Whannel and Stuart Hall, art—in this case film—becomes merely "sugar on the pill."[9]

In the past few decades, a number of theoretical approaches to film, like structuralism and semiology, have held that film is "a system of conventions and codes, a set of structures dictating and circumscribing the ultimate possibilities of any individual film."[10] According to these theoretical perspectives, it's the underlying cultural patterns, not the individual artist, that create meaning in a film. The emphasis in semiology is on sign systems and structuralism—more on broader organizing principles (e.g., the antimony between civilization and the wilderness that runs through the western film) than on the individual artist's vision or the work's aesthetic value or its virtues and weaknesses. As a result, the distinction between high art and popular art and between art and artifact becomes of little or no interest to the critic—all being equally open to structural and semiological analysis.

In the wake of structuralism and semiotics, there has been a stream of diverse theoretical developments that are usually placed under the rubric of deconstruction. Influenced by the writings of Foucault, Lacan, and especially Jacques Derrida, "the most far-reaching consequence of a deconstructive perspective on film concerns the act of interpretation."[11] According to film theorist Peter Brunette,

> Ultimately, deconstruction shows that it is strictly speaking, impossible to spec-
> ify what a "valid" interpretation would look like. In this sense, it might be said
> that deconstruction's most important work has been the investigation of the in-
> stitutions that allow or restrict reading, or meaning-making of any sort.[12]

What deconstructionists questioned were all claims to universal truth—
seeing them "as self-serving deceptions perpetrated by wielders of power."[13]
And most deconstructionists repudiated the idea that a work of art conveys
"meaning, beauty, and authorship"[14]—sometimes ending with an extreme
skeptical perspective where any critical interpretation could be seen as equally
valid. However, during the past 10 years, the contemporary theoretical landscape seems quite fragmented, and there seems no unified theory in the offing.
Some theorists have posited a cognitive approach that derives from neurosci-
ence and doesn't have much continuity or dialogue with the more politicized,
sociological forms of film theory. It goes back to the idea that responses to cinema are near universal and tries to explain how certain filmic conventions
trigger responses in the brain.

Though our book does not embrace semiological, structuralist, and decon-
structionist theoretical perspectives, we are aware that they have at times
given us new ways of seeing the underlying cultural codes inherent in film.
For example, the idea of the camera's gaze in classical Hollywood film as a
male one—that sees women as objects of voyeuristic pleasure (modified since
then by its author, Laura Mulvey)—alters one's way of thinking about familiar films. If, on the one hand, however, modernist and postmodernist theory
leads to fresh insights into the role that culture plays in shaping films, then,
on the other, it remains abstracted from the particularity of the individual
film and its historical context. In their attempt to get the respect of the hard
sciences, the postmodernist theorists have constructed a specialized and ob-
fuscating vocabulary of their own (e.g., words like "valorizing" and "multiva-
lent"). In addition, in their contempt for subjectivity (despite their deriding
any claims to objective knowledge), the contemporary theorist often tends
to be removed from the concrete act of viewing a film—an emotional experience that makes one see how often the complex texture of a film undermines
those structures and theories that have become the lifeblood and ultimate
trap of academic film study.

In writing this book, however, we have been influenced by genre, auteur,
feminist, psychoanalytic, Marxist, structuralist, multicultural, poststructural-
ist, and other critical perspectives but are not wedded to any one critical system. Our aim is to depict and evaluate, both politically and aesthetically,
the way American films convey their social and cultural values and commitments. Given our belief in film's historical and social significance, it is the

particular purpose of this study to look at American films from 1945 to the present and analyze how they perceived and conjured up the American social and cultural landscape. In addition, we have included a brief rendering of some of the major political events and social and cultural trends that dominated a decade and left a mark on its films.

To accomplish this, our method is a simple one. For one thing, since American screens—and a large percentage of foreign ones as well—are dominated by Hollywood films, we have treated Hollywood and American film as being synonymous. And for the purpose of this study, we have left out a discussion of avant-garde and most documentary films. We are also aware of the hazards of adopting a decade-by-decade approach, for clearly the culture and politics of the 1960s did not end on December 31, 1969—and the Cold War and the anticommunist crusade were not limited to one decade. The general tone, concerns, and beliefs of one decade often overlap into the following one. Despite the somewhat arbitrary nature of our book's structure, it has the advantage of convenience and popular acceptance—references to decades like the 1950s and 1960s continue to denote a particular set of social and cultural norms and patterns.

One serious difficulty in writing the book was making a selection of films that best illuminated these trends. In order to accomplish this, we have relied in the main on a large body of films that could be called "public classics"[15]— films whose box office grosses awards and critical reputation (which have either stood the test of time or grown with it) indicate, by their broad acceptance, that they have a connection with the popular consciousness. Undoubtedly, there are many other films that might point in different directions or deal with the themes we have analyzed in a clearer, sharper manner or that were perhaps visionary in their ability to herald future trends and themes. Nevertheless, it does seem to us that some degree of consensus exists about the importance of specific films and their relation to the society of their times, such as films like *The Best Years of Our Lives* and the 1940s, *Rebel Without a Cause* and the 1950s, *Bonnie and Clyde* and *Easy Rider* and the 1960s, *Nashville* in the 1970s, *Do the Right Thing* in the 1980s, *Philadelphia* in the 1990s, and *The Hurt Locker* and *Up in the Air* in the first decade of the 21st century. We have included in our study a number of films of this type. In addition, since this book was intended as both an introduction and a guide to American film and culture for students, we have tried to include films that are accessible to them through DVD, online, and by mail rental services, video stores, and available archives, although this was by no means the decisive factor in our choice.

Finally, as far as the theme of this study goes, it is important to return for a moment to *Let There Be Light*. When that film is placed alongside some films of the 1970s dealing with similar problems and themes like *The Deer Hunter* and *Coming Home* (1978) and a documentary like *Hearts and Minds* (1974), one cannot help but see what a different portrait the 1970s films provide of American life and how that image has radically changed over time. In *Let There Be Light*, for example, the officer informs (without irony) the just-discharged patients, "On your shoulders falls much of the responsibility for the postwar world." It is the sort of uplifting sentiment that traumatized Vietnam War veterans, like Nicky (*The Deer Hunter*) and Bob (*Coming Home*), would greet with the stony stare of suicidal despair. Throughout the book, we have attempted to show how American films moved from the relatively self-confident affirmation of the American Dream in the late 1940s (Hollywood at its zenith) to the films of the 1960s and 1970s and even the politically retrograde and nostalgic Reagan 1980s, where, despite the continued emphasis on big budgets, stars, and genre formulae, the films in general grew increasingly more anxious, alienated, and nihilistic. (One trend that makes one feel hopeful is that by the end of the 1990s and into the first decade of the 21st century, despite all the high-concept, big-budget films like *Independence Day* [1996], the *Mission Impossibles* and *Batmans*, and *Avatar* [2009], there seemed to be a great deal more room in theaters for low-budget and idiosyncratic films.) In constructing this pattern, we have tried to avoid subsuming the contested meanings of individual films and the often-contradictory history of cinematic cultural trends under reductive and rigid sociological categories. We have been conscious of the feelings of doubt and loss that began to appear beneath the buoyant surface of 1940s films and the preservation of American dream imagery in the darker, more pessimistic work of the 1960s, 1970s, 1980s, and 1990s and into the first decade of the 21st century.

Ultimately, what we have written is only one more step in the ongoing and complex study of the multiple and diverse interactions of culture and society and, more specifically, film and society. We have not conceived this book as a definitive work but rather as one among a number of possible ways that help illuminate the nature of American society and culture. The book is based on the anachronistic idea that a passion for and a personal commitment to the imaginative life of films can be an integral part of the critical process and that the critique can be conveyed in a language that any intelligent person who cares about film can understand. It is best summed up in the humanist perspective of Raymond Williams, which holds that art is a means to "learn, describe, to understand, to educate"[16]—a way of heightening one's perception of self, others, the larger social and political world, and the human condition itself. To that list, we would add that the capacity of film to grant aesthetic pleasure in the contemplation of camera movement, composition, editing, color, sound, and other formal elements is as significant as any other end. We finally believe, as did James Agee on writing his first film review in *The Nation*, that the final function of any review or critical study is to aid those "who watch any given screen, where the proof is caught irrelevant to excuse, and available in proportion to the eye which sees it, and the mind which uses it."[17]

NOTES

1. Andrew Sarris, "Hobgoblins of Reality," *The Village Voice* (January 21–27, 1981), p. 45.

2. Erwin Panofsky, "Style and Medium in the Motion Pictures," in G. Mast and M. Cohen (eds.), *Film Theory and Criticism* (New York: Oxford University Press, 1974), p. 152.

3. Ibid.

4. John E. O'Connor and Martin A. Jackson (eds.), *American History/American Film: Interpreting the Hollywood Image* (New York: Frederick Ungar, 1979), p. x.

5. Thomas Schatz, *The Genius of the System: Hollywood Filmmaking in the Studio Era* (New York: Pantheon, 1988), pp. 3–12.

6. Robert Warshow, *The Immediate Experience* (Garden City, NY: Anchor, 1964).

7. Tim Bywater and Thomas Sobchack, *Film Criticism: Major Critical Approaches to Narrative Film* (White Plains, NY: Longman, 1989), p. 121.

8. Siegfried Kracauer, *From Caligari to Hitler: A Psychological History of the German Film*, 3rd ed. (Princeton, NJ: Princeton University Press, 1970), p. 6.

9. Stuart Hall and Paddy Whannel, *The Popular Arts* (New York: Pantheon, 1965), p. 28.

10. Bywater and Sobchack, *Film Criticism*, p. 175.

11. Peter Brunette, "Post-Structuralism and Deconstruction," in *Film Studies: Critical Approaches* (Oxford: Oxford University Press, 2000), p. 92.

12. Ibid., pp. 92–93.

13. Andrew Delbanco, "The Decline and Fall of Literature," *New York Review of Books* (November 4, 1999), p. 36.

14. Ibid.

15. Michael Wood, *America in the Movies; or, "Santa Maria, It Had Slipped My Mind!"* (New York: Basic Books, 1975), p. 11.

16. Raymond Williams, *Communications*, 3rd ed. (London: Pelican, 1976), p. 11.

17. James Agee, *Agee on Film: Reviews and Comments* (Boston: Beacon Press, 1966), p. 23.

2

THE 1940s

In 1936, President Franklin D. Roosevelt announced that Americans had a "rendezvous with destiny." The war years turned that prophecy into a reality as America emerged from its traditional isolationism and became an imperialist, interventionist nation—the most powerful nation in the world. The political energy that had once gone into the struggle against the Depression was now concentrated on the war effort. And that undertaking granted to many people on the home front a sense of purpose, exhilaration, and community that was rare in American history.[1]

The same energy and optimism that helped bring about victory carried over into the postwar years. However, this optimism had more to do with people's material well-being (in the 1940s the average American enjoyed an income 15 times greater than the average foreigner)[2] and national pride than with any new political and social commitments. In fact, most Americans had become weary of the long years of economic depression and foreign wars and, in general, bored with politics. Constricted by the enforced savings of World War II, Americans wanted to enjoy their newfound prosperity and victory. A new era seemed about to open, offering ordinary Americans not only increased income but also a chance for education and greater social and economic status.

One of the driving forces behind this new mood was the GI Bill of Rights, which became law in 1944, helping returning veterans to borrow money to set up businesses and attend universities that they had once viewed as preserves of the upper-middle class. In addition, a baby boom gave evidence that

Americans felt freed from the social anguish of the past decade and a half and had begun to feel that the future held infinite promise.[3]

Another key factor in this changing climate was the accession to the presidency, upon the death of Roosevelt in 1945, of Vice President Harry S. Truman, who was a moderate, Democratic Party organization stalwart from Missouri. At first, Truman's presidency suffered by comparison with the charismatic Roosevelt. In addition, he was beset by a resurgent conservative congressional coalition of southern Democrats (Dixiecrats) and Republicans, who frustrated his attempts to extend the New Deal and forced him to watch helplessly as they overrode his veto of the antilabor Taft-Hartley bill in 1947. However, even when he came into his own, after a startling come-from-behind victory in the presidential campaign of 1948, he merely introduced a Fair Deal program that was only a pale copy and codification of the New Deal. Thus, despite his political triumph, the Truman era was dominated by the profits and developing prestige and power of the corporations rather than by the forces of social reform.[4]

Nevertheless, although feelings of both material abundance and the irrelevance of social conflict were prime cultural themes of the 1940s, there were darker signs. A crippling strike wave, culminating in a coal strike led by Roosevelt's nemesis John L. Lewis, served notice that labor was no longer willing to continue its rather unequal collaboration with business and wanted a larger share of the wealth generated by the war. The labor insurgency, coupled with high inflation, caused ripples of anxiety in the economy. Equally significant, though largely beneath the surface, were a pair of major demographic changes. One was the great migration of poor blacks to the North to work in defense plants during World War II where they exchanged the certainties and oppression of southern rural life for the anxieties and higher wages of the northern cities. Paralleling this black migration was the movement of whites (aided by low-interest Federal Housing Administration and Veterans' Administration loans) to the suburbs. Hand in hand, the twin migrations would alter the entire social fabric of America.[5]

However severe these labor problems and demographic changes were, they were merely minor irritants compared to the turmoil caused by foreign affairs. Long used to neglecting foreign relationships, the Americans were thrust by the war into a leading international position. It also moved the United States into an alliance with the Soviet Union—a nation considered in some prewar American circles as a greater menace than Germany, Italy, or Japan. Nonetheless, most Americans were little disturbed by the wartime alliance with the Soviet Union. In fact, many liberals saw that alliance (with the Soviet Union as the junior partner) as the basis of an enduring peace where postwar social reforms would become the prime commitment of both nations. Yet among conservatives there were always undercurrents of suspicion of the Soviet Union and the U.S.-Soviet alliance. And when Stalin, in quest of greater security, broke the 1945 Yalta agreements, conservative unease and anger toward the Soviet Union increased, a wariness that many liberals soon began to share.[6]

During the next few years, despite the dream of a new international order embodied in the United Nations, the Cold War (as it came to be known) escalated and relations between the United States and the Soviet Union were permeated with fear, suspicion, and distrust. As a result, the two ideologically expansionist powers, their wartime cooperation seemingly forgotten, confronted each other with neither side genuinely seeking peace or rapprochement. On their side the Americans continually evoked images of an "iron curtain" and the threat of Soviet expansion, while the Russians talked of "American imperialism" and the constant threat to their borders and security.[7]

The conflict was not solely confined to rhetoric. In 1947, breaking with a long-standing American tradition against peacetime military and political alliances, President Truman gained congressional approval for $400 million in military and economic aid to Greece and Turkey to help them in their struggle against communist guerrillas. This action, soon to be dubbed the Truman Doctrine, had broader implications—including the seeds for later American interventions—for, in the words of Truman, America was now committed "to support free people who are resisting attempted subjugation by armed minorities or by outside pressure."[8]

The crisis between the two former allies deepened as a Soviet-sponsored coup in Czechoslovakia in 1948 eliminated the last vestiges of democracy in eastern and central Europe, and the Marshall Plan and the North Atlantic Treaty Organization established an American-backed cordon sanitaire in western Europe. The cordon sanitaire was worked out by diplomat-scholar George F. Kennan and his State Department policy planning group and given political sponsorship by Secretary of State George C. Marshall, reasoning that an anticommunist foreign policy was not enough to impede the spread of communism in Europe. They believed that it was only with the recovery of the European economy (one that would also provide markets for the United States) that the Soviet threat could be thwarted. Indeed with the passage of the Marshall Plan in 1948 western Europe took a giant step toward economic recovery and enhanced its capacity to resist communism.[9]

However, even with western Europe stabilized by 1949, American anxieties about communism hardly lessened. The fear of communist aggression from abroad was soon replaced by terror over a native communist fifth column whose task was seemingly to ferret out military secrets as they subverted

America's will to resist. These feelings were reinforced by a succession of spy ring revelations—Igor Gouzenko, Judith Coplon, Elizabeth Bentley, and Whittaker Chambers. The explosion of a Soviet atomic bomb, coupled with the fall of mainland China to the communists, transformed these fears into a full-fledged anticommunist hysteria. Angered by their sense of a growing visible and invisible communist menace and becoming anxious over their own survival, Americans sought facile explanations for what they saw as an imminent threat. Rather than confront the long-term economic and social causes that produced both wars of "national liberation" and communist takeovers (at the time they were neatly equated), Americans found the reasons for the success of the left in a supposed international communist conspiracy.[10]

In the vanguard of this search for traitors was the House Un-American Activities Committee (HUAC). Dormant during the war years, the committee saw its chance to regain the limelight in 1947 when it held hearings investigating communist influence in the motion picture industry. Drawn by the prestige and glamour of the film industry, the committee was more interested in the political affiliations of its 10 "unfriendly" witnesses—some of whom were the most talented and politically active writers and directors in Hollywood (e.g., Dalton Trumbo, Albert Maltz, and Ring Lardner Jr.)—than in the supposedly subversive content of their films.[11]

At first the moguls and liberals in the industry protested about the committee's actions, but seeing the witnesses take the first amendment regarding their politics, they quickly succumbed to expediency, fearing that their profits and careers might be threatened. In a meeting at the Waldorf-Astoria Hotel soon after the 10 witnesses appeared before the committee, the moguls issued their craven Waldorf Statement, which was in essence a tacit agreement to establish a blacklist refusing to either reemploy the "Hollywood Ten" or other members of the Communist Party.[12]

Of course the HUAC investigations of Hollywood were just one element of the growing fear of and attack on the presumed communist conspiracy. In 1949 the leaders of the U.S. Communist Party were convicted under the Smith Act for conspiracy and sent to prison. More significantly, the deeply symbolic Hiss-Chambers affair, which saw the former high-level New Deal bureaucrat Alger Hiss accused of espionage and convicted of perjury, brought the New Deal under attack for being soft on communism. The 1940s concluded with a portion of the American public, dominated by midwesterners, recent immigrants, and Catholics, holding that New Deal liberalism and communism were one and the same thing.[13]

Nevertheless, despite the growing fear of the "red menace," the 1940s were still essentially a time of optimism and consensus, and nowhere was this more evident than in American film. For although they had a dark side touched with pessimism and self-doubt, the movies basically endorsed and reflected a feeling of national triumph. Moreover, for the industry itself the postwar era was a bloom time. From 1942 to 1944, Hollywood produced about 440 films a year, and 1946 was the most commercially successful year in its history. The 1940s were a time of big stars and big audiences where the studios, with their armies of talented technicians and performers, reigned supreme. The last years of the decade did see Hollywood beset by labor troubles, adverse Supreme Court decisions (the *Paramount* case), and the aftereffects of the HUAC hearings—leading to the blacklisting of a large number of major creative contributors to the industry. But the forties were still "the last great show of confidence and skill" by Hollywood before it became paralyzed by competition from television and the death of the studio system.[14]

Nowhere was this optimism more evident than in the war films that the studios churned out through the war years. The overriding purpose of these films was patriotic uplift, and despite the fact that an occasional hero lapsed into *Casablanca*-like (1942) cynicism or malaise, they were all eventually aroused to a commitment to the collective struggle against fascism. With Hollywood helping to shoulder the wartime burden of maintaining morale, there were few films that dealt with the reality rather than the romance of combat or with the psychological effects of the war. Those that did, like John Huston's pacifistic documentary *Battle of San Pietro* (1945), which evoked haunting and harrowing images of the war with great immediacy and intensity, were prevented by the Pentagon from reaching the public. Neither the Pentagon nor Hollywood wanted films that filled the screens with images of exhausted soldiers, cemeteries of dog tags, and terrified peasants. They desired war films that exulted in America by creating mythical—ethnically, regionally, and occupationally heterogeneous—platoons to personify American democracy.

By the end of the war, however, with victory clearly in sight, self-righteous propagandistic films like *God Is My Co-Pilot* (1943) and *The Purple Heart* (1944) were replaced by more sophisticated and realistic films. Among the first of these was Lewis Milestone's *A Walk in the Sun* (1945), which provides a realistic treatment, through its subtle and moving use of close-ups and light and shadow, of an infantry unit's battle fear and anxiety. The soldiers are fallible human beings, not Hollywood heroes, though the film still contains the usual sentimentalized melting pot of "dogfaces" who engage in tiresome, colloquial banter and even go in for self-conscious interior monologues. But if *Walk in the Sun* indulges in antifascist and pseudodemocratic (Popular Front) clichés and rhetoric about the "mighty Joes" and the people's folksy wisdom and capacity for artistic feeling, its images of long lines of soldiers walking in the darkness are vivid and poignant. And its generally unromantic treatment of a war where men become frightened and die placed it far above the run-of-the-mill war films with their bloodthirsty and barbaric "Nips" and "Krauts" being put to route by the derring-do of an Errol Flynn or John Wayne.

William Wellman's *The Story of G.I. Joe* (1945) was a much leaner and more solemn film than *A Walk in the Sun*. Based on Ernie Pyle's Pulitzer Prize–winning dispatches, this dry, understated, quasi-documentary work avoids almost all the inflated political rhetoric, histrionics, and stereotyping that characterized most other World War II films. The film is constructed, without a driving narrative to propel it, as a series of abruptly terminated scenes that powerfully capture the pathos and tragedy of the war. Wellman's infantrymen are not clean shaven or well fed, and the war takes a palpable toll—all the men are exhausted by the day-to-day slogging and fighting; a tough sergeant, obsessed with home and his son's voice, has a breakdown; and the strong, quietly dignified captain of the platoon, Bill Walker (Robert Mitchum), who is a towering figure, dies. Watching this film, James Agee was sufficiently moved to compare it, especially its final, somber, dark moments, to a Whitmanesque war poem.[15]

In a far different mode was John Ford's romantic and leisurely *They Were Expendable* (1945). Ford's film displayed little interest in the psychology or sociology of his PT boat officers and crew but was deeply committed to paying homage to a community of men who were portrayed as gallant and heroic in defeat. The film was filled with epic long shots of almost painterly sea battles and of the men's ritualistic arrivals from and departures into battle. Ford believed in the virtues of the military, conceiving it as a community built on a hierarchic code of power, self-sacrifice, responsibility, and obligation. The film's officers are viewed as heroes, men free of any fear or anxiety about the war, best illustrated by the impetuous, tough Captain Rusty Ryan (John Wayne), who is unwilling to allow mere wounds to prevent him from going into battle. They also understand that leadership demands that they subordinate individual desires for the good of the squadron—to become "team players."

Ford's film was a celebration, not a critical portrait, of the American war effort. *They Were Expendable* is filled with patriotic and elegiac sentiments—a sound track playing "The Battle Hymn of the Republic" and "Red River Valley"; an affecting montage of wounded men, one of them who is blind, smoking a cigarette with trembling hands; and a melancholy full shot of exhausted, courageous nurses seen in silhouette walking through a hospital corridor. Consequently, it should come as no surprise from such a paean to the military that the film's apotheosis is the appearance of an actor embodying Ford's personal deity, General MacArthur, accompanied by a series of reaction shots of sailors with glowing faces standing in awe of this American icon.

In the hands of another director without the pictorial or narrative gifts of Ford, these rituals and stereotypes might have become mere historical tableaux. However, Ford's treatment of military rituals and codes is so profoundly felt and his images so grand and stately that the conventional and sentimental emotions and characters are transformed into archetypes and the clichés into myths.

No less important in raising morale and maintaining commitment to the war effort than some of the flag-waving combat films were the home-front melodramas. In fact, a film such as David O. Selznick's *Since You Went Away* (1944) actually opened with this announcement: "This is the story of an unconquerable fortress, the American home, 1943." What followed was Hollywood's sanitized version of American women's commitment to the war effort. The plot has a typical suburban housewife, played by a miscast Claudette Colbert, leaving her comfortable home for a job in a welding factory. There she becomes a mentor in Americanization for the immigrant women who work beside her and who see her as the embodiment of the American dream. It's not only the immigrant women who view her in this manner, for the film itself idealizes Colbert's family and friends, portraying their world as clean, unruffled, and innocent. The dream is made complete by a black mammy cook (Hattie McDaniel) who, though the family can no longer afford her, returns each night after a full day's work to provide free housework, comic relief, and consolation. It's an image of racial unity that provides a fitting capstone to this relentless celebration of the home-front United States.

Nevertheless, despite its saccharine, wish fantasy quality, *Since You Went Away* did touch on one very important home-front reality: the new role for women as workers in defense industries. There were more than 4 million in 1943, with many more working in other industries. Mass-circulation magazines reacted to this new development by creating the symbol of "Rosie the Riveter," and Hollywood responded by having its female stars play women who go to work (e.g., Lucille Ball as a defense plant worker in *Meet the People*, 1944). Hollywood's casting its stars as workers beautifully encapsulated the fact that everything shot in Hollywood during the years 1942–1945, be it combat films such as Walsh's *Objective Burma* (1945), the Tarzan series, or Donald Duck cartoons, reflected or was actively committed to the war effort.

However, as the war came to a close, Hollywood began to turn from making films about the war to those that would help ease the transition from war to peace. Here it was the symbol of the returned veteran who became the embodiment of those issues. As a matter of fact, as Dr. Franklin Fearing wrote in the first issue of the *Hollywood Quarterly* (predecessor of the present *Film Quarterly*),

"When Johnny Comes Marching Home" is not only the title of a popular Civil War song, it is a symbol and a situation. It is a symbol with curiously ambivalent meanings, it signifies the return of heroes, or wars ended, of happy reunions after hardwon but glorious victories, and of peace after battle. It is also a sign of dissension, of nervous uncertainty lest, in truth, we have not prepared a "land fit for heroes," of anxiety regarding possible capacity to adjust and even curiously of fear and hostility. The laughter and tears which welcome Johnny home reflect honest joy and relief, but there is an undertone of nervous tension. Has he changed? How much have I changed? Can we get along together? What is ahead?[16]

It was this type of anxiety that a film such as *Pride of the Marines* (1945) was intended to assuage. The film itself was taken from the real-life experiences of marine hero Al Schmid (John Garfield), who was blinded at Guadalcanal. After detailing Al's early life and his being wounded, the film presents his subsequent withdrawal into a shell of rage and resentment. In the hospital ward other veterans with problems like Al's overcome them by believing that the country will take care of them with the GI Bill or that just standing up for your rights will get you heard. Al, however, remains unconvinced that there is a place for him in civilian society, and it's made clear that it's his personal problem, not America's. With the issue defined in psychological terms and society absolved, the conventional Hollywood solution is easily achieved. His fiancée confronts his self-pity and tells Al she needs him; predictably, his neurosis (as does our concern about the fate of the returned veteran) then quickly dissolves.

The same theme of postwar adjustment was taken up by *Till the End of Time* (1946), where the crippled veteran has no girlfriend but rather a mother and a friendly army officer who rouse him from his anger and withdrawal to enter the world again. These films paled by comparison with Samuel Goldwyn and William Wyler's *The Best Years of Our Lives* (1946), which dealt with the return home of three World War II veterans from different social backgrounds and the psychological, economic, and physical problems of readjustment they confronted.

The Best Years of Our Lives swept the Academy Awards, was the top box office attraction of 1947, and garnered great critical praise. James Agee, for one, wrote that it was "one of the very few American studio made movies in years that seem to me profoundly pleasing, moving and encouraging."[17] The Marxist and soon to be blacklisted writer-director Abraham Polonsky wrote that "the era of human character which *The Best Years* makes available to its audience is a landmark in the fog of escapism, meretricious violence and the gimmick plot attitude of the usual movie."[18]

Praise like this catapulted the film into the realm of an instant masterpiece. And though that judgment was probably inflated, for the film tended to take few intellectual risks and be somewhat sentimental, *The Best Years*

The Best Years of Our Lives (1946). (Courtesy of RKO Radio Pictures/Photofest.)

still contained more truth and insight about the readjustment of veterans to peacetime than any other forties' film. Moreover, its subtle and eloquent use of deep focus, flowing camera movements, and moving reaction shots that caught the emotional nuances of the characters' behavior made it an un-self-consciously beautiful and lyrical film as well.

The Best Years was an intelligent, humane, deeply felt attempt to deal with the problem of the readjustment of veterans in postwar American society. At the same time, it was a stately, carefully balanced, and shrewdly manipulated tribute to the American way of life. It paid homage to American institutions like the small town (the camera lovingly providing a montage of American icons like hot dog stands, ballparks, and Woolworth's), the family, and Hollywood's own belief in the redemptive power of love. And the film tended to obfuscate social issues—dismissing class as a factor in American life by constructing a world where the comradeship of veterans, who run the gamut from bank officers to soda jerks, could un-self-consciously carry over into civilian life. It also personalized social problems such as the difficulties that GIs without capital had when they wanted to own a business or some land. Of course, the answer the film offers is not built on any institutional or structural reform.

In the Capra tradition (e.g., *American Madness*), it's politically sufficient that the film's liberal banker, Al Stephenson (Fredric March), grant small loans without any collateral to respectable and hardworking veterans. Implicit in that act is the film's belief that the system can be made to work by good-natured, "regular guy" bankers (Al tells a nervous applicant for a loan, "Don't sir me—I'm just a sergeant") and that in America anybody with enough drive can make it.

In the same fashion as the other veterans' films, the family and a woman's love help Al adjust to civilian life. Al comes home to his comfortable apartment and to the warm embrace of an urbane, supportive wife, Millie (Myrna Loy), and two almost grown children who now have lives of their own. However, he feels generally uneasy about his familial role and sexually tense, drinking and bantering compulsively to avoid confronting his feelings of alienation from both family and job. Al's behavior suggests more complex and tortured emotions about job, family, marriage, and self than the film is willing to explore (feelings that can't have all been caused by his war experience). By the film's conclusion, it is all neatly righted, and though Al may still drink too much and have some genuine discontent with the way his life has evolved, the domestic warmth and love of his family will ease his return without too much difficulty.

What is true for Al holds true for both the other veterans, Fred and Homer. Fred Derry (Dana Andrews) returns home a war hero with ribbons, citations, and nightmares from living so close to death. He also comes back without any qualifications for a decent job (the ribbons doing nothing to help him) except for the soda jerk position he had left and feels degraded working at. Fred is sharp, cynical, tough, and filled with middle-class ambitions, but the good jobs don't seem available to him. He also carries the added burden of marriage to a brassy, sexy blonde who is that particular symbol of anxiety that bedeviled so many GIs—the unfaithful wife. Too narcissistic and independent, Marie (Virginia Mayo) cannot offer Fred any support and only makes him feel worse about himself. However, a good woman's love ultimately suffices to rescue Fred from despair, as Al's pert and sensitive daughter Peggy (Theresa Wright) offers him female understanding and support.

Although Fred's rescue by Peggy and the offer of a job recycling old bombers into prefab housing is rather contrived, the subplot provides one of the best reasons why *The Best Years* has been assigned a niche in the pantheon of American films. In one of the film's most formally dazzling and powerful scenes, Fred walks into an airplane graveyard overrun with weeds and containing rows of bombers that are going to be turned into scrap (a metaphor for the now obsolete Fred) and climbs into one of the cobwebbed planes. Camera movement, sound, and editing then work together to reconstruct the sensation of takeoff and flight. There is a close-up of a sweating, feverish Fred; the sound of engines on the sound track; and a nightmarish shot of Fred through the blurred glass of the cockpit. It's a sequence that provides a profound insight into Fred's relationship to a war that gave him both a sense of power, self-esteem, and pain. By reliving the war in this one scene, both Fred and the movie audience get a chance to exorcise the war experience.

The postwar adjustment of the third veteran, the inarticulate, vulnerable Homer (Harold Russell), is sensitively and honestly rendered. The poignancy of his story is heightened by the fact that Homer is played by a real amputee (an example of the care that Wyler took in casting the film) who exudes great naturalness in the role. Homer's problem is not his handicap—he has already achieved a great deal of good-humored self-sufficiency using his hooks—but the unwarranted fear that his passive, loving fiancée, Wilma (Cathy O'Donnell), will be unable to deal with him. Homer does not want to be pitied or treated as a freak; in turn, he rejects Wilma and, as a result, begins to feel isolated and angry. Of course, in the context of the film, all he needs to be happy is to be willing to accept Wilma's love. However, before this foreseeable conclusion is reached, there are tender, understated scenes where Homer's father undresses him and takes off his hooks and one where Homer sitting somberly in the shadows puts Wilma to the test by removing his hooks and describing how helpless he is: of course, maternal, caring Wilma comes through.

Despite its limitations, *The Best Years'* emotionally moving scenes, its formal luminosity, and its well-defined characters did provide a genuine glimpse of postwar American life. And though it ultimately allowed each of its characters a graceful, albeit predictable, reentry into postwar American society, it suggested that there were genuinely real and traumatic problems inherent in returning home from the war. There were also hints that underneath the film's essentially optimistic surface there existed some feelings of doubt about America's future. (The film's brief portraits of the civilians who stayed home and prospered during the war are so repellent that one begins to wonder about how benign American society could be if it was populated by people of this type.)

This anxiety about America was not merely confined to the returned veteran, but it also extended to other areas of American life. The traces of it could even be found in the work of that apostle of Hollywood optimism, Frank Capra. In Capra's very first postwar film, *It's a Wonderful Life* (1946), he began to modify his normal optimism and belief in the "little people" with a vision of a nightmare world. Capra's usual mythic, tranquil, small town, Bedford Falls, is destroyed by selfish materialism and turned into a raw, industrial, neon-lit Pottersville (a fantasy possibly inspired by the squalid boomtowns that grew up across America in the wake of the wartime industrial explosion). Even his archetypical common man, George Bailey (James Stewart), is beset with feelings of self-doubt and resentment. Nevertheless, Capracorn and the spirit of Christmas eventually do triumph, the whole cast of characters ultimately singing in unison "Auld Lang Syne," and the significance of each man's life, no matter how ordinary, is reaffirmed. In this Capra film the act of affirmation becomes more difficult, and Capra must contrive the deus ex machina of a cute, folksy angel, Clarence (Henry Travers), to bring this film to its benign and joyous conclusion.

It's a Wonderful Life (1946) was Frank Capra's favorite film and probably his most personal.[19] Its hero, George Bailey, is the most individualized and psychologically complex of Capra's heroic everyman. George is decent, intelligent, caring, and doomed to living a life he finds constricting, devoid of adventure or great success. In fact, despite the good he does in town (he builds a subdivision of clean, inexpensive new homes), George sees himself as having no real identity, a failure.

Unlike some of Capra's earlier films, especially his populist trilogy (*Mr. Deeds Goes to Town*, *Mr. Smith Goes to Washington*, and *Meet John Doe*), this film is more meditative, less dependent on montage, and more dependent on lengthy close-ups of George Bailey isolated within a frame. Previously, Capra had questioned the value of his form of populist political vision in *Meet John Doe* (1941), and there were moments of anguish in his other films, but in *It's a Wonderful Life*, the despair becomes more personal and deeply felt. And in the style of 1940s films, the doubts expressed deal more with the nature of identity and self than with social or political abuses. As a result, there is no steely-eyed Edward Arnold to play a corrupt political boss or a forbidding fascist tycoon who in the film can ominously threaten Bailey and Capra's ethics and politics. Instead, there is only Mr. Potter (Lionel Barrymore), the "meanest man in town," a solitary, Scrooge type who owns slum tenements. Potter is a Dickensian cartoon, a small-town tyrant in a wheelchair whose threats cannot really be taken too seriously. George's nightmare, though supposedly brought on by Potter's villainous machinations, comes from inside himself, carrying the sort of intense rage that has him cry out to his cloyingly sweet wife Mary (Donna Reed), "Why do we need all these kids!" George's anger is finally defused, but it takes all of Capra's genius at manipulating an audience to achieve it, and a trace of his anguish cannot be fully erased.

What is more, Capra's nightmare sequence, filled with flashing neon lights; gin mills; harsh, pained characters; and a dark shadowy ambiance, contained most of the elements that characterized a whole genre of 1940s films. For many of Hollywood's films, especially those dealing with contemporary American life, conveyed, through their somber black-and-white photography, a tone of claustrophobia and entrapment. Obviously some of this dark, oppressive mood derived from the budgetary limits placed on wartime filmmaking, where light-

ing had to be cut down and sets substituted for location shooting. Nevertheless, the eerie menace inherent in the films' look was more than an adjustment to industry economics. It was a conscious choice made by the films'
directors, many of them expatriates who had been at Germany's UFA (the
largest single pre–World War II European studio) and received basic training
in the German expressionism of the 1920s, with its emphasis on the visual
evocation of emotional and intellectual states (e.g., *The Cabinet of Dr. Caligari*
and *Nosferatu*). Other significant influences were the murky atmospherics of
French prewar poetic realist films (e.g., *Port of Shadows*), the Warner gangster
films of the 1930s, and a strain of 19th-century romanticism.

Some leading figures among these expatriate directors were Billy Wilder
(*Double Indemnity*, 1944), Otto Preminger (*Laura*, 1945), Robert Siodmak
(*The Killers*, 1945, and *Cry of the City*, 1948) and Fritz Lang (*Woman in the
Window*, 1944, and *Scarlet Street*, 1945). They made films that tended to, in
stylistic terms, deliberately disquieting editing, low-key lighting, night for
night shooting, subjective view shots, voice over and flashback, and oblique
camera setups. Their films were also characterized by images of rain-swept,
foggy-night streets, shadowy figures, seedy bars, flickering street lamps, isolated
coast roads, and rooms dominated by mirrors. Postwar French critics identified the films containing many of these elements as a genre that they dubbed
film noir.[20]

Many of these film noir works constructed worlds where paranoia was the
dominant feeling, and almost nobody could be trusted. It was a world where
women, often in the central role, were glamorous and dangerous—seductive
sirens whose every action was marked by duplicity and aimed at satisfying a desire for wealth and power—while the male protagonists were frequently weak,
confused and morally equivocal, susceptible to temptation, and incapable of
acting heroically. In turn, the villains were often superficially sympathetic figures whose charm masked malevolence and perversity and on occasion operated as alter egos or doubles for the films' heroes. Film noir also contained
bizarre and seedy minor characters, ritualized violence, sadomasochistic behavior, sexual alienation, and a general sense of the perverse, and when the
good triumphed at the film's climax (for the genre was still dominated by Hollywood conventions), its triumph was usually ambiguous.[21]

The film noir style encompassed a wide range of works of varying quality.
For example, there were films like Fritz Lang's visually powerful *Woman in
the Window* (1944) and *Scarlet Street* (1945), where a lonely, repressed, conflicted male (Edward G. Robinson) is victimized by a beautiful temptress (Joan
Bennett) who is also a victim. Both films were especially striking in their elegant mise-en-scène—more interested in the precise projection of a pessimistic
worldview through high overhead shots, low-key lighting, and emotionally

charged objects than in an evocation of beauty. Lang's cold, nightmarish films envisioned a corrupt world where people are trapped by abstract forces—fate, instincts, and society—and nobody really escapes punishment. The films also had a special gift for both imagining sadomasochistic encounters and creating vicious, insidious villains like those played by Dan Duryea in the two films.

There were also less successful films like Robert Siodmak's *Cry of the City* (1948), which had a pungent, quasi-documentary feeling for low-life locales: perennially wet streets, neon lights reflected in windows, sinister cocktail lounges, and decaying tenements. It also contained some imaginatively constructed noirish set pieces: a gross six-foot masseuse (Hope Emerson) seen both in close-up devouring her breakfast or through a glass door, in full shot, ominously striding through a house switching on the lights in room after room; a police interview of a group of émigré abortionists that is enveloped in squalor and pathos; and a meticulously executed escape scene, accompanied by a swelling drumbeat on the sound track, as the film's corrupt and charming villain slips right past the police. However, the film turns out to be no more than the sum of its carefully constructed and calculated tensions, a work of strong surface effects and style based on a banal, cliché-ridden script and dominated by characters devoid of internality or genuine interest.

Much of the same film noir style also dominates Michael Curtiz's *Mildred Pierce* (1945), adapted from a novel by James Cain. *Mildred Pierce* charts the rise, through hard work, of a housewife, Mildred (Joan Crawford), from a waitress to becoming the wealthy owner of a chain of restaurants in southern California. Elements of film noir—stylish low-key lighting; seedy, smoke-filled police stations; pools of shadows; and avaricious, venal characters—permeate the film. *Mildred Pierce* could also be seen as a women's picture, romantic films designed to offer women, especially housewives, a cathartic experience. Glamorous Hollywood stars like Bette Davis (*Deception*, 1946) and Joan Crawford (*Possessed*, 1948) portrayed women who had to lie, scheme, or even murder to get what they wanted from life. The films gave expression both to alluring wish fantasies about love and luxury and to the frustrations of housewives by dealing with women who led self-sacrificial lives, had ungrateful children, or had to deal with chronic and terminal illnesses. Though often hopelessly soap operatic and melodramatic, the women's films often featured strong women fighting for their own identities in a world controlled by men.[22]

In many ways, *Mildred Pierce* fit the women's films pattern. It carried a predictable narrative about a mother's self-destructive love for her daughter, tended toward overstatement and hysteria, and contained major characters who lacked even a hint of psychological nuance. A prime example was Zachary Scott's cardboard cutout Monte—an aristocratic, decadent, heel recycled from innumerable Hollywood melodramas. For all its lack of subtlety, however,

Mildred Pierce was a work that resonated culturally and socially beyond its conventional narrative.

Crawford's Mildred is supposedly an ordinary, lower-middle-class house-wife (though Crawford can never quite convince audiences that she is any-thing but tough-minded and glamorous) who escapes household drudgery and an enervated husband to become a successful entrepreneur. Warned early that the pursuit of success (it would have been interesting if the film had really begun to question the whole American obsession with success) and the ab-dication of her maternal role will prove destructive, she is punished by see-ing her sweet, perky, younger daughter die of pneumonia and by having a relationship with the feckless, parasitical Monte, who is unfaithful and lives off her money.

But her ultimate punishment for being a strong, independent women is to be treated with contempt and betrayed by her monstrous, eldest daugh-ter, Veda (Ann Blyth). Mildred has spoiled Veda, compulsively sacrificing her-self so that Veda can be raised to become a lady. In fact, Veda becomes so absurdly pretentious that despite Mildred's success, she continues to treat her as if her own life has been irrevocably tainted by Mildred's having to work for a living. And Veda's contempt for Mildred's being merely a waitress—and, in turn, Mildred's own embarrassment about her job—feels emotionally true and conveys some insight into the sort of status and class anxiety that the usual Hollywood mythology of a classless America rarely would recognize or deal with.

On another level, as mentioned before, the film's treatment of career women is the most powerfully suggestive aspect of the work. Hollywood films usually treated career women (especially in the post–World War II era) as peo-ple who had to be domesticated and made to see the error of their ways when they competed with men. Even Katharine Hepburn, Hollywood's most noted feminist, had to accept ritualistic degradation and defeat (*Adam's Rib*, 1949) in her classic bouts with Spencer Tracy.[23] In a similar fashion, Joan Crawford's Mildred is clearly superior to the men who surround her but is still supposedly enough of a traditional woman to allow herself to be manipulated by these same callow males. Nor does the film even allow Mildred to pursue a career for profit, power, or a sense of self—it is conceived of merely as a means to ac-quire and hold Veda's love. And Veda's behavior itself can possibly be viewed as an extension of Mildred's success drive or a demonic variation on it.

At the film's conclusion, there is a tacked-on happy ending with Mildred now bravely facing the future with her passive, dull, chauvinistic husband, who looks even more inadequate when forced to stand next to her. But given Hollywood conventions, he is there to save her from being a single woman. To underline this chauvinistic point, the film allows Ida (Eve Arden), Mildred's handsome, sarcastically witty friend and workmate, to be treated by men as if she were not a "real woman," the moral being that aggressive, intelligent career women are usually doomed to lonely and asexual lives and in Ida's case would trade all their independence for the right man.

Obviously, Joan Crawford's career woman owed more to the conventions of the women's pictures than to film noir, but in both genres women often enjoyed a great deal of power over the imagination and will of men. There were a number of possible reasons for the diverse and powerful images of female menace, power, and maternal patience and sacrifice that pervaded these films. For one thing, female stars had a great deal of prestige in Hollywood of the 1940s, and the films reflected that fact. Another explanation for their taking on the image of murderous wives and lovers may have partially derived from the American soldier's nightmare of infidelity at home during World War II. Of course, the narrative, no matter how much the camera focused on the predatory sexuality or the psychological strength of the female, always restored male dominance by the film's climax.[24]

It was Rita Hayworth, a pinup favorite of American males in the 1940s and Columbia Pictures' only major film star and sex symbol, who became the apotheosis of these dangerous females. In fact, the effect of her role as the sensual, nightclub singer in *Gilda* (1946) was so strong that it inspired the U.S. Air Force to place Gilda's name on the atomic bomb dropped on the Bikini Atoll. That role was shortly followed by her playing the character of a mysterious, seductive Circe, Elsa, in the intricately murderous plot of *The Lady from Shanghai* (1947).

The Lady from Shanghai, directed by her then-husband Orson Welles, is a virtuoso piece of baroque filmmaking filled with striking and bizarre aural and visual images and metaphors (e.g., the symbolic intercutting between the film's characters and flamingos, crocodiles, and snakes), unusual camera angles, and the rich use of depth of focus. The world it depicts was an embodiment of film noir, a dark, nihilistic universe of men and women who deceive and destroy each other, this time in exotic settings, such as the Caribbean and Acapulco. Although there are moments when the film seems like nothing more than stylish nonsense—all windy rhetoric and meaningless confusion—the bewitching Elsa's manipulation of Michael O'Hara (Welles himself), a romantic innocent and aspiring novelist, is touched with interesting ambiguities. Elsa is motivated by both greed and a feeling of being utterly adrift in the world, and while caring for Michael, she is also willing to use and destroy him.

Throughout the film, Welles takes pleasure in his cinematic virtuosity and creates original images and sequences to evoke Elsa's lethal charm. For example, there is an overhead shot of Elsa languidly lying down and singing on the deck of the yacht, luring O'Hara from the bowels of the boat, and an aquarium scene where her face is juxtaposed with an octopus, a metaphor for her preda-toriness. For a grand finale, Welles constructs a playland sequence with gro-tesque laughing dolls, chutes, masks, and a house of mirrors—a labyrinth of refracted and reflected multiple selves. Elsa is the incarnation of film noir's femme fatale whose snares are difficult to escape. And although her image is figuratively and literally destroyed, Michael, although escaping her trap into the light of day, we know, as in many other 1940s films, is bound to her image for life. As he states, "Maybe I'll live so long that I'll forget her. Maybe I'll die trying."

O'Hara's final lines were characteristic of the romantic despair and angst that was so much a part of film noir. The films projected a world that was al-most universally corrupt and morally chaotic but gave little sense of how par-ticular social values and institutions helped shape or contribute to this vision (though there were exceptions like Abe Polonsky's *Force of Evil*, 1948). Corrup-tion was defined primarily in metaphysical—and, at moments, psychological—terms, though the monstrosity of characters, like Veda in *Mildred Pierce*, was too outsized for the film's psychological explanations. Many characters in film noir were impotent and helpless in the face of evil, bending to its force, which seemed to reside in an inalterable human nature. Others struggled against it but in the process were tainted by evil even when they achieved a victory. And there were still other characters who acted as if they were the personifi-cation of that corruption.

One of them, a prep school teacher Charles Rankin (Orson Welles) in Welles's third feature film (following *Citizen Kane* [1941] and *The Magnificent Ambersons*), *The Stranger* (1946), can be viewed as the embodiment of evil. In the film, Rankin turns out to be a notorious Nazi war criminal Franz Kindler—a fictional architect of the Holocaust. Rankin/Kindler had somehow managed to escape the fall of the Third Reich and landed in the picturesque, classic New England small town of Harper, Connecticut—evil invading an American dream-scape. As the film opens, he is about to marry Mary Longstreet (Loretta Young), the daughter of a Supreme Court justice. After listening to Rankin's chillingly ironic monologue advocating the total genocide of all Germans, a pipe-smok-ing, preternaturally calm and perceptive Nazi hunter Wilson (Edward G. Rob-inson), who has been pursuing him, brings him down. Supposedly, Rankin has given himself away by referring to Karl Marx as a Jew. Neither the film's script—too many rhetorical speeches—nor its characters—Loretta Young's Mary is unbelievably naive (we are forced to believe that she is so besotted with love for the glowering, controlling Rankin that she picks up nothing about him)—are convincing. Still Welles's characteristically compelling, ominous shadows, chiaroscuro images, and striking camera angles and set—the church tower and clock—remain beguiling. In addition, while most of Hollywood shied away from dealing with the horrors of the Holocaust, *The Stranger* was the first American film to even touch on the issue.

However, a writer like Barbara Deming could still suggest in her book *Running Away from Myself: A Dream Portrait of Americans Drawn from Film of the 40's* that 1940s films (not only film noir) revealed a crisis of public faith: "A vision of hell in which we are bound."[25] Of course, she qualified that perception by stating that the theme and the audience's response to it were mainly unconscious. Other critics speculated that the bleak mood of film noir derived from the cumulative anxieties of the Depression, World War II, and the Cold War, though it was difficult to see, by a close analysis of these films, how public events may have directly influenced or shaped the perspective.

If we took a critical leap and suggested that these films may, on some level, have been a revelation of an unconscious public despair, they could just as easily be seen as works that were mere derivations from other popular arts, such as the successful hard-boiled detective novels of Hammett (*Maltese Falcon*, 1941), Cain (*The Postman Always Rings Twice*, 1946), and Chandler (*The Big Sleep*, 1946). On yet another level, like many Hollywood film trends, they could be viewed as a popular genre that, since it made a profit at the box office, was adopted by the industry. And though a number of film noir works may have expressed a genuine directorial sensibility, the look of them—lighting, sets, and camera angles—often seemed more significant than their perspective on the world. In fact, many of these films were potboilers that seemingly did no more than adopt a successful set of formal and narrative codes.

Even more interesting and ironic is that the existence of film noir served only to highlight the essential optimism of the 1940s. Despite the hopelessness, cynicism, and sense of universal decay that film noir projected, both the filmmakers and the audience were readily prepared for and even desirous of avoiding their implications. As a result, even though the logic of the film's imagery demanded an opposite conclusion, the happy ending and even justice often triumphed. Of course, much of this had to do with Hollywood's system of self-censorship and genre conventions. On the other hand, it was possible to conclude the films in this manner because of the audience's willingness and desire to suspend belief—an attitude that was probably aided by the war-inspired conviction that sufficient energy and goodwill existed in society to solve any problem and triumph over any evil. In fact, film noir's evocation of evil may have served only as a delicious contrast, making the victory of goodness that much more grand and satisfying. Consequently, though film noir portrayed the darker side of human nature, it was one based as much on cinematic form and style as on the expression of a genuine moral or personal vision, and the films and the audience's response to them hardly affected the basic self-confidence of the era.[26]

Nowhere is the era's basic optimism better illustrated than in some of the 1940s films that dealt with social problems, particularly discrimination and racism. In the postwar years, a number of Hollywood producers, directors, and writers were determined to extend the democratic ideals that ostensibly underlied the war effort into an examination and attack on racism and bigotry in America. Films like *Crossfire* (1947) and *Gentleman's Agreement* (1947) were probably two of the first Hollywood studio products to confront anti-Semitism as a serious social problem. For, although almost all the Hollywood moguls were Jewish, they were Jews who craved assimilation and made films that "reinvented the country"[27]—creating their own myth of America. Except for films like *The Jazz Singer* (1927), Jews were usually seen as secondary characters—often comic ethnic types in films usually dominated by the moguls' upper-middle-class White/Anglo-Saxon/Protestant (WASP) ideal (though 1930s Warner Bros. films had many ethnic, working-class, but not Jewish protagonists). Thus, even when films like *Crossfire* and *Gentleman's Agreement* proved profitable, no other films dealing with the subject followed.

Crossfire was an edgy thriller whose visual texture—its mise-en-scène—was much stronger than its script. The film is filled with film noir shadows—razors so gleamingly polished that characters can be reflected in them—and a number of ominous low-angle and overhead shots. There is also a psychopathic villain, Montgomery (Robert Ryan), who is a deceptively soft-spoken sadist, seething with feelings of inferiority, resentment, and anti-Semitism—"Jewish people live off the fat of the land."

The power of the film lies in Ryan's performance and in its gift for evoking a tense, seedy night world of smoky bars, all-night movie theaters, and cheap apartments inhabited by characters such as Gloria Grahame's Ginny, a tough, exhausted woman, and her odd, pathological-liar boyfriend. The bitterness and venom that is exchanged between the two of them and the feeling that most of the characters are living near the precipice are much more striking than the film's attack on anti-Semitism.

Crossfire's social vision is timid and evasive. The anti-Semite is conceived as an uneducated psychopath, distancing the situation from the audience's own experience and values and absolving them of any guilt. The Jewish victim, Samuels (Sam Levene), is a war hero and an empathetic good guy, the film seeming to suggest that an ordinary Jewish scapegoat would be unable to elicit audience sympathy, only the extraordinary Jew being capable of eliciting moral or social concern. And by turning the homosexual victim of the novel into a Jew, the film demonstrated Hollywood's timidity and fear during this period (homosexuals could not be dealt with in a sympathetic light in films of the 1940s). Finally, in its implicit belief that all problems of prejudice and racism are interchangeable, Hollywood manifested an unwillingness to deal with the particular historical and social experiences of different groups. The films expressed a faith that tolerance—a decent, liberal principle—was sufficient to encompass and solve a variety of complex social problems. Both compounding and illustrating this mixture of intellectual and political timorousness and vagueness was Crossfire's tendency to be awkwardly and superficially didactic. Its liberal spokesman, pipe-smoking police Lieutenant Finley (Robert Young) stops the action and provides a vaporous sermon about standing up to prejudice. It's an editorial that safely invokes 19th-century discrimination against the Irish as a historical parallel to anti-Semitism rather than the more charged and contemporary issue of race.

In contrast to Crossfire, Elia Kazan's Gentleman's Agreement (which won the Oscar for best picture in 1947), though lacking the former's visual style and texture, examined and dramatized facets of anti-Semitism that Crossfire never touched on. In the film, a WASP magazine writer, Phil Green (Gregory Peck), pretends to be a Jew for two months so that he can write an exposé of bigotry. In pursuit of his story, a gallery of anti-Semites make their appearance, running the gamut from raging bigots to genteel WASPs ("nice people") who indulge in polite prejudice and to self-hating Jews who object to Jews who are too ethnic ("kikey").

Despite Gentleman's Agreement's more complex perspective on anti-Semitism, it is characterized by the same political superficiality endemic to social-problem films. Its use of a Gentile journalist to confront anti-Semitism evaded the whole issue. It made it seem that the distinct social and cultural history and ethnic characteristics that distinguished Gentile from Jew never existed. And a Gentile being the victim gave the audience the chance to express anger without having to confront the moral wrongness of prejudice. They now could get upset because an innocent man—a non-Jew—has by mistake become a victim of prejudice.

It was not only Jews who got a touch of liberal optimism from Hollywood in the 1940s. Blacks, from Birth of a Nation (1915), had usually been seen by Hollywood either as brutal, savage bucks or as good toms and mammies. In 1930s films, two new black stereotypes began to appear: sympathetic victims who were symbols of general rather than racial oppression (the black janitor who is brutally questioned by the police in They Won't Forget, 1937) and "tragic mulattoes" (e.g., Imitation of Life, 1934) whose skin color allowed them to pass into white society. However, until the 1940s problem, films' blacks were confined mainly to minor roles, and racism was never explored as an issue.

By the end of the decade, Hollywood began to deal with the issue, and a number of films dealing with race prejudice were released. In one of these, Home of the Brave (1949), an educated, emotionally disturbed black GI, Peter Moss (James Edwards), is cured of a trauma (psychosomatic paralysis) by a white psychiatrist. Moss's character is in the tradition of the noble martyr (though the film deals directly with racism, not generalized oppression), a passive, self-effacing figure who embodies white values. He is the perfect black to exemplify the liberal ideals of the film since he is a war hero and a success-ful professional. He is a man who can be viewed by the white audience as someone whose character and lifestyle are no different than any white's. Just as in *Gentleman's Agreement*, Hollywood again affirmed tolerance and inte-gration, provided it was for blacks and Jews who behaved like or really were WASPs. *Home of the Brave* defined racism as a psychological problem—racists being pathological and blacks being oversensitive to prejudice. For 1940s Holly-wood, there was no such thing as institutional racism—where racist practice permeated, consciously and especially unconsciously, the dominant politi-cal and economic institutions of the society—and almost no sense of how profound a role racism played in the daily life of both the whole society and blacks. It was conceived of as a problem that neurotic individuals suffer from and that could be simply resolved with a dose of shared sympathy and under-standing between whites and blacks.

In films like *Lost Boundaries* (1949) and *Pinky* (1949), a somewhat similar so-cial perspective was communicated. *Lost Boundaries* was produced by documen-tary filmmaker Louis de Rochemont (creator of the *March of Time* newsreels) and shot on location in New Hampshire and Maine, using a largely non-professional cast. Based on a true story, the film deals with a dedicated black doctor, Dr. Scott Carter, and his family, who in the tradition of Hollywood's tragic mulattoes pass for white in an idyllic New England town. The only seem-ing legacy of Dr. Carter's racial past is his children's gift for music (the "natu-ral rhythm" of blacks)—though he still guiltily goes to Boston once a week to practice at a ghetto clinic. Ultimately, the family secret is revealed when Dr. Carter is rejected for a naval commission because he is black, and the fam-ily is forced to deal with the mild social prejudices of the town and, more im-portant, their sensitive son's confusion (the children were never told) over his racial identity.

Lost Boundaries is a well-intentioned film, but it is limited by a neat Holly-wood formula that turns the problem of racism into a peripheral racial prob-lem and totally blurs even that issue by having the black Carters played by white actors (Mel Ferrer and Beatrice Pearson) in the Hollywood tradition of *Showboat* and *Imitation of Life*. Hollywood was unwilling to take the risk that audience sympathy could be elicited for black actors passing for white, so it made it easy for them. It gave them white actors, playing characters, who by some imperceptible accident of fate may have some black blood.

The film concludes with the town's Episcopal minister giving a sermon af-firming Christian principles ("I am my brother's keeper") and announcing that the navy has seen the light and has begun to grant officers' commissions to all people of all races. The sermon has a magical effect, moving a number of townspeople to apologetically welcome the Carters back into the community.

Liberal optimism triumphs, and though black social and economic conditions are alluded to in some affecting documentary footage of Harlem squalor and violence and there is a self-conscious speech by a black police officer of the pernicious effect of an impoverished environment on black lives, it is in no way the core or prime concern of the film. The political essence and hope of the film lies in the acceptance of one upper-middle-class, churchgoing, white-black family by white society.

In a similar fashion, Elia Kazan's *Pinky* (1949) also focused on a tragic mulatto passing for white (again played by a white actress, Jeanne Crain), but the film lacks even the surface realism of *Lost Boundaries*. *Pinky* takes place in a studio-set southern town, all wisteria and willows, and trades in racial stereotypes and clichés: an irascible but just and independent white matriarch (Ethel Barrymore); a traditional, strong, wise nanny (Ethel Waters); a hypocritical, fat clubwoman bigot; white-trash rapists; and a lazy, no-account black with his razor-carrying wife. At the film's conclusion, Pinky has refused to pass for white any longer and affirmed her racial identity by starting a nursery-hospital for blacks. In rediscovering her black roots, Pinky's triumph is a personal rather than social one. Its victory is achieved with the assistance of paternalistic whites and gives no sign that the South's repressive and segregated order will ever be confronted, much less changed.

Other social-problem films during the period dealt with subjects like mental illness, such as Anatol Litvak's *The Snake Pit* (1948), which did bring about reform of some state mental hospitals, and juvenile delinquency, such as Nicholas Ray's *Knock on Any Door* (1949). But none of them really broke from the Hollywood norm.

In retrospect, the intellectual faintheartedness of these 1940s social-problem films seems even more blatant. Of course, the films were, as always, constrained politically by the industry's prime commitment to making a profit. However, not only were these films pallid, evasive, and sentimental in their handling of social issues, but most of them also had little cinematic energy, style, or dramatic life of their own. The characters inhabiting these works were usually impersonal figures, lacking a semblance of internality or psychological nuance and operating as mere representations or symbols of social problems. The films conceived of their characters' behavior as being shaped by external forces or problems rather than being people with genuine inner lives who reacted to charged social situations, the result being that the characters' existential or political choices never seemed to stem from their own reflections or feelings.

All the same, despite their shallowness, these films must be seen and evaluated within the context of their own times. For one thing, they strongly suggest how deeply a politically committed culture of liberalism had taken root in historically conservative Hollywood since the 1930s (one shortly to be decimated by HUAC and the blacklist). They also attest to the economic security enjoyed by the industry, a security that enabled it to feel confident enough to touch on previously taboo themes. Indeed, the very existence of these social-problem films testifies to a shift away from the conventional Hollywood wisdom about social issues, which was, "if you want to send a message, use Western Union," to an equally crude belief in the power of the image and a vague form of liberalism to produce instant social change. In fact, the lack of subtlety and complexity in these films can in some ways be seen as yet another sign of the overwhelming optimism of the era—a sanguine belief that no problem was insoluble.[28]

A few films departed from this facile optimism. *Force of Evil* (1948), written and directed by Abraham Polonsky (who was soon to be a victim of the blacklist), was a sharp contrast to films like *Lost Boundaries* and *Gentleman's Agreement*. On the surface, *Force of Evil* was a formula melodrama about the numbers racket—complete with a head racketeer and his femme fatale wife—whose violent confrontations were awkwardly edited and devoid of dramatic tension. However, there was much more to the film than the predictable tale of a bad-guy, good-guy lawyer, Joe Morse (John Garfield), who is ready to go straight at the film's climax. Polonsky crafted an ambiguous and imaginative work that uses Hollywood conventions to evoke on one level a portrait of American society dominated by greed and acquisitiveness; on another level, it's the story of a passionate, guilt-ridden, love–hate relationship between Joe and his older brother, Leo (Thomas Gomez), who had given up going to college to send Joe to law school. The brothers share both a profound resentment of and love for each other.

Though all of Polonsky's characters are caught in the coils of the social system and its pernicious values, they are not simply symbols of a corrupt society. They have inner lives that are both shaped by and independent of social forces, the characters being people who choose the direction of their life. In this small, poetic, near masterpiece, Polonsky has successfully fused Marxist and Freudian strains. The film's protagonist, Joe Morse (John Garfield), is a tough, perceptive lawyer who is aware of his inability to resist being part of the rackets and becoming corrupt. But Joe is adept at rationalizing his choices by asserting that everybody is guilty—that they all hunger for "the ruby." And in *Force of Evil*, all the characters, including sweating, apoplectic, self-righteous Leo and even Leo's naive, dreamy stenographer, Doris, are tainted by the seductions of money and success.

Polonsky's direction is characterized by extremely long overheads of minute, isolated figures dwarfed by Wall Street buildings (seemingly based on a Paul Strand photo)—a metaphor for monolithic and alienating capitalist power—and by the film noir images of seedy numbers parlors, opulent winding staircases, and shadows augering doom. Much more original than the film's imagery is Polonsky's use of language—both dialogue and narration—which he aims to make play an equal, sometimes dialectical relationship with the visual images. And though at moments the words become overly literary and self-conscious, its Joycean repetitions, city argot and inflection, and metaphors (e.g., "money spread over the city like perfume") convey a genuine street poetry and set the film apart from almost all other 1940s films.

Force of Evil concludes with Joe Morse descending on a gray morning to the "bottom of the world" to discover Leo's dead body left looking like an "old dirty rag." Polonsky does not have Joe indulge in grand, heroic gestures, nor does he insert polemics for radical change. There is only a solitary Joe, willing to make his own understated moral stand, ready to help if he can. Polonsky's film offers no easy solutions. It knows how powerful the capitalist ethos is. Polonsky holds not only that it is Wall Street that pursues a capitalist-gangster ethic but also that the consciousness of most Americans is suffused with capitalist dreams.

Besides *Force of Evil*, other films that dealt with some insight and intelligence about political and social themes were Robert Rossen's *All the King's Men* (he had directed a boxing film *Body and Soul*, 1947, with a script written by Abraham Polonsky) and Billy Wilder's *A Foreign Affair* (1948). *All the King's Men* was based on a novel by Robert Penn Warren dealing with the career of populist demagogue and Louisiana governor Huey Long, here called Willie Stark (Broderick Crawford in a flamboyant, forceful Academy Award performance). Stark begins his political career as a man of the people, but, thwarted by the political machine, he adopts its corrupt tactics to achieve and sustain his power.

All the King's Men is an intellectually ambitious but clumsy film. Stark's transformation into a power-mad megalomaniac is too abrupt and extreme; the reasons for the alcoholic, drifting journalist-narrator Jack Burden's (John Ireland) continuing loyalty to Stark are never really illuminated; and the script tends to telegraph its point of view. But despite the melodramatic turns and the choppy continuity, the film trenchantly captures the perniciousness of political power and how the use of corrupt means in pursuit of social change can ultimately become an end in itself.

In *A Foreign Affair*, Wilder displayed a talent for mordant, cynical comedy satirizing the foolishness and naïveté of an American congressional committee investigating the morale of American troops (who are entwined in black market dealings and affairs with German women) in postwar occupied Germany. Wilder is particularly nasty about American provincialism and ethnocentrism and shows how easily the committee's self-righteousness is subverted when confronted by European cynicism and sophistication. However, the portrait of the Germans, who are interested only in self-preservation—personified by a ruthless, sensual, ex-Nazi collaborator played by Marlene Dietrich—is not a sympathetic one. Yet, as is Wilder's wont, by the climax he has thoroughly softened the film's bite, endorsing the American values that he, at first, so savagely poked fun at.

Clearly, the compromises inherent in *A Foreign Affair* were the Hollywood norm since the industry rarely had the courage or the imagination to deal truly with controversial political and social themes. It was much easier for Hollywood to work in genres that provided comforting fantasy images, such as the musical—a genre that, ever since its "All Talkin', All Dancin', All Singin'" days of the late 1920s and early 1930s, had become one of Hollywood's glories. During the late 1930s, various studios vied for the honor of producing the best musicals, but by the 1940s, the undisputed leadership in the genre had fallen to MGM. There the Arthur Freed unit, with talents like Gene Kelly, Judy Garland, Fred Astaire, Vincente Minnelli, and others, turned out hit after hit.[29]

Though often considered the most escapist of the Hollywood genres, the musical nevertheless succeeded in striking emotional chords that few other films could match. Its tunes became the hallmark of particular eras. For example, Judy Garland's *Wizard of Oz* (1939) rendition of "Over the Rainbow" became a worldwide hymn of a hoped-for postwar world of peace and prosperity. The same film's "We're Off to See the Wizard" became the anthem of the British army as it chased Rommel across the sands of North Africa, and "Ding Dong the Witch Is Dead" was danced the world over on VE Day.

On another level, the film's singing and dancing intimated that a great deal of energy lurked beneath the everyday surface and seemed ready to burst forth at any moment. During the war years, that energy seemed to nestle softly in a nostalgic evocation of a turn-of-the-century America, an idealized world that was perhaps never better realized than in Vincente Minnelli's vividly colored and stylized *Meet Me in St. Louis* (1944). Except for the momentary anxiety over the family's possible uprooting because of the father's new job in New York, some nervousness about whether the boy next door, John Truett (Tom Drake), loves Esther Smith (Judy Garland) and the strikingly visualized Halloween night terrors of little "Tootie" (Margaret O'Brien), the Smith family lived on the surface a warm, almost idyllic existence. The film constructed an Edenic past centering on home and family and topped off by a vision of an ever-progressing future embodied in the 1903 St. Louis World's Fair.

This version of a bright, promising new world was fully realized in Gene Kelly and Stanley Donen's MGM film *On the Town* (1949). The tale of three sailors on a three-day pass in New York, the film uses real locations—the Brooklyn Bridge, the Statue of Liberty, and Washington Square—and artfully designed sets to turn the city into a magical place where all of one's dreams can be fulfilled.

The film begins serenely with a long crane shot of a longshoreman lazily on his way to work at dawn, singing "I feel like I'm not out of bed yet," and then cuts to three animated sailors (Kelly, Sinatra, and Jules Munshin) bounding off their ship ready to take on New York. The sailors are "ordinary Joes"— innocents filled with a sense of wonder and exhilaration as they move naturally from everyday speech to sing "New York, New York, it's a wonderful town." There is nothing serene or simple about the city that they're hungry to experience. But they are filled with confidence that all of New York can be absorbed, the camera tracking after them as they sing, "We're really living, we're going on the town." Their energy is so infectious that it allows them to liberate three young women—an overworked taxi driver (Betty Garrett), an oversexed socialite (Anne Miller) (class differences are no obstacle), and a pert ballerina reduced for financial reasons to kootch dancing at Coney Island (Vera Ellen). As they romp through New York, the city becomes a metropolis of grandeur, romance, vitality, and sentiment (even the cops are softhearted), the exuberant center of an even more buoyant America.[30]

It is this inexhaustible sense of energy, joy, and confidence that more than anything else characterizes the 1940s and its films. Certainly, there were dark clouds looming, such as HUAC's threat to sap Hollywood's vitality. In addition, film noir had raised the curtain on a darker side of the American psyche and character. Nevertheless, for most Americans, the 1940s—particularly the late 1940s—were the first relatively unruffled period of peace and prosperity that they had enjoyed in almost two decades. Despite the fact that there were fears of Russia and a native communist fifth column, there was also the faith that America had both the material and the moral capacity to deal with the "red menace" and any other problem it confronted. For example, films like Howard Hawks's epic western about the first cattle drive up the Chisholm Trail, *Red River* (1948), conveyed great confidence in the strength of the American character. The film's monomaniacal, forbidding hero, Tom Dunson (John Wayne), easily masters the land, cattle stampedes, and Indian attacks. And this exemplar of American individualism can even learn to temper his rigidity and rage and reconcile himself with his more flexible, feelingful (but still tough) stepson, Matt Garth (Monty Clift).

Hollywood had emerged from the war with its coffers, audience, and prestige at an all-time peak. As a result, 1940s films were perhaps the last time that Hollywood had sufficient self-confidence to create an insulated coherent world that could un-self-consciously endorse the American dream. For most Americans and for Hollywood, the 1940s were truly "The Best Years of Our Lives."

NOTES

1. Godfrey Hodgson, *America in Our Time: From World War II to Nixon, What Happened and Why* (New York: Vintage Books, 1978), pp. 17–64.

2. Ibid., p. 20.

3. Ibid., p. 54.

4. Eric F. Goldman, *The Crucial Decade—and after, America 1945–1960* (New York: Vintage Books, 1960).

5. Ibid., pp. 46–70.

6. Stephen E. Ambrose, *Rise to Globalism: American Foreign Policy 1938–1970* (Baltimore: Penguin Books, 1971), pp. 102–35.

7. Ibid., pp. 136–66.

8. Dean Acheson, *Present at the Creation* (New York: W. W. Norton, 1969), p. 297.

9. Ambrose, *Rise to Globalism*, pp. 136–66.

10. Alistair Cooke, *A Generation on Trial* (Baltimore: Penguin Books, 1952).

11. Walter Goodman, *The Committee: The Extraordinary Career of the House Committee on Un-American Activities* (Baltimore: Penguin Books, 1969), pp. 207–25.

12. Ibid., p. 300.

13. Cooke, *A Generation on Trial*, pp. 337–41.

14. Charles Higham and Joel Greenberg, *Hollywood in the Forties* (New York: Paperback Library, 1970), p. 18.

15. James Agee, *Agee on Film: Reviews and Comments* (Boston: Beacon Press, 1966), p. 173.

16. Franklin Fearing, "Warriors Return: Norman or Neurotic," *Hollywood Quarterly* (October 1945), pp. 91–109.

17. Agee, *Agee on Film*, p. 229.

18. Abe Polonsky, "The Best Years of Our Lives: A Review," *Hollywood Quarterly* (April 1947), pp. 91–92.

19. Frank Capra, *The Name above the Title* (New York: Bantam, 1972), pp. 418–26.

20. Higham and Greenberg, *Hollywood in the Forties*, pp. 19–39.

21. Ibid.

22. Molly Haskell, *From Reverence to Rape: The Treatment of Women in the Movies* (Baltimore: Penguin Books, 1974), pp. 153–88.

23. Ibid., pp. 189–230.

24. Ibid.

25. Barbara Deming, *Running Away from Myself: A Dream Portrait of American Drawn from the Films of the Forties* (New York: Grossman Publishers, 1969), p. 6.

26. Joseph G. Goulden, *The Best Years, 1945–1950* (New York: Atheneum, 1976).

27. Neal Gabler, *An Empire of Their Own: How the Jews Invented Hollywood* (New York: Crown, 1988), p. 7.

28. Peter Roffman and Jim Purdy, *The Hollywood Social Problem Film* (Bloomington: Indiana University Press, 1981).

29. Hugh Fordin, *The World of Entertainment! Hollywood's Greatest Musicals* (Garden City, NY: Doubleday, 1975).

30. Richard Dyer, "Entertainment and Utopia," in R. Altman (ed.), *Genre: The Musical* (London: Routledge & Kegan Paul, 1981), pp. 175–89.

3

THE 1950s

The 1950s began on an ominous note with the United States, as part of a nominally UN force, becoming involved in a war in Korea and the repressive and paranoid investigations of Senator McCarthy and company in full throttle. The decade, however, ultimately evolved into one permeated by a broad political and cultural consensus.[1]

The first years of the decade were dominated by the stalemated Korean War, where the Truman administration was willing to eschew military victory for a limited war and a negotiated settlement. Truman's military policies were challenged by World War II hero General Douglas MacArthur, who was then commander of the UN forces. Cloaking himself in his own sense of omniscience and his 19th-century patriotic pieties, MacArthur saw Truman's policies as the appeasement of communism and committed himself to total victory in Korea. Truman, in turn, responded by firing MacArthur for insubordination and subsequently discovered himself the object of intense public rage.[2]

That rage soon found a home in the McCarthy, the House Un-American Activities Committee (HUAC) and Senate Internal Security Subcommittee investigations of a domestic communist conspiracy. This conspiracy was seen as a threat to take over a number of American institutions, such as the church, universities, private industry, and Hollywood. During the 1950s, the anticommunist crusade elicited the involvement either out of fear, political self-interest, or conviction of a number of liberal groups and individuals. It included the American Civil Liberties Union, which from 1953 to 1959 refused to defend communists who were under attack or lost jobs, and Hubert Humphrey, who as a senator proposed a bill to outlaw the Communist Party.[3] Interestingly enough, many liberal intellectuals placed the blame for men like McCarthy on the actions of the left rather than on the right, at times even supporting the general public's view that the rights of communists and communist sympathizers should be denied.

The leading and most brazen figure in the anticommunist crusade was Senator Joseph McCarthy, a crude Wisconsin Republican who opportunistically manipulated the issue to promote his own power and career. For four years, he successfully used smears, innuendoes, and lies to trample on individual rights and helped create a climate of political fear and conformity that even had establishment institutions on the defensive. But in 1954, when McCarthy went after the army and even dropped hints that President Eisenhower was soft on communism, he overreached himself and initiated his own rapid fall from power and celebrity. McCarthy's decline did not signify a turn to the left. There was no sudden opening of public discussion on such issues as the admission of China to the United Nations or talk about a social commitment to the poor, but it did mean a moderation of the repressive and divisive impulses that dominated the early 1950s.[4]

The prime American political symbol of the 1950s, however, was not Joe McCarthy but General Dwight Eisenhower, from 1952 to 1960 the Republican president. Ike was a World War II military hero whose calm, avuncular, optimistic public presence helped create a nonideological political mood that muted controversy and offered something both to liberals and to conservatives. Though disliking the welfare state, Ike accepted the reforms of the New Deal without extending them and was prepared to use fiscal and monetary measures to maintain full employment. Despite believing in the Cold War and unable to see the difference between communist and nationalist revolutions (e.g., CIA interventions in Iran and Guatemala occurred during his administration), he believed in a nuclear truce, refusing to engage in an arms race with the Soviets and studiously avoided getting the United States involved in a war.[5]

Eisenhower was a cautious president who, though unsympathetic to the growing civil rights movement, reluctantly sent troops to Little Rock, Arkansas, to ensure school desegregation in 1957 and in crisis after crisis kept political tensions beneath the surface. By dint of his confident cautiousness and political skills, Eisenhower was able to preside over a national political consensus that excluded only paranoid right elements, southern reactionaries, segments of the Old Left, and the few independent radicals who were still functioning as critics.[6]

This political consensus was built on and reinforced by an intellectual consensus shared by most American intellectuals. Some, like John Kenneth

Galbraith, believed in a theory of "countervailing power" where big-business power would be balanced off by the power of big labor and government.[7] Others held that the age of ideology was over (e.g., Daniel Bell, *The End of Ideology*) and in its place substituted an optimistic faith in capitalism, political pluralism, and the uniqueness and perfectibility of American society. These tough-minded anti-ideologues had constructed their own ideology—building it on a belief that economic growth and the practical application of social science principles would provide social justice and solve social problems. In this social vision, there would be no need for economic redistribution (many of them were ex-radicals and leftists who out of a complex of motives rejected their own political past), for the American people were supposedly becoming more economically equal. And poverty, during the rare times it was acknowledged to exist, was seen as gradually disappearing. In turn, they also read the idea of class conflict—and even the significance of class—out of the American social and political landscape, promoting their own liberal mythology that in a totally middle-class society everybody had an equal opportunity to succeed. The other prime element of this ideological consensus was the previously mentioned rise of liberal anticommunism (e.g., *The Partisan Review*, once a critical, sophisticated Marxist journal, became an avid defender of the West), which viewed Cold War politics as far more significant than domestic affairs. This commitment was so potent that even the newly merged American Federation of Labor and Congress of Industrial Organizations gave more attention to the anticommunist struggle than to organizing the mass of workers who remained outside the unions.[8]

However, though most intellectuals either were utterly at home with the direction of American politics or turned to contemplating existential and religious questions emphasizing the limitations of human nature and simply ceased to be political dissenters and critics, there were still a number of intellectuals who preserved their critical skills by analyzing and attacking the character of American mass culture. In the 1950s, the economy of abundance helped create a powerful suburban and consumer culture where the pursuit of success and an emphasis on social conformity became the dominant values of the era. As novelist Edmund White wrote about growing up in the Midwest in the 1950s, "That was a time and place where there was little consumption of culture and no dissent. . . . It felt, at least to me, like a big gray country of families on drowsy holiday, all stuffed in one oversized car and discussing the mileage they were getting."[9]

College students were in harmony with this mood and were for the most part apolitical ("a silent generation")—interested in a fraternity/sorority-based social life and in preparing for future careers. The Reverend Norman Vincent Peale, with his message of "positive thinking," became the country's most popular moralist and preacher, and the country's growing religious interest seemed built on sociability rather than spirituality.

The mass media of the 1950s reflected and reinforced these values. Television was dominated by entertainers like the droning, folksy Arthur Godfrey, who became one of its most powerful personalities; by the skilled slapstick of *I Love Lucy*; and by the naked greed of quiz shows such as *Twenty-one*. And though there were imaginative comedy programs like *Your Show of Shows* and original television drama on *Playhouse 90*, the most popular programs were often built on the most inane premises and on the marketing of personal comfort and instant gratification. One interesting statistic that conveyed something of the anti-intellectual taste of the times was that "about four times the expenditures on public libraries were paid out for comic books."[10]

In books like William H. Whyte's *The Organization Man* (1956) and David Riesman's more scholarly and complex *The Lonely Crowd* (1950), American middle-class life was criticized for its penchant for uniformity, social role playing, and privatism. Other critics, both liberal and conservative, poked fun at the mass media, advertising, the automobile culture, and the anxiety-laden drive for social status and material goods. However, though the banality and tastelessness of much of what appeared on television and the blandness of suburban life were criticized, there was no attempt by these critics to break from the political and social consensus of the 1950s. For the most part, they accepted the political and social system that helped shape the culture, and most of the targets they attacked were not particularly controversial ones.[11]

Nevertheless, despite the serene and confident veneer of the Eisenhower years, there were subversive currents that, though sometimes unrecognized, coexisted with the dominant mood of stability and complacency. The threat of nuclear war shadowed the period, creating among a number of people a sense of fatalism and despair and leading to protests in the late 1950s against the civil defense program. The program was seen as treating nuclear war as an acceptable military alternative that people had to prepare themselves to survive.

The 1950s also saw the civil rights movement begin to take shape. Whites may have been content with the political and social world of the 1950s, but black needs and problems were clearly left unmet by an indifferent Republican administration and a Congress paralyzed by the southern Democratic bloc. The only arm of government responsive to black grievances was the Supreme Court led by Chief Justice Earl Warren. In 1954, the Court came to a monumental decision. In *Brown v. Board of Education of Topeka*, it outlawed segregation in the public schools. There were violent reactions in the South, but de jure segregation of the schools (de facto segregation is a continuing and deepening reality) was at the beginning of its end.

The Court decision led to the 1955 Montgomery bus boycott—a grassroots black protest against segregation in public transportation. The boycott was followed by protest movements in other southern cities and, most important, marked the ascent to national black leadership of Martin Luther King Jr.

The movement to the suburbs by urban whites also carried a critical, even dark, undercurrent. For though it was viewed either satirically—as a flight to a sterile, tedious, and vulgar world—or sympathetically—as ordinary Americans achieving their small portion of the American Dream—the radical consequences (by 1950, 40 to 50 million Americans lived in the suburbs) of this flight for the inner cities of the 1960s and 1970s were not foreseen. The departure of the white middle class and lower-middle class from the cities and their replacement by black and Hispanic poor led in the following decades to the erosion of the urban tax base (built on the sales and property taxes of its inhabitants), the escalation of often insoluble urban problems, and even greater residential segregation than existed in the past.[12]

There were also other 1950s currents that indicated resistance to the conservatism of the decade. The beat movement, which was an attack on the middle-class conformity, the hypocrisy of the Eisenhower years, and the elite literary culture of the universities, came of age in the 1950s. Led by serious poets like Allen Ginsberg and Gregory Corso and novelists like Jack Kerouac (*On the Road*), the beats modeled their writing on poets like Walt Whitman and novelists like Henry Miller and on the improvisation of jazz musicians like Charlie Parker. In their writing and lives, they emphasized spontaneity, personal freedom, contempt for authority, and spiritual exploration. The beat movement did not consist only of artists. There were other young people— beatniks—who, taking their lead from the Kerouacs and Ginsbergs, adopted or mimicked a more natural, antibourgeois (i.e., some pot, jazz, and freer sex) lifestyle. And though the beats were never a part of a political or social movement, their writings rejected racism and the nuclear arms race and treated homosexuality without contempt or condescension.[13]

The 1950s also saw the development of a distinctive youth culture accompanied by a new (though derived from black rhythm-and-blues music) form of music—rock and roll. For many older Americans, rock music was too loud and overtly sexual and sounded to them like aimless noise. However, at its best and most innovative (e.g., the rock of Chuck Berry and Elvis Presley), the music had an energy, freedom, and earthiness that offered the possibility of an undefined, new lifestyle that strongly contrasted with 1950s conventionality. Of course, by the late 1950s, much of rock music's class and regional identity had been bleached out and transformed into the mass-produced, soporific sound of Frankie Avalon and his clones.[14]

Clearly, these deviant currents and dark strains were not the preeminent ones in 1950s America. It is important, however, to recognize that the era was more complex than the usual images and descriptive phrases evoking a time supposedly dominated by a passive "silent generation."

Similarly, the films produced in Hollywood also defied facile labels and categories. In the early 1950s, as they did in the late 1940s, HUAC garnered publicity by investigating the film industry. Its hearings helped buttress the already powerful blacklist of actors, writers, and directors and created in its wake a "clearance"[15] industry that passed on the political purity and future employment of the people worked in Hollywood. And just as in the late 1940s (*I Married a Communist*, 1949), cheap genre films were produced to purge the Hollywood image of any taint of radicalism. A film like *Big Jim McLain* (1952) used a documentary style, including an authoritative narrator, to exult the FBI and HUAC while condemning communists more for their character traits (they were either criminals, idealistic dupes, nymphomaniacs, or disturbed fanatics) than for their ideology. In fact, the ideology was never defined or explored. Communists were reduced to caricatures who saw human life as dispensable, had no room for private feelings, and were even in opposition to God and motherhood.

The most hysterical of these films—and probably the one least bound by genre conventions—was *My Son John* (1952). Its director was Leo McCarey (e.g., *The Awful Truth*, 1937), who had distinguished himself during the 1947 HUAC hearing by replying to a question about why the Russians had banned his last film (*Going My Way*, 1944): "Because it had God in it." In addition, in 1950 he joined Cecil B. DeMille in urging all members of the Directors' Guild to take a loyalty oath. *My Son John* differed from other anticommunist films by focusing on the conflict between father and son rather than the usual exposé of communist crimes and conspiracies. The film operated most powerfully on a barely acknowledged Oedipal level where both father and son struggle for the wife-mother's time and respect. However, it is clear that what McCarey tried to do in *My Son John* was to pit the all-American "Jefferson" family's communist son John, an unathletic, sexually ambiguous intellectual, played in his insidious, contemptuous *Strangers on a Train* (1951) style by Robert Walker, against his modest, down-to-earth parents (Helen Hayes and Dean Jagger) who believe in football, the Bible, the American nation, and the flag.

It is obviously an unequal struggle since the sullen, slick John is seen by McCarey as a monster, and though the overpossessive mother is a mass of neurotic tics—rolling eyes, tense smile, and flapping hands—and the father is a rigid, banal legionnaire, they are totally vindicated at the film's conclusion. In an unbelievable final scene, the dead John (killed by communist agents) leaves a tape recording of a commencement speech that, enveloped in almost divine light, plays from the lectern to his former university's graduating class. The tape affirms his faith in his father and mother and informs the students how the communist serpent numbed his brain and led him to become a traitor.

In McCarey's feverish world, being an intellectual was clearly a dangerous, un-American vocation, and redemption could be found only in the moralisms of John's elementary school principal father and the hysterical religiosity of his mother. For McCarey, it is the heart and emotions, no matter how pathological, that won't lie or lead you astray. But the intellect is dangerous—it makes you question and doubt and leaves you open to subversive ideas and the rejection of commonsense wisdom.

Nor was McCarey alone in this view of the perfidy of the intellectual. It was a perspective that was shared, albeit with greater subtlety and complexity, by Elia Kazan, who also played a leading role before HUAC. Kazan had joined the Communist Party in the 1930s but resigned, feeling intense bitterness and hostility toward it. However, he continued to see himself as a man of the left.[16] And in 1951, at the height of the Cold War and close to the time he delivered his infamous cooperative testimony before HUAC, he made *Viva Zapata*, a film dealing with the heroic leader of the Mexican Revolution. It was Kazan's first truly personal and structurally cinematic work—an intense film characterized by highly stylized and powerful imagery and lighting and a political perspective open to a variety of conflicting interpretations. That was a sign of either its profound ambiguity or its intellectual confusion.

Nevertheless, at the HUAC hearings, *Viva Zapata* was viewed as a sustained anticommunist film, and Kazan himself promoted it as an anticommunist work. What could be considered anticommunist in the film was evoked most vividly by the character of Fernando (Joseph Wiseman), a Machiavellian, professional revolutionary, and intellectual. Kazan conceived him as a sterile, cold man—an antilife force—dangerous not only because of his political opportunism but also because of his lack of capacity for human connection. In fact, Fernando is portrayed as a revolutionary devoid of any political ideology excepting a commitment to power—a common stereotype that Hollywood used to provide a negative portrait for revolutionaries. He is willing to shift from the political left to the right without a moment's hesitation or reflection. It is clear that Kazan wanted Fernando to be seen, despite the vagueness of his ideology, as the apotheosis of the Communist Party commissar—a man who could use and betray both the people's demands and his personal relationships and loyalties to achieve power.

Kazan's evocation of the intellectual's power hunger is, however, only one example of the film's prime theme: the oppressiveness and meaninglessness of political power. For example, in a key scene, Zapata (Marlon Brando) is depicted occupying the presidential palace and continuing both to temporize and to intimidate the peasants as the tyrant Diaz had done before him. Obviously, in this somewhat abstract, schematic sequence, Kazan wished to demonstrate to the audience that power corrupts and that revolutionary regimes have sustained the tyrannical patterns of their right-wing predecessors.

However, *Viva Zapata* cannot be reduced to an anticommunist polemic on the lines of *My Son John* since it is filled with diverse (sometimes half-developed) strains that lead to often contradictory interpretations. Given this fact, it is understandable that the *Daily Worker* would have attacked the film for being Trotskyist,[17] that a number of film critics could condemn it for its Cold War anticommunism, and that a great many people in the 1960s New Left could love and embrace it.[18]

Viva Zapata conveyed both populist and anarchist sentiments along with its anticommunism. The film was filled with images of peasants acting heroically and collectively to promote the revolution. For the most part, Kazan tended to romanticize them, portraying them in static, archetypal images and in silhouette as models of innocence and solemn dignity. But Kazan's populism also had an underside in the person of Eufemio (Anthony Quinn), Zapata's brother, who is a barbarian desiring the fruits of the revolution—booty, women, and the land—without any other commitment beyond self-gratification. And the power of the people is often undermined by the charismatic figure of Zapata. Though Zapata is able to inform the people that "there is no leader but yourselves," he is depicted as a mythic figure whose instinctive nobility and life energy dwarfs the noble peasants that surround and follow him. The mixture of Brando's larger-than-life performance and Kazan's conception of Zapata make it difficult to believe that with Zapata's death the peasants have become a populist force—the "strong people that don't need a strong man."

If Kazan's populism is bound by contradictions, his anarchism exists much more as a personal response, a belief in acting spontaneously and passionately rather than a politically coherent idea of state and society. There are no hints of Kropotkin, Bakunin, or some form of anarchosyndicalism inherent in the film. There is just Kazan's personal disdain for bourgeois repression and respectability and his ambivalence about the quest for middle-class success. And if in *Viva Zapata* there exists a genuine antagonism to political structures and hierarchies, it is more out of a commitment to the revolutionary image and emotion than to the political and social ends of revolution. Kazan is finally more interested in heroic myth (Zapata heroically astride his white horse) and the act of rebellion than in history or politics.

Clearly, *Viva Zapata* was not the unequivocal anticommunist polemic some critics perceived it to be. But Kazan did pay his dues to HUAC with his next film, *Man on a Tight Rope* (1953). The film was neither a commercial success nor a personal favorite of Kazan's. Filled with Cold War speeches and stereotyped characters, it deals with a Czech circus fleeing to the West. It pits communist thugs and bureaucrats against the cosmopolitan life force and artistry of the circus performers. The communists are seen as stupid, petty, and anti-intellectual, committed to stifling all individuality and shaping it to fit the party line. *Man on a Tight Rope* was a conventional melodrama, devoid of real people, whose main aim was to propagate an anticommunist line and help Kazan escape the committee's hook.

In 1954, however, Kazan's craft revived with his Academy Award–winning direction of *On the Waterfront*—on one level an emotionally charged and moving melodrama dealing with both one man's personal redemption and the nature of union corruption on the New York waterfront. On another level, Kazan used the film to justify being an informer before HUAC with his protagonist, Terry Malloy (Marlon Brando), acting as a heroic stand-in for himself. Malloy becomes an informer in an extremely difficult situation—where he could be dubbed a Judas for breaking the neighborhood code of silence. But it is also a situation where the decent and virtuous characters (along with the audience) would view his unwillingness to talk as an act of moral cowardice. In fact, Kazan stated, "Terry Malloy felt as I did. He felt ashamed and proud of himself at the same time. . . . He felt it was a necessary act."[19] In addition, Kazan partially sanitized the HUAC investigations by having their film counterpart, the crime commission, represent all that was benign and honest in governmental action.

However, in *On the Waterfront*, the parallels to Kazan's experience with HUAC and the social significance of the film are overshadowed by the powerful and complex portrait of Terry Malloy that Brando and Kazan created. Malloy is a mumbling, shoulder-shrugging, boy-man who raises pigeons, pals around with adolescents who worship him, and survives as the condescended-to pet of the egotistical and vicious union boss Johnny Friendly (played in a roaring, larger-than-life style by Lee J. Cobb) on the periphery of the longshoremen's community. He is also a gum-chewing, alienated, tough, urban wise guy with scar tissue over his eyes from his earlier stint as a prizefighter who masks his vulnerability by upholding a code that is based on the notion that the world is a jungle where your first obligation is to look out for yourself.

As the film evolves, Kazan turns Terry from a comic-reading bum into a moral and social hero. It's a change seen most poignantly and concretely in his relationships with the fragile, protected, "good girl" Edie (Eva Marie Saint); the morally tough Father Barry (Karl Malden); and his opportunistic, shyster brother Charlie (Rod Steiger). Terry is barely articulate, but Brando is able to totally inhabit the role and with every gesture and word grants the character a complex inner life. Malloy is composed of a variety of parts: a profound sense of personal failure and lost dignity, a powerful loyalty to his brother and corrupt union boss, and a mixture of tenderness and brutality in his character. It all comes together in such a manner that the change in Terry is utterly believable.

On the Waterfront is also a film that deals with the world of the longshoremen and their corrupt union. The film's cinematography, though self-consciously pictorial, does evoke the physical surface of a world of heavy mist, haunting boat whistles, seedy pocket parks, garbage-ridden backyards, tenements covered with clotheslines, television antennae, pigeon coops, and an omnipresent river filled with boats. There are also painful glimpses of longshoremen rituals, such as the soul-destroying shape-up, where the men scramble on the ground for tokens that provide them a day's work. But it is all more an expression of Kazan's sharp eye for dramatic detail than his interest in the social texture and dynamics of the docks. Kazan's longshoremen are never really particularized; they are "more social masks than people."[20] They are seen as a mass, first intimidated and submerged by the union boss and his goons, and by the film's conclusion, following a bruised and martyred (though Kazan denies that there is more than a hint of Christian symbolism in the film), Malloy back to work.

Aside from trying to vindicate the role of the informer, On the Waterfront is a much less political film than Viva Zapata. Kazan is not really interested in exploring the politics of one type of American unionism. The relationship of the longshoremen's union to the shipping interests and the political machine is barely touched on. The populist strain that is found in Zapata doesn't exist here. The workers are cowed by the union and docile—incapable of generating any collective political action on their own. It's the character and redemption of Terry Malloy that is the film's stunning centerpiece, and although in the film's operatic climax Malloy leads the workers against Johnny Friendly, there is no political dimension to his victory. (There is even a note of warning about the nature of the triumph inserted, with a beaten but still defiant Johnny Friendly screaming, "I'll be back." And in the real world, his counterparts continued to control the docks.)

The heroic attack against corrupt power and repression of Zapata has become a purely personal and moral act. There is no suggestion that Malloy has developed a political and social vision like Zapata's; he is merely a more alienated and resentful version of that classic American hero, the courageous individual who stands up for the good against those who would degrade and threaten our lives, though this time there is an upright government to be of some help to the hero.

On the Waterfront can be seen as a conventional Hollywood film, filled with stock villains, overly theatrical sequences (e.g., Father Barry's speech in the hold attacking the mob), and a manipulative and intrusive score. However, listing the film's weaknesses fails to convey Kazan's characteristically driving energy and passion and genius with actors. And in Brando's Malloy, the film brought to life one of the most striking manifestations of the anti-hero, who began to appear frequently in the films of the 1950s.

In contrast to the implicit anticommunism of *Viva Zapata* and the defense of informing in *On the Waterfront*, Kazan's *Face in the Crowd* (1957) was a truly prophetic work on the growing power of television and the merging of politics and entertainment. It was a combination that would ultimately transform American politics. Kazan's film follows the rise and fall of a hillbilly singer who moves inexorably from a local radio station in Arkansas to network television stardom in New York. The singer, Lonesome Rhodes (an inspired performance by Andy Griffith), is viewed as a media natural—a spontaneous and even genuinely honest figure—but he is also someone with a touch of a con man's seductive duplicity, displaying contempt for the public he captivates.

By the film's overdrawn second half, there is no longer any ambiguity surrounding Lonesome. His rebellious charm has disappeared, and he has turned into a power-hungry monster. He feels now that he can ignorantly pontificate on a variety of social and political issues. He even turns into a political mentor, prefiguring the age of Reagan, by advising a group of right-wing fat cats that what's important for political success is to be photogenic and being able to deliver lines rather than take cogent political positions.

Lonesome ultimately has a television program where a chorus of ersatz rubes mouth familiar platitudes about the flag, the need for family values, and the dangers of the welfare state. It's right-wing populism at its most repellent and insidious.

The film can feel too strident, including a final scene where a defeated Lonesome, seen in a variety of extreme camera angles, bellows in front of a backdrop of giant, blown-up photos of himself, a roaring applause machine, and a banner, emanating heavy-handed irony, reading, "There's nothing as trustworthy as the ordinary mind of the ordinary man." Still, the film provides an almost visionary portrayal of the future political power of entertainers, television personalities, and actors, who seem perfectly prepared for an age where media politics is triumphant (e.g., Trump).[21]

Kazan was hardly alone among 1950s directors that dealt either directly with communism or indirectly with the ideology and psychology surrounding the anticommunist crusade. Even Alfred Hitchcock, in his commercially successful, charming chase film *North by Northwest* (1959), added a Cold War spy story to its stylish mix of romance, wit, and suspense.

Early in the decade, with the advent of the Korean War, Samuel Fuller made *The Steel Helmet* (1951), a crude, earnest, low-budget film that on one level seemed determined to be second to none in its portrayal of communists as the last word in bestiality and savagery. Fuller has the North Koreans leaving booby-trapped corpses of dead GIs around, killing innocent children, and indulging in human-wave attacks that give clear evidence of their contempt for the value of human life. Nonetheless, Fuller, in his primitive anarchic fashion, gave ample hints that he was wary of all ideologies: finding fault with his American GIs' racial and cultural blindness and depicting his alienated hero Sergeant Zack (Gene Evans) as a cynical, sadistic, cigar-chomping figure, interested only in survival and untouched by the slightest hint of humanitarian impulse (except for his love for his South Korean ward). *The Steel Helmet*, despite its tabloid script and cartoonlike characters, had a great deal of bite and reality. It also gave evidence that the war film could simultaneously mouth and subvert patriotic platitudes and convey that the anticommunist side was no community of saints.[22]

To a degree, this flexibility allowed some directors and writers to use genres as a means of commenting on American politics. In 1952, director Fred Zinnemann (*The Search*, 1948, and *From Here to Eternity*, 1953) and scriptwriter Carl Foreman (who had been cited by HUAC in 1951, refused to cooperate, and was subsequently blacklisted) made *High Noon*, a popular western that was clearly a left-liberal parable about HUAC's attack on Hollywood. *High Noon* was a "mature western" about an aging, weary marshal (Gary Cooper in an Academy Award–winning performance) who has a deeply lined face and sagging flesh and admits to being scared. Uncharacteristically for a western hero, he asks for the assistance of the townspeople but is deserted by them and left alone to confront a murderous psychopath and his henchman. The craven townspeople find a variety of reasons why they cannot stand up to this threat to law and liberty: the parson cannot commit himself to killing, the old sheriff is paralyzed by despair, the judge is a smooth careerist whose only loyalty is to self-preservation, and the others just hide or flee from the confrontation. We are left with the lone American hero who must face and, of course (for some of the genre conventions are maintained), defeat the villains.

High Noon is a skillfully directed, gripping, and intelligent film that uses incisive crosscutting and an exciting sound track—an Academy Award–winning score by Dimitri Tiomkin—and the rhythmic ticking of a clock (the film's running time runs parallel to this time of crisis in the marshal's life) to successfully build narrative tension. However, it is a film whose images are merely functional and whose characters are intelligently conceived types without any genuine individuality. The film's moral heroism does not quite translate into political terms, for the hero has no politics and the villains have no institutional connections. Nevertheless, in its commitment to individual moral responsibility and courage, the film did convey to a portion of its audience that evils such as McCarthyism could no longer be rationalized or evaded and must be resisted.

Given the political mood of the period, *High Noon* was a bold film, but its use of metaphor and allegory and its emphasis on moral rather than political courage made it a relatively oblique one.[23] A film that dared to criticize American capitalism directly stood the risk of having its production disrupted by vigilantes and even if completed would find few distributors or theaters willing to exhibit it. Such a film was *Salt of the Earth* (1954), which was independently made by blacklisted writers Herbert Biberman (who also directed it), Michael Wilson, and Paul Jarrico and sponsored by the Mine, Mill, and Smelter Workers, a union that had been expelled from the Congress of Industrial Organizations in 1950 for its communist ties. The film focuses around the strike of a group of primarily Mexican American zinc miners against a racist, exploitative, and repressive mining company. There are moments that the film was crudely polemical and stilted, more socialist than social realism, particularly in its use of militant music, heavy-handed crosscutting, and stereotyped villains; a clownishly crude and violent sheriff and his deputies; a callous pipe-smoking superintendent; and a company president who goes on African safaris. Of course, the Mexican workers are seen as spontaneous and brave, and the film's heroine Esperanza (Rosaura Revueltas, who was deported three times during the film's shooting) is a shy, glowing beauty who conveys great warmth and courage.

On the other hand, *Salt of the Earth* projects a feminist consciousness unique for either the left or the right during the 1950s, for the film centers on the conflict between the sexes on the workers' side as well as with class oppression. The miners have never thought about the feelings and lives of their wives, who are taken for granted, traditionally bound to home and children. But as the strike develops, the women, who are forced to take the men's place on the picket line, assert themselves, asking to be treated as equals. The men's pride and machismo is hurt, but eventually they begin to accept the change in traditional patterns, and they not only win the strike but also transcend their chauvinist notions of sexual identity. It is a pat conclusion, but the images of women gathering on a hill to join the picket line and some men struggling with the laundry are moving ones and pre-date anything Hollywood was to conjure up until the feminist-conscious 1970s and 1980s.[24]

With its unabashed left perspective, *Salt of the Earth* was an aberration in the 1950s. A film more in tune with the spirit of the decade was Don Siegel's *Invasion of the Body Snatchers* (1956), a low-budget, witty, science-fiction film dealing with the subject of alien infiltration and mind control that pervaded so many of the science-fiction films of the decade.

In *The Thing* (1951), a U.S. scientific expedition is threatened by a ferocious monster that they thaw out of a spaceship. In William Cameron Menzies's *Invaders from Mars* (1951), a small boy is unable to convince adults that Martians are kidnapping important figures and placing crystals in their brains that will force them to commit brutal acts. Of all these films, however, *Invasion of the Body Snatchers* was the most subtle. Its most distinctive quality stems from its director Don Siegel's matter-of-fact, realistic style, which eschews violence for still, silent, ominous images. The film projects a world where ordinary objects are strangely illuminated and people's faces remain unlit and where light signifies safety and hope and darkness and shadows mean danger. The paranoid plot focuses on an invasion of alien pods (a product of atomic mutation) of a small, neighborly town where everybody knows each other's first name. As the pods possess the people in the town, they turn them not into violent monsters but into bland, expressionless vegetables who are incapable of love, rage, pleasure, or pain.

It is the depiction of the pods that opens *Invasion of the Body Snatchers* to a variety of interpretations. In one interpretation, the pods can be seen as a symbol of a society where alienated people flee their individuality and seek refuge in mindless mass conformity—an exaggerated version of Riesman's *Lonely Crowd*. In another, more probable interpretation, the pods could be seen as communists, the omnipresent aliens of the 1950s who are everywhere conspiring to turn people into robots. Of course, it is doubtful if *Invasion of the Body Snatchers* was perceived by its audience as anything more than a conventional entertainment film. Nonetheless, the anxiety, hysteria, and paranoia it tapped about the threat of communist totalitarianism made it a perfect expression of some of the decade's obsessions.[25]

Undoubtedly, a direct or even an oblique commitment to dealing with political issues was far from the dominant force in the Hollywood of the 1950s. Given the competition from television and decreasing movie theater attendance, Hollywood gave a great deal of thought to recapturing its audience. Using color more heavily and then seeking out new technological processes, the studios attempted by overwhelming the viewer to attract him back to moviegoing. Processes such as Cinemascope, Vista-Vision, Cinerama, and 3-D were introduced, exploiting the size of the film image and experimenting (unsuccessfully) with the creation of the illusion of depth.[26]

Ultimately, the wide-screen processes led to a number of expensive, lengthy blockbuster films like *The Robe* (1953), *The Ten Commandments* (1956, which cost $13.5 million to make), and *Ben-Hur* (1959). These epics were on one level part of the religious revival of the 1950s—cartoons of religious piety—and, more important, with their color, crowds, chariot races, and crucifixions they were the last great flings of studio excess (where "only too much is really sufficient"),[27] allowing these films to fully exploit the vastness of the new screen.

The new Hollywood could be glimpsed in Billy Wilder's smart *Sunset Boulevard* (1950). The plot centers on an aging, once famous and glamorous silent-screen actress, Norma Desmond (Gloria Swanson), who lives in a decaying mansion as if time has stood still. She fantasizes about making a comeback film with the aid of a decent, weary, and hungry screenwriter, Joe Gillis (William Holden), who becomes first her collaborator and then her lover and kept man. *Sunset Boulevard* follows a number of the conventions of film noir, using voice-over narration and flashback and centering on a possessive, hysterical, sexually devouring heroine and a morally ambiguous hero. However, the film's prime focus is not on the corruption of Joe Gillis but on the contrast between the old Hollywood and the new—not necessarily to the latter's advantage.

Though Billy Wilder and his co-writer Charles Bracket depict Norma Desmond as something of a wild-eyed, campy grotesque, the film is still an idiosyncratic homage to the absurdity, excess, and graciousness of the flamboyant, old Hollywood. Luminaries of the old Hollywood like Buster Keaton, Cecil B. DeMille, and Erich von Stroheim (who plays Max, Norma's first-director, ex-husband, and present-day protector and servant) are treated sympathetically, while in the plainer, sharp-tongued, grasping new Hollywood, producers dismiss the "message kids," want to make Betty Hutton musicals out of baseball stories, and have no time for truth or art. For Wilder, the old Hollywood, if nothing else, had style, making the more pragmatic, businesslike Hollywood of the 1950s (which he was an integral part of) pale in comparison.

Contrary to *Sunset Boulevard*'s sour view of the contemporary Hollywood scene, many producers still felt optimism about the future. Some of that hopefulness was based on the success of big-screen musical comedies, particularly adaptations of Broadway hits like *Oklahoma* (1955) and *Guys and Dolls* (1955).[28] However, these musicals, though commercially successful, suffered from ponderous and inflated production values. It also began to seem ridiculous for characters to break into song and dance at the slightest provocation. The best musicals of the decade appeared in the early 1950s and came from the illustrious Freed unit at MGM. These medium-budget original musicals included Vincente Minnelli's decorative and stylized *An American in Paris* (1951) with an athletic Gene Kelly, his somber and witty *The Bandwagon* (1953) with the elegant and feathery Fred Astaire, and Stanley Donen and Gene Kelly's classic show-business musical *Singin' in the Rain* (1952).

Singin' in the Rain is a breezy, good-natured satire of Hollywood's Busby Berkeley musicals, film premieres, star biographies, and the introduction of sound, written by the urbane Betty Comden and Adolph Green and starring Gene Kelly as an earthy, dynamic, ordinary American Hollywood star, Don Lockwood. Kelly is, as always, brashly self-confident and jaunty, and in the film's stirring title number, he wistfully stamps around in rain puddles, and holding his sole prop, an umbrella, he exultingly embraces the studio rain. With its pastel colors, cheerful songs ("Good Morning"), and acrobatic pratfalls (Donald O'Connor energetically dancing through cardboard sets), *Singin' in the Rain* created a world where any action can spontaneously, calmly, and naturally be turned into music and dance. It was a world where despair and doubt do not exist and where the happy ending continues to survive. And if *Singin' in the Rain*'s plot about the transition to sound is a metaphor of the challenge that Hollywood faced from television, it is also an indicator of just how much carefully honed optimism still dominated the studio product.[29]

A few years later, a much more melancholy and despairing note was conveyed in Donen and Kelly's final collaboration, *It's Always Fair Weather* (1955). In many ways a successor to *On the Town*, its three GI buddies (Dan Dailey and Michael Kidd re-creating the Jules Munshin and Frank Sinatra roles) decide to get together 10 years after the war is over. It is a measure of the sour mood of the film that the three find they have very little in common and do not really like one another. Although both Dailey and Kidd are better dancers than Munshin and Sinatra, there is very little chemistry between the three— even their bravura garbage-can dance together, though clever, has none of the inspired warmth of the numbers in *On the Town*. Indicative also of the darkening Hollywood mood is the film's negative response to the world of media and television. It takes satiric pot shots at advertising—Dan Dailey as an ad executive singing the drunken "Situationwise"—and at television shows like *This Is Your Life*.[30]

Even if *It's Always Fair Weather* did sound a despondent chord and few 1950s films had *Singin' in the Rain*'s charming airiness and feeling of being at home in the world, the era still contained many genre films that upheld traditional virtues and values and were commercially successful. In George Stevens's carefully composed, beautiful *Shane* (1955) a blond, mysterious stranger in white named Shane (Alan Ladd) is befriended by a group of homesteaders and protects them in turn from a predatory rancher and his psychopathic, hired killer dressed in black (Jack Palance). In a sense, *Shane* is no ordinary western. It is a self-conscious attempt to create a mythic West populated by archetypes—with the enigmatic, perfect-featured, sententious Shane seen continually from the perspective of a hero-worshipping young boy (Brandon de Wilde).[31] However, despite its portentousness, it was a more conventional film (for all his grandiosity, Shane is not that much different from the more pedestrian radio and television hero the Lone Ranger) than the 1950s westerns of Anthony Mann (*The Naked Spur*, 1953), austere, bleak films built around a revenge motif or John Ford's epic western *The Searchers* (1956) with John Wayne as the most ambiguous of Fordian heroes.

Ford's later films like *The Searchers* depicted a darker, less morally defined world than earlier works like *Stagecoach* (1939) and *My Darling Clementine* (1946). The plot of *The Searchers* revolves around a driven, ex-Confederate soldier Ethan Edwards (Wayne), who searches for years for his niece Debbie (Natalie Wood). Debbie has been kidnapped by the Indians after her family members (including Ethan's brother and sister-in-law) were massacred. Edwards still has enough left of the classic Wayne–Ford hero to display indomitable courage, rescuing Debbie from the Indians he passionately hates, and returning her to Ford's ideal world of family and community—the garden in the wilderness.

But nothing is quite the same in Ford's world in this film. Everything has become grimmer: the landscape is more threatening, Ford's beloved cavalry both less noble and more absurd, and his sullen, violent hero consumed by murderous rage and racist feelings. Ford's heroes can usually reconcile their individuality with community—nature with civilization. But Ethan is the "man who wanders" and is unable to enter the door of the hearth again. The stirring long shot of his walking away, framed by the doorway of the house, is not an affirmation of the romance and freedom of a Shane-like hero who can never be domesticated but rather a tragic, desolate image of a man doomed to solitude. (In the 1980s, *The Searchers* became a model for films like *Rambo: First Blood Part II*, where the freeing of MIAs from the barbaric captivity of the North Vietnamese followed the pattern of Ethan's quest to free Debbie from the Indians.) It also inspired rock 'n' roll icon Buddy Holly's hit song "That I'll Be the Day," after a catch phrase used repeatedly by Wayne in the film.

Despite this tragic denouement, Ford's gift for poetic imagery is still in evidence. Ford creates scenes wherein a single gesture can speak volumes. For example, Martha (Dorothy Jordan), Ethan's sister-in-law, strokes his cape with such tenderness that the Rev. Capt. Samuel Johnston Clayton (Ward Bond) has to avert his eyes from the intimacy of the moment. Ford also includes mythic themes of the American culture such as the captivity literature and the works of James Fenimore Cooper by making Ethan a "Man who knows Indians." In a scene where the Texas Rangers come upon the grave of one of the Indians they are pursuing, the vengeful Ethan shoots out the eyes of the corpse, condemning him to wander the earth after death. Ford also attempts to provide motivation for the Indians' depredations by having the chief Scar (Henry Brandon), who abducted Debbie, explain that the white man killed his sons. In addition, Ford tries to be morally even-handed (not his wont) in showing that the Indian atrocities were balanced by the cavalry's massacre of entire Indian villages.

There is an aspect of *The Searchers* that seems not fully comprehensible but is still especially moving. Ethan, who only a few scenes earlier was ready to kill Debbie because he felt her becoming one of Scar's wives made her too tainted to be allowed to live, suddenly takes her in his arms and says, "We're going home." This moment, when Ethan transcends himself, moved director/critic Jean-Luc Godard, whose politics were the antithesis of Wayne's, to remark that until that moment he hated him, but after it he loved him.

Despite the sense of unease that began to creep into 1950s films, neither Hollywood nor the public was particularly open to films that took formal or intellectual risks. Exemplifying this attitude was the popular comedy team of the 1950s, Martin and Lewis (*Artists and Models*, 1955), whose slapstick routines and Jerry Lewis's twitchy, idiotic, victim's persona did not differ much from the style of earlier B-film comic teams like Abbott and Costello.

Just as indicative of the basic conservatism of popular taste and values were films dealing with woman's consciousness and identity. During the decade, there were not only fewer films about independent women than in the 1930s or 1940s but also fewer films dealing with women at all. In the literate, epigrammatic Academy Award–winning *All About Eve* (1950), a temperamental, sarcastic, ambitious star of the theater, Margo Channing (Bette Davis), is also a vulnerable, insecure woman underneath all her wit and drive. She ultimately sees her career as insufficient, as something separate from being a real woman, and opts for marriage, children, and retirement. And her mousy and devoted protégé Eve (Anne Baxter) turns out to be a predatory and manipulative actress who wants to be a star and is willing to use any means to supplant Margo. In *All About Eve*, successful women are either unhappy or so distorted by their ambition that they lose their humanity in the process.

In a minor role in the same film, Marilyn Monroe, the sex symbol of the 1950s, plays another of her dumb blondes, a woman-object whose sexuality is unthreatening, guileless, and childlike. Toward the end of the decade, in films such as Billy Wilder's brilliant, frenetically paced, transvestite sex farce *Some Like It Hot* (1959), she added vulnerability to her victim's persona.

While Monroe was more a male fantasy figure than a woman that other women could identify with, the freckled, eternally sunny Doris Day was one female star who was capable of eliciting both male and female sympathy. In a period where being popular had become a prime cultural value, Day's persona in battle-of-the-sexes comedies, such as *Pillow Talk* (1958) with Rock Hudson, conveyed a superhygienic, wholesome cheerfulness. However, though these comedies were built on an extremely puritanical, timorous form of sexiness, with Day remaining always the virgin, her supposed sexual innocence was less significant than her drive, ambition, and spunkiness. In fact, so potent were those qualities that as a tailored-suited journalism professor in *Teacher's Pet* (1958), she is tough enough to even put to rout Hollywood studs (albeit he had begun to age) like Clark Gable. Despite Day's girl-next-door looks and behavior, her characters often had jobs and projected a tougher, more independent persona than most of the other major female stars (e.g., Grace Kelly and Audrey Hepburn) of the decade.[32]

However, though the characters Doris Day played may have held down jobs, most women in the 1950s films were housewives or women seeking to avoid spinsterhood who found salvation in marriage. In one traditional genre, however—the soap opera—German-born director Douglas Sirk made films that used the genre's conventions to make oblique criticisms of traditional female roles and middle-class conformity.

Backed by one of the most commercial Hollywood producers, Ross Hunter, *All That Heaven Allows* (1955) was characterized by artificial studio landscapes and townscapes, melodramatic, fortuitous accidents, a saccharine score, and a predictable, neat conclusion. Despite the clichés that permeated the film, Sirk was a consummate stylist who could use color, light, clothes, and furniture to express his sensibility—through capturing his heroine's state of mind. Throughout the film, Sirk uses both reflections on television screens, mirrors, and piano tops and ubiquitous screens and doors both to evoke a middle-class world dominated by gleaming surfaces and appearances and to catch the heroine's feelings of imprisonment. It's an eloquent use of cinematic form to comment on content[33] and, at moments, transcends the lack of subtlety and soap operatic quality of the script.

The film presents the world from the point of view of an older heroine, Carrie (Jane Wyman)—an upper-middle-class widow with few interests, little emotional connection between herself and her unpleasant, grown-up children, and a number of acceptable men desiring to marry her. She breaks from the mores of her country club set and the disapproval of her children, becoming involved with a young, passive, handsome hero Ron Kirby (Rock Hudson). He is not only much younger than her, but he is also a landscaper who lives a comfortably bohemian life that is dimly committed to simplicity, a love of nature, an uncompromising belief in being autonomous, and a disdain for snobbery and status seeking. But he's college educated and refined, and his home and friends look more like models for a Norman Rockwell magazine cover—cute and unnaturally wholesome—than some bohemian enclave.

For all that, Kirby is not the usual alternative for heroines in 1950s and women's pictures. Carrie chooses to fulfill her own emotional and sexual needs and not only rejects her friends but also decides that she won't be a Stella Dallas (heroine in Vidor's film of same name in 1937) or Mildred Pierce and sacrifice her life for her children. Sirk's film, however, was clearly no feminist work. Carrie's choice of a new way of life is predicated on the existence of a man to provide her with an alternate set of values and a refuge in marriage; in terms of the narrative, it is a very safe sort of rebellion. But its criticism of middle-class materialism, hypocrisy, and emptiness (more telling in the film's mise-en-scène than its narrative) was symptomatic of much less oblique works that rebelled against the complacency and conformity of Eisenhower America. In these films, male stars such as the previously mentioned virile, angry Brando (*On the Waterfront*); the brooding, vulnerable Monty Clift (*A Place in the Sun*, 1951, and *From Here to Eternity*, 1953); and James Dean (Kazan's *East of Eden*, 1955) played antiheroic heroes who in different ways were at odds with the prevailing social order.

In *A Place in the Sun* (1951), Clift plays a haunted, sensitive outsider in a dark, romantic version—all dramatic tight close-ups, shadows, superimpositions, and dissolves—of Dreiser's naturalistic novel *American Tragedy*. George Eastman (Clift) is a quietly ambitious, uneducated young man who wants to escape his street missionary boyhood and enter the world of his wealthy relatives. However, the film's emphasis is much less on the nature of social class and the hunger for success in America than on Eastman's doomed relationships with a clinging, drab, working-class woman (given texture and poignance in Shelley Winters's performance) and with Angela Vickers (Elizabeth Taylor), who is the embodiment of glamour and wealth. In the Oscar-winning *From Here to Eternity* (1953), Clift played another vulnerable, doomed outsider (Prewitt), brutalized by a corrupt army on the eve of Pearl Harbor. Prewitt is a man of courage and integrity who is unwilling to bend to the dictates of an institution he loves.

The rebellion expressed by three actors, was, however, neither political nor social in nature, nor were the characters they played artists, beats, or bohemians. They were just sensitive, sensual, and often anguished young men seeking to discover and define their identities. In the process, they raised doubts about the values and behavior that dominated American culture and society and indirectly conveyed some of the undercurrent of dissatisfaction that existed during the decade.

Rebel Without a Cause (1955). (Courtesy of Warner Bros./Photofest.)

Of the three stars, James Dean had the most profound effect on the consciousness of the young in the 1950s. Dean had an aura—a mythic presence—and,
with his abrupt and tragic death in a car crash in 1955, generated a cult and became a legend. His film career was a brief one, but in Nicholas Ray's extremely
popular *Rebel Without a Cause* (1955), he left his unique mark on the 1950s.

Rebel Without a Cause was less about rebellion than about the anger of Jim
Stark (James Dean) toward his middle-class parents and the world. Jim is a
brooding, suffering, isolated, high school student who hates his apron-wearing
father's (Jim Backus) flaccid amiability and weak submission to his self-
involved, backbiting wife. Mumbling, slouching, hunching his shoulders, and
curling up in a fetal position with a cigarette dangling from his mouth, the tormented Jim is like a coiled spring ready to cry and rage. Surrounding Jim are
two other pained, rejected adolescents: Judy (Natalie Wood), stunned and
emotionally thrown by her father's sudden rejection, and Plato (Sal Mineo), a
morbid, friendless boy who lives alone with a black maid because his divorced
parents have deserted him.

Rebel Without a Cause's uniqueness rests more in its cinematic style and
Dean's performance than in its script. Ray uses a variety of camera angles, a
dislocated mise-en-scène, tight close-ups, point-of-view shots, intense color, and
rapid, turbulent cutting to successfully project the tension, anger, and sense of almost metaphysical alienation that permeates the film. There are also luminous,
metaphoric sequences, such as the "chicken run," with a pinkish-white specter, Judy, signaling the beginning of the race in the center of a pitch-black run-
way lit by car headlights—an initiation rite or journey confronting death; and
the scene shot in the vastness of the planetarium (which is located on a precipice) with its apocalyptic, end-of-the-world images of the galaxy exploding—as
the three alienated kids sit alone in the dark watching—provides a powerful
metaphor for the insecurity and isolation of adolescence.

Rebel Without a Cause's dialogue and narrative are much more pedestrian
than its imagery. In terms of the narrative, the film sees the causes of adolescent
turmoil as solely psychological—caused by both the instability and conflict
within families and their failure to communicate and provide understanding.
There is an implicit critique of upper-middle-class status striving and conformity, but the script's emphasis is not on social or class reality. In fact, the film
even introduces an understanding detective who acts as a social worker (the
helping professions, such as psychologists, social workers, and so on, became
common in 1950s films) and surrogate father to Jim.

The film's conclusion is both clichéd and sexist: the submerged father taking off his apron and asserting his authority and embracing Jim and reconciliation and love triumphing over fragmentation. However, what is most
memorable is not Jim's opting for a 1950s affirmation of domesticity—shedding

his asocial self for a responsible familial one—but those powerful existential images of lostness, of being a romantic outcast and alone in the world.[34]

Dean departed from this image in his third and last film, George Stevens's *Giant* (1956), which was adapted from Edna Ferber's novel. He plays Jett Rink, a sullen, inarticulate ranch hand who becomes an oil millionaire. Rink is the only character in the film with the suggestion of an internal life—a tribute to Dean's gift for giving nuance and complexity to even this most seemingly stereotypical of characters. Although in *Giant* Dean continued to mumble and slouch, he is transformed from a hostile, arrogant outsider, filled with resentment of those who have power, to a wealthy but pathetic power wielder consumed by alcoholic self-pity, racism, and the resentments of youth. Dean's Jett is not a particularly sympathetic figure, but the tension and energy he conveys in the role is one of the few vital elements in this inflated and trite epic about Texas culture and society.

However, in contrast to Dean's earlier films, *Giant* does make some interesting social points, albeit they are built on a sentimental, liberal point of view characteristic of the Hollywood social films of the mid-1950s. *Giant* is both a ponderous soap-operatic chronicle about a wealthy ranching family and a critique and a bit of a satire of Texas materialism, anti-intellectualism, machismo, and racism. Unfortunately, the critique is subverted both by the long shots exalting an almost mythic Texas landscape and by the beautiful and somewhat progressive, eastern heroine Leslie's (Elizabeth Taylor) ultimate embrace of Texas and its ethos. And her acceptance of that world after years of ambivalence occurs only when her stolid rancher husband Vic (Rock Hudson) displays his humanness and manliness by brawling for the rights of his half-Mexican grandchild. *Giant* contains no real political critique. Leslie does not want to give up her privileges or make changes in the political and economic structure, for she merely wants the elite to be more paternalistic (to sustain the values of her Maryland adolescence) and demonstrate some kindness to the poor Mexicans who work for them. However, she is bold enough to accept intermarriage, and the film clumsily suggests, through its final shots of Leslie's and Vic's white and copper-skinned grandchildren sitting together in their playpen, that the answer to racism may lie in the coupling of the races—the traditional Hollywood embrace of personal rather than political solutions.

Richard Brooks's *Blackboard Jungle* (1955) was a 1950s film carrying more social bite and tension than *Rebel Without a Cause* or *Giant* and dealing with similar issues—delinquency and racism. In fact, when the film was screened at the Venice Film Festival, it elicited a diplomatic protest from Claire Booth Luce (ambassador to the Vatican) because she felt that it exported a squalid, unfavorable image of American life.[35]

Blackboard Jungle centers on a tough, crew-cut idealistic teacher, Mr. Dadier (Glenn Ford), who believes in education and democracy and must tame a group of violent young hoods. In true 1950s style, the actions of the hoods are given no social roots or explanation, merely psychological chatter about permissive child rearing. Nevertheless, these hoods are no Bowery Boy cream puffs, but are alienated, resentful, and vicious—especially their leader, West (played with an imitation Brando–Dean posture by Vic Morrow). *Blackboard Jungle* is a perfect example of what in Hollywood passes for social realism and social exposé. New York is reduced to a studio set devoid of any sense of texture or place, and the teachers in the main are stereotypes, ranging from Murdoch (Louis Calhern), a cynic who calls the school a "garbage can," to the frustrated Miss Hammond, who wears tight, sexy clothes and is almost raped by one of the students. The plot is also built on a series of contrived, mechanical twists, featuring sudden shifts of destructive or cynical characters to the side of virtue and, of course, offering Hollywood's usual solution to complex social problems: the concern and commitment of one courageous, caring individual—Dadier.

Despite these discordant elements, the film was still capable of capturing some of the difficulties involved in teaching tough, disruptive adolescents (it uses the dissonant sounds of a machine shop class and the passing elevated subway train to help evoke feelings of oppression). The potent use of one of the first rock hits, "Rock Around the Clock," conveys a strong feeling of the unbridled energy and antagonism of 1950s youth culture. The issue of racism is also raised with the introduction of the character of Miller (Sidney Poitier in one of his early, more complex roles). Miller is a sensitive, strong, intelligent underachiever who at first is angry and resentful of what he perceives to be a white-dominated education system and then baits and torments Dadier. But by the film's climax, he turns into a noble hero joining Dadier against West and his brutish allies.

Blackboard Jungle is filled with embarrassing clichés about the promises of equal opportunity in America—Dadier attempts to get Miller to continue to go to school by invoking the successful careers of black stars Joe Louis and Ralph Bunche. Nevertheless, the film does touch on the reality of black anger, and that is a positive step in a decade where, excepting *No Way Out* (1950)—Poitier as a middle-class doctor—there were no other films dealing with black consciousness and problems until Martin Ritt's *Edge of the City* (1957). However, in *Edge of the City*, Poitier plays a longshoreman-saint who sacrifices his life for a confused, neurotic, white friend, played by John Cassavetes, and no real feelings of black life or problems are conveyed.

In Stanley Kramer's *The Defiant Ones* (1958), Poitier plays an escaped convict (Cullen) in the South whose character is given enough pungency and reality to directly express his anger at southern racism. Being a symbol of virtue, Poitier's rage is balanced by qualities like intelligence, tenderness, loyalty, and courage. *The Defiant Ones* is a conventional, contrived work of liberal poster art whose key image—a close-up of two hands, black and white, manacled together—is an obvious metaphor for Kramer's view that blacks and whites are inescapably linked to each other in America. Cullen has escaped chained to a white convict, Jackson (Tony Curtis), who is morally and physically much weaker than him. Jackson is an insecure, petty criminal who dreams of big money and lives by the southern racist code. But it is predictable from the very beginning that Jackson will be transformed and that the hate between him and Cullen will be turned into concern and love.

The Defiant Ones, like *Blackboard Jungle*, has a great deal of surface excitement and even some dramatic punch—the crosscutting between the convicts on the run and the liberal sheriff (Theodore Bikel) in pursuit is especially effective. However, like *Blackboard Jungle*, it offers a simplistic social answer—the achievement of racial solidarity through the commitment of individual blacks and whites to each other. And there is no attempt in the film to depict or even suggest the complex economic, political, and cultural dimensions of the race problem. Of course, integration is made easy for whites because the black character is Sidney Poitier, a charismatic, seductive, and superior presence who at the film's climax even sacrifices his freedom for his white friend (invoking jeers from the blacks in the audience). Indeed, it was this dignity and transcendent humanness that made Poitier the one black star who was consistently successful and acceptable to white audiences. Poitier never bowed or scraped to whites, but he was so reasonable and humane that the white audience knew that his anger would always stay within acceptable bounds and that there was nothing to fear from the characters he portrayed. They were men who could arouse the hatred or abuse of only the most ignorant or reactionary of whites.

Later on, during the more militant 1960s, blacks often put down Poitier's persona as middle-class, masochistic, and liberal.[36] Nevertheless, he was one black actor who no longer had to sing, dance, and roll his eyes to have his image appear on the screen. And though Hollywood's handling of the race problem was neither bold nor imaginative, given the conformist political tenor of the time, the emergence of a token black star could still be viewed as a minor triumph.

Ultimately, it was this lack of political and artistic ferment or originality in 1950s Hollywood that allowed an opening for a group of independently produced films, such as the Academy Award–winning *Marty* (1955). Ironically, it was Hollywood's bête noir, television, that was the inspiration of *Marty* and other films of this type, for along with the hours of dross that dominated 1950s television, there were some moments that broke the mold. Under the inspiration of innovative spirits such as NBC's Sylvester "Pat" Weaver, new forms, such as the magazine concept show (*Today*), talk shows (*Tonight*), and spectaculars (*Peter Pan*), were produced on television. Producers such as Fred Coe and Worthington Miner created original live drama shows such as *Studio One* and

Philco Playhouse featuring the talents of new writers (Paddy Chayevsky, Rod Serling, and Horton Foote), directors (Sidney Lumet and John Frankenheimer), and actors (Paul Newman, Kim Stanley, and Rod Steiger).

Marty was the first and most commercially successful of these films adapted from live television. Written by Paddy Chayevsky and made on location in the East Bronx in low-budget black and white, it dealt with the daily lives of ordinary people. *Marty*'s major achievement was in evoking the tedium and loneliness that permeates the life of an unattractive Bronx butcher (Ernest Borgnine) who ultimately finds happiness by going out with a shy, homely teacher.[37] Although Chayevsky claimed that his work opened up the "marvellous world of the ordinary," *Marty* was a dialogue-bound, formally inexpressive film whose camera did not probe deeply into the faces and behavior of lower-middle-class life. It was merely a quietly sentimental story, characterized by a fine ear for Bronx dialogue and syntax—answering a question with a question (e.g., "What do you feel like doing tonight? I dunno, what do you feel like doing?") and offering Hollywood's predictable, all-purpose solution—love—to give Marty's life some purpose.

It was *Marty*'s commercial success that led to other small films, the most distinctive being Sidney Lumet's *Twelve Angry Men* (1957), adapted from a television play be Reginald Rose. *Twelve Angry Men* is an account of a jury's deliberations over a murder case where the defendant is a Puerto Rican boy. Using a single set of a New York City jury room on the hottest day of the year, Lumet succeeded in adapting most of the conventions of the television play—tight close-ups, medium group shots, panning, and fluid and precise cutting from sweating face to face to build a dramatically effective film. He was especially gifted directing actors and a cast that included a combination of New York character actors (Lee J. Cobb, Jack Klugman, and E. G. Marshall) and a Hollywood star, Henry Fonda, as the jury gave a seamless illustration of ensemble playing.

Twelve Angry Men was a socially committed work that raised questions about the nature of the jury system and, by extension, the nature of American democracy itself. The jury was a gallery of social types: bigots; a shallow, spineless advertising man; a decent working man; an immigrant deeply committed to the democratic process; a cold, logical stockbroker; and the hero, an intelligent, decent, liberal architect (Henry Fonda) who must convince the rest of the jury members that what seems like an open-and-shut case is liable to reasonable doubt. He is a resolute man with a soft, cultivated voice who ingeniously and logically succeeds in convincing the other jury members that the prosecution's case has holes. Despite the doubts the film raises about a system where bigotry, complacency, and convenience (one juror wants to resolve the case quickly so that he can get to a Yankees game) become the sole basis for deciding the guilt or innocence of a defendant, the film ends on a positive note, with the defendant allowed to go free and the American system of justice affirmed.

Twelve Angry Men's strength lies in its dramatic fireworks and its well-drawn social types rather than in the depth of its social critique or the psychological complexity of its characters. It is a film where the villains sweat, rage, and bellow a great deal and the hero is a totally admirable and reasonable man. Every scene in the film is neatly choreographed and calculated for dramatic impact, with all the characters given a single note—the old man on the jury is observant and notices details—to define themselves and a significant moment where they shift their vote. And though the film does not gloss over the fact of how ambiguous and complex the meting out of guilt and innocence in a criminal case can be, it still holds that for our institutions to be just, they merely need one good person who will tap the basic virtues of other ordinary Americans. It is the type of Hollywood political fantasy that such vastly different directorial sensibilities as Frank Capra and Sidney Lumet could share.

Besides *Marty* and *Twelve Angry Men*, there were other small films that elicited critical attention during the late 1950s, such as Richard Brooks's *Catered Affair* (1956) and Delbert Mann's *Middle of the Night* (1959). One of the most striking was Alexander Mackendrick's hard-boiled, atmospheric, bracingly colloquial (script by Clifford Odets) *Sweet Smell of Success* (1957) depicting the relationship between a vicious, megalomaniacal Broadway gossip columnist (Burt Lancaster playing a version of Walter Winchell) and Tony Curtis as a slimy, hungry, publicity man who obsequiously serves and is victimized by him.

However, the production of these small films began to decrease at the same time as live drama was replaced on television by filmed series. And although good, small, realistic films were still produced during the next three decades—*The Luck of Ginger Coffey* (1964), *Hester Street* (1974), and *El Norte* (1984)—after the 1950s there never again was a time where the small film seemed capable of becoming one of the dominant cinematic forms in Hollywood.

The small, realistic films did not attempt to subvert either Hollywood conventions or the dominant political and cultural values of the 1950s. However, in the late 1950s, two films were made that were critical of the military mind and of the development of nuclear weapons—*Paths of Glory* (1957) and *On the Beach* (1959).

Of the two, the more formally distinctive and politically subversive was Stanley Kubrick's independently produced *Paths of Glory*. Despite the fact that the film takes place within the confines of the French army of World War I rather than in the more charged and contemporary setting of the U.S. Army of the Korean War, *Paths of Glory* trenchantly conveys the cynicism, hypocrisy, and careerism of the French officer class and provides a powerful indictment of war.

In what was to become his characteristically cool, dazzling, and original style, Kubrick evokes an unjust and death-saturated world through sound (drumbeats and whistles), camera movement, lighting, and vivid imagery rather than through antiwar sermonizing. The two prime villains of the film are the calculating, subtle, and insidious General Broulard (Adolph Menjou) and the neurotic, murderously ambitious General Mireau (George Macready), who live in opulent chateaux and hold glittering formal-dress balls. They are totally contemptuous of their men treating them like chess pieces to be manipulated or ants to be casually slaughtered—"scum" who can be sacrificed to their own career ambitions. Mireau watches the battle through binoculars (one of Kubrick's many devices conveying war as a voyeur's sport of the officer class) and hysterically rages at the soldiers' retreat.

Though the film puts greater emphasis on the class structure and inequity of the war machine than on the horrors of the war, Kubrick still evokes the advance and retreat of the soldiers in nightmarish, richly textured battlefield scenes. The battlefield is a lunar landscape of craters, mud, and puddles, littered with bodies, barbed wire, and the wreckage of a plane, punctuated by whistling shells and enveloped by a flare-lit sky. The camera relentlessly tracks the men as they scramble to their anonymous deaths through the debris and smoke.

The hero of *Paths of Glory* is the granite-faced, courageous, and compassionate Colonel Dax (Kirk Douglas), who is at one with the men. Dax is an uncomplicated idealist who can openly say to Mireau that "patriotism is the last refuge of scoundrels." He also defends three innocent, court-martialed soldiers—he is a defense lawyer in civilian life—who have been chosen arbitrarily from the mass of soldiers to be punished for their supposed cowardice (in reality to cover the general's mistakes) in battle. Though Dax is a jut-jawed hero and idealist, the three soldiers are fallible, frightened men who cry and rage and whose death is absolutely barbaric and meaningless. Kubrick concludes the film without a glimmer of hope—Dax not only failing to prevent their deaths but also, almost immediately after the court-martial, being forced to lead the exhausted troops, who are longing for home, back to the murderous trenches. The system has him in its hands, and there is no escape.

Stanley Kubrick went on to make much more mordant and outrageous films where strong, noble figures like Dax not only rarely appear but also would be parodied and undermined if they did (e.g., *Dr. Strangelove*, 1963, and *Clockwork Orange*, 1971). For the smug 1950s, a film that portrayed the military hierarchy as moral monsters and maintained such a bleak view of the human condition was a radical work and, of course, doomed to commercial failure.

Paths of Glory did not offer the facile, personal, and liberal solutions of *Blackboard Jungle* and the *Defiant Ones* or the leftist optimism of *Salt of the Earth*. It was a profoundly pessimistic work that offered only contempt for the conduct of war and the corruptions of power and privilege and nothing more.[38]

In contrast, Stanley Kramer's disaster movie *On the Beach* (1959), although it is built around the notion that the world is on the verge of extinction by nuclear war, ends on a curious note of hope. Based on Australian novelist Nevil Shute's best-selling book, the film was seen in some ways as a small step toward the easing of Cold War tensions by being screened almost simultaneously in Moscow and Washington. But despite its political pretensions, this tale about the aftermath of World War III and a last surviving American submarine arriving in Australia just ahead of a postnuclear exterminating cloud seems nothing more than a backdrop for a doomed love affair between Ava Gardner, an alcoholic war widow, and Gregory Peck, the submarine commander.

Stanley Kramer's aim to make a star-laden film (Fred Astaire also had a role in the film) that would act as a warning about the consequences of the nuclear arms race had good intentions. In fact, few people could take exception to the film's decent instincts, but only in Hollywood would bromides like the need to preserve the wonder of life be seen as socially significant. There is also something bland and antiseptic about the images of the nuclear holocaust that the film projects. However, there are moments when the film captures the kind of despair that might become an integral part of the lives of the doomed survivors, particularly in a car race in which the drivers drive with a consciously suicidal recklessness and abandon. These scenes are rare, and *On the Beach*'s real purpose is revealed in its final image of a Salvation Army banner proclaiming the message that "there is still time, brother!"[39]

Though intended as a cautionary message about the apocalyptic consequences of the arms race and nuclear war, the implications of this message might also serve as a convenient summary of Hollywood's passage from the optimism of the 1940s to the anxiety of the 1960s. On the one hand, it evokes the complacency of an industry that despite economic decline and political problems still went on churning out the same films built on the ersatz emotions, melodramatic conventions, and evasive political and social formulae of previous decades. On the other hand, however, a number of these films managed to contain a deeper sense of uneasiness, an urgency, and a greater sense of the imperfections of American society than in the past. Of course, the 1950s ended with Eisenhower in the White House and Doris Day starring in *Pillow Talk* (1958), but inherent in all that manufactured calm and good cheer was a sense of disquiet, perhaps even of time running out on a period of stability and consensus.

NOTES

1. Eric F. Goldman, *The Crucial Decade—and after, America 1945–1960* (New York: Vintage, 1960).

2. Ibid., pp. 292–311.

3. Richard Rovere, *Senator Joseph McCarthy*, rev. ed. (New York: Harper and Row, 1973).

4. Ibid.

5. Ronald Steel, "Two Cheers for Ike," *New York Review of Books* (September 24, 1981), pp. 10–12.

6. Richard Rovere, "Eisenhower over the Shoulder," *The American Scholar* 21 (Spring 1962), pp. 34–44.

7. Frederick F. Siegel, *Troubled Journey: From Pearl Harbor to Ronald Reagan* (New York: Hill and Wang, 1984), p. 99.

8. William L. O'Neill, *Coming Apart: An Informal History of America in the 1960s* (New York: Quadrangle, 1971), pp. 3–24.

9. Edmund White, *The Beautiful Room Is Empty* (New York: Ballantine, 1988), pp. 7–8.

10. Eric Goldmen, *The Crucial Decade*, p. 291.

11. O'Neill, *Coming Apart*, p. 4.

12. Godfrey Hodgson, *America in Our Time: From World War II to Nixon, What Happened and Why* (New York: Vintage, 1978), pp. 54–64.

13. Morris Dickstein, *Gates of Eden: American Culture in the Sixties* (New York: Basic Books, 1977), pp. 3–12.

14. Charlie Gillet, *The Sound of the City: The Rise of Rock and Roll*, rev. ed. (New York: Pantheon, 1984).

15. Victor S. Navasky, *Naming Names* (New York: Viking, 1980).

16. Michel Ciment, *Kazan on Kazan* (New York: Viking, 1973), p. 94.

17. Ibid.

18. Peter Biskind and Don Georgakas, "An Exchange on Viva Zapata," *Cineaste* 7, no. 2 (Spring 1976), pp. 10–17.

19. Ciment, *Kazan on Kazan*, p. 110.

20. Ibid., p. 108.

21. Leonard Quart, "A Second Look: A Face in the Crowd," *Cineaste*, 17, no. 2 (1989): 30–31.

22. Nicholas Garnham, *Samuel Fuller* (New York: Viking, 1971).

23. Nora Sayre, *Running Time: Films of the Cold War* (New York: Dial Press, 1982), p. 176.

24. Deborah Silverton Rosenfelt (ed.), *Salt of the Earth* (Old Westbury, NY: Feminist Press, 1978).

25. Stuart Samuels, "The Age of Conspiracy and Conformity: Invasion of the Body Snatchers," in John E. O'Connor and Martin A. Jackson (eds.), *American History/American Film* (New York: Frederick Ungar, 1979), pp. 203–17.

26. Pauline Kael, *Kiss, Kiss, Bang, Bang* (New York: Bantam, 1969), pp. 446–47.

27. Michael Wood, *America in the Movies; or, "Santa Maria, It Had Slipped My Mind!"* (New York: Basic Books, 1975), pp. 180–81.

28. Robert Sklar, *Movie-Made America: A Cultural History of American Movies* (New York: Vintage, 1975), pp. 283–84.

29. Wood, *America in the Movies*, pp. 146–64.

30. Ibid.

31. Phillip French, *Westerns* (New York: Oxford University Press, 1977), p. 70.

32. Molly Haskell, *From Reverence to Rape: The Treatment of Women in the Movies* (Baltimore: Penguin, 1974), pp. 231–76.

33. Jon Halliday, *Sirk on Sirk* (New York: Viking, 1972), pp. 97–98.

34. Venable Herndon, *James Dean: A Short Life* (New York: Signet, 1974).

35. Garth Jowett, *Film: The Democratic Art* (Boston: Little, Brown, 1976), p. 385.

36. Sidney Poitier, *This Life* (New York: Ballantine, 1980), pp. 331–41.

37. Eric Barnouw, *Tube of Plenty: The Evolution of American Television* (New York: Oxford University Press, 1977), pp. 154–65.

38. Norman Kagan, *The Cinema of Stanley Kubrick* (New York: Grove Press, 1972), pp. 47–67.

39. Donald Spoto, *Stanley Kramer: Filmmaker* (New York: G. P. Putnam's Sons, 1978), pp. 207–15.

4

THE 1960s

In 1848, revolutions broke out almost simultaneously in Paris, Berlin, Vienna, and Milan that toppled long-established reactionary regimes and attempted to institute political and social reforms. Historians referring to this period call it the "springtime of the nations." These revolutions were ultimately crushed or gave way to even more sophisticated autocratic governments that were in many ways more repressive than the ones they replaced. Nevertheless, in their brief moment of triumph, these revolutions exposed some of the most glaring contradictions of their societies—most notably, the growing, almost unbridgeable, gulf between the bourgeoisie and the newly emergent industrial working class—laying to rest the myth that Europe was moving toward a harmonious era of the golden mean.[1]

If the events of 1848 sound familiar to modern ears, it is because a somewhat similar pattern of events took place during and after 1968. That year saw concurrent riots, insurrections, and near rebellions in the streets of New York, Chicago, Detroit, Paris, Mexico City, and Prague. This "'68 Spring" was also crushed in successive waves of assassinations, Russian tank invasions, police and army tear gas, and bullets. However, like their 1848 predecessors, these revolts also exposed a number of the contradictions inherent in their societies.[2]

In America, 1968 was merely the most apocalyptic year of a momentous decade. During that period, the myths underlying the foreign policy of containment, the belief that domestic affluence ensured social peace, and the basic optimism that dominated American life and spirit since World War II were buried forever. For many Americans, their image of themselves, their society, and their place in the world underwent a painful transformation. Despite the fact that it ultimately ushered in a period of intense social and political con-servatism (whose force and grip on power have still clearly not abated), it left hope that this was no permanent state of things—that some form of social and cultural rebellion could arise again.[3]

The decade was ushered in with a growing sense of possibility for political change. Symbolic of that hope was the presidency of the handsome, youthful John F. Kennedy. He projected an image of energy and eloquence that veiled his militant Cold War postures and other political assumptions he shared with his Republican opponent in the 1960 election, Richard Nixon. Kennedy was elected on his promise to "get the country moving again" and his vision of a "New Frontier." The public had become a bit tired of the malaise and apa-thy of the last years of the Eisenhower administration: the constant economic dislocations (recessions and unemployment), foreign policy disarray (the U-2 incident, Japanese student riots, and the Cuban revolution), and missile gap myths. Still, the reaction to the cool, stylish senator from Massachusetts wasn't overwhelming—he won the presidency with the slim mandate of only 118,000 votes.[4]

In his inaugural address, Kennedy neglected to mention domestic issues but promised a renewed dedication to world leadership and proceeded to convert his mandate into a foreign policy of constant challenge to the Soviet Union and its allies. Kennedy and his crisis-management teams ranged worldwide con-fronting the communists in Laos, Berlin, and Cuba until they almost brought the world to the brink of nuclear disaster with the 1962 Cuban missile crisis.

Sobered by this flirtation with the apocalypse, Kennedy negotiated a long-awaited nuclear test ban treaty and raised hopes for further detente with a thoughtful foreign policy address at the American University in Washington, D.C., in June 1963. His assassination, however, tragically cut short more con-certed attempts to bring about disarmament and disengagement.[5]

Kennedy's capacity for exciting the public's expectation of a breakthrough in the Cold War was paralleled by his seeming encouragement of black American hopes for some form of civil rights legislation. Initially for Kennedy, hardly a radical on the issue during his senatorial career and barely mentioning it in his Churchillian inaugural address (one brief sentence), race was not a major con-cern. However, equality for black Americans was "an idea," in the words of Victor Hugo, "whose time had come."[6]

Ever since the 1940s, blacks had almost imperceptibly made significant so-cial and economic gains and become more critical of racist and discrimina-tory policies and practices. Their migration to the urban North led them to become one of the mainstays of the Democratic Party's political coalition and provided the margin of victory for both Truman and Kennedy. In the 1950s, the National Association for the Advancement of Colored People, which had diligently struggled in the courts against segregation and discrimination in education and voting, won the previously mentioned landmark decision in the Supreme Court against segregation in the schools (the 1954 *Brown* decision) and established racial equality as one of the prime and unavoidable political and moral issues facing the United States.[7]

What is more, the black community had produced leaders in the 1950s and 1960s such as Martin Luther King Jr., James Farmer, Roy Wilkins, Whitney Young Jr., Bayard Rustin, and the younger "new abolitionists" of the Student Non-Violent Coordinating Committee (SNCC). Beginning with the successful Montgomery bus boycott, through sit-ins, freedom rides, and voter registration drives, blacks made clear their demand for integration and equal rights. It was a demand that peaked during the Kennedy administration in the 1963 March on Washington, where blacks made a highly visible, well-organized, and disciplined bid for their demands to be heard, culminating in Martin Luther King's eloquent and evangelical "I Have a Dream" speech.

Though the March was probably the apotheosis of liberal optimism and self-confidence, in its midst there were the seeds of discord symptomatic of tactical, ideological, and programmatic differences within the black leadership and community. The most fully reported of these episodes was the radical speech attacking the Democratic Party leadership that John Lewis, executive secretary of the SNCC, intended to make, which was so objectionable to other members of the March coalition that it almost caused their withdrawal.[8]

However, even if the March on Washington maintained its facade of harmony, it did not prevent a northern black leader, scornfully dismissing the march's goals of civil rights legislation, from commenting, "What difference does it make if you can sit at a lunch counter with whites if you didn't have the money to order a hamburger?" This remark neatly summarized the feelings of many northern blacks who for years had de jure civil rights but were deprived of jobs, adequate education, and housing and were imprisoned in a psychology and ethos shaped by racism that no amount of civil rights could allay or transform.[9]

It was this oppressive and alienating situation that propelled blacks into a series of violent ghetto riots that engulfed numerous major cities in the 1960s. The riots resulted in a diminution of white liberal support for (and in some cases a backlash against) the civil rights movement—edging the movement farther away from its integrationist philosophy. The move away from both nonviolent resistance and a commitment to integration had already begun to take place. Continued violent southern resistance—the murder of three civil rights workers in Mississippi in 1964—and a feeling that institutions such as the Democratic Party and the labor unions were hesitant about dedicating themselves to social change helped bring about this shift. There emerged a number of militant, angry black leaders, such as Malcolm X and Stokely Carmichael, who repudiated acceptance by and integration into white America for an ideology of black nationalism and separatism.[10]

The task of Kennedy's successor, Lyndon B. Johnson, was to respond to demands that went beyond mere civil rights. Johnson was a complex man of immense energy, virtuoso political skills, and genuine compassion whose crudely manipulative and abrasive personality and ideology of globalism were ill suited to the demands of the time. A southern moderate who in his senatorial career had been more conservative than Kennedy, he nonetheless fully committed himself to the task of civil rights legislation. He succeeded in winning the passage of laws, like the Voting Rights Act, that assured blacks of their rights as no other political figure, including Kennedy, could have accomplished. In an attempt also to deal with black as well as white economic and social deprivation, he updated the New Deal and fashioned a program (e.g., community action groups, aid to minority businesses, and so on) that he called the "War on Poverty," intended to be a link in creating for all Americans what he dreamed would be a "Great Society."[11]

Unfortunately, from its inception Johnson's war fell victim to underfunding, administrative chaos, rip-offs, and an insufficient understanding of how complex and profound were many of the social problems confronting the poverty war. The program also caused resentment and anger among white working-class and lower-middle-class people who felt that the government was neglecting their needs in favor of blacks—a problem that still confronts almost any social program that seems exclusively aimed at helping minorities. This set of circumstances ultimately became terminal as the United States became more and more enmeshed in a futile 10-year war to stop "communist aggression" in South Vietnam and the poverty program in turn began to lose both funding and the president's attention and commitment.[12]

The Vietnam War dominated political debate and policymaking during the second half of the 1960s, and the assumptions that guided this struggle were the same as those that had directed American policy in Europe since 1945. The United States continued to believe that Soviet Russian–controlled communist movements were seeking to expand at the expense of weak liberal-democratic regimes and must be contained by the military and economic power of the United States. The corollary of that notion was that if one nation fell, all would collapse—the "domino effect."

However, the principles of containment did not apply to Southeast Asia and particularly South Vietnam. Here the communist monolith had long been stalled on the shoals of divergent Moscow–Peking versions of communism, ancient distrusts, and even ethnic and racial hostility. There was no evidence that Ho Chi Minh had any desire to do more than create a unified Vietnam. And the governments that the United States tried to support were never demo-cratic and hardly liberal. Finally, the war was also not quite a naked communist power grab but at first largely the result of indigenous communists and national-ists attempting to wrest power from the hands of increasingly isolated, dictato-rial, and corrupt neocolonialists.[13]

Instead of confronting communist expansionism, the United States self-destructively thrust itself into a civil war. This meant little to the policy plan-ners of the State Department and the Pentagon, who saw the war as a way of both extending the Pax Americana to Asia and testing their new military tac-tics against the post–World War II "wars of national liberation."[14]

To accomplish this policy, the government had to hide its purposes behind carefully built-up subterfuges, such as claiming that the United States was helping the Vietnamese to help themselves and by instigating provocations that inflamed American patriotic feeling (the Tonkin Gulf and Pleiku inci-dents) as a pretext for a military buildup. Indeed, as a consequence of this pol-icy, the government had more than 500,000 troops in South Vietnam by 1968 and was spending nearly $27 billion a year on the war.

The inconsistencies and contradictions of this well-orchestrated escalation were not lost on a growing number of middle-class white American youth whose commitment to activism and social change had been inspired by the early idealism evoked by the rhetoric and style of the Kennedy administration and the actions of the civil rights movement. In the early 1960s, a group of college students formed Students for a Democratic Society and elaborated and attempted to implement a program of political and social reform based at first on nonviolence and participatory democracy. This "New Left," as it was called, took the lead in recruiting and politicizing an effective and dynamic antiwar movement numbering thousands of Americans (most of whom were far from being new leftists) repelled by the U.S. conduct of the war, the growing num-ber of American casualties, and the rising draft calls.[15]

The New Left was the most politically conscious section of a larger move-ment of students—young and not-so-young men and women who were not only estranged by the war but also alienated from what they perceived as American culture's spiritual emptiness and puritanical repressiveness. A product of the baby boom of the postwar era, the expansion of education, and the growing suburban affluence of American life, the "hippies" or "flower children" (most accurately the counterculture or adversary culture since most of its most in-fluential spokesmen were well over the dread age of 30) gained intellectual awareness and legitimacy from the writings of 1950s intellectual radicals such as Norman Mailer, Paul Goodman, and C. Wright Mills and the novelists and poets of the "beat generation." Nonetheless, the basis of the counterculture's ethos was not intellectual (indeed, many were aggressively anti-intellectual) but rather the shared experience of drugs like marijuana and LSD, personal style (long hair and army cast-off clothes); folk and rock music (the Beatles, Bob Dylan, and the Rolling Stones), and a burgeoning, assertive underground press (*Los Angeles Free Press, Berkeley Barb,* and *East Village Other*).[16]

Though there were stylistic and intellectual differences between the amorphous counterculture and the chaotic but more self-conscious and organized New Left, they existed in uneasy coalition with each other. The coalition reached its apogee of political power and influence when their shared antagonism to the war helped lead to Johnson's dropping out of the 1968 presidential race. They were also able to join together in the demonstrations and riots that engulfed Columbia University in the spring of that year and the Democratic Convention in Chicago that summer. A similar public expression of the communal spirit of the 1960s, though much more affected by the values of the counterculture, was the Woodstock Music Festival in the summer of 1969.[17]

However, both the New Left and the counterculture quickly splintered as Martin Luther King Jr. and Robert Kennedy were assassinated and demonstrations did not bring the instant collapse of the Pentagon or the war effort. Revolution-intoxicated leaders turned from community building and constructing a resistance to the war to nihilistic terrorism or sterile neo-Stalinist and Maoist dogmatism. At the same time, the counterculture found itself usurped by hip capitalists and a sensation-hungry media who marketed and trivialized some of its more innovative and original elements. And the simplistic counterculture ethic of "doing your thing" was used by criminal elements to penetrate the milieu and exploit its ingenuousness. In addition, the antiwork, antifamily, antipatriotic, and antiwhite working-class rhetoric and image of the New Left and the counterculture aroused an aggressive backlash that first manifested itself in the populist racism of the Wallace movement and then became an integral part of the conservative coalition that elected Richard Nixon to the presidency in 1968.[18]

The last years of the decade saw what was left of these movements destroy themselves and most of their appeal in a paroxysm of violent "Weatherman" demonstrations, the bloody Rolling Stones concert at Altamont, and the paranoid and murderous destruction of the Manson family (which could be seen as a pathological parody of the counterculture). Helping to also bring it to the ground were the cunning policies of the Nixon administration. Nixon manipulated Vietnam troop withdrawals and began to end the draft while at the same time intensifying the air war in Vietnam and expanding the ground war into Laos and Cambodia. It was all done to give the public the impression that the war was gradually winding down and to lead to its removal as a prime element in the national consciousness.[19]

Despite ending on such discordant notes, the 1960s nevertheless had positive results. Among the most permanent of these was a revisionist impulse that stimulated many Americans to look critically at themselves, their history, and social and political ideas and institutions. Of course, this did not guarantee that real change would come about, but it did make political and social non-conformity more difficult to repress and the simplistic pieties of the past harder to sustain.

Nowhere was this tendency to ignore reality or bend it to its will more firmly entrenched than in Hollywood at the beginning of the 1960s. Nonetheless, even in Hollywood, the 1960s was a force for renewal and transformation. The spirit of optimism may have marked the opening of the decade for the rest of the country, but the film industry was at its nadir. The most startling victim of that decline was the vaunted studio system, whose final demise was symbolized in the 1970 MGM auction of artifacts like Judy Garland's *Wizard of Oz* ruby slippers.

Taken over by financier Kirk Kerkorian in 1969, the studio (which once boasted "more stars than in heaven") was promptly turned into a hotel-gambling enterprise with only incidental filmmaking interests. MGM was only one (albeit the most prominent) of a number of studios that went completely out of the filmmaking business (RKO) or became part of the leisure-time divisions of conglomerates like Gulf and Western (Paramount), Transamerican (United Artists), MCA (Universal), and Warner Communications (Warner Bros.).

Gone forever were the dream factories with their armies of contract actors and actresses, writers, directors, craftspeople, technicians, and publicists. Instead, the new studio head, who operated under the logo of the old studio, was likely to be a former talent agent (Ted Ashley and Barry Diller) who could put together talented packages of superstar actors, actresses, and directors. By the end of the decade, the studios were no longer interested in making films; they had assumed merely the marketing and financial end of the process.[20]

Nevertheless, not every change during the 1960s was an unmitigated disaster. Indeed, as a result of relaxing societal sexual standards and court rulings overturning rigid obscenity laws, the sexual taboos long governing Hollywood began to fall by the wayside. Gone were the twin beds, and in to replace them came full-frontal nudity. Though this freedom was used by some filmmakers as an excuse for sexual titillation and spawned a successful independent cottage industry of hard- and soft-core film pornography, it did permit a widening of the range of permissible film topics. American films now had a greater chance to convey aspects of human relationships that they previously had little freedom to depict.[21]

In addition to sex, other Hollywood blind spots were breached by the protest movements of the 1960s. Blacks could no longer be either totally ignored or merely cast in subservient and stereotypical roles—though no great breakthrough for films dealing with black life took place. And the deviant lifestyles and political ideas of the young, though often exploited and adulterated by

Hollywood, still had to be dealt with, especially since they had begun to make up the largest portion of the cinema audience.[22]

One of the first intimations of a new mood in Hollywood was Hitchcock's extremely successful *Psycho* (1960). It was a formally dazzling and brilliantly perverse film—oriented to a new generation of filmgoers—more erotic, violent, and macabre than any of Hitchcock's previous work. In this bleak black-and-white film, Hitchcock, working with his usual obsessions (i.e., guilt, voyeurism, Oedipal complexes, and misogyny) utilizes the iconography of the horror film—an isolated motel; an old, forbidding Victorian house; a sensational murder sequence (using an Eisenstein-like montage) that arouses feelings of terror; a chilling musical score; and a murderer who is a transvestite and psychotic. *Psycho* marked the introduction of the formula thriller "which redefined the limits of sex and violence in films"[23] and would in a decade or more overrun the theaters with mediocre slasher films.

An early 1960s film that both prefigured the style of other films during the decade and had an almost prophetic quality was John Frankenheimer's *The Manchurian Candidate* (1962). *The Manchurian Candidate* was based on the 1950s liberal conceit that suggested that "if Joe McCarthy were working for the communists, he couldn't be doing a better job."[24] In a rather intricate, ironic script, adapted by George Axelrod from the novel by Richard Condon, chilling, odious Sergeant Raymond Shaw (Laurence Harvey) comes back from the Korean War a Medal of Honor winner. However, it turns out that the incident for which he was awarded the medal is a fabricated one and that Shaw is really a programmed communist assassin (the brainwashing done in Manchuria by murderous Russian and Chinese Pavlovian psychologists) controlled by his communist agent mother (Angela Lansbury). This monstrous manipulator of a mother turns out to be merely using him as a weapon to put her buffoonish, McCarthy-like senator husband into the White House and acquire absolute power for herself. *The Manchurian Candidate* allows Frankenheimer to succeed in constructing a neat, liberal balancing act, condemning McCarthy while simultaneously invoking the specter of a vicious "red menace" and conspiracy.[25]

Within this inventive but somewhat hysterical thriller framework, Frankenheimer sought to create the ultimate send-up of McCarthy (a bit belated since McCarthy was already dead and his power long since curbed) with war heroes, senators, and even the ne plus ultra of American virtue—Mom—revealed as communist agents. He also succeeded in creating an almost absurdist sense of American politics, where irrationality is the norm, plots abound, mother-dominated sons are turned into robotlike assassins, overwrought liberals denounce right-wingers as "fascists," right-wingers parade around at costume parties in Abraham Lincoln outfits, and most figures of authority and power are never what they seem to be. Frankenheimer may have succeeded beyond his own expectations in creating a film of political prophecy. In it, he augured not only the media politics of the 1960s with scene after scene dominated by the almost baleful gleam of the television screen but also, most ominous of all, its political assassinations, particularly the Oedipal and vengeful Madison Square Garden shootings of Raymond's parents, linking private pathology with public and political action.

Unfortunately, Frankenheimer's skillful, flashy, sometimes gratuitous blending of 1950s political issues with prefigurings of the late 1960s "put-on" style—the use of bizarre effects and outrageous overstatement to make a point and get a laugh—did not inspire a host of films that struggled to illuminate American politics. Instead, the key issue in films such as Otto Preminger's *Advise and Consent* (1962) and Franklin Schaffner's version of Gore Vidal's cynical, literate novel *The Best Man* (1964), with its political convention battling between Stevensonian and Nixonian candidates, was homosexuality.

However, there was more to *Advise and Consent* than its melodramatic, prurient treatment of homosexuality. With his cool, objective, and lucid style—characterized by long takes, deep focus, and fluid tracks and pans—Preminger was able to successfully evoke the atmosphere of the Senate and its procedures—pages, the gallery, quorum calls, and the workings of the committee system. Preminger endorsed the American system's gift for compromise and flexibility—the film's hero being the honorable, decent majority leader, Senator Munson (Walter Pidgeon), who is committed to the civilities and rules of "the Club"—the Senate. Munson affirms the system of checks and balances and is repelled by the behavior of the film's villain—a tactless, vile, left-liberal opportunist who respects nothing but his own drive for power. Preminger's idea of a left-wing senator is a crude caricature, but the film tries to balance him off with a florid, manipulative, reactionary southern Senator Seab Cooley played with such flair by Charles Laughton that he is able to elicit audience sympathy. However, *Advise and Consent* was not interested in either senator's ideological stance—the film never really explored the rights and wrongs of the issues. Its concern was with honorable behavior, and for Preminger that sort of conduct comes from understanding that the political world is built not on moral purity and pride but rather on a sense of ambiguity and compromise.

Advise and Consent was a generally intelligent film that, like many less sophisticated Hollywood products, saw political conflict as primarily a struggle between personalities. However, its personal dynamics were more complex than the usual heroes versus villains. But in its affirmation of political flexibility, the film never questioned the truism that the system serves all segments of the American population or asked about the nature of the social ends that the governmental process is geared to. In fact, Preminger's complacency smacked of 1950s consensus thinking about the effectiveness of American democracy.

Nevertheless, Preminger's satisfaction with the workings of the government was supplanted by films dealing with the apocalyptic terror aroused by the possibility of nuclear attack and annihilation. In *Seven Days in May* (1964) a statesmanlike, peace-oriented president (Fredric March) signs a nuclear nonproliferation treaty with the Soviet Union, prompting a group of right-wing generals led by a megalomaniacal zealot, General Scott (Burt Lancaster), to plot a coup. The villains are no longer communist fifth columnists, like in early 1950s films, but a charismatic general who believes the country can be saved from the Russians only by a man on a white horse. Decent men who believe in the democratic process and the Constitution predictably subvert the coup.

Seven Days in May was a much less imaginative work than films made the same year about the actual threat of nuclear destruction. In the words of Susan Sontag, films about nuclear war struck the audience's "imagination of disaster"—their sense of participation—"in the fantasy of living through one's own death and more the death of cities, the destruction of humanity itself."[26] It was a vision of the world that certainly contributed to the success of two films with radically different styles: *Fail-Safe* (1964) and *Dr. Strangelove: Or How I Stopped Worrying and Learned to Love the Bomb* (1964).

Unlike *Dr. Strangelove*, released earlier that year, *Fail-Safe*, adapted from a best-seller by Eugene Burdick and Harvey Wheeler, saw nuclear disaster as resulting from the probable malfunctioning of nuclear weaponry's safeguarding technology rather than from the actions of paranoid generals. In *Fail-Safe*, it is a technological breakdown that launches American bombers on a full-scale attack of the Soviet Union. Hoping to avert a catastrophe, the decent American president (Henry Fonda) negotiates with the Russian premier over the hotline. However, the bomber does get through to bomb Moscow, and the American president, to save the world, winds up having to trade the destruction of New York for the obliteration of the Russian capital. Despite this rather far-fetched conclusion, Sidney Lumet's semidocumentary approach and his powerful and horrifying final montage of the destruction of New York and Moscow give the film a chilling measure of reality.

The most compelling moments of the film are the image of Fonda framed in almost total isolation, trying in his characteristic dry, almost laconic tones to assure the Russians that it was all a mistake, and his shedding a tear after hearing the shrill sound of the telephone that signals the bomb exploding in Moscow. These scenes capture a sense of the unbearable tragedy that hangs in the balance as men representing very different power structures and interests try, against imponderable odds, to reason with each other about the dire consequences of both nations' nuclear arms policies. An audience viewing these scenes would be hard pressed to avoid feeling how close to the brink we were and what slender resources existed to avert such a disaster.

Fail-Safe is a cautionary film about an out-of-control technology that makes men its pawns and disciples. It is not particularly subtle, turning most of its characters into ciphers who merely serve its theme. In Walter Matthau's overstated, Dr. Strangelove–like political science professor (Groteschele), the film has a character who conveys genuine political substance. Matthau represents the 1960s Cold War intellectuals (e.g., Kahn and Teller) who expressed their vision of realpolitik and their machismo fantasies by indulging in "thinking about the unthinkable." These were men who could talk casually and obsessively about building advanced weaponry and the possibilities and necessary risks of nuclear warfare without any moral or humane constraints or qualms about the consequences of these policies.[27]

It is this assault on murderous realpolitik that was one of the prime themes of Stanley Kubrick's sardonic black comedy *Dr. Strangelove*. The director of one critically acclaimed antiwar film, *Paths of Glory* (1957), Kubrick had long been interested in the problem of nuclear war and its effects. At first, he tried to do a faithful adaptation of Peter George's novel *Red Alert*. However, each time he attempted to write it, the whole notion seemed more and more "ridiculous," and he decided to do a black-comic film instead.

Kubrick was able to enlist the mimic and comic talents of Peter Sellers, who played three roles (the stiff-upper-lipped British Group Captain Mandrake; the balding, literally eggheaded President Merkin Muffley; and the bizarre, Nazi-refugee scientist Dr. Strangelove). He also blended the talents of George C. Scott as the General Curtis Lemay–like, adolescent, gravelly voiced, platitude-spouting Air Force Chief of Staff Buck Turgidson and the deadpan of Sterling Hayden's mad, grim General Jack D. Ripper, the man who initiates the unauthorized bomber raid.

Complementing this ensemble acting was Kubrick's genius for creating striking images and settings. This talent is maintained from the opening scene, where the B-52 is seen copulating with its refueling plane (to "Try a Little Tenderness" on the sound track), to the black-comic finale, where the doomsday mechanism has exploded and what results is a void with only mushroom clouds filling it. On the sound track, Vera Lynn can be heard singing the World War II favorite "We'll Meet Again." Kubrick also constructs three imaginative settings, cutting from one to another throughout the film: the extremely realistic and intricate-looking technology of the B-52 cockpit; the war room in Washington whose flashing lights, big board, large circular table, and vast empty space skirt the line between realism and surrealism; and Burpleson Air Force Base, where the psychopathic General Ripper is shot in tight close-up from a low angle and his troops' violent defense of the base against other American troops is shot with a handheld camera in grainy cinema verité style.

These elements came together in a narrative that describes the destruction of the world by a Soviet-constructed doomsday machine ignited by a nuclear attack launched by General Jack D. Ripper. He initiates the attack because he absurdly fears that the nation's sexual potency is on the brink of being undermined by a communist-inspired plot to fluoridate the American water supply. Terry Southern's antic screenplay served Kubrick brilliantly in satirizing a world of well-meaning but ineffectual liberal politicians, warmongering generals, espionage-obsessed Russian ambassadors, and demonic nuclear-war strategists.

Dr. Strangelove went beyond satire of the foibles of the power structure and its thinking about nuclear war, linking their behavior to the primal instincts of sex and death—eros and thanatos. There are scenes of the president talking over the hotline from his cryptlike war room to a drunken Russian Premier Kissoff, who can't comprehend what's being said because he's dallying with his mistress; Turgidson in turn getting calls from his mistress in the midst of a war room discussion; and Colonel Kong (Slim Pickens) astride the B-52's nuclear bomb (looking like a monstrous phallus) as it descends to penetrate and destroy the Soviet Union and the world.

Of course, the humanistic tradition presumes that the forces that kindle these passions can be held in check by reason. However, *Dr. Strangelove*'s most caustic barbs are aimed not only at the deadly logic of thinking about the unthinkable but also at sweet, humane reason itself. Time after time, we hear President Muffley's bland, decent conversations with the Russian premier ("Now Dimitri, you know how we've always talked about the possibility of something going wrong with the bomb—the bomb, Dimitri, the hydrogen bomb") or his shouting, "You can't fight here, this is the war room," as the Russian ambassador and air force chief of staff wrestle on the floor, and we are reminded of the futility and impotence of reason as men try to cope with the enormity of the forces they have unleashed.[28]

Kubrick posits no alternative to an insane world whose leaders are either ineffectual, stupid, infantile, or obsessional personalities. There is no plea for sanity or belief in social change inherent here. There is only the monstrous Dr. Strangelove, who is the personification of scientific reason gone amok. Strangelove, with his self-propelled Nazi-saluting arm, his belief in the divinity of computers, and his gleeful plans for a postnuclear holocaust society of subterranean polygamy (the ultimate expression of America's obsession with macho potency and power), emerges as a brilliant parody of the worst strains in American politics and culture.

In allowing us to take this black-comic peek at the apocalypse, Kubrick succeeded more in creating an inoculation against the fear of annihilation (laughter providing a means for coping in a world perched on the abyss) than in providing even a hint of some sane strategy for dealing with nuclear weapons. Kubrick's world is a mad, hopeless one, and as Pauline Kael wrote in her review of *Dr. Strangelove*, "What may have been laughed to death was not war, but some action about it."[29]

Despite this sort of criticism, Kubrick's film was able to sum up the anxieties about nuclear disaster that haunted the 1950s and, with the Cuban missile crisis, almost turned into reality in the 1960s. And by making both sides responsible for the state of affairs, it cut through the Gordian knot of Cold War mythology.[30] As social philosopher Lewis Mumford, writing in the *New York Times*, noted, it was "the first break in the cold war trance that has so long held this country in its rigid grip."[31]

Dr. Strangelove's breakthrough may not have changed the nature of nuclear policy, but it allowed film directors to use black comedy and irony to make social and political points. (The use of black humor reflected the influence of savagely satiric novelists like Joseph Heller, Thomas Pynchon, and Kurt Vonnegut.) It gave directors and the industry the opportunity to critically confront controversial issues without alienating an audience.

Besides films like the previously mentioned *Manchurian Candidate*, there were works like Billy Wilder's Oscar-winning *The Apartment* (1960). It was an acidic seriocomic take on corporate sexual politics and success; the film's central figure, an innocent but ambitious insurance clerk, C. C. Baxter (Jack Lemmon), lends his apartment to his married corporate superiors so that they can have assignations with their mistresses. Nevertheless, though the film concludes sentimentally with a pathetic Baxter both finding true love and finally standing up to his bosses (he refuses to loan his apartment out any longer and gives up his promotion), the film's vision of corporate behavior was an uncompromisingly dark one.

There was also *The Americanization of Emily* (1964), which, ironically, celebrated cowardice and was a film clearly ahead of its time. The only stir it initially created was by virtue of Julie Andrews's post–*Mary Poppins* dramatic debut. However, when it appeared again in 1967, its attacks on war and heroism fit nicely into the spirit of the 1960s. There was a ready-made audience for its cynical, wheeler–dealer, antihero, Naval Lieutenant Commander Charles Madison (James Garner), whose credo was that cowardice does more for humanity than courage.

The film doesn't just pay homage to cowardice, but it takes potshots at the madness of war, especially Madison's superior officer, who wants the first dead man on Omaha Beach to be a navy man. This sort of satire may not have been profound or radical, but it broke from the conventions that dominated films about the military in the preceding decades.

Nevertheless, the industry preferred, in the main, to grind out its usual quota of genre films led by the Cold War–inspired, superspy exploits of James Bond and his imitators like *Our Man Flint* (1966) and the Matt Helm series

(*The Silencers*, 1966; *Murderers Row*, 1966; and *The Ambushers*, 1967). Occasionally, these films were buttressed by a prestige picture like the anti-Nazi but essentially Grand Hotelish *Ship of Fools* (1965); the theatrical, message-bloated *A Man for All Seasons* (1966); or Sidney Lumet's *The Pawnbroker* (1965), an overemphatic but moving work that evoked the Holocaust survivor experience in a way that no other Hollywood film has ever done.

The Pawnbroker centers on a haunted, emotionally frozen concentration-camp survivor, Sol Nazerman (Rod Steiger), who owns a pawnshop among the violent, broken, and defeated in New York's East Harlem. The film's emphasis is on the isolated Nazerman's anguish and his catharsis, but there are also some vivid, unsentimental portraits of customers whose lives are also bound by suffering. However, influenced by Alain Resnais's *Hiroshima Mon Amour*, the film indulges in a great deal of parallel cutting from the teeming, inner-city ghetto streets to harrowing memory images of Auschwitz. The film doesn't quite attempt to equate the camps with East Harlem, but the trenchant cutting between the two experiences suggests that the people of East Harlem are on one level prisoners just like Nazerman is, though the streets project a great deal of life energy that coexists with their oppression.

However, even if *The Pawnbroker*'s prime interest was not in evoking inner-city reality, it was one of the few Hollywood films of the 1960s that gave us images of the way those streets (e.g., pool halls, cramped apartments, tenement stoops, nightclubs, and indoor markets) looked. Just how far out of step Hollywood was could be seen in the films that focused on black life, for despite the civil rights movement, there had been no great surge in the direction of making films about blacks or black life in either the late 1950s or the early 1960s. However, in films like *The Defiant Ones* (1958) and *A Raisin in the Sun* (1962), there was an attempt at least to portray blacks in a positive manner and to wrestle with some social and economic issues (especially in *A Raisin in the Sun*) but all within the context of an optimistic, integrationist philosophy. These were films that suggested that the American Dream was open to blacks if white attitudes shifted and blacks pursued their ambitions more relentlessly.

A film we should mention though it did not deal directly with black life is the film version of Harper Lee's Pulitzer Prize–winning novel *To Kill a Mockingbird* (1962). What it did do was evoke a time and place, where the words "desegregation" and "civil rights" were not yet part of anyone's vocabulary and older black men were still called "boys."

Set in the dusty dirt roads and vine-covered town of Maycomb, Alabama, in the 1930s (a striking studio set), the film is initially a coming-of-age story of the two children of the widowed and saintly lawyer Atticus Finch (the always dignified and remote Gregory Peck). The spirited tomboyish Scout (Mary Badham) and her intrepid 10-year-old brother Jem (Phillip Alford), joined by their diminutive neighbor "Dill" Harris (John Megna), spend their days and nights making up stories and trying to get a look at the almost invisible neighborhood bogeyman Boo Radley (Robert Duvall), and in the case of feisty Scout, getting into frequent fights at school.

Their world is dramatically altered when Atticus is called upon to defend a crippled black sharecropper Tom Robinson (Brock Peters) against the false charge of rape. Atticus stands down a mob of racist rednecks and prevents Robinson from being lynched. He also eloquently defends Robinson with his final summation, which is a model of white liberalism: "In this country our courts are the great levelers, and in our courts all men are created equal." The speech adheres to Atticus's personal credo that one should understand people by getting inside their skin. Nonetheless he can't convince the all-white jury of Robinson's innocence (this is after all 1930s Alabama.)

Atticus's defense of Robinson earns the ire of an alcoholic bigot, Tom Ewell (James Anderson), the presumed victim's father, and in a culminating, beautifully edited, menace-filled scene, he attacks the children, only to be killed himself by the supposedly monstrous, but morally innocent and ultimately sympathetic Boo Radley—illustrating too neatly Atticus's belief that no one's essence should be merely understood from the outside, through stereotype and public reputation, but from the inside.

Given that To Kill a Mockingbird's vision of Atticus is a child's point of view, it's both moving and overly sentimental. Atticus is a flawless hero, who stoically stands up to racist taunts, and is treated almost reverentially by the black population. But the film gives no sense that his liberalism is somewhat paternalistic. He operates at a distant remove from the black world, linked to the town's white hierarchy. He may brave danger, but nothing he does—his commitment to law and fairness—attempts to change the status of blacks in this segregated, racist society.

However, despite the fact that the fantasy of equity and integration was being destroyed no further away from Hollywood than the streets of Watts, the film industry still clung tenaciously to its sentimental and reductive vision of black–white relations. In the Oscar-winning crime melodrama In the Heat of the Night (1967), a stiff, dignified, black Philadelphia homicide detective Virgil Tibbs (Sidney Poitier) solves a murder case in a Mississippi town and predictably wins the respect of the bigoted, bellowing, lonely police chief (Rod Steiger). Tibbs, of course, is smarter and more professional than any of the local cops—a man toward whom only the most benighted could display any racist feelings. What is distinctive about the film is not the script or performances but Haskell Wexler's cinematography, which captures the oppressive heat and tension of summer nights in a racist, rural southern town.

Nowhere was the faith that social change could be brought about through personal understanding and affection between blacks and whites more evident than in Stanley Kramer's *Guess Who's Coming to Dinner* (1967). Kramer's liberal credentials were already well established with his portentous, social-problem productions of the antiracial prejudice such as *Home of the Brave* (1949), the anti-Nazi *Judgment at Nuremburg* (1961), *On the Beach*, and *The Defiant Ones*. In the glossy *Guess Who's Coming to Dinner*, Kramer and scriptwriter William Rose decided to tackle the subject of interracial marriage.

However, "tackle" is hardly the right word since there rarely has been such a field of straw men and women. The black male lead was again Sidney Poitier, who had already established himself as a worthy and successful missionary to white folks in a great many films (e.g., *Lilies of the Field*, 1963, and *A Patch of Blue*, 1965) and in this film portrays a handsome, chaste, and charming doctor well on his way to someday winning the Nobel Prize. In fact, he is too good a catch for the innocent, simpering daughter (Katharine Houghton) of liberal millionaire presslord Matt Drayton (Spencer Tracy) and his feisty, gallery-owning wife, Christina (Katharine Hepburn).

Although there are objections to the marriage, ranging from the bigoted snobbishness of one of Christina's art gallery employees to the comic protests of the Drayton's cute black maid ("civil rights is one thing, but this here's another!"), they are easily brushed aside. More difficult to sweep away are the more serious doubts expressed by Matt Drayton about the social problems the young couple will have to face. However, even his reasonable concerns are effectively bypassed by Beah Richard's (Poitier's mother in the film) suggestion that it is not race that is preventing the marriage but rather the fact that he and her husband (who also opposes the match) have forgotten what it was like to be young.

As a result, what ostensibly emerges as a prime issue in *Guess Who's Coming to Dinner* is not race but the clash of generations. Of course, it's a situation that is immediately rectified in Tracy's valedictory to Christina, about love conquering all, which is as much a commentary on his own 27-year relationship with Hepburn as it is to his fictional wife since Tracy was to die within weeks of the conclusion of the film.[32]

And though the issue of the generation gap feels totally bogus, especially in a film ostensibly dealing with the complex issue of intermarriage (not to mention the total blindness and irrelevance of the film's liberal, integrationist impulses to the rage and despair of the black community), it nevertheless superficially touched on something significant, namely, the growing polarization between generations. It was this polarization, resulting from the Vietnam War and the rise of the New Left and counterculture, that intensified and helped divide America in the late 1960s.

Already, the coming of the young into American politics had been celebrated in the prose of authors such as Norman Mailer, who saw them as "those mad middle class children with their lobotomies from sin . . . their innocence, their lust for the apocalypse."[33] However, their image had still not been forged in film, nor would it be until Arthur Penn's *Bonnie and Clyde* (1967).

Bonnie and Clyde not only shifted the focus of film to the young but also defined a unique 1960s cinema and sensibility in ways that *The Manchurian Candidate* and *Dr. Strangelove* had only hinted at. The best indicator of how far it went in accomplishing this was the vehemence of the attacks on it by the critical establishment, led by *New York Times* critic Bosley Crowther. Nevertheless, audiences flocked to it, copied its clothing styles, and made it one of the year's top grossers.

Vindicating the judgment of audiences over film critics is only one of the film's minor achievements. Its greatest success was in both introducing the ideas and techniques of the French "New Wave" into the Hollywood mainstream and firmly fixing the gaze of American filmmakers on the lives and styles of the alienated and discontented.

Written by two young *Esquire* writers, David Newman and Robert Benton, it was originally seen by them as a possible project for either François Truffaut or Jean-Luc Godard, a hope based on their appreciation of the French New Wave's understanding of the poetic and mythic nature of the American genre film. However, neither director was available, and the film was ultimately produced by Warren Beatty and directed by Arthur Penn.

Penn had also been influenced by the New Wave, so little was really lost by the change, and he was able to incorporate many of their techniques into the film. Thus, along with free intercutting of time and space—the use of slow and accelerated motion—he also used little vignettes ending in visual and verbal puns à la Truffaut and the alternating of comic and violent moments apropos of Godard. In fact, it was the irony and humor of *Bonnie and Clyde*—like the chase scene where careening and zigzagging cars comically pursue each other accompanied by a wildly twanging banjo sound track or the gang's picnic with a middle-class couple who, though at first terrified, ultimately refuse to leave them—that helped prevent the film from turning into conventional social melodrama.

These techniques updated a story that was done before by Hollywood in Fritz Lang's *You Only Live Once* (1937) and Nicholas Ray's *They Live by Night* (1949). Yet this time-worn tale of two youthful outsiders who choose a life of crime held a powerful attraction for an audience who felt they were living cut off from the channels of power and incapable of bringing about social and political change.

This restless quality is caught right from the opening Depression-era scene, in which the beautiful and bored Bonnie (Faye Dunaway) sees the limping, toothpick-chewing, handsome Clyde (Warren Beatty) attempting to steal her mother's car, and, attracted by his bravado, she becomes involved in a life of

Bonnie and Clyde (1967). (Courtesy of Warner Bros./Seven Arts/Photofest.)

crime. It takes them on a number of botched and bumbling robbery attempts, and after the addition of Clyde's crude, guffawing brother Buck (Gene Hackman), his bovine, pathetic wife Blanche (Estelle Parsons), and a nose-picking, hero-worshipping rustic driver named C. W. Moss (Michael Pollard), they go on a bank-robbing rampage that makes them celebrated and notorious figures.

Despite their violent and criminal acts, Penn never allows the audience's sympathy to leave Bonnie and Clyde. On the one hand, they are seen as outlaw-rebels (though never social victims) against an unjust social order represented here by the banks and police; on the other hand, they are innocent, awkward clowns who in one robbery can't get the attention of their victims. Penn also attempts to reinforce our positive feelings for them through his use of shallow Freudianism. Clyde is sexually impotent, which supposedly provides the character with a measure of vulnerability and gives his gun a crude, symbolic significance.

In depicting Bonnie and Clyde as ordinary folk, seeking to be immortalized, Penn sometimes catches the pathos underneath their posturing and bravado. The sheepish, slow, inarticulate Clyde—match in mouth and permanent limp—and the slatternly, poetess manqué Bonnie—constantly looking at her image in a blurred mirror—are nothing more than a yokel sharecropper and a waitress who hunger for the American Dream of glamour and success. No matter how often Bonnie may dress in expensive clothes and obsess about her image and making the headlines, she still longs for her mother and settling down in a home. And though the scene where Bonnie returns to the family picnic is overly stylized and filled with soft-focused, sentimentalized, pastoral imagery (e.g., an almost too picturesquely weathered and stark-looking farm woman mother), it succeeds in evoking the rural and church-bound social world they both come from.

What is most striking in the film, however, is not their ordinariness or the social reality that helps shape them but rather their mythic quality. It is a quality conveyed both by the glamour of stars like Beatty and Dunaway and by Penn's camera, which captures in long shot and close-up the outlaws' vitality, spontaneity, and style. Penn frames their actions with painterly, beautifully composed, melancholy images of sweeping wheat fields and prairies and Walker Evans–like small towns. It is topped off by their slow-motion death, dressed in white (innocence?), twitching like rag dolls in a montage of violence. Their death is both mythic, the tragic death of a heroic duo, and concrete, for the bullets are real and leave them truly dead.

The myth of Bonnie and Clyde works for Penn in aesthetic terms—the beauty of alienation and outlawry—and captures something of how integral violence and the unfettered assertion of both self and will were to American mythology and the 1960s. It is when Penn wants his outlaws to be seen as romantic rebels against an unjust social order—Clyde returning money he stole from a bank to a poor farmer or the gang being embraced as people's heroes at a migrant camp (straight out of *The Grapes of Wrath*)—that the film becomes most simplistic and even dangerous. It is clear that Penn wants Bonnie and Clyde to stand as symbols for the rebellious and high-spirited youth of the 1960s, while the banks, Deputy Sheriff Hammer, and Pa Moss represent a callous, rigid, and hypocritical adult world. There are also suggestions, in the exaggerated, murderous use of police firepower (e.g., a bloody shoot-out where the police use an armored car), of the American military's penchant for overkill in Vietnam.

However, no matter that Clyde talks about protecting poor folk, their social consciousness is no more than a contrivance of Penn's. The only community Bonnie and Clyde are members of is the criminal one, and though the film might not have had any more pernicious influence than getting somebody to buy a snap-brim hat, it did give symbolic sanction to certain nihilistic values and strains permanent in both the counterculture and the New Left. The film fed the contempt many of the young had for the adult world and its work ethic. More significantly, by affirming crime as a viable means of social, political, and cultural protest, it fed the growing contempt that many of the young felt for more orthodox forms of political organization and action and ominously romanticized sociopathic violence by confusing it with acts of social rebellion.[34]

These objections aside, *Bonnie and Clyde* was still the landmark film of the 1960s. Along with revitalizing the formal dimensions of the Hollywood film, its focusing of attention on the young and the alienated gave some Hollywood luster to the 1960s revisionist impulse, which saw American history and society from the bottom up. Once launched on this road, the facile shibboleths about American society that had been Hollywood's stock in trade since World War II became harder and harder to sustain. And while much of this new perspective was transformed into films expressing a kind of bankable and facile pessimism accompanied by the same superstar actors as before, nevertheless, the films projected a vision of a fragmented America no longer as secure of itself and its values as had once been the case.

Nowhere is the crumbling of these values more clearly illustrated than in Mike Nichols's homage to the young, *The Graduate* (1967), a commercially and critically successful film whose most compelling moment is the postnuptial abduction of the beautiful Elaine Robinson (Katherine Ross) by the romantically obsessed Benjamin Braddock (Dustin Hoffman in his first film). Not only did this scene break with a whole genre past that upheld the sanctities of the marriage vow above everything else, but it was merely the shrewdest—it gave Hollywood a breakthrough into the 18- to 25-year-old market—assault in a whole series of attacks on the values of the affluent, upper-middle-class American.

The embodiment of this challenge in *The Graduate* is somber, bright, and inexperienced Benjamin Braddock, who returns to the emptiness and sterility of his parent's vulgar southern California world of swimming pools and material comfort. Out of a sheer sense of ennui and alienation, Ben begins a sexually satisfying but emotionally starved and mechanical affair with the bored, cynical wife of his father's law partner, Mrs. Robinson (Anne Bancroft). It is the first stages of this affair that allow Hoffman to display his talent for giving richly textured performances. Before his transformation into a romantic hero, Hoffman's Braddock is filled with anxiety and self-doubt—speaking in half-finished phrases, wheezily expelling breath, and never quite sure of what his hands are doing—while fending off Mrs. Robinson's seductive wiles. The affair is simultaneously comic and pathetic and probably is the most poignant section of the film.

The deadness of his affair with Mrs. Robinson is contrasted with the spontaneity and openness he finds with her daughter Elaine. It is a relationship that the predatory Mrs. Robinson violently objects to. And Nichols skillfully evokes empathy from the youth audience for both Elaine's freshness and vulnerability and Benjamin's truth seeking and rejection of a plastic, unfeeling adult universe.

Combining the New Wave techniques of jump and flash cuts, extreme close-ups, and subjective view and telephoto lens shots (throughout, one senses Nichols's eclectic, stylistic borrowings from Antonioni, Fellini, and Godard) with the music of youth-culture heroes Simon and Garfunkel, Nichols successfully creates a world of honest young people surrounded by stereotyped adults who are either predators or fools. The gilded surfaces of the adults predictably cover empty lives and dead marriages all echoing, in the words of Simon and Garfunkel, the "sounds of silence."

In such an emotional and moral void, the mere act of honestly being in love is perceived as liberating and capable of shattering old taboos, even the supposed eternal links of "I do." Consequently, Mrs. Robinson's shriek at the runaway Elaine, that it's "too late," can be met with the reply "not for me." This hardly guarantees a "they live happily ever after" fade-out, and the film ends with the couple's blank and ambiguous stares as they leave the scene of the wedding in the back of a municipal bus.[35]

Regardless of this final seed of doubt about the future, *The Graduate* still remains a hymn to the young. Like *Bonnie and Clyde*, it grants all vitality and integrity to the young. However, in contrast to the origins of Bonnie and Clyde's revolt, which was loosely tied to the poverty of the Depression, the reasons for Ben's alienation supposedly can be found in the sterility of upper-middle-class affluence. Taken together, both films affirmed the discontent of the young. *The Graduate* underlined that dissatisfaction by locating it precisely at the moment when the American Dream seemed to have reached its peak of material fulfillment—creating a paradigm for the type of 1960s film that attempted to subvert the values that had dominated American films since the 1940s. Not only were the language and sexual detail more frank in *The Graduate*, but the insistence on a moral perspective that unambiguously repudiated social convention and mores was relatively new to Hollywood. With its oblique references to 1960s radicalism when its locale is shifted from southern California to Berkeley (where a harried Benjamin follows Elaine) and a comic landlord who dislikes outside agitators makes a brief appearance, *The Graduate* hinted that there might be even more to Benjamin's anguish than alienation from the values of the upper-middle class and existential angst. However, *The Graduate* was based on a 1950s novel by Charles Webb, and the film's few 1960s allusions did little to update the novel and illuminate the sources of student rebellion and alienation in the 1960s.

Still, there was something about the intensity of *Bonnie and Clyde*'s violence and the extremity of Benjamin's alienation that suggested that political events had some effect on the nature of the two films. The event that had the most profound effect on the politics of the young and American politics in general was the war in Vietnam. Aware of the divided nature of American public opinion about the war, producers hesitated to tackle the subject directly. However, for a right-wing superstar and patriot like John Wayne, a film about the Vietnam War, *The Green Berets* (1968), with himself as star, was a means of winning the hearts and minds of the American people.

Since the 1940s and films like *Wake Island* (1942), *They Were Expendable* (1945), and *Sands of Iwo Jima* (1949), John Wayne had become the symbol par excellence of the tough, efficient, patriotic, American fighting man. The Wayne image was indelibly imprinted on every American schoolboy's imagination and every raw recruit's dreams. Nor was there anything ironic or calculating in Wayne's own devotion to the image, as exemplified by his red-baiting leadership in the McCarthyite Motion Picture Alliance for the Preservation of American Ideals and his support of bellicose right-wing politicians like Barry Goldwater and Ronald Reagan.

Choosing as the subject of his Vietnam film the elite, military unit the Green Berets, Wayne was returning to the world of John Ford, his mentor. Ford's cavalry units, perched at the edge of the frontier, were bastions of communal honor, tradition, camaraderie and pride, fighting an often little appreciated and less understood battle for civilization and decency against the barbarians. Wayne's notion of the Green Berets was similar; he saw them as a fortress of muscular and professional anticommunist values whose most serious challenge came, ironically enough, not from the communists but from a liberal, skeptical reporter, George Beckwith (David Janssen). For Wayne, those soft liberals who undermined our patriotic will were far more dangerous than regiments of savage Vietcong. However, Beckwith's piddling doubts are suppressed as soon as he is exposed to the murderous brutality of a Vietcong raid on a desolate Vietnamese village.

If the first half of the film is mediocre, John Ford—the Vietcong even scale with ladders the Green Berets' fort, which is aptly named Dodge City—the film's second half is pure Richard Nixon. In this section, Wayne uses all manner of advanced technologies and dirty tricks, including a Hollywood-style Mata Hari female decoy, and he kidnaps an enemy Vietcong general. The general's aristocratic and decadent values make even the revolutionary politics of the Vietcong suspect. Through all this, Wayne's hero (Colonel Mike Kirby) hovers about like a good paterfamilias, granting absolution to the liberal columnist for his political sins and providing fatherly comfort to a cute Vietnamese orphan who in Wayne's fade-out comment is "What this is all about."[36]

Although *The Green Berets* (1968) turned out to be financially profitable, rather than setting Americans' minds at ease about the righteousness of their cause, it produced new evidence of the national split on the war. Indicative of that polarization was some of the critical reaction to the film. In previous years, a Wayne film rarely raised anything more than a critical ho-hum. However, *The Green Berets* provoked *New York Times* critic Renata Adler's withering comment that

> *The Green Berets* is a film so unspeakable, so stupid, so rotten and false that it passes through being funny, through being camp, through everything and becomes an invitation to grieve not so much for our soldiers or Vietnam (the film could not be more false or do greater disservice to them) but for what has happened to the fantasy-making apparatus of this country.[37]

Adler's comment recognized that Hollywood's mythmaking abilities had lost power and resonance, and consequently the old Hollywood formula could no longer capture and spur the nation's imagination to a greater commitment in the war. No longer could Wayne's war-loving, patriarchal figure, spouting the old patriotic and macho certainties and clichés about decent, freedom-loving Americans and brutal, totalitarian Vietcong, capture and dominate the moral center of the American imagination as it once had. Instead, Wayne's values existed in uneasy proximity to Hollywood's new revisionism featuring genre films that not only undermined Wayne's most cherished certitudes but also covertly and slyly evoked a Vietnam war that had horror rather than honor as its dominant motif.

One such film was Sam Peckinpah's (a descendant of pioneers) brilliantly cut and richly composed western *The Wild Bunch* (1969). Paradoxically, *The Wild Bunch* drew much of its power from working against the Ford–Hawks tradition that had done so much for Wayne's reputation. For instance, *The Wild Bunch* took place when the frontier was closed physically and the ethos of the Old West was disappearing fast in the wake of new technologies such as the motorcar and machine gun. Also fading with it were the elite band of mythic professional good–bad Robin Hoods that often populated the moral landscapes of Hawks and Ford. In *The Wild Bunch*, we have the interminable wranglings and whorings of Pike Bishop's (William Holden) gang of bank robbers and payroll snatchers who are in turn pursued by a group of craven, rednecked, lumpen bounty hunters led by Pike's old confederate, the melancholy, trapped Deke Thornton (Robert Ryan). In addition, the traditional Hollywood western town, which often contained some people who could express communal pride, concern, and virtue, has been replaced by a passive, foolish citizenry, too cowed and confused to make even more than a token protest when the streets of their town erupt with bloody, chaotic violence. The only seemingly active members of the town are its children who mimic the shoot-out and are demonically amused by burning to death the scorpions and ants they have been playing with.

With society corrupt and rapacious and the mythic West gone, the film follows Bishop's bunch involvement in the Mexican Revolution (whose political issues Peckinpah cares nothing about) and in the process trying to establish some kind of rough set of principles. The one most valued is group loyalty, the kind embodied in Bishop's comment, "When you side with a man, you side with him all the way—otherwise you're an animal." Ultimately, this sense of loyalty grows among the outlaws and even includes the primal, savage Gorch Brothers (Ben Johnson and Warren Oates) and the Mexican bandit Angel (Jaime Sanchez). Almost as significant is the value placed on genuine authority in a world of corrupt betrayers where traditional institutional power is dominated by debauchees like the gross, murderous Mexican general Mapache (Emilio Fernandez) and the ruthless railroad executive Harrigan (Albert Dekker). Society's corruption makes it imperative, according to Pike's lieutenant Dutch (Ernest Borgnine), to heavily weigh the fact of not only giving your word (the old code) but also considering "who you give it to."

However, whatever scrupulousness the outlaws exhibit toward their code is not matched by any restraint on Peckinpah's part in his depiction of violence in the film. For a supposed moralist, Peckinpah's use of graphic, elongated, and sensational violence throughout the film—a horse stomping on a woman and dragging a man along the ground and countless bodies falling in slow motion with blood gushing from them—raised again questions about the origins and effects of screen violence. The answer this time was not only the usual talk about the psychology of the director and Hollywood's tendency to indulge in and exploit blood and gore but also a crediting of responsibility to the audience's increasing receptivity to violence, some of it caused by the nightly scenes of Vietnam bloodletting they saw on the television screen.

The climax of The Wild Bunch, with its stylized, orgiastic massacre, raised questions not only about the often incoherent blend of moralism and nihilism pervading Peckinpah's work but also about the hopelessness reflected in many of the films of the late 1960s. Although The Wild Bunch ends on a supposedly revolutionary note with the last survivors both of the outlaws and of the bounty hunters, wise Old Sykes (Edmond O'Brien) and Deke Thornton, joining with the revolutionaries, the gesture seems a hollow afterthought following the more emotionally and aesthetically intense and compelling slaughter scenes. In fact, Peckinpah's deepest and most sentimental loyalties clearly have nothing to do with social commitment. It is men like Pike, seen in low-angle shots walking tall to a drumbeat and resolving to die heroically, who elicit Peckinpah's deepest feeling. Pike and the men of the wild bunch may be brutal killers who belong to the past, but Peckinpah grants them a final, heroic eulogy (shades of Ford's Fort Apache, 1948) as he superimposes them over the film's last images, watching them, in their moment of transcendence, riding out of a Mexican village to the applause and serenades of its inhabitants.[38]

The Wild Bunch's mixture of intellectual incoherence and imaginative and powerful imagery was symptomatic (though in exaggerated form) of the problems that many of these late 1960s films exhibited. The filmmakers reveled in the freedom they had to pursue previously forbidden subject matter and imagery but were often incapable of doing more than evoking a portrait of a world gone awry. They were clearly at home more with images and feelings of human corruption, alienation, confusion, and rebellion than with incisive and complex social and political critiques. And they were more attuned to feelings of anger and resentment toward established institutions and the desire for "freedom" from conventional mores than to any overviews of the social malaise and political and cultural movements of the 1960s.

There were a number of films that touched on aspects of the counterculture. Films like Richard Lester's psychologically suggestive and self-consciously stylish *Petulia* (1968)—excessive flash cuts and a splintered narrative—were interested primarily in satirizing the callousness, crassness, and obliviousness of American society of the 1960s. However, the film does provide brief glimpses of the counterculture, but as a social alternative it holds out little hope. Lester depicts its adherents as being just as uncaring and mean-spirited as conventional middle-class society. And Paul Mazursky's box office success *Bob and Carol and Ted and Alice* (1969) gently satirizes the southern California, upper-middle-class version of the counterculture. Mazursky's well-heeled professionals go to Esalen (for primal scream, 24-hour marathons, and other pop therapies), smoke pot, and struggle to achieve emotional and sexual liberation. The film has charm and wit, and Mazursky conveys an insider's knowledge of his characters' foibles. It never, however, probes beyond the externals of their behavior, asking larger social questions about why they behave as they do—Mazursky playing it safe and muting his satiric jabs.

Arthur Penn's elegiac and loosely episodic *Alice's Restaurant* (1969) goes a bit further. Its prime purpose was to provide a critical but loving evocation of the counterculture. Using a balladlike structure and centering the film on a solemn, honest, pure Arlo Guthrie (playing himself with consummate impassivity), the film touches on Arlo's relationship with the Old Left (via visits to his dying father, the legendary Woody Guthrie), his conflicts with the establishment (college, the police, and the army), and his involvement with the counterculture.

Arlo has long hair, plays a guitar, smokes dope, and takes refuge in a counterculture commune presided over by his more animated and complex surrogate parents, sensual earth-mother Alice (Pat Quinn) and her insecure, hostile, dreamer husband Ray Brock (played with manic intensity by James Broderick). Penn's sympathies are clearly with the counterculture as he wittily portrays Arlo's victories over the police (he beats a conviction for littering) and the draft. These scenes wryly and satirically (the film re-creates the 20-minute talking-blues hit "Alice's Restaurant Massacre") capture the estrangement between the generations in America. Nonetheless, though Penn likes the young's openness and spontaneity, he sees the counterculture having its own painful limitations, for, though Arlo can serenely triumph over traditional institutions, another member of the commune dies of an overdose of heroin. And the image of the commune as a beatific refuge (they even reconsecrate an abandoned church) coexists with a profound sense of the whole venture's futility and failure. The film concludes with a despairing Ray desolately fantasizing about creating one more commune and with Penn's camera tenderly panning around Alice, who stands vulnerable and alone with both the commune and her marriage heading for disaster.

Alice's Restaurant is filled with luminously poetic and painterly images and exhibits a real empathy for the counterculture. Penn can grace us with scenes that catch both the absurdity—the dim, clichéd talk about getting one's head together—and the sense of human possibility and community of the counterculture. However, at times it seems that there are too many tones inhabiting the work—comic, pathetic, and ironic—ultimately dissipating some of the film's emotional and intellectual impact. *Alice's Restaurant* also never gets sufficiently close to the Brocks or especially to the other members of the commune—who are merely colorfully dressed, hippie extras—to get to the heart of the film's personal and communal breakdowns.[39]

If *Alice's Restaurant* is not a fully realized and coherent portrait of the counterculture, a film like the left-leaning, strikingly cinematic *Medium Cool* (1969) tends to sacrifice its narrative and characters to the evocative documentary footage that its director had amassed. *Medium Cool's* hard-boiled, apolitical, hero is a television cameraman, John (Robert Forster), who views contemporary events with professional detachment; he treats the nature and substance of the event as much less significant than the process of getting the story—until he discovers that the FBI is being allowed to use his footage to identify radicals. He suddenly realizes that the act of pointing a camera is itself a political gesture.

John's job as a television cameraman allows *Medium Cool's* director Haskell Wexler to mix cinema verité—documentary and neodocumentary footage (a reconstruction of the assassination of Bobby Kennedy)—with a loose fictional narrative in order to create a telling portrait of 1960s social reality. And though there are scenes that go in for easy ironies (e.g., "Happy Days Are Here Again" can be heard on the sound track as protestors are beaten by Chicago police) and take facile potshots at targets like insensitive, white, middle-class liberals, the film is filled with incisive sequences depicting angry, knotted-up black militants subtly playing with white fears and guilt, Illinois National Guardsmen receiving riot training, and the chaos and repression of the Chicago 1968 Democratic Party Convention and police riot. However, the purely fictional scenes lack conviction and are often left aimlessly suspended as the more powerful verité scenes are inserted between them.

Even in the verité scenes, *Medium Cool* sometimes indulges in awkward Pirandello-like effects—the actors wandering past the Chicago police and protestors and the audience viewing Wexler and his crew self-consciously shooting the final fatal accident scene and turning the lens toward the audience. That final scene, where John and a woman friend, Eileen (Verna Bloom), die in a car crash, ends the film on a dark note, one that both conveys a sense of the fatality and destruction of the 1960s[40] and suggests that "we are implicated both as voyeuristic viewers and as potential victims of the camera's imaging of violence and death."[41]

Wexler is unambiguously on the side of the 1960s protestors, but he knows full well that the exposure of repression on film, including his own, may merely titillate its audience. That "the whole world may be watching" on television the brutality of Mayor Daley's police, but their actions will probably arouse little concern in the audience. For a committed filmmaker like Wexler, the feeling that politically engaged films may ultimately make no more social difference than the most detached, commercial works was not a hopeful sign for the success of the 1960s movements.

Easy Rider (1969), which was the most culturally significant and commercially successful of cinematic attempts at capturing the rebellious and alternate lifestyles of the 1960s, was no more sanguine about the future. Initially conceived of as a kind of American International Pictures' exploitation quickie about the hippie scene like the *Wild Angels* (1966) and *The Trip* (1967), it had to be finished with independent financing by its star Peter Fonda. Its subsequent box office success compared to its small initial investment made it a model for what became known as the New American Cinema. Their characteristic products were independently financed, low-budget films, made by non–studio-trained directors who combined highly personal or politically radical stories that broke with conventional Hollywood narrative techniques while borrowing heavily from the respective styles of New Wave, cinema verité, and avant-garde films. Offshoots of this tendency were *Wild 90* (1968), Brian De Palma's *Greetings* (1968), *Hi Mom* (1970), *Putney Swope* (1969), *Coming Apart* (1969), *Ice* (1970), and other films of the late 1960s and early 1970s.

Crucial to *Easy Rider*'s enormous commercial success and cultural significance was its ability to capture on a visceral level certain prime themes and concepts of the counterculture and the 1960s—mysticism, personal freedom, "the land," drugs, and communes. It begins as a reverse road film in which a pair of hippie motorcyclists—the cool, detached, oracular Wyatt (Peter Fonda) and the tense, angry, and comic Billy (Dennis Hopper)—sell a kilo of dope to a Los Angeles hippie capitalist and then head east to New Orleans for Mardi Gras in what ostensibly is a search for freedom. Along the way, *Easy*

Rider becomes a laid-back bildungsroman as the duo visit old-time ranchers and hippie communes, spend time in jail and in brothels, and take acid trips. The journey is enhanced by the film's exciting use of landscape, space, light, movement, and sound (especially the contemporary rock music of Jimi Hendrix, the Byrds, Steppenwolf, and others).

Unfortunately, the film is often painfully inarticulate, shallow, and pretentious when it forgoes its tracking camera and tries to turn its vision into words. Most of it takes the form of particularly banal and pretentious pronouncements by the hippie saint Wyatt who gives a benediction to a rural commune that has faced hard times—"they're gonna make it"—or pays pious reverence to the simple lifestyle of a toothless old rancher with a beaming Mexican wife who is "doing his own thing, in his own time."

However, in its depiction of "us against them"—the supposed free, longhairs versus the vicious, and redneck straights who universally treat Wyatt and Billy with murderous contempt—the film does strike a powerful social and emotional chord. In the process, the film gave up its penchant for indulging in ersatz and sentimental beatitudes and connected itself to the disillusionment felt by many, especially the young, about 1960s America. Its most poignant expression came in the comments of an articulate, witty, alcoholic lawyer, George Hanson (Jack Nicholson), who joins the two on their quest. After they are attacked by local goons, Hanson points out that "this used to be a helluva country," but it seems to have lost its way. He adds that though the rednecks may ostensibly believe in the idea of freedom, they are scared of free individuals.

Hanson's remarks set the tone of the second half of the film, which is pervaded with as much of a sense of failure, doom, and despair as the opening half was a paean to the exhilaration of traveling on the open road. Wyatt and Billy's own violent fate is prefigured in George's murder by a group of rednecks. And, although they do make it to the Mardi Gras and take an extravagantly filmed acid trip (fish-eye lens, overexposed images, and overlapping dialogue) with some prostitutes in a cemetery, their pathetic destiny seems so sealed that we get hints of it in flash-forwards. It is a climax that not only acted as a judgment on their personal quest but also seemed to extend to the American experience as a whole.

Such was the outrage of some critics at this judgment, that an elite, cultural custodian like Diana Trilling (who had not raised more than an eyebrow at films since her tenure as a reviewer for *The New Republic* in the 1940s and 1950s) was moved to call the film "devious." She particularly questioned the appropriateness of Wyatt and Billy as symbols of our social and cultural condition and complained that "Wyatt and Billy lack the energy to create anything, comment on anything, feel anything, except the mute, often pot-induced pleasure of each other's company."[42]

However, though one may clearly quarrel with the presumptuousness of two dope-dealing drifters standing as symbols of freedom and making judgments on something as vast as the "American experience," there is little doubt that *Easy Rider* captured the sense of foreboding and doom that dominated many of the films of the sixties and heralded those of the 1970s. In fact, the deaths of Wyatt and Billy seemed a reflection of what had been the fate of Martin Luther King, Malcolm X, and Robert Kennedy, and some felt could be the lot of anyone whose dissent and protest truly threatened the power structure of America.

Of course, Billy and Wyatt were far from being political rebels or critics, but in their dim, self-destructive way, they were searching for some alternative vision to the dominant culture. *Easy Rider* is a tongue-tied film that succeeds in evoking the mood of a decade. In its mixture of intellectual simplemindedness, striking imagery and editing, and conscious and unconscious intuition into the decade's confusion and alienation, it was one of the most representative of late 1960s films. In fact, Wyatt's despairing comment grants unintentional pop-cultural symmetry to a decade that began with the unequivocal optimism embodied in lyrics of songs like "Blowin' in the Wind" and ended with the pessimism of a line like "We blew it."

NOTES

1. William L. Langer, *Political and Social Upheaval, 1832–1852* (New York: Harper and Row, 1969).

2. Godfrey Hodgson, *America in Our Time: From World War II to Nixon, What Happened and Why* (New York: Vintage, 1978).

3. Ibid., pp. 491–99.

4. William L. O'Neill, *Coming Apart: An Informal History of America in the 1960s* (New York: Quadrangle, 1971), pp. 29–103.

5. Ibid.

6. Hodgson, *America in Our Time*, pp. 179–99.

7. Ibid.

8. Ibid.

9. Hodgson, *America in Our Time*, pp. 200–24.

10. Ibid.

11. Doris Kearns, *Lyndon B. Johnson and the American Dream* (New York: Signet, 1976), pp. 220–62.

12. Kearns, *Lyndon B. Johnson and the American Dream*, pp. 263–323.

13. Frances Fitzgerald, *Fire in the Lake* (New York: Vintage, 1973).

14. David Halberstam, *The Best and the Brightest* (New York: Fawcett, 1973).

15. Kirkpatrick Sale, *SDS* (New York: Vintage, 1974).

16. Morris Dickstein, *Gates of Eden: American Culture in the Sixties* (New York: Basic Books, 1977), pp. 51–88, 128–53.

17. Hodgson, *America in Our Time*, pp. 326–52.

18. O'Neill, *Coming Apart*, pp. 396–428.

19. Ibid.

20. James Monaco, *American Film Now: The People, the Power, the Money, the Movies* (New York: Oxford University Press, 1979), pp. 1–48.

21. Ibid.

22. Ibid.

23. Thomas Schatz, *The Genius of the System: Hollywood Filmmaking in the Studio Era* (New York: Pantheon, 1988), p. 489.

24. Pauline Kael, *Going Steady* (New York: Bantam, 1971), p. 115.

25. Gerald Pratley, *The Cinema of John Frankenheimer* (Cranbury, NJ: A. S. Barnes, 1969).

26. Susan Sontag, *Against Interpretation* (New York: Dell, 1969), p. 215.

27. Norman Kagan, *The War Film* (New York: Pyramid Publications, 1974), p. 142.

28. Norman Kagan, *The Cinema of Stanley Kubrick* (New York: Grove Press, 1975), pp. 111–44.

29. Pauline Kael, *Kiss, Kiss, Bang, Bang* (New York: Bantam, 1969), p. 79.

30. Albert Auster and Leonard Quart, *How the War Was Remembered: Hollywood and Vietnam* (New York: Praeger, 1988), p. 25.

31. Lewis Mumford, quoted in Kagan, *The Cinema of Stanley Kubrick* (New York: Grove Press, 1972), p. 132.

32. Donald Spoto, *Stanley Kramer: Filmmaker* (New York: G. P. Putnam's Sons, 1978), p. 2.

33. Norman Mailer, *Armies of the Night* (New York: Signet, 1968), p. 47.

34. Robin Wood, *Arthur Penn* (New York: Praeger, 1969), pp. 72–91.

35. Hollis Alpert and Andrew Sarris (eds.), *Film 68/69: An Anthology by the National Society of Film Critics* (New York: Simon and Schuster, 1969), pp. 235–41.

36. Alan G. Barbour, *John Wayne* (New York: Pyramid, 1974), pp. 121–22.

37. Renata Adler, *A Year in the Dark* (New York: Berkley, 1969), pp. 199–200.

38. Joseph Morgenstern and Stefan Kanfer (eds.), *Film 69/70: An Anthology by the National Society of Film Critics* (New York: Simon and Schuster, 1970), pp. 148–56.

39. Wood, *Arthur Penn*, pp. 92–116.

40. Morgenstern and Kanfer, *Film 69/70*, pp. 165–72.

41. Robert Sklar, "When Looks Could Kill: American Cinema of the Sixties," *Cineaste* 16, no. 1–2 (1987–88), p. 51.

42. Diana Trilling, *We Must March, My Darlings* (New York: Harcourt Brace Jovanovich, 1977), pp. 175–86.

5

THE 1970s

On March 18, 1969, newly elected President Richard Nixon ordered the secret bombing of neutral Cambodia. It was the first in a series of events whose consequences were to dominate American politics and society during the first half of the 1970s. Given Nixon's past history—his hawkish foreign policy views and his gift for manipulating anticommunism to further his political career—there should have been little surprise that he ordered the bombing. But in 1968, Nixon had come to power primarily on the strength of the vague promise that he knew how to end the war in Vietnam, understanding that at this point in the Vietnam War, neither Congress nor the public would approve its escalation.[1]

Despite his political promises, however, Nixon was clearly not ready to abruptly terminate American involvement. Nixon and his advisers had no use for the Johnson–Humphrey idea that the war was fought for democracy and "winning the hearts and minds" of the people and displayed little interest in geopolitical rationales like the fear of toppling Southeast Asian dominoes. The Nixon–Kissinger justification for continuing U.S. involvement was summed up in the strategic concept of "credibility." They believed that the war was being fought to maintain America's reputation "as a guarantor"—to assure her allies and more particularly her enemies that the United States would be firm in confronting a crisis.[2]

Inextricably connected to the idea of "credibility" was the notion of "American will." The Nixon administration felt they had to assure the world that America would take the necessary painful steps, like the bombing of

Cambodia, to back up words with action. After the American people finally became aware of the bombing, the president affirmed the notion of credibility by stating, "It is not our power but our will and character that is being tested tonight."[3]

To the Nixon administration, that will seemed badly shaken after years of interminable bloodshed, the investment of billions of dollars, and the often violent political debate and struggles of a profoundly divided nation. There were people in the administration who felt that the national will had been permanently damaged not only by the war but also by social welfarism, government intervention in the economy, and the leadership of a decadent elite and establishment.

In order to renew America, Richard Nixon set about attacking the media, liberal-left intellectuals, and government bureaucrats—institutions that he viewed as bastions of an enemy establishment. It was a campaign motivated almost as much by Nixon's own sense of personal powerlessness and private grievance as by his ideological and political commitments. In the process of initiating this attack, Nixon dismantled much of the "Great Society" legislation of the Johnson presidency, stacked the Supreme Court with supposed judicial conservatives (though Blackmun surprisingly turned out to be a liberal on a number of issues), and attempted the political mobilization of a segment of the American population he dubbed the "silent majority." They were supposedly ordinary Americans who adhered to traditional verities like patriotism and were antagonistic to the values of both the establishment and the war protesters.

Given that Nixon's policies were dependent on smears, innuendo, confrontation, and polarization, they succeeded only in fragmenting any semblance of an American will. They pitted race against race, old against young, class against class, and region against region, leaving division rather than unity in their wake. This further disruption of the American will did not contradict the goals of the Nixon administration, for what he and his associates were really interested in creating was not a harmonious and cohesive American society and spirit but rather an administration that embodied and defined the national will. It was this confidence (megalomania?) that his administration really was an expression of the American will that provided Nixon with the rationale to indulge in whatever he felt politically necessary: to concentrate power in the White House, to use war methods against domestic enemies, and to use the power of the federal government to promote and maintain the image and reputation of the administration. In fact, for Nixon and his cohorts, the image the administration projected was more significant than the substance, a notion that was far from new to American politics but clearly gained much strength during the 1970s.[4]

In promoting their image, the Nixon administration initiated a campaign of illegal activities. In 1971, after the release of the Pentagon Papers, the administration created a group of undercover operatives nicknamed "the plumbers." It was the covert activities of this group that led to the break-in at Democratic headquarters in June 1972 and the resulting Watergate scandal. The public revelation of the scandal and the administration's cover-up led to the resignation of Nixon—though even in his final days of power, Nixon was unable to confront and admit his own responsibility in the whole affair. The forcing of Nixon and his hatchet man out of office (e.g., Vice President Agnew—for bribe taking) undermined both the institution of the presidency and the whole American political ethos. The public began to distance itself from politics, expressing only cynicism about the rhetoric and programs that politicians proposed. By 1973, it was clear that the political passions and polarization of the 1960s had died, replaced by a general sense of political alienation and apathy.[5]

Paralleling that shift in the public mood was the replacement of Nixon by his appointed Vice President Gerald Ford, the perfect figure to preside over a period of political stagnation. In 1976, Ford led a bicentennial celebration of American independence. The frenetic activity and the overblown rhetoric were a self-conscious attempt by Americans to demonstrate their confidence in the country despite almost 15 years of wars, recessions, riots, and the assassinations and resignations of its leaders. The most poignant expression of this need for self-congratulation occurred in New York City. In 1975, perhaps symbolic of American society and especially of its older urban areas, New York had been brought to the brink of bankruptcy by a combination of such factors as middle-class flight, rising crime, a reduced tax base, increased demands for public services from a growing poverty population, economic demands of municipal unions, and the callousness and rapacity of the city's major banks. Only a last-minute loan guarantee by the federal government staved off financial catastrophe.

However, despite—or more likely because of—these economic and social conditions, New York staged "Operation Sail," one of the most impressive of the bicentennial ceremonies. During this celebration, a fleet of white-sailed schooners and frigates from all over the world sailed up and down the Hudson River to the applause of immense crowds. New York's elaborate ceremony seemed to embody the nation's desire to affirm the power and resilience of the American will—no matter what the social realities were like.[6]

In fact, Jimmy Carter based his campaign for the Democratic presidential nomination in 1976 on just this national need to renew its belief in itself. Carter, a man of deep religious convictions (he was a "born-again Christian"), was aware of the country's need for spiritual talk rather than political rhetoric and programs. In his standard speech, he talked about a government as good as

its people, implicitly affirming a belief that the American will and spirit were
still strong and vital. He also shrewdly sensed that after Nixon, the "character
issue" was a prime one for the American public, and he promised in Sunday
school terms never to lie to the people.

In addition, Carter benefited from other American social and political
strains. A "New South" had emerged since the 1960s, for with de jure elimi-
nation of racial segregation, Carter no longer had to deal with the southern
politician's albatross of the Civil War, Reconstruction, and Jim Crow. Second,
Carter was not a national politician or party chieftain; he was an outsider (one-
term governor of Georgia) who could be projected as a fresh face untainted by
Watergate. Finally, the all-pervasive power of the media had made it possible
for a political figure to jump from obscurity to celebrity merely by making a
number of successful television appearances.[7]

Carter's campaign avoided dealing with the issues or taking hard positions,
and by invoking moral pieties and capitalizing on his outsider status, he won a
narrow victory over Ford in the 1976 election. However, though he was a skilled
diagnostician of the public's yearnings, Carter's political talents did not seem
to extend beyond the pursuit of power and the winning of elections. His first
year in office was committed more to populist symbolism than to substance.
Informal state dinners, telephone talks with ordinary citizens and spending
the night at their homes, and wearing a cardigan sweater while announcing an
energy plan that he conceived as the moral equivalent of war did not help him
with Congress. Carter confronted an assertive Congress, which after Vietnam
and Watergate was profoundly wary of the executive branch. Furthermore,
Carter carried over from his campaign a blurriness over issues and an inability
to make hard decisions. He equivocated in the Bert Lance scandal, tarnish-
ing his image for integrity, and seemed to lack control over his cabinet and his
low-comic brother, Billy. More and more there existed a growing feeling that
Jimmy Carter was too small a man to handle the presidency.[8]

In July 1979, after repeated attempts to untangle his administration, Carter
tried to liberate himself from his ineffective and incompetent image by firing a
number of cabinet members (Califano, Blumenthal, and others) and making a
speech updating his energy policy. It was more than just a speech about energy;
it was in typical Carter style an expression of moral concern that attempted
to rouse the American people from their malaise. It was a call to strengthen
the American will by ridding it of its self-indulgence: "The erosion of our confidence in the future is threatening to destroy the social and political fabric
of America . . . we have learned that piling-up material goods cannot fill the
emptiness of lives which have no confidence or purpose."[9]

Though this ministerial oratory was no substitute for a coherent energy
policy, Carter's rhetoric did have cultural resonance and significance for the

1970s. It paralleled the writing of culture critics such as Christopher Lasch and Tom Wolfe who had called the 1970s a narcissistic era, the "me decade." They conceived the age as a period when people went about polishing, cultivating, and doting on themselves and their relationships without regard to politics, society, or posterity. The 1970s had produced a culture built on a cult of personal relations that was often simply an expression and a result of a chaotic, destructive social order and devastated and empty private lives. This culture was characterized by a craving for intimacy without genuine human connection and sacrifice, material plenty without productivity, and success without real content or accomplishment. Hedonistic consumerism and the ethic of self-preservation—including an interest in the body ("working out" and natural diets)—had become the order of the day.[10]

To some extent, this collective narcissism was partially brought on by the failure and collapse of the New Left and counterculture in the early 1970s. The "Movement" always differed from the Old Left by being concerned with problems of personal identity and authenticity. These problems, especially for those who were political or social activists, were rarely separated from their commitment to transforming American society. Of course, there were always activists who treated political action as merely a substitute for personal therapy. But by the 1970s, many of the survivors of the Movement had decided that one of the reasons for its failure (neglecting or dismissing historical and political explanations) was the nature of political commitment itself. What was now necessary to achieve some sense of peace and fulfillment was getting directly to the bottom of the self or losing oneself in various self-awareness movements (EST, Rolfing, and Arica), oriental gurus, and religious cults like the Moonies and Jim Jones's suicidal People's Temple and bioenergetics.[11]

The premise underlying this intense preoccupation with the self was the assumption that unlimited personal growth would coincide with unlimited material prosperity. The belief was based on the post–World War II notion that continuous expansion was inherent in the very nature of the American economy and that though blatant racial and economic inequities existed in America in the years from 1945 through the early 1970s, America had the resources to create an economy successful enough to satisfy the material needs and yearnings of the majority of the people. Within that expansionist framework, American capitalism could vitiate resentment by keeping unemployment low, increasing social services, and mediating between the interests of capital and labor.

However, in the mid-1970s, a change in public consciousness occurred. For the first time in American history, public opinion polls reported that the American people were no longer optimistic about the nation's future. The country was beset with an economic crisis, which in fact was an underlying cause of Carter's 1976 victory. But Carter was ultimately unable to turn the economy around. By the end of his term, rising oil prices, a debt-laden balance of payments, and the lack of competitiveness of the motor and steel industries had again thrown the American economy into severe recession.

In the 1980 election, Carter was soundly defeated, and the ex-actor and California governor Ronald Reagan was elected by a landslide to the presidency. There were many reasons for the repudiation of Carter and the Democrats—a recoil from big government and liberalism (though Carter was no liberal), personal rage and resentment toward Carter's supposed weakness and incompetence, and, most important, the hope that Reagan would resurrect the American will from its malaise. The public craved a candidate untouched by a sense of complexity and ambiguity who could successfully package a simple belief in American might, power, and opportunity to right the ills of the nation. However, in 1980 the rebirth of the American will existed only in the realm of political rhetoric; the country was beset with perilous economic, social, and international difficulties that clearly would not be resolved by the intoning of patriotic and moralistic platitudes.[12]

During the 1970s, the film industry and its product reflected the confusion and malaise permeating the American will. At the beginning of the decade, the industry was a chronic invalid, with studios losing a combined aggregate of $500 million between 1969 and 1972, only to renew itself financially during the second half of the decade with grosses of almost $3 billion. Early in the decade, the old studios connected their fortunes to those of huge conglomerates like Kinney National Service. As a result, the men who produced the films had their eyes glued to the balance sheets rather than to the rushes. That meant fewer pictures, but those that were made had generous publicity budgets geared primarily to a youth audience between the ages of 12 and 26.

Another element in this process was the changing relationship between the movie industry and television. It began with a period of all-out war in the 1950s and moved to the casual embrace of the 1960s, and by the 1970s, the film industry's relationship with television had become a passionate one; by preselling their films to both pay and commercial television and cashing in on new video software (cassettes, discs, and so on), the possibility of Hollywood losing immense sums of money on films had become slight. No longer did a studio have to worry about possible bankruptcy if one heavily financed film failed.[13]

There was at least one beneficial result from the financial difficulties of the 1970s. In groping around for any means to make a comeback, the studios began to take chances and reach out to relatively untried filmmakers such as Robert Altman, Martin Scorsese, Brian De Palma, Peter Bogdanovich, Steven Spielberg, Michael Ritchie, and Francis Ford Coppola.[14]

What distinguished these directors was their awareness of film history, technical competence (sometimes gained from working on small-budget quickies or being trained in university film schools), and self-conscious, personal visions. A number of these directors made films that were self-reflective in nature and veered from the formal stateliness and order and even, at moments, the sense of verisimilitude of the classical narrative. For instance, Robert Altman directed films that were highly personal, idiosyncratic versions of popular genres (i.e., film noir) like *The Long Goodbye* (1973), engaged in social comment and satire in *Nashville* (1975), and made dreamlike, European-style art films like *Three Women* (1977). Brian De Palma's varied output included the anarchic *Hi Mom* (1969) and the Hitchcockian *Obsession* (1976), and Francis Ford Coppola transformed the gangster film (*The Godfather I* and *The Godfather II*) into a tragic epic about the nature of Americanization.

In stark contrast to the old studio days when these directors and their cinematic styles and themes would have been subordinated to a whole battery of executive producers, they now retained a great deal more control over scripts and actors. They often even had the power of the final cut. The studios had become primarily financiers and distributors, treating film more as a business than an industry and consequently taking more interest in profit margins than in the substance of their product.

The transformation of the studios and the success of this more personal form of filmmaking did not mean that Hollywood had opted for dispensing with the traditional genres. Genre films with their well-defined characters, actions, and iconography still resonated with American audiences. In the 1960s, a number of films (e.g., *Easy Rider*) both cut across and modified the traditional genres focusing on buddies (rather than Hollywood's usual solitary hero), the counterculture, and blacks. However, despite *Easy Rider* becoming a landmark for the directors of the 1970s, these new genres did not sustain their audience appeal. A number of the 1970s directors did make films that turned back to conventional genres like the gangster film and the thriller, but the effects of the counterculture and the New Left of the 1960s and the sense of alienation and anomie were too great to make films that adhered to the structure and rules of classics like *The Big Sleep* (1946) and *Little Caesar* (1930). The genre conventions often existed now as a springboard for social commentary, psychological revelation, or parody and satire.[15]

The best example of this use of genre was the protean Francis Ford Coppola's *The Godfather* (1972) and *The Godfather II* (1974). In their emphasis on the murders, violence, and Machiavellian manipulations of criminals, these films indirectly reflected American involvement in Vietnam and the political crimes of Watergate. The films also echoed Balzac's famous comment that behind every great fortune there rested a crime. But beyond these images of American corruption, the two films used a driving narrative rhythm, a luxurious use of light and shadow, and voluptuous camera movements to evoke the destruction of the American Dream.

The Godfather: Part II (1974). (Courtesy of Paramount Pictures/Photofest.)

Coppola based the films on Mario Puzo's commercially successful pulp novel and used it to invert the whole tradition of the gangster film. As Robert Warshow once wrote of the gangster film, "Since we do not see the rational and routine aspects of the gangster's behavior, the practice of brutality—unmixed criminality—becomes the totality of his career."[16] In *The Godfather* films, Coppola begins with the very rituals and emotions that have been left out of the traditional gangster film—baptism and marriage, family solidarity, and love—all of which serve as the foreground for the life of criminality, violence, and murder to which the characters remain committed.

The *Godfather I* centered on the idea of family and those rites of passage that celebrate and validate it. Dominating the film is gravelly voiced Don Vito Corleone (Marlon Brando), an almost mythological figure—a murderer who is totally at ease with his authority and power. He is a man whose prime goal is to keep his family from dancing to another's strings and who is committed to maintaining their security, dignity, and independence. Don Vito is a powerful force who can absolve people of their guilt and protect them from hurt. He is a monster but in Coppola's view an almost sacred one. In *The Godfather*, for every dark, shuttered room where business and murder are plotted, there are still scenes where children play, marriages are held, and familial and communal warmth and light exist. The don may live by violence, but Coppola allows him to die peacefully, playing with his grandson among the tomato plants in his garden.

Some of *The Godfather*'s audience appeal must have derived from the sense of order it evoked. During a time when many Americans felt the world had gone mad with assassinations, war, corrupt politics, and economic recession, there was a longing for a sane place where experience was relatively coherent and secure. In a nostalgic film like George Lucas's *American Graffiti* (1973), the time of innocence—of cruising and proms—is placed in the 1950s, and in *The Godfather* that haven was the ethnic family. *The Godfather*, however, was a film drenched in blood, and neither the depiction of strong family roots nor the Don's rough, natural sense of justice could quite cancel out the image of a family whose business and success were totally involved in intimidation, violence, and murder.[17]

In *Godfather II*, Coppola decided to pursue the underside of the American success ethic in much greater depth. Using Don Vito's son and heir, Michael (Al Pacino), as the central character, the film captures the transformation of the American Dream into a nightmare of alienation and dissolution. In *Godfather II*, the old tribal Mafia of Don Vito's New York–based Genco Olive Oil Company—with its numbers, juke boxes, and prostitutes—has begun to transform itself into a Lake Tahoe–based, acculturated, depersonalized, multinational corporation. And with the abandonment of the old traditions, the quest for a veneer of corporate respectability and legitimacy has only tragic consequences.

Michael and "the family" have made it in America and are powerful enough to command the support of a hypocritical and venal U.S. senator and to gather with the heads of other ("legitimate"?) multinational corporations to divide up the spoils in pre-Castro Havana. However, the family's mobility and new status has brought neither happiness nor repose, just pain and fragmentation. Michael is somber, remote, and unfeeling; all his life energies are projected into the "business." His success results only in his sister Connie's (Talia Shire) hatred; betrayal by his ineffectual, envious brother, Fredo (John Cazale); and estrangement from his White/Anglo-Saxon/Protestant (WASP) wife Kay (Diane Keaton).

The decline of the family is filmed in dark, dimly lit interiors and in sterile, luxurious rooms where people can often be seen only in silhouette. It is a joyless world, and by intercutting and counterpointing luminous flashback sequences of the life of the young Don Vito (Robert De Niro), Coppola succeeds in vividly heightening the bleakness and desolation of Michael's universe, for though the immigrant world of Don Vito's Little Italy may be impoverished and murderous, it is enveloped in golden-toned colors and light and shot in soft focus, nostalgically evoking a world of warmth and community. Don Vito himself is depicted in a heroic mold, a venerated, urban Robin Hood—courtly, self-possessed, and courageous—a man who can help his fellow immigrants by frightening the rapacity out of exploitative landlords. Coppola does not hide the fact Don Vito is a criminal, but he is one whose profound familial feelings and natural grace make his criminality almost socially acceptable.

However, in the move from the world of tenements, pushcarts, and religious processions to the armed fortress in Lake Tahoe, the personal and the familial have been lost. The haven of the family and the ethnic community (however claustrophobic and prescriptive) cannot be sustained under the fragmenting pressures of the capitalist success ethic. Coppola depicts Michael as attempting to hold on to aspects of the code—he believes in machismo and the sacredness of the family—but they exist for him primarily as abstract and formal ideals, and he is never able to convey the love for his children that the young and old Don Vito basks in. In fact, it is Fredo who acts as surrogate father for Michael's unhappy, melancholy son, Anthony. By the end of the film, the unforgiving Michael has murdered and lost almost everything he has cared for and is seen in close-up sitting in tragic isolation, his face turned into a ghostly death mask.

The *Godfather* films did not pretend to provide a sophisticated left critique of capitalism and its ethos. However, while operating within the genre conventions, they were able to convey some of the perniciousness of the American success ethic. The films projected an epic of dissolution conveying how Americanization and mobility turned the murderous passion and loyalty of the immigrant Mafia into an impersonal, rootless nightmare. Implicit in the films was the feeling that the nightmare extended far beyond the parochial confines of the Mafia into the center of American history and society itself.[18]

Another film that, in a similar fashion, was consciously influenced by the political and cultural ferment of the 1960s was Robert Altman's *Nashville* (1975). The film was Altman's epic and ironic attempt at capturing both middle-American consciousness and the perniciousness and life energy of America's popular culture that helps both shape and express it.

Indicative of the film's importance was that the *New York Times* assigned then associate editor Tom Wicker to write a think piece about it. In it he called *Nashville* "a two and half hour cascade of minutely detailed vulgarity, greed, deceit, cruelty, barely contained hysteria and the frantic lack of root and grace into which American life has been driven by its own heedless vitality."[19] In *Nashville*, Altman interweaves 24 characters who both are participants or dream of entering the world of country-and-western music. Using an openended, improvisatory style that centers around the actors, *Nashville* is built on privileged, seemingly disconnected moments, filled with dazzling aural effects and visual images and demanding close viewing from his audience (to pick up the elusive detail in frames packed with overlapping actions). Altman evokes a callous, grasping, violent world in which everyone either gropes for stardom or lives off the fantasies and myths popular culture creates. The country-and-western stars are manipulative, absurd, hysterical—in the main, empty, vain people obsessed by crowd applause and their own status, while their public's behavior ranges from breathless adulation and emulation to petulance and rage.

Among Altman's "Grand Hotel" of stars is the doyen of country-and-western music, Haven Hamilton (Henry Gibson), a self-important, narcissistic, and petulant tyrant stuffed into a tailored, sequined cowboy suit with a slightly askew toupee. Hamilton is a tough, ambitious little rooster whose songs "We Must Be Doing Something Right" and "For the Sake of the Children" embody the soporific and saccharine values of Nashville. The prime singing star, Barbara Jean (Ronee Blakley), a madonna dressed in white, is a childlike, fragile, and neurasthenic figure. She is the film's symbol of how media success can help victimize and destroy a performer, exemplifying the agony that lies between an unstable private self and a star's public role. Altman's other characters run the range from a handsome, totally egoistical, stud rock singer who plays tapes of his songs while he sleeps to a pathetic off-key singing waitress; a dim, bizarre-looking, promiscuous groupie; and a ridiculous and pretentious BBC journalist. They inhabit a world where relationships are subordinated to hustling for the main chance or to promiscuous scoring. It is a fragmented and alienated world where the characters, in the main, exist from moment to moment, and there is almost nobody in the film capable of listening to or caring about what another person is saying. Altman's cool sensibility succeeds in turning Nashville's country music world into a metaphor for American life—a chaotic din where everybody is struggling for or has their own gold record.

In *Nashville*, everything is packaged, including politics. From the opening frame, when the sound track of the Replacement Party's presidential candidate, the pseudopopulist Hal Phillip Walker, patrols the predawn empty streets to the final shot of his limousine leaving the climactic assassination scene, politics play a significant role in the film. It is a politics built on a canned voice and an invisible candidate (we never see Walker, just the detached, quietly contemptuous advance man, Triplette [Michael Murphy]). And the party, with its slogan "new roots for the nation" and platform calling for a new national anthem and the removal of lawyers from Congress, seeks national moral renewal by selling nostalgia and bumptious iconoclasm. The party is one more image without substance: boosters and a sound truck hawking the vagaries of the platform in the same way as the record albums are hyped over the opening credits.

Altman has created, through dynamic and seamless cutting and unrelenting movement within his densely packed frames, a frenzied world. It is a landscape he simultaneously loves and despises. One thinks of Whitman's catalogs of America now gone amok; sound tracks overlap as cars crash, planes roar, marching bands perform, and television newsmen drone on. This grasping, frenetic universe has its apotheosis in the assassination of Barbara Jean at a benefit concert for the Replacement Party in Nashville's Parthenon. In this dazzling set piece of a finale, a seemingly innocuous boy with a guitar, acting out of some Oedipal rage or possibly out of the violence that permeates every pore of the society, shoots Barbara Jean. The act is an echo of the Oswalds, Sirhan Sirhans, and Arthur Bremers—the assassins and psychopaths that wander and menace the streets of contemporary America.

In the aftermath the crowd, stunned and milling about, begins to participate in the ironic and chillingly repeated lyric, "You may say I ain't free, but it don't worry me." What sounds at first like a stirring song of solidarity and the courage to go on is one more turn of the screw, accentuated by the fact that a black choir leads the singing. The camera pans to close-ups of people in the crowd giving voice to the words and then zooms away to a long shot of the stupefied, acquiescent mass. The song is a hymn to apathy and accommodation, a metaphor for an America that unthinkingly accepts its bondage to the media's plasticity, artifice, and banality.

Altman is a director who is in love with the ambiguity and complex texture of his images, behavioral tics, and social surfaces. His work is built on observation rather than exposition, intuition rather than analysis, and on a vision of a society based on chance rather than on one whose values can be systematically traced to a set of causes. Consequently, Altman is not interested in exploring popular music's historical and cultural content or dissecting the power groups that help shape the music industry. But he understands just how bountiful and destructive American popular culture is and how the world of appearances and hype often beguiles and rules Americans. When his suggestive metaphors and images come alive, as they do in *Nashville*, they conjure up a monstrous and irrational America that is vivid, resonant, and true.

Nashville's vision of the role of the media—especially in the political arena—has grown more apt and pointed with each passing decade, though there was no denying the power of the media to shape American public opinion during the late 1960s and 1970s. In fact, there were other films made during the decade, like Michael Ritchie's *The Candidate* (1972) and Sidney Lumet's *Network* (1976), that criticized the power of the media.

The Candidate used a semidocumentary technique—natural sound, panning and tracking with a handheld camera, and a mixture of professional and nonprofessional actors—to richly evoke the mechanics of the political process and the power of the media to shape it. The film's protagonist is an idealistic, Kennedy-style, public service lawyer, Bill McKay (Robert Redford), who runs for the Senate in California against a glib, right-wing conservative. As the campaign evolves, the frank-speaking, socially committed McKay acquiesces to being transformed into a handsome commodity who hedges on the issues and learns to speak in empty political slogans and vaporous rhetoric about "courage and compassion" so that he can win the election.

The film does little with McKay's private self or marriage, but it has a political insider's knowledge of how to produce 30-second spots, write position papers, win endorsements, and engage in campaign debates, rallies, and speeches. The television cameras are ubiquitous in the campaign, and the candidates must learn to gear their persona and positions to the camera eye and sound bite. *The Candidate* is satirical about the nature of a media-governed politics, but it's too shrewd and knowing to offer quick-fix alternatives to a political process with a genius for co-optation.

Network—winner of four Oscars—is utterly different intellectually and stylistically than *The Candidate*. Written by Paddy Chayevsky, it is a dark, shrill, sometimes expressionist comedy filled with television lampoons, rousing monologues, collective primal screams, and savage portraits of freaked-out anchormen and television revolutionaries. Shot mainly in close-up and medium shot, *Network*'s images are totally subordinated to Chayevsky's speeches. In them, he brings his wrath down on a corrupt and dehumanizing television world built on corporate jockeying and an obsession with Nielsen ratings. In Chayevsky's pessimistic vision, the left is totally absurd, "the people" mesmerized sheep, and there is only one weary, honest news department head, Max Schumacher (William Holden as an Edward R. Murrow clone), to stand for what is honest and true.

Network is a moralistic, overstated film that strains for significance. But there are moments it draws blood—it is especially good on the media's capacity for turning everything into a marketable commodity and conveying the feeling that the television image has become reality for many Americans, though in its desire to be outrageous, the film ironically often seems to be doing what television does—merchandising iconoclasm.

The two films may have savaged the role of television, but it's clear that without television, the antiwar and women's movements in the 1970s would have had a lesser impact. Television covered feminist sit-ins at leading women's magazines, mass marches, and demonstrations and held debates on men and women's changing roles and identities. Of course, television also vulgarized and merchandized feminism in various sitcoms and commercials, such as the one for Virginia Slims cigarettes.[20] And its underlying attitude toward women and feminism was at best ambivalent and at worst destructive, but it succeeded in forcing the movement into the consciousness of the American public.

Hollywood in turn had no journalistic function, so it had even more difficulty in dealing with women's issues, especially since they went far beyond equal rights and equal pay and challenged sacred movie industry canons about the nature of sexuality and the family. For a time in the 1970s, Hollywood seemed to have banished most women from the screen and replaced them with buddy films such as *Little Fauss and Big Halsy* (1970), *Scarecrow* (1973), and *The Sting* (1973), works that concentrated on macho exploits and homoerotic bonds.

At the same time, however, Hollywood was being prodded to pay attention to changes in women's consciousness, both by the women's movement and by powerful and popular actresses like Barbra Streisand and Jane Fonda. In addition, the rise of an independent women's cinema that produced documentary films like *Joyce at 34* (1973), *Nana, Mom and Me* (1974), and *Union Maids* (1976) and features like Joan Micklin Silver's film about Jewish immigrants' adjustment to America, *Hester Street* (1975) and Claudia Weill's *Girlfriends* (1978), dealt with women defining themselves through work and in other ways where their relation to men did not have primacy. These varied influences moved the mainstream film industry to make a stab at producing films where a women's exploration of identity was a central theme. One of the first of these, *Klute* (1971), was not only a box office success but an Academy Award winner as well.[21]

Klute is John Klute (Donald Sutherland), a strong, silent, small-town policeman who comes to New York to pursue leads in the disappearance and possible murder of a close friend. The film is stylishly directed by Alan Pakula (*All the President's Men*, 1976), creating a paranoid, noirish New York of wiretaps, dark hallways, and lurking silhouetted figures. Pakula's compositions are nervous with his characters often placed on the extreme edge of the frame, and he often blacks out part of the screen to create feelings of isolation and tension. But the real focus of the film is not urban paranoia or the sadistic, murderous violence that lies behind respectable, corporate facades; it lies in the struggle for self-definition of a prime suspect—in the case, a call girl, Bree Daniels (Jane Fonda).

Bree is a witty, seemingly confident, cynical, and self-destructive woman who wants to control her life but can maintain only some equilibrium when she operates as a call girl. It is a life she knows is going nowhere. Nevertheless, as she tells her therapist about her tricks, "I'm in control. When they come to me they're nervous, I'm not. I know what I'm doing. I know I'm good." In contrast to her power over the johns who share her bed, she has little control over the rest of her life. Although able to simulate sexual excitement and manipulate male fantasies as a call girl, she is merely an object or image, a commodity to be dismissed when she pursues her acting and modeling careers.

What little control Bree has in her life is increasingly threatened by her love for Klute, an emotion she tries to fend off by continually manipulating and hurting him. Some of the film's best moments take place during Bree's sessions with her therapist, where she describes how she tries to destroy her feelings for Klute for fear they will engulf her and she will lose whatever autonomy she has. It is one of the few times in the history of American film that a therapeutic session seems natural and irreducible to psychological clichés and magical resolution.

Unfortunately, Klute's character does not quite transcend Hollywood stereotypes. He is portrayed as a man whose self-sufficiency is merely a muted affirmation of traditional Hollywood rites of machismo and whose passivity is a form of aggression. But the character of Bree gives the film a genuine sense of the problems of the 1970s "new woman." Breaking away from the old roles based on female dependency and commitment to domesticity and family means all sorts of new and anxiety-laden relationships and situations. At the end of the film, Bree gives up her compulsive need to manipulate and control and leaves with Klute for his hometown. But she remains ambivalent about the relationship and informs her therapist in a voice-over, "I may be back in a couple of weeks."[22]

While Bree does not make the complete break with the traditional women's role in Hollywood—her possible happiness is predicated on her having a man to emotionally support her—the film does provide some feeling of a woman's struggle for a new identity. In a faltering manner, the film industry made a number of other gestures toward confronting the social and psychological issues raised by the women's movement. Films such as Paul Mazursky's satiric sex comedy *Blume in Love* (1973) and Martin Scorsese's film about a working-class widow who seeks to create a life of her own, *Alice Doesn't Live Here Anymore* (1974), reflected, in a compromised and commercialized fashion, the industry's struggle with constructing an image of the "new woman." There was also the lushly romantic—a great many soft-focused close-ups and reaction shots—Streisand–Redford film *The Way We Were* (1973) about the doomed love affair of a passionate, Jewish leftist with a cool, handsome, uncommitted WASP. Streisand's aggressive heroine is a committed activist who is willing to lose her love over a matter of moral principle, but the film subordinates its feminist and political strains to its romantic nostalgia.

Some of the women's films made during the second half of the decade tended to trivialize the problem by tying it to outworn genres like the "weepie" (*The Turning Point*, 1978) or a literate, female version of the buddy film (*Julia*, 1977). There were also films that dealt with supposedly liberated women, such as the comfortably feminist *An Unmarried Woman* (1978) and *Kramer vs. Kramer* (1979), which either provided talented, loving Prince Charmings to ease the pain of "liberation" or implicitly criticized the callousness of the newly emancipated women.

Kramer vs. Kramer was 1979's biggest commercial and critical hit, winning five Oscars (including ones for best film, best director, and best actor) and grossing more than $60 million domestically. It was the kind of work that *Time* could tout as a minefield of contemporary social issues. And though it did indeed deal with the breakdown of traditional concepts of marriage and family and with the male assuming the maternal role, much of its massive success rested with its remaining human and cozy in the old Hollywood style. It is a film that keeps under control the despair and chaos inherent in the abandonment by the liberated wife-mother Joanna (Meryl Streep) of her husband Ted (Dustin Hoffman) and her son, emphasizing instead the growing warmth and love between father and son. It also comforts rather than disturbs the audience, assuring them that in a time of fragmentation where egoism had become a prime virtue, humane qualities, such as loyalty, decency, and self-sacrifice, still exist.

Despite these limitations, *Kramer vs. Kramer* is an intelligent and accessible work that succeeds in conveying fresh and unsentimental truths about parents and children; the relationship between father and son is evoked in all its anguish, pleasure, and complication. The intensity of the father's love is most powerfully communicated in a scene where the boy receives a severe cut by falling off some playground monkey bars. The camera then focuses on Ted's despairing and guilt-ridden face as he races wildly with his son in his arms to the hospital. There are also perceptive scenes where Ted not only must try to be patient and compassionate with his son but also must feign affection and interest when he does not feel it or has his mind on other matters. And though Ted is clearly depicted as a caring, devoted father, he also can at times become prickly, tense, and easily irritated.

Nevertheless, *Kramer vs. Kramer* is a film that takes few formal or intellectual risks. Its emotions and images don't reverberate beyond what is presented within the frame. There is also a strain of antifeminism inherent in the film. It is Ted who garners the film's sympathy and applause by displaying the humanness and emotional strength (not without difficulty) that makes him capable of both pursuing a career and being a nurturing, committed parent. The wife's consciousness is never explored (except for the opening moments where in desperation and sorrow she prepares to tell her husband that she is leaving), and she is given relentlessly packaged feminist clichés (which in the context are unsympathetic): anguished-women-submerged-by-domesticity-careerist-husband-in-search-of-self.[23]

Despite these limitations, there were clear advances for women in the films of the 1970s. Women's issues were consciously foregrounded and built into the narrative of the films in ways the Joan Crawford and Bette Davis films about strong, well-defined women rarely did. For example, in *Norma Rae* (1979), a sentimental liberal film about a successful textile strike, the interest is more on the unformed heroine (Sally Field) realizing her potential than on labor issues. Spunky Norma Rae has spent much of her life being used and abused by men, but the strike grants her the opportunity to discover that she is a courageous, intelligent, and independent woman. Still, it's a man, an articulate, aggressive, New York Jewish labor organizer, Reuben (played with broad, ethnic strokes by Ron Leibman), who acts as her intellectual and political mentor and guide. Though Norma Rae does not end the film in a classic romantic clinch with Reuben—submerging her identity in his—the majority of the other 1970s films still saw women usually back in place next to their man at the climax despite the struggles for autonomy they engaged in through the body of the narrative.

In sharp contrast to the increasing number of films about women's quest for selfhood was the disappearance of the few serious films about black life (it was as if Hollywood decided to echo the Nixon–Moynihan notion of "benign neglect"). Black films had been commercially successful in the early 1970s, with movies about heroic black studs and pimps like *Shaft* (1971) and *Superfly* (1972) ushering in a whole new genre called blaxploitation films (though they began to disappear by the mid-1970s).

There was also writer-director Melvin Van Peebles's more outrageous and controversial hit *Sweet Sweetback's Baadasssss Song* (1971), whose hero (played by Van Peebles) transforms himself from an apolitical black stud who works in a whorehouse into an indomitable avenging angel at war with and in flight from the police. The film is contemptuous of whites, who are seen as murderous brutes and buffoons, while it romanticizes the communal spirit of ghetto blacks. The anger and defiance at the heart of the film is more an expression of black rage toward whites than a coherent politics; the film is "dedicated to all those who have enough of the man." And among those who have had enough are a group of ghetto inhabitants—prostitutes, campy preachers, unwed mothers, and gamblers—whose lives Van Peebles does not prettify but still affirms and even exalts.

Sweetback is an overheated, overdirected film—inundated with flash cuts, tilts, freeze frames, voice-overs, double exposures and the use of a split screen. However, it's a vivid and vital work, and though it's politically counterproductive to turn a sauntering pimp into a superhero and attempt to frighten and intimidate whites, the film's abrasiveness and rhetorical commitment to black power was successful in reaching a large black audience in 1971.

Films that in turn involved much less action and dealt with less sensational aspects of black life, such as *Claudine* (1974), *Conrack* (1974), and *The*

Bingo Long Traveling All-Stars (1976), did not do well at the box office. With rare exceptions, black films needed a star personality such as Diana Ross (*Lady Sings the Blues*, 1972) or Richard Pryor (*Greased Lightning*, 1977), to get the crossover audience—whites who would not normally go to see a film about blacks. And although these stars could generally sell a film, they tended to be well-crafted escapist works rather than films that dealt with the psychological and social reality of black life. Hollywood clearly sensed in the 1970s both that white guilt about the social status and problems of blacks had begun to disappear and that black civil rights organizations had lost much of their political potency and power. As a result, beyond the few black stars that had crossover appeal, black actors played mainly minor character roles. Hollywood's decision to avoid dealing with the complexity of black life and lives was clearly in tune with the dictates of the market and the political and social climate of the 1970s.

Of course, early 1970s Hollywood films did not speak in one voice. Not all films engaging in a critique of American society and culture were made from the perspective of women or blacks or by people adhering to left-liberal politics or the counterculture. There were a great many people in the 1960s and early 1970s who were appalled by what they perceived as a period dominated by permissiveness and social breakdown. Their answer to the political protests and alternative life styles was a return to traditional values of home, family, and law and order. Part of this yearning was turned by Hollywood into a nostalgia for a lone man with a gun bringing law and order to an untamed frontier, only this time that frontier included the city as well. *Death Wish* (1974) and *Walking Tall* (1974) were two prime examples of this film genre, but the best and most archetypal one was Don Siegel's brilliantly edited *Dirty Harry* (1971), starring Clint Eastwood.

Dirty Harry was a film about an avenging knight, a San Francisco police inspector, Harry Callahan, whose major targets besides criminals were the liberals and politicians whose laws and sentiments helped create a permissive social climate. In the film, Harry pursues a psychopathic, hippie killer who has tortured and killed a number of people and culminated his series of atrocities by kidnapping a bus filled with children. Harry is a solitary, lean, indefatigable figure who will not be deterred by mere legalities, like civil liberties or police rules, until he has killed this personification of pure evil—there are no psychological or social explanations for the killer's behavior. Using heroic low-angle and full shots of the demigod Harry, the film totally identifies with his perspective, making his superiors seem lame and weak and Harry's skill at providing vigilante justice the only protection against a violent, demonic world. At the film's climax, in a scene reminiscent of *High Noon*, Harry throws his badge into the water where the killer's corpse is floating. Obviously, it is only a beau geste, for in sequels like *Magnum Force* (1973) and *The Enforcer* (1976), Harry continues to relentlessly wage all-out war against radicals, homosexuals, and other groups he perceives as flotsam of a permissive society.[24]

Many of the films of the early and mid-1970s nicely illustrated how long it took for major cultural changes and trends to register in Hollywood. Whether or not their points of view were inspired by the political right or the left, many of these films were a spillover from the political conflicts and social tensions of the 1960s. For example, Alan Pakula's *Parallax View* (1974) was a stunningly visual thriller (e.g., a wonderful use of wide screen space and unique settings) about a politically nebulous right-wing conspiracy's assassination of a Kennedy-style politician that a government commission (i.e., the Warren Commission) whitewashes by attributing the murder to a lone psychopath. The conspiracy is all-encompassing, and the sullen, unflappable reporter Joe Frady's (Warren Beatty) heroics are insufficient to defeat this omnipresent, evil power. Another skillful, paranoid thriller and commercial success was Sydney Pollack's *Three Days of the Condor* (1975), which evoked a desolate world of betrayers who work for the CIA. The film's last scene sees its isolated hero played by Robert Redford going off to take his story about this renegade organization that has gotten inside of the CIA to the *New York Times*—a variation on Daniel Ellsberg and the Pentagon Papers. However, in this case, the film bleakly suggests that even the good, respectable *Times* could be part of the conspiracy and may not publish the story.

One film that acknowledged some of the major political and social trends of the early 1970s was Alan Pakula's big box office hit *All the President's Men* (1976). The film was based on the Woodward–Bernstein book, which painstakingly followed their investigation for the *Washington Post* of the Watergate burglary and all its more ominous political ramifications. Shot in the characteristic Pakula mode—shadowy night streets and apartment interiors, parts of the screen blackened out, and the reporters seen isolated on the frame in extreme long shot or dwarfed by Washington's buildings—the film combines the style of the thriller and the television-style documentary drama that dramatizes actual events.

The two dogged, driven reporters—Woodward and Bernstein (Robert Redford and Dustin Hoffman)—are treated here as icons, using the freedom of the press to preserve our constitutional rights and democracy. Their private lives and individual personalities—except for sketching the surface of Bernstein's tense, aggressive, chain-smoking persona—are totally subsumed in the detailing of the investigation. The film tries and sometimes succeeds in adding drama to the endless car rides, phone calls, and meetings with the editors by creating an all-pervasive sense of danger. It sets a number of scenes in the murk of an underground garage—complete with threatening footsteps and screeching car tires—where Woodward meets his prime informant, Deep Throat (Hal Holbrook). In this Pakula film, the conspiracy is, of course, defeated, and we are made to feel good about the press and the American system. Still, the film eschews a full exploration of the political motivation and institutional accommodation that was at the root of Watergate for the usual Hollywood emphasis on the courage of two individuals—Woodward and Bernstein.

Despite these conspiracy films, the industry sensed that the public sought some release from the years of Vietnam and Watergate. It turned, in the main, to mirroring political slogans like Ford's "time of healing" by relentlessly packaging escapist entertainment. Some of the films, such as the bicentennial blockbuster *Rocky* (1976), resurrected traditional American values like the Horatio Alger dream of "rags to riches." The fairy-tale dimensions of the film were projected both on and off the screen for it was written by an unemployed and practically destitute actor, Sylvester Stallone, who became an overnight sensation and superstar and won an Academy Award.

Rocky was a film about a broken-down pug who also moonlights as an enforcer for a mob loan shark. However, in this fairy tale, Rocky was depicted as combining the body of a circus strongman with the saintliness of St. Francis. He was kind to animals and small children and gave a break even to those who were behind in their payments to the loan shark. Rocky's big moment comes when the black heavyweight champion grants him a shot at the title. The scenes of his training and his Dionysian struggle with the champion Apollo Creed turn into a crudely stirring evocation and endorsement of the importance of honesty, perseverance, and hard work.

Rocky not only revived the Alger myth but also made ethnic, working-class Americans the prime actors and agents of the dream. In Rocky, the film had created a character who existed as some prepsychoanalytic being, a man who could invoke nostalgia for a purer, simpler past. For the general filmgoing audience, working-class lives had, for the moment, become a preserve of spontaneity, warmth, and masculinity.

In fact, the success of *Rocky* made the white working class briefly fashionable in Hollywood again. The trend took off into solid, commercial hits like *Saturday Night Fever* (1978) and less successful films such as Paul Schrader's *Blue Collar* (1977), *F.I.S.T.* (1978), and *Bloodbrothers* (1978), all of which highlighted working-class characters and situations though were more interested in exploiting genre conventions than in exploring class realities.[25]

In *Saturday Night Fever*, the hero, Tony Manero (John Travolta), conveys on the surface much of the same mixture of macho charisma, gentleness, and vulnerability as Rocky. But instead of the heroics taking place in the ring, his arena is the dance floor, where he is the local king of the disco. His undulating energy and dynamism on the dance floor, however, aren't sufficient to grant him a way out of his neighborhood wasteland. Tony is bound to a world composed of a

stereotypical Italian American mother and unemployed construction worker
father, both of whom spend much of their time either putting him down or
shouting at each other; a pill-popping, gangbanging, and fighting, oafish group
of friends; and a job without a future as a clerk in a hardware store.

Saturday Night Fever is a more complex and suggestive film than *Rocky*.
Though *Rocky* cannot escape touching on certain social realities, such as decaying ethnic neighborhoods and racial conflict (Rocky as "the great white
hope"), it still blurs, even obliterates, those tensions in a magical act of transcendence. However, *Saturday Night Fever* allowed much more of the anxieties
of working-class life to intrude before submerging them in the romantic music
of the Bee Gees and disco scenes shot through multicolored filters by a fluidly
zooming and panning camera.

Tony, however, though more sensitive, decent, and perceptive than his
friends, is not another saintly Rocky. His character is built on a blend of crude
street humor, macho posturing, and self-absorption. He can use and dismiss
friends (male and female) without much sensitivity to their feelings. The film
also touches on working-class sexism, frustration, rage, and the sense of social
inadequacy that working-class people feel when dealing with an upper-middle-
class culture. *Saturday Night Fever* is still primarily a commercial, escapist work
that does not delve too deeply into the full meaning of these problems and
emotions. In fact, like *Rocky* (though in much more muted fashion), the film
offers a second chance to Tony, a romance with an upwardly mobile secretary, Stephanie (Karen Lynn Gorney), and the repudiation of his Brooklyn
world for a supposedly more humane and exciting life in an upper-middle-class
Manhattan.[26]

Along with *Rocky*'s affirmation of the American Dream came a revival of the
traditional Hollywood theme of the uncommon common man. For example,
in Steven Spielberg's *Jaws* (1976), the family man as hero is affirmed amidst
blockbuster technical effects and a consummate building of tension and suspense. The most memorable elements in *Jaws* are the skillfully edited scenes of
a killer shark's attack on a summer resort. However, though the ominous shark
has a great deal of life, the film's central characters are thinly sketched. Among
them is a middle-class family man, police chief Martin Brody (Roy Scheider),
who battles against the cover-ups of the town's corrupt mayor and ultimately
kills the shark. He only does that after the upper-class technologisms of ich-
thyologist Matt Hooper (Richard Dreyfuss) and the working-class machismo
of the Ahab-like sailor Quint (Robert Shaw) have failed. By turning Brody
into the film's hero, *Jaws* implicitly celebrated the virtues of fidelity and family
instead of glorifying the heroic loner.[27]

But even *Jaws* was touched with the anxieties of the real world. In George
Lucas's *Star Wars* (1977), the ultimate in escapism was achieved by creating a
magical world, somewhat similar to the American West, where heroic action

could find its proper setting. The audience no longer had to be bothered by images of real streets, problems, and people; it could lose itself in outer space. In *Star Wars*, Lucas threw everything he knew into the picture—a catalog of genre entertainments of the past 30 years—and capitalized on America's passion for technology. The film is populated with almost human, cuddly robots, computers and alien beings (looking like an ape version of the *Wizard of Oz*'s Cowardly Lion), and scenes of glorified combat with rocket fighters right out of World War II films—all of it placed in a fantasy galaxy. Lucas's inventiveness is framed within a story of a "quest" for the "force" in a hierarchical world that not only consists of robots but also contains knights, villains in black, princesses, and priests, all of which were staples of adventure fiction, comic books, and fairy tales. Even if Americans were no longer willing to follow the lone cowboy as he eternally cleaned up the frontier, they flocked in record numbers to Luke Skywalker and his cohorts as they blasted through space and shot it out with Darth Vader.[28]

Shoring up this return to past values and genres were films evoking occult dread and divine power. Starting with *The Exorcist* (1973), a terrifying film directed by William Friedkin (*The French Connection*, 1971), these works began to denounce the sins of modernism and implied that only true faith could ensure peace and tranquility. *The Exorcist* was conceived by its scriptwriter, the Jesuit-trained, former U.S. Information Agency writer William Peter Blatty, as part of his "apostolic work."[29] The film describes how two gentle, heroic priests invoking Christ's name cured or exorcised (at the expense of their own lives) the young daughter of a freethinking, divorced actress of demonic possession after all else, including impotent doctors and psychiatrists, had failed. Besides preaching the true faith, *The Exorcist* and other similar works (e.g., *The Omen*, 1976, and *Exorcist II*, 1977) also undermined the idea of individual or moral responsibility for one's behavior. *The Exorcist*, though primarily a work of well-crafted horror—using sound and elaborate makeup to evoke anxiety and fear in its audience—still projected in a cold and impersonal manner that the acts of human beings are determined by powerful demonic forces.

Though little intellectual credibility could be given to a belief in demonic forces, *The Exorcist* was symptomatic of a number of Hollywood films of the second half of the decade. In contrast to films of the first half of the decade that either attacked American capitalism and culture for its corruption, murderousness, and creation of ersatz values or saw criminality aided by liberalism overwhelming traditional institutions, many of the second-half films affirmed traditional American values, such as a belief in mobility, family, technology, and religion.

That is not to say that there weren't a number of major films that didn't quite fit into either category. One of the best American directors of the 1970s and 1980s was Martin Scorsese, whose work was built on emotional extremity, pulsating energy, and formal boldness. Two of his most original and imaginative works were critical successes and starred Robert De Niro. *Mean Streets* (1973) is an edgy, violent, semi-autobiographical film that fuses realist and expressionist imagery to unsentimentally evoke the codes and rituals of "the boys" in New York's Little Italy.

Taxi Driver (1976) was a more murderous, alienated, and hallucinatory film than *Mean Streets*. It centered on a paranoid, solipsistic, and strangely innocent New York City cab driver, Travis Bickle (De Niro), who, isolated behind his glass partition, drives all night around nightmarishly beautiful Manhattan streets filled with junkies, pimps, and 12-year-old hookers. Bickle is a man who carries "bad ideas in his head" and with an arsenal of weapons wants to clean the city—"an open sewer"—of its scum. *Taxi Driver* is not *Dirty Harry*—Scorsese is not advocating vigilante justice—nor is the film a social reformer's portrait of urban squalor and disintegration or a critique of the condition of 1970s America.

Scorsese's obsessions are primarily psychological and aesthetic rather than social and political in nature. *Taxi Driver*, with its cinematic allusions, voice-over, restlessly moving camera, high overhead shots, semiabstract sequences, extremely tight close-ups of Bickle's mad eyes, use of slow motion, and sweltering night city of shadows, neon lights, shimmering shapes, and manhole covers emitting steam, is not interested in providing a documentary or social realist view of the city. The emphasis here is on one alienated man's personal hell—most of the film shot from Bickle's point of view—which is shaped by the dark ambience of film noir and Scorsese's own personal demons and fantasies and fragmented view of the world. Scorsese has made a riveting, virtuosic work where, breaking from classical Hollywood conventions, he creates no truly redeemable characters and concludes the film on an ambiguous, open-ended note.

Another major director of the 1970s whose work could not easily be placed in either category was Woody Allen, America's prime comic auteur. By the late 1970s, Allen's films were no longer nightclub-based, cartoon-style works filled with one-liners and pratfalls (e.g., *Bananas*, 1971) but comedies with serious moral intentions and characters capable of genuine suffering. The best of them was *Manhattan* (1979), a tragicomedy with a coherent narrative and a distinctive visual style. The film opens with a glorious, loving montage of Manhattan icons and avenues—Lincoln Center and Park Avenue—the final image being a spectacular fireworks display over Central Park. Allen's New York is not Scorsese's; it's chic, comfortable, and romantic, and it sways to a Gershwin tune. His urban New Yorkers, however, may live in a city whose beauty can "knock you out," but they are neurotics—irresponsible and egoistic individuals—unable to sustain commitments to work or to other people.

Allen, of course, still remembers how to be funny. He wittily satirizes the cultural games that New York intellectuals and demi-intellectuals engage in: Mary's (Diane Keaton) seamless flow of pretentious art-crit jargon and talk of the wrong kind of orgasm at a Museum of Modern Art fund-raiser. But in *Manhattan*, he never allows a sight gag or a one-liner to disrupt the film's moving, comic-pathetic portrait of intelligent people who are given over to self-deception and who live unrealized lives.

Allen's film, like Scorsese's, could be read on one level as a critique of contemporary American urban life, but his perspective was neither shaped by nor derived from the movements of the 1960s. As an antidote to contemporary moral decay, Allen constructs a personal pantheon that includes Willie Mays, Ingmar Bergman, Groucho Marx, and Louis Armstrong. His heroes aren't hip or politically radical; they have a sense of purpose, discipline, and genius—virtues that Allen clearly sees as having been lost by the often emotionally flabby and intellectually compromised characters that inhabit his cinematic universe.

Allen's and Scorsese's films were anomalies; *Rocky* came much closer to what the Hollywood mainstream was all about in the second half of the decade. The ultimate test of this renewed commitment to patriotism and the American Dream was to see how Hollywood would handle the Vietnam War. All through the war, it had shied away from any films that dealt directly with the conflict. Despite some films (*Bonnie and Clyde* and *The Wild Bunch*) that could be seen as oblique metaphors for the war, there was doubt whether Hollywood would ever directly confront the issue. In an industry whose basic operating premise is that an appeal to the lowest common denominator is one of the keys to making a profit, dealing with a war that was so divisive and controversial was seen as a recipe for financial disaster.

However, as a number of successful novels and memoirs on the war came out and people's passions about Vietnam cooled, films dealing with the war began to seem less risky. Moreover, books such as Tim O'Brien's National Book Award–winning novel *Going after Cacciato* and Michael Herr's dazzling, feverish *Dispatches* projected the feeling that only a film could convey the nightmarish and absurdist imagery of the war—making the ultimate statement about Vietnam and integrating it into the national consciousness. Consequently, after the release of a number of smaller films about Vietnam (*Boys in Company C*, 1978; *Tracks*, 1978; and *Go Tell the Spartans*, 1978), the war and its impact were treated in three big-budget films: *Coming Home* (1978), *The Deer Hunter* (1978), and *Apocalypse Now* (1979).

Coming Home, directed by Hal Ashby, was a film structured around a traditional love triangle that mixed a touch of feminism and some painful Vietnam realities to give the film political and cultural significance. The prime focus is on a romantic affair between a Marine Corps captain's wife and former cheerleader, Sally Hyde (Jane Fonda), and a paraplegic Vietnam veteran, Luke Martin (Jon Voight). Sally is transformed by her love for Luke from a repressed, conventional wife into a sexually liberated and somewhat independent woman, while Luke moves from an embittered, totally dependent cripple into an empathetic, politically and sexually active handicapped person. And the third person in the triangle, eager, ambitious marine captain Bob Hyde (Bruce Dern), goes off to Vietnam without any hesitation and returns submerged in suicidal despair, evoking the alienation and moral disintegration that often accompanied frontline service in Vietnam.

The romantic triangle and the radical transformations of character, in the main, seem simplistic and unconvincing. Sally's changes lack internality and are built on her achieving orgasm with Luke (aided by the Beatles' "Strawberry Fields" on the sound track) and are expressed primarily through stylistic changes in dress and hairdo. Luke's emergence as a caring, almost saintly figure is too sudden to be credible and makes the film seem smug about America's capacity to turn the resentful vets into symbols of postwar hope.

Despite the facile Hollywood touches, there are moving moments where the film captures a great deal of the texture of the war's terrifying legacy. The scenes in the veterans' hospital of the crippled GIs oppressed by nightmares, talking unselfconsciously and often with black humor about the war and the pain they experience, seeing them being sponged, fed, and getting high, carries a great deal of emotional resonance and authenticity. The hospital's physical condition and medical care are no horror show, but the vets feel walled in—they see themselves as carrying too much of the war's reality for ordinary people to deal with except by treating them as objects of pity.[30]

Coming Home is a film openly critical of the war that never quite goes to the heart of the Vietnam experience. The nightmare of combat is left to our imagination and whatever can be gleaned from Bob Hyde's memories. More important, the film shies away from the war's political and historical context—emphasizing its link to American machismo—and tries to mute the specific terrors of the war by providing overly neat moral and psychological transformations and an upbeat final image of Luke and Sally spending a joyous, sunny day on the beach.

The terror of Vietnam was clearly not purged from Michael Cimino's *The Deer Hunter*. Cimino's controversial epic was alternately condemned as being racist or a total distortion of the truth or praised for being cinematically brilliant and emotionally devastating by critics and Vietnam War correspondents. The film even brought on hostile demonstrations by antiwar activists when it won the Academy Award in 1978.

The three central figures in *The Deer Hunter* are three apolitical, young Russian American steelworkers—Michael, the film's central figure (Robert De

Niro), Nicky (Christopher Walken), and Steven (John Savage)—from a mill town in western Pennsylvania who go off, without qualms, to fight in Vietnam. These are men who are linked to each other and their ethnic community not by words but by a number of visible and invisible strands of ritual and memory. Cimino is in love with their rituals and turns every experience (e.g., lip-synching rock songs, drinking, and hunting) into an elaborate ceremony. And he is concerned more with constructing images of a warm, working-class community than with illuminating the social structure and culture of that world. The apotheosis of Cimino's homage to traditional working-class life is the ethnic wedding sequence. It is lovingly detailed with the camera dollying around the wedding participants, who include young children, stocky Slavic housewives, grizzled older workers, and all the film's major characters, evoking the joy, energy, cacophony, and brawling stupidity of the celebration.

Despite Cimino's use of long takes, natural sound, and nonprofessional actors to capture the formlessness of authentic experience, he gives a sentimental gloss to his working-class milieu. It's a more intact and satisfied community than ever graced *Rocky*, *Saturday Night Fever*, or factory towns in the late 1960s. *The Deer Hunter*'s steel mill is no "dark satanic mill" filled with alienated and resentful workers but rather an elegant monolith where sooty, sweating workers labor with gusto and even pleasure amid intense noise and blast furnace flames. The three steelworkers are untouched by dreams of mobility and feel that all they have ever desired in life "is right here."

This almost Edenic image of the working class community serves to make what follows in the second half of the film in Vietnam even more horrific. The second half begins with the use of a handheld camera to make the audience viscerally feel the terror of Vietnam combat. There are no limits in this war—everyone, including civilians and soldiers, women and children, can be either shot or burned alive. However, Cimino's focus is not on combat but on the emotional effects of the war on the three steelworkers, whose point of view the film embraces.

Vietnam's abattoir disrupts them all to different degrees, and their connection to each other and their community is almost totally torn apart. The only one of the trio who comes out of Vietnam able to function (though disoriented) is Michael, the deer hunter of the title. Cimino conceives Michael as a working-class superman in the romantic tradition of James Fenimore Cooper's *The Deerslayer*, a frontiersman who stood on the periphery of his society and struggled with nature to define his manhood. Michael, in turn, is still one of the boys who wrestles, jokes, guzzles beer, and has a deep link to his friends. But like Cooper's Bumppo, he is silent, stoical, sexually chaste, and given to inarticulate poetic yearnings beyond the emotional understanding of his friends. He is also a man of almost superhuman will—an indomitable, fearless figure who is able to calmly confront and triumph over death. It is his will that saves the trio, by slaughtering their NLF captors, when they are tortured in an emotionally draining, politically manipulative, and stunningly edited Russian roulette session (purely a fictional conceit of Cimino's).

If the film lacks a conscious coherent political ideology, its total identification with Michael's rectitude and heroism has the politically invidious effect of inverting history, making the Americans innocent victims and the Vietnamese the aggressors in the war. In close-up, the Vietnamese (including the South Vietnamese) are seen as "the other," demonic or decadent variations of "the yellow peril." The film suffers from a case of political and moral amnesia, forgetting that it was the Americans who were the aggressors and extended the basically civil and colonial conflict and who carpet bombed and napalmed the Vietnamese and adulterated and destroyed the social fabric of South Vietnam. *The Deer Hunter* personalizes history, constructing a war where good Americans struggle to survive against bad Vietnamese rather than one where political ideology, Cold War politics, and nationalism play a determining role.

The film's final scene provides a perfect illustration of Cimino's gift for moving us emotionally with action that is politically and intellectually callow. After Nick's funeral, Michael and his friends sit in numbed silence and suddenly begin to sing "God Bless America" in tremulous voices. Their singing uneasily affirms a tattered American will and community. One wants to believe that Cimino is providing, on one level, an ironic commentary on their continued patriotism, but there is no sign of it in the sequence. Given that *The Deer Hunter* gives no reason for Americans to be participants in the Vietnam charnal house that it depicts, it is impossible to simply empathize with this ritual of reconciliation. Obviously, Cimino's strength is a gift for using mise-en-scène and editing to create striking images and arouse us emotionally. What he lacks is the kind of political intelligence that would allow for greater insight and coherence into the Vietnam experience.[31]

Despite its intellectual limitations and distortions, *The Deer Hunter* did convey a sense of the spiritual desolation and destruction that Vietnam caused for many Americans. However, the film not only raised a great deal of controversy but was often taken by audiences as an homage to the American cause in Vietnam. As a result, it made the final release of Francis Ford Coppola's *Apocalypse Now* (1979) that much more eagerly awaited. There was a feeling that this film would provide for the public an emotional catharsis and be the final word about the war. Coppola reinforced these expectations when he equated the making of the film with the war itself. He said that he had made *Apocalypse Now* just the way America made war in Vietnam—that there were too many people, that too much money was spent and equipment used there, and that little by little the cast and crew went insane.

Apocalypse Now was loosely based on Joseph Conrad's *Heart of Darkness*, particularly its evocation of the emotional and moral rot of imperialism. It opens with an image of apocalyptic flames superimposed over a sweating, drunken Willard—the novella's Marlow (Martin Sheen). Willard has the mad eyes and ravaged looks of a man who has lived and seen too much. In the film, he is a burnt-out government hit man with six kills to his credit whose mission is to terminate the life of Colonel Kurtz (played with little sign of real involvement by a bulging, mumbling Marlon Brando), a rogue Green Beret colonel who had set himself up as a tribal god, engaging in a private war against the North Vietnamese and Vietcong in the Cambodian jungle.

Using Willard's pilgrimage as a framework, Coppola constructs a hallucinatory, surreal Vietnam—the war as absurdist epic. The film is filled with spectacular scenes touched with a sense of the absurd: an exhilarating *Gotterdammerung* helicopter attack led by Colonel Kilgore (Robert Duvall as an exaggerated version of General Patton), to whom napalm is the perfume of victory and the purpose of destroying a Vietcong village is to discover the perfect wave for surfing; the revolt of sex-starved soldiers as they rush the stage after being tantalized and provoked by a garish USO bump-and-grind show of undulating Playboy bunnies; and an officerless and forgotten platoon of anxious black GIs despairingly shooting into the darkness (accompanied by atonal music, disembodied voices on the sound track, and flares lighting up the sky) in the "asshole of the world"—the last American outpost on the border between Vietnam and Cambodia. These set pieces and a number of Coppola's other terrifyingly luminous images grant the film great visual power and a genuine feeling for the chaos and lunacy of the war. Still, there is something excessive about much of it—not enough repose and moral balance to give some perspective on the almost unrelieved madness and abundance of special effects that fills the frames.

What hurts the film most is that the ultimate confrontation between Kurtz and an empty and exhausted Willard is anticlimactic. Willard is too saturated in death and a sense of nothingness to be morally transformed (as Marlow is in Conrad's version) by meeting Kurtz. In fact, there is little interaction between them, as an imprisoned Willard sits passively listening to Kurtz's gnomic and pretentious monologue, which is permeated with literary allusions ranging from Eliot's *The Hollow Men* to *The Golden Bough*.

In Kurtz, Coppola has created a metaphysical abstraction—the superman incarnate—a man who speaks of himself as transcending conventional opinion and morality. He advocates, in almost Nietzschean terms, that judgment defeats us, and "we must make friends with moral terror." And Coppola's superman engages in the ultimate assertion of will: he wills his own and his followers' deaths.

Nevertheless, all Kurtz's philosophic musings and imperial posturing turn him into such a self-conscious symbol that the particular historical and social reality of the Vietnam War and America's role there is replaced by a vaporous notion of civilization's madness. The terror is universalized—it is seen as a part of the human condition, not as a product of concrete political forces. In constructing his version of Kurtz, Coppola strains for significance, trying to sum up the highly charged and sometimes overly spectacular imagery of the film's first two-thirds with a symbol that has little emotional or political resonance.

In addition, Coppola demonstrates little critical distance from his conception of Kurtz. One senses that though Coppola may, on the one hand, morally recoil from the war's murderousness and madness; on the other hand, he identifies, even embraces, Kurtz's megalomania and extremity. So when Dennis Hopper's manic photojournalist speaks of Kurtz as a "great man," as an archetypal figure who has his own "dialectic logic," he is not parodied for his portentous babbling but is seemingly expressing one strain in Coppola's vision. In *Apocalypse Now*, that vision itself was often blurred, as Coppola sacrificed clarity for stylistic effects.

There is a German proverb that states that a war creates three armies: an army of cripples, an army of beggars, and an army of the unemployed. The Vietnam War had created a fourth army: one of filmmakers. But in the 1970s, these were directors who substituted a gift for inventive metaphors and symbols and startling images for an ability to penetrate the heart of darkness that was Vietnam.[32]

Of course, Hollywood has rarely tried to penetrate that heart—in either Vietnam or at home in New York or other American cities. It has usually used well-honed conventions and ceremonies to mute those profound anxieties and avoid looking too closely at what is. The Academy Award ceremonies of 1978 were just the sort of occasion where Hollywood utilized its genius for shaping public rituals and neutralizing what was politically or emotionally threatening. John Wayne (in his last public appearance before his death) was called to present the Oscar for best film to Michael Cimino for *The Deer Hunter*. In the 1960s and 1970s, Wayne had become synonymous with the traditional American verities and with virulent, jingoistic right-wing politics. Though *The Deer Hunter* was clearly no left-wing film, its alienated and maimed soldiers (though there was still a stoical, courageous hero) caught in a futile war were a far cry from the tough, confident, and uncomplicated fighting men portrayed by Wayne in *They Were Expendable* (1945) and *The Sands of Iwo Jima* (1946). The ceremony brought together the two Hollywoods: Wayne, who had gone through the ranks from bit player to icon, and Cimino, who, without the long apprenticeship common to the old studio system (he had made only one previous film, *Thunderbolt and Lightfoot*, 1974), found himself with a multi-million-dollar picture in his hands. As it had done so often in the past, Hollywood had found the appropriate ceremony to absorb, exploit, or mute what could be seen in some ways as deviant and new.

Even without the death of John Wayne giving the decade a symbolic cap-stone, the 1970s was the end of an era in American films. Gone forever were even the remnants of the old Hollywood production system, and in its place the studio had become a financial clearinghouse, dependent on independent producers rather than a rationalized assembly line. The old Hollywood, which could produce family pictures cheerily affirming individual mobility and suc-cess, family, and patriotism, had almost disappeared. Its values were now open to question or even repudiation, and the films conveyed a greater sense of un-certainty about what was true and right than in the past. None of these changes, however, meant that much of the old Hollywood had not survived. It was still an industry where big-budget films were dominant, where stars called the shots as much or more than they ever did, and where television staples like situation comedies provided a large portion of the creative models for film-makers. And in a faltering and confused way, Hollywood still had the com-mercial magic and potency to create worlds that could simultaneously hint at what American social reality was like and skillfully obscure it.

NOTES

1. Jonathan Schell, *The Time of Illusion* (New York: Alfred A. Knopf, 1976).

2. Godfrey Hodgson, *America in Our Time* (New York: Vintage Books, 1978), pp. 239–40.

3. Ibid., p. 398.

4. Schell, *The Time of Illusion*, pp. 77–134.

5. Theodore H. White, *Breach of Faith* (New York: Dell, 1975).

6. Gerald R. Ford, *A Time to Heal* (New York: Berkley, 1980), pp. 378–80.

7. James Wooten, *Dasher* (New York: Signet, 1978).

8. Ibid., p. 298.

9. Ibid., p. 301.

10. Christopher Lasch, *The Culture of Narcissism* (New York: Warner Books, 1979).

11. Ibid.

12. Lou Cannon, *Ronald Reagan* (New York: G. P. Putnam's Sons, 1982).

13. James Monaco, *American Film Now* (New York: Oxford University Press, 1979).

14. Diane Jacobs, *Hollywood Renaissance: The New Generation of Filmmakers and Their Works* (New York: Delta, 1980).

15. Monaco, *American Film Now*, pp. 54–68.

16. Robert Warshow, *The Immediate Experience* (Garden City, NY: Anchor, 1964), pp. 38–39.

17. Jacobs, *Hollywood Renaissance*, pp. 115–18.

18. Leonard Quart and Al Auster, "The Godfather, Part II," *Cineaste* 6, no. 4 (Winter 1976), pp. 38–39.

19. Tom Wicker, quoted in Judith M. Kass, *Robert Altman: American Innovator* (New York: Popular Library, 1978), p. 193.

20. Leonard Quart, "Altman's Films," *Marxist Perspectives* 1 (Spring 1978), pp. 21–33.

21. Molly Haskell, *From Reverence to Rape: The Treatment of Women in the Movies* (Baltimore: Penguin Books, 1974), p. 366.

22. Ibid., p. 369.

23. Leonard Quart and Barbara Quart, "Kramer vs. Kramer," *Cineaste* 10, no. 2 (Spring 1980), pp. 37–39.

24. Stuart M. Kaminsky, *Don Siegel, Director* (New York: Curtis Books, 1974), pp. 268–83.

25. Leonard Quart and Albert Auster, "The Working Class Goes to Hollywood," in Philip Davies and Brian Neve (eds.), *Cinema, Politics and Society in America* (Manchester: Manchester University Press, 1981), pp. 163–75.

26. Albert Auster and Leonard Quart, "Saturday Night Fever," *Cineaste* 8, no. 4 (Winter 1978), pp. 36–37.

27. Peter Biskind, "Jaws," *Jump Cut* 15, pp. 3–4.

28. Dan Rubey, "Star Wars," *Jump Cut* 18, pp. 9–14.

29. Josh Rofkin, "The Exorcist," *Screen Talk* (September 1975), p. 54.

30. Albert Auster and Leonard Quart, *How the War Was Remembered: Hollywood and Vietnam* (New York: Praeger, 1988), pp. 50–52.

31. Ibid., pp. 58–65.

32. Ibid., pp. 65–71.

6

THE 1980s

The politics of the 1980s were dominated by Ronald Reagan's serene, amiable personal style and right-wing politics. Reagan's political "philosophy" was built around aggressive anticommunism and an antagonism to big government and the welfare state. These commitments, ironically, made this enemy of state intervention the best friend in government that the American military-corporate power structure ever had. The 25 percent tax cut enacted in his first year in office delighted business, and the almost 10 percent increase over inflation in military spending pleased the Pentagon. And his cuts in domestic spending—health care, low-cost housing, and income maintenance programs—elated conservatives who saw them as the beginning of their long-hoped-for counteroffensive against five decades of the welfare state.

At first, however, Reagan's economic policy—critics named it "voodoo economics" as a contemptuous substitute for its original "supply-side" title—resulted in the worst bout of unemployment (one factor in the creation of a subculture of homeless people who continue to wander and often sleep on the streets of American cities), bankruptcies, and corporate deficits since the Great Depression. Nevertheless, despite the growing income gap between the rich and poor and the failure of what were essentially his "trickle-down" economic tenets, Reagan rigidly held onto his beliefs, shoring them up with anecdotes about welfare "cheats" and a philosophy of voluntarism that seemed to owe as much to Frank Capra (a Capra without a social conscience) as to Herbert Hoover.

Nor was this film-based political vision confined to economic affairs. In foreign policy, Reagan's "Darth Vader" speech referred to the Soviet Union as an "evil empire" and extended the Star Wars metaphor even further by justifying his massive military buildup with allusions to as-yet-unbuilt space weapons that would presumably deter Soviet aggression. It seemed as if America had finally acquired a president who was deeply committed to all the crackbrained fantasies and mindless, empty rhetoric peddled by Hollywood ever since it became the center of America's popular culture.

Obviously, Reagan's saber rattling (which included the arming of a rebel force, the contras, against the leftist Sandinista regime in Nicaragua and the overthrow of an ultraleft revolutionary government on the island of Grenada in 1983) had a disquieting effect on America and its allies. If nothing else, it helped relaunch antinuclear and disarmament campaigns that had lain dormant for a number of years. In small towns and large cities, people all over the world began again to protest against the Strangelovian nuclear policies of the past 45 years. In a similar fashion, by unleashing free-market forces, particularly on the air, on the land, and in the workplaces of America (dismantling the Environmental Protection Agency) and placing people in charge who unblinkingly served the special interests, Reagan incurred the ire of the nation's environmentalists.

Nonetheless, despite these problems, midterm election losses, and an unemployment rate of more than 10 percent, Reagan continued to gain the approval of the majority of Americans. Much of it had to do with his undoubted charm, his quickness with a quip, and his calming nice-guy demeanor, media assets that, when coupled with his actor's talent for assuming the presidential role and playing the "Great Communicator," led him to an easy election victory over a serious, uncharismatic Walter Mondale in 1984. Reagan's triumph clearly demonstrated that the American public's obsession with imagery and personality went so deep that this politically unreflective and callow figure—this shallow man who seemed all persona—could do no wrong in their eyes.[1]

Of course, by 1984 the economy had revived, though there was an immense budget deficit and economic weak spots in the old industrial areas of the Northeast and Midwest, and blacks and the poor were clearly economically worse off. In fact, in the 1980s the living standard for the bottom fifth of the population dropped by 8 percent, while the top fifth's standard of living rose by about 16 percent.[2] Wealth became increasingly more concentrated as a result of Republican policies. The public, however, cared little about the difficulties of the poor—the poor living at a great remove from most people's daily experience. They also felt that times were prosperous and that success was open in America to anybody who worked hard at achieving it. And even a precipitous decline of the price of farm commodities in 1985 and a trade shortfall of $170 billion in 1986—with protectionist Japan flooding America with better-quality VCRs and autos (though it aroused the anger of unions and business groups)—did little to undermine the public's sanguine mood about the American economy. Of course, union opposition had little effect on Reagan's policies, as they had, in the main, allied themselves with the Mondale campaign and were in a weakened state, their membership declining by 1985 to 19 percent of the workforce. Reagan's base of support also included members of Protestant fundamentalist groups (e.g., the Moral Majority) whose prime political aims were not in the economic sphere but in the active promotion of a social agenda, including prayer in the schools, prohibition of abortion, traditional family values, and law and order. Reagan paid constant lip service to this constituency in innumerable presidential pronouncements but did little concrete to put their program into effect beyond taking their interests into account in his Supreme Court nominations (e.g., Scalia and Bork).

The last years of his administration saw a scandal—"Irangate"—finally stick to Reagan (the "Teflon president") personally. This was a secret arms-for-hostages deal with Iran where profits from weapons sales were covertly shifted to the contras—a deal that broke the law and overrode the Constitution. Reagan attempted to deny his own responsibility for the affair by claiming total ignorance of the activities of subordinates like chief of the National Security Council, Vice-Admiral John Poindexter, and superpatriot Colonel Oliver North. Of course, denying knowledge of the affair made Reagan look publicly like a bumbling, ineffectual figure incapable of controlling his underlings. Some of his diminished popularity was regained at the Gorbachev–Reagan summit conference in Iceland in 1986 when for the first time the superpowers agreed to eliminate a whole weapons system (all medium-range missiles in Europe).

Nevertheless, by 1987 the Reagan administration seemed moribund: the president vague and detached, some former aides indicted for influence peddling, and the president and Congress at a stalemate over Star Wars, the budget, and other issues. But the Democrats were incapable of transforming the troubles of the Reagan administration into a victory in the presidential election of 1988. The Democrats, led by Michael Dukakis, an intelligent but inexpressive and rigid technocrat who emphasized "competence" rather than social vision, ran an inept, defensive campaign that helped turn lightweight George Bush into a formidable candidate and Republican winner.

Bush was also aided in his victory by some skillful debate preparation and well-crafted, vicious, and racist negative campaign ads. In its first year, the popularity of the Bush administration benefited greatly from being in power as the Cold War wound down and revolutionary political changes in Eastern Europe, the Soviet Union, and Nicaragua took place (though the political and economic future of almost all these countries remains uncertain and even precarious). Bush demonstrated little talent or imagination for using the historical moment to project an inspiring vision of democracy, but his affable, cautious style also meant that he did not say or do anything that could undermine these momentous developments. On the domestic front, Bush's tepid, consensual, right-of-center politics muted much of the ideological abrasiveness of Reagan conservatism without breaking the faith on issues like abortion or tax policy. He also indulged in rhetorical gestures of concern for the poor and homeless and made a legislative commitment to educational and environmental reform—without any of it being sufficiently far reaching to make even a dent in social problems (e.g., drugs, crime, housing, and teenage pregnancy) that grew more profound and explosive with each passing year.

More significant than any specific Republican legislation during the 1980s was Reagan's ushering in a culture of unbridled greed and materialism—where lining your own pocket was the primary goal. The public realm was devalued and treated negligently and contemptuously. There is, of course, the close to $2 trillion debt that the federal government built up over the previous decade. More than that, there is the corruption and influence peddling that permeated the Department of Housing and Urban Development, the money necessary to clean up waste from nuclear plants like Hanford in Washington, and the exorbitant cost (estimates run as high as $500 billion) to the public of the savings-and-loan spree that was supported by both the Reagan administration and Congress casting a blind eye to ongoing abuses. Conversely, the marketplace and the private realm and pleasure were deified. In a sense, it was a second Gilded Age, where conspicuous consumption was the norm—a great many stretch limousines and a great deal of nouvelle cuisine—an age whose commitment to profit, hedonism, and modern technology basically subverted its conservative political rhetoric. Its heroes—and Reagan's speeches promoting individual heroism—were vulgar, aggressive entrepreneurs like Donald Trump and sharp Wall Street pirates like Ivan Boesky, whose operations skirted and went over the line into illegality. In fact, the people who did best financially during the decade were paper entrepreneurs (e.g., investment bankers) who made their money through deal making and asset rearranging—hostile takeovers, leveraged buyouts, and junk bonds—rather than creating anything of value. The tone for the decade was set by Reagan's first inaugural, which cost $8 million, opening with an $800,000 fireworks display at the Lincoln Memorial, followed by two nights of show business performances and topped off by nine inaugural balls serving 14,400 bottles of champagne. The inaugural exemplified both Reagan's aesthetic and his moral perspective, which was based on the notion that the "beautiful was the expensive, the good was the costly."[3]

This distorted moral vision gave sanction to an age of narcissism whose most representative figure was the yuppie. Yuppies may have been subjects of jokes and social satire, but in their emphasis on financial success, consumption, and self-development, they embodied the period. The archetypal yuppie jogged, ate health food, was obsessed with brand names and what was fashionable, and was a workaholic. Work was a means to greater status and a more affluent lifestyle, and happiness could be realized only by relentlessly pursuing one's own needs. And little sense of larger social, moral, and communal concerns were allowed to intrude on this hunger for personal mobility. Of course, not every yuppie neatly fit this complacent archetype or, should I say, stereotype, but enough conformed to the type to help define the social character of the decade.

It was not clear, however, that his old industry, Hollywood, reaped any immediate benefits from the Reagan era. Not that times were bad—overall income and profits being up for most of the major studios. Yet, as always in an insecure industry, anxieties were heightened by Reagan's economic policies, especially since they swelled interest rates. Since the lifeblood of Hollywood is borrowed capital, the number of films produced each year suffered a severe cutback. At the same time, Hollywood looked for economic shelters, usually in the arms of huge conglomerates that had enough internal excess capital to avoid high interest rates. So the conglomeration of Hollywood that started in the 1960s and 1970s continued apace, with the gobbling up of previously unattached studios like Columbia by Coca-Cola in 1982 (the studio has just been bought by Akio Morita's Sony) and the mergers of old giants like MGM and United Artists. In the process, tycoons like Kirk Kerkorian, Ted Turner, and Rupert Murdoch (he picked up Twentieth Century Fox in 1985) all got into the movie business.

The conglomerates positioned themselves to take control over some of the theaters they had lost long before—acquiring since 1985 more than 3,500 of the country's 22,000 screens.[4] They also took advantage of the explosion in new telecommunications technology—cable, cassettes, and video discs—and their need for product by selling their old film libraries to them at a great profit. Despite the mergers, independent production companies (e.g., Island and Vestron) grew in the 1980s until the stock market crash of 1987.[5] But by 1988, many of these independent companies were on the verge of collapse, unable to produce the box office hits that would keep them solvent. However, by the end of the decade, Hollywood was under the tight domination of the entertainment combines, who, in the main, eschewed innovative and risky filmmaking for conventional blockbusters with established stars—there were still independent production and distribution companies, like Miramax and New Line, functioning and making films that were too idiosyncratic and personal for the mass market.

At the beginning of the decade, industry insecurity was heightened by the failure of Michael Cimino's intellectually vacuous and inchoate western epic *Heaven's Gate* (1980), a total economic and critical disaster. Suddenly, studios were calling into question the whole policy of allowing big-budget laissez-faire to directors with only one or two hits to their credit. A search was initiated for highly marketable properties based on presold reputations—sequels like *Superman II* and *Rocky III* (the latter a film that exploits racial fears and stereotypes by creating a villain who is a brutal, black boxer with an intimidating, baleful look).[6]

It was perhaps this insecurity and the quest for bankable commodities that made it easier for Robert Redford to direct a film. Redford had been the producer of well-received and even financially successful films like *Downhill Racer* (1960), *The Candidate* (1972), and *All the President's Men* (1976) and this time around decided himself to direct a film based on Judith Guest's novel, *Ordinary People* (1980).

To some extent the material of *Ordinary People* was made to order for Redford with his Hollywood image of the White/Anglo-Saxon/Protestant (WASP) golden boy in films like *The Candidate* (1972) and *The Way We Were* (1973). The film evoked the dark side of an upper-middle-class, suburban WASP family—the Jarrets. The family's placid, comfortable life is disrupted by the accidental death of their eldest son, Buck, and the subsequent suicide attempt and hospitalization in a mental hospital of his guilt-ridden, bright, and sensitive younger brother, Conrad (Timothy Hutton).

The villain of the film is not the middle-class materialism or the conformist wasteland of the suburbs of a film like *The Graduate* but rather WASP repression and control as epitomized by Conrad's handsome, compulsively neat mother, Beth (Mary Tyler Moore). She is conceived as a woman so obsessed with appearances and so fearful of allowing her emotions to get out of control that she deals with the family tragedy by remarking, "We'd have been alright if there hadn't been any mess." The Jarret family "mess" and, in particular, the terror in self-lacerating Conrad's eyes begins to be worked out only when Dr. Berger (Judd Hirsch), a warm, commonsensical, and iconoclastic Jewish psychiatrist, starts getting through to him. Berger not only helps Conrad but also, as a bonus, shakes his passive, somewhat unconscious but loving father Calvin (Donald Sutherland) out of his bondage to his wife's rigidity.

Ordinary People is a small, intelligent film that has an assured feel for the cocktail chatter and the green lawns and backyards of the insulated, all-white Lake Forest suburb where the film was made. However, the film is primarily a work of two shots and interiors, a domestic work much more interested in the tensions of family life than the world of the upper-middle class (there is no evidence in the film that Calvin's values are much different from Beth's). Despite subtle touches such as Dr. Berger's office becoming darker as Conrad gains more insight into his problems, the film is marred by Redford's habit of sometimes reducing the complexities of familial conflict to pat formulas.

From Conrad getting just the right, jargon-free psychiatrist to his meeting up with the most understanding and loveliest of high school coed girlfriends (Elizabeth McGovern), the film has a tendency to be too pat. What helps *Ordinary People* transcend some of its clichés and melodramatic contrivances (the boating accident itself) is Redford's gift for having his actors use their faces and body movements to convey a wide range of emotions. In an especially inspired bit of casting, Redford garnered Mary Tyler Moore (America's sitcom sweetheart) to play against type, giving a performance that avoids turning her frigid, golf-playing, napkin-folding mother into a mere stereotype. She is able to successfully communicate the profound desperation and insecurity that lies underneath her need to cleave to the surfaces of life and to coerce the people around her to do the same.[7]

However, though her ability to project feelings of anxiety adds nuance and dimension to the role, the mother is still the film's villain, bearing primary responsibility for Conrad's problems. It is Beth who is unwilling to contemplate changing and going to therapy and incapable of giving any love to Conrad. And it is the mother's cold-bloodedness and egoism that links the implicit point of view of *Ordinary People* with sophisticated, often unconscious feminist backlash strains inherent in films like *Kramer vs. Kramer* and even *Tootsie* (1982). Like the wife in *Kramer*, Beth flees home and familial responsibility and leaves her husband to assume the nurturing, maternal role—the family becoming a male preserve. In both films, the central female characters are portrayed as being either irresponsible or uncaring, with Beth carrying the added burden of being insidious as well.

Tootsie, of course, is a very different sort of work from the other films we have linked it with. It was one of the big box office hits of 1982, a genuinely clever and funny film with beautifully timed gags, witty one-liners, and a virtuoso performance by Dustin Hoffman. It is built around the classic comic gambit of the man who dresses up as a woman and then cannot have his identity revealed (e.g., *Some Like It Hot*, 1959). However, Hoffman and the film's director, Sydney Pollack, were not satisfied with merely making a film that left audiences howling, and they began to make serious claims for the film as an exploration of gender and sexual roles.

Tootsie is the sort of film that baldly states that each of us carries both maleness and femaleness and that a man can acquire greater sensitivity and humanness by getting in touch with his femaleness. It also touches on other feminist issues and insights by dramatizing the insults and patronizing behavior constantly bestowed on women at work by their bosses and, of course, asserts that women must stand up for their dignity. However, despite the film's self-conscious feminism, the reality of *Tootsie* is much more conventional than its ambitions. As Dorothy Michaels, soap opera star, Hoffman continuously affirms his maleness beneath the female impersonation; there is little sense of Hoffman having truly experienced his female side. And Dorothy Michaels's feminism is troubling since it ends up that the strongest and, in fact, the only feminist in the film is a man, the other female characters being either neurotically insecure or vulnerable and dependent on a man to provide direction. *Tootsie* is a skillful, entertaining film that breaks little new ground, for it ultimately demonstrates how a man can become a feminist and leave the traditional sexual patterns in place. Just as in *Kramer vs. Kramer* and *Ordinary People*, the new hero-heroine of *Tootsie*'s brand of feminism turns out to be a man.[8]

Though small personal works like *Ordinary People* and a farce with pretensions to social significance like *Tootsie* were popular in the early 1980s, probably more symptomatic of the period were the works of Steven Spielberg. In the 1970s, Spielberg directed blockbuster hits like *Jaws* and *Close Encounters of the Third Kind* (1977) and almost single-handedly resurrected the fortunes of Columbia Pictures. But after the failure of his comedy *1941* (1980), his career seemed on the wane until, aided by his friend and University of Southern California schoolmate George Lucas (the film's executive producer), he directed *Raiders of the Lost Ark* (1981).

As in his previous films—the hunt for the malevolent shark in *Jaws*, the extraterrestrials in *Close Encounters*, and the Japanese submarine in *1941*, *Raiders* is essentially a story about a quest. The search focuses on the competition between an intrepid and invulnerable American archaeologist, Indiana Jones (Harrison Ford), and the Nazis to find the lost ark of the covenant, which will give its possessor unlimited power.

Although the film does go in for an awesome though nonsensical religious display at its finale and there is talk of the gleaming gold ark having infinite power, the film's appeal and even its subtext aren't built around religious belief. *Raiders* is a reflection of the old Hollywood and its skilled manipulation of an audience's need to feel anxiety, lose itself in harmless fantasy, and become nostalgic.

In fact, from the film's opening credit, where the Paramount fades into a snow-covered Andean peak, to a fade-out where it re-creates the final scene in *Citizen Kane*, we are treated to a whole host of images and themes borrowed from old Hollywood—particularly the cliffhanging serials of the 1930s. Following the genre conventions, the whip-snapping, unreflective Indiana and his hard-drinking, tough but dependent girlfriend, Marion (Karen Allen), face down poison darts, snakes, rotting corpses, and assorted gun-toting villains and finally outsmart and outfight the inhuman Nazi hordes. The upshot of it all is not so much to reassure us about good triumphing over evil—Indiana's only real commitment is to adventure and acquiring the ark (even Marion is an afterthought)—as to enclose us in a claustrophobic world of action for its own sake. The result is that *Raiders* comes as close as a film can to being a children's comic book.[9]

It is that very same child that exists in all of us that Spielberg appealed to so imaginatively and skillfully in *E.T.* (1982). Written by Melissa Mathison, who wrote the scenario for the lyrical children's film *Black Stallion, E.T.* managed to hit on a mine of primal fantasy. It is basically the story of a benign extraterrestrial (who looks very much like one of the aliens in *Close Encounters*) who is left behind when his spaceship takes off without him and a young boy, Elliot (Henry Thomas), who befriends, protects, and helps him return to his home. The story is as simple and familiar as any about a boy and his pet dog. However, there is more to the film than a bare sketch of the plot would suggest. *E.T.* contains numerous references and images invoking children's films (i.e., *Bambi*, 1943; *Peter Pan*, 1953; and *Mary Poppins*, 1964). The film also carries a feeling of religiosity that alternately transforms the cute, doll-like extraterrestrial into a loving father substitute and, possibly pushing its significance a bit too far, a Christ figure (E.T. dies and is resurrected in the midst of a family where the mother's name happens to be Mary).

Of course, the qualities that made *E.T.* a great commercial success—within less than a year of its release it was assured of becoming one of the top-grossing films of all time—went far beyond its *Bambi*-like forest imagery or its possible religious resonances. Among the most significant of these was the emphasis it gave to the need that all of us have for unwavering affection, which is conveyed in the spiritual union between E.T. and Elliot. Pervading the whole film was Spielberg's commitment to childlike innocence, reinforced by his ability to visualize the world the way a child does.

As a result of the film's emphasis on a child's perspective, adults and adult authority are either treated warily or distrusted altogether. Even Keys (Peter Coyote), the benevolent and sympathetic head of the government scientists sent out to find E.T., wants to subject him to scientific scrutiny, and that alone places him in the adult realm. None of the adult males in the film, including Keys, are ever shown beyond their midriffs; they are a faceless, ominous, and an almost malevolent group—the real aliens. Elliot's mother is portrayed as ineffectual—she has difficulty coping with being a single parent—and his father as irresponsible—he causes Elliot distress by running off to Mexico with another woman. In *E.T.*, the children ultimately triumph over the adults, helping E.T. elude their grasp and reach his home—the victory of feeling over rational and scientific thought.

E.T. was essentially a fairy tale, sometimes a bit too cute and sentimental for its own good—a film whose meaning is much less significant than the feelings it elicits. Still, its general mood paralleled a number of cultural tendencies in early 1980s America. In its affirmation of innocence, its simple optimism, and its distrust of authority, particularly the state, it unconsciously mirrored some of the certainties and pieties offered to the American public by Ronald Reagan. Indeed, both E.T. and Ronald Reagan were eminently lovable, and just as Spielberg's Elliot found solace from his problems in a fantastic creature, Reagan mouthed platitudes about traditional values and fled the complexities inherent in bringing about social change or reshaping the economy.[10]

The fact that the audience also shared this nostalgia for old verities need not rest solely on the election returns but can be confirmed from the grosses and awards to a film like *On Golden Pond* (1981). In fact, if nothing else, *On Golden Pond*, with its saccharine shots of rippling water and loon-filled lakes, evoked the sterile aura of a Norman Rockwell illustration. Despite the banal imagery, the film did have an important theme and moments of truth about a rite of passage—aging and the confrontation with the imminence of death. Nevertheless, by casting Henry Fonda and Katharine Hepburn in the leading roles as the 80-year-old, ailing Norman Thayer and his radiant, vital wife Ethel, the film paid less attention to gerontology than to Hollywood iconography.

It is not that Fonda's portrayal of the dying Norman was not a fitting culmination to a brilliant career. In fact, his characterization of the surly curmudgeon with a soft streak, who delivers lines like, "I think I'll read a new book—see if I can finish it before I'm finished. Maybe a novelette," is letter perfect. Likewise is his confusion and anxiety when a well-known path suddenly becomes unknown to him because of his failing memory.

It was not the characters or the neatly turned, sentimental narrative that drew audiences. What did was the teaming of Fonda and Hepburn and the cinematic memories it evoked of her costarring roles with icons like Grant, Tracy, and Wayne and their combined five decades of starring roles from Mary, Queen of Scots, to Tom Joad and Mr. Roberts. In addition, in casting herself as his estranged daughter Chelsea, Jane Fonda stirred resonances of her real-life, often embattled relationship with her father. Finally, it also gave Hollywood the chance to make amends to an actor who had given so much to the industry and audience over the years by granting him an Academy Award for best actor.

The long-overdue award to Fonda (Hepburn also won for best actress) was yet another symptom of Hollywood doting on its past. The problem was that this tendency was more than mere nostalgia, for it indicated not just a sentimental longing for the past but also an active use of its ideas and images in lieu of any new subjects, themes, or forms. Hollywood's yearning after its past almost seemed symptomatic of a more general longing for an America of a vigorous work ethic and powerful, growing industries whose policy of speaking softly and carrying a big stick was enough to keep any foreign government, at least the Latin American ones, in line. It was a simpler, more buoyant and heroic past that stood in sharp contrast to a contemporary America where smokestack industries decayed and closed, leaving its workforce standing in unemployment lines and a seemingly growing number of Central American Fidelistas thumbing their noses at American power.[11]

To some extent, it was this yearning after a heroic past that contributed to a decidedly peripheral but still minor trend in the early 1980s—the impulse to make epic films dealing with grand themes. It was a thread that ran through *Heaven's Gate* (1980), a muddled, inarticulate attempt to deal with class warfare in the American West, and Milos Forman's respectful, intelligent but stolid effort in *Ragtime* (1981), based on E. L. Doctorow's jaunty, ironic, cinematic novel of the same name, to deal with the American success myth and American racism—a trend that finally regained some critical if not economic respectability with Warren Beatty's *Reds* (1981).

In many ways, *Reds* was as much a personal film for Warren Beatty as *Ordinary People* was for Robert Redford. Like Redford, Beatty's previous successes as the producer-star of *Bonnie and Clyde* (1967), *Shampoo* (1975), and *Heaven Can Wait* (1978) insured him the industry clout necessary to make a film about, of all things, an American radical and communist. Also in line with Redford's work, Beatty's film was inspired by personal experience. In the late 1960s, Beatty had taken a trip to Russia, where, whenever he met older communists, they told him how much he physically resembled John Reed. When he returned home, Beatty delved into doing research about Reed, which set off an almost two-decades-long campaign to do the film about him.[12]

Ultimately, it was a combination of this personal obsession, coupled with his awareness of what made for success and failure in the film business, that deeply influenced *Reds*. First of all, Beatty (who won an Oscar for direction) decided to limit the focus of the film to the last four years of Reed's life, concentrating on his love affair and marriage to Louise Bryant (Diane Keaton), their experience and reporting of the Russian Revolution, and Reed's subsequent commitment to building an American Communist Party. Of course, this left out important aspects of Reed's life: his equally intense involvement with wealthy Mabel Dodge Luhan, who ran a literary salon in the Village, and his participation in the Mexican Revolution and World War I, struggles of which we get only brief glimpses. In addition, Beatty's decision to portray Louise as a poor little woman who clings to her man offended many feminists who saw her as much more forceful, defined, and talented than the Keaton role conveyed.

Significant as these omissions were, even more glaring was how basically safe the film truly was—especially on a formal level. Of course, Beatty faced an insurmountable problem in making a commercially viable film with a $35 million budget that at the same time treated two American communists sympathetically. In making *Reds*, except for his inspired use of the "witnesses," Beatty never strayed beyond the conventional romantic epic. In fact, despite its links to Stieglitz photos and Eisenstein's *Ten Days That Shook the World*, it owed its greatest debt to David Lean. In one episode, Beatty had Louise, in her attempt to unite with an imprisoned Reed, doing a pointless reprise of Dr. Zhivago's trek across the frozen tundra to Lara. The film also had a tendency to transform the chaos of the revolution and the squalor and poverty of war and communism into Hollywood operatics and glamour. In *Reds*, historical credibility is sacrificed so that the revolution can become a carefully choreographed magical tableau.[13]

Unfortunately, in this quest for commercially viable elements, Beatty often skirted perilously close to romantic comedy, complete with cute puppy dogs and running gags, like Reed bumping into a chandelier. The most problematic element, however, was the film's depiction of two main characters and their relationship. Keaton is able to bring some complexity into the role of Bryant when she communicates both her insecurity and her resentment at being treated as a mere adjunct to Reed during their early Village days—especially when Emma Goldman curtly dismisses her as she painfully struggles to find the right words. Still, there is nothing in her performance of the passion and sensuality of the woman whose touch, according to Eugene O'Neill, could set you afire. Indeed, the only time she conveys a bit of that intensity is in her scenes with O'Neill, played with great brio and force by Jack Nicholson. In addition, the scene where Bryant begins to offer trenchant political criticism of the relationship between the American Communist Party and the working class feels utterly incongruous, as if a ventriloquist's dummy is doing the talking.[14]

Beatty in turn struggles to capture a life of the scale that Reed lived—his romantic individualism, his contentiousness, and the passion and intensity of his political commitment. Though he makes him an attractive figure, nowhere does one get the sense of a man whom Walter Lippmann described as "Many men at once ... there is no line between the play of his fancy and the responsibility to fact: he is for the time the person he imagines himself to be."[15] Beatty, with his boyish charm, winsome smiles, and sheepish looks, is not so much protean as eager to please. And the complicated, painful, and contradictory relationship between Reed and Bryant, which is made the focus of much of the film, is superficial and seen primarily from the outside through meetings, partings, and passionate reconciliations rather than through illuminating its intricate internal life and motivation.

Despite these limitations, *Reds* remains both stirring and provocative. It was one of the rare times a Hollywood film both had at its center an appealing hero who was fully committed to left politics and made the history of the American left accessible and engaging. And though the film may concentrate too much on the Bryant–Reed relationship, *Reds* successfully captures the feeling of two people living on the rim of a new world that will usher in a cultural and sexual revolution as well as a political one. Of course, it may be absurd to hear *The Internationale* played with such exaltation while Reed and Bryant make love and at the same time the Bolsheviks take over the government. But it is also striking to see an image of politics, more American 1960s than Communist Party, that merges the personal and the political—as much a revolt against bourgeois culture as against capitalism itself.

Coinciding with this image of a utopian—thoroughly romantic, impulsive, and exhilarating—political commitment is the most incisive and lucid political dialogue to appear in an American film. Undoubtedly the contribution of Beatty's screenwriting collaborator, British leftist playwright Trevor Griffiths (*Comedians*), there are moments, particularly in the film's second half, chronicling Reed's political battles within the American left and with the Comintern that carry a dialectical electricity. For instance, in one especially insightful moment, a weary and disillusioned Emma Goldman (Maureen Stapleton) and Reed debate the effects of the Russian Revolution. Goldman attacks the decline of the revolution into tyranny, stating, "The dream we had is dying, Jack. The centralized state has all the power. They're putting anarchists like me in jail, exterminating all dissenters. I want no part of it." To which, justifying himself, Reed replies, "What did you think anyway? It was all going to work right away? It's war, Emma. And we have to fight it with discipline, terror, firing squads—or give up." Then pausing and expressing his own internal conflicts and misgivings, Reed ruefully says something with as much relevance to himself as to her: "Otherwise what has your life meant?"[16]

Unfortunately, when this sort of exchange is fused with brief portraits of Reed's political struggles with Comintern ideologues and political Czars Zinoviev (played by chic, Polish-born novelist Jerzy Kosinski) and Radek, there was not so much the image of a man analyzing and brooding over the nature of the revolutionary process or of a man conflicted between the bohemian writer and the disciplined revolutionary in himself as the simpler, less introspective question of whether Reed was ultimately disenchanted with the revolution. It was not that Beatty did not bravely begin to pose the other questions, but the film never truly pursues them. Of course, even the question of Reed's disenchantment is never really answered and is made to seem less significant by the only genuine unconventional formal technique in the film (a chorus and self-reflexive device)—the use of real "witnesses" who were contemporaries of Reed and Bryant.

Like "petals on a wet black bough,"[17] as one critic, quoting Ezra Pound, referred to them, the poignant, intelligent, aged faces and voices of Adela Rogers St. John, Rebecca West, Dora Russell, Henry Miller, and other famous and once-famous figures comment on Reed and Bryant ("I'd forgotten all about them.

Were they Socialists?") and their times ("There was as much fucking then as there is today."). And the one inescapable conclusion drawn from these meandering and fragmented comments is the elusiveness and selectivity of human memory. Whether Reed would have turned against the revolution (as many of his friends like Max Eastmen did) is probably less important than the larger truth that a person's historical place and role is difficult to discover and define. If nothing else, *Reds* at least rescued the figures of Reed and Bryant from historical obscurity and assured them a place in popular mythology.

There were other films during the Reaganite 1980s that dealt with the nature of the American left. Writer-director John Sayles made his first feature film *The Return of the Secaucus Seven* (1980)—a low-budget ($40,000), independent work about a group of 1960s activists who get together for a reunion in the late 1970s. The group were never hard-line, movement ideologues, nor had they been hippies. In Sayles's words, "they were the people who went to the marches, not those who planned them"[18]—strongly committed, issue-oriented activists who liked to smoke dope. By the time of the reunion, most of them are no longer activists—they are teachers, doctors, folk singers, or speechwriters for liberal politicians. But the political values and culture of the 1960s still have a powerful effect on their lives, without their ever losing a sense of perspective and some ironic feelings about the period.

Sayles's film had little camera movement, contained a number of scenes that needed editing, and was generally very raw and awkward on a technical level. However, it was a fresh, authentic, and open-ended work, made by a man who understood the 1960s from the inside—capturing its consciousness, language, and humor—and who did not dismiss or parody the significance of the experience. Sayles's wondrously attuned ear and eye for the way different people speak and behave was extended also to a "straight" liberal visitor and two working-class townies. Almost all his characters carried the kind of behavioral nuance that defied stereotyping.

It was, however, Lawrence Kasdan's popular hit *The Big Chill* (1983) rather than *The Return of the Secaucus Seven* that conjured up memories of the 1960s for the general public. Using a somewhat similar plot device to *Secaucus*, Kasdan structures the film around the reunion of a group of 1960s friends for the funeral of their friend and guru, Alex—the only one who kept the 1960s faith—who has committed suicide.

Starring rising Hollywood stars like William Hurt, Kevin Kline, Glenn Close, Tom Berenger, and Jeff Goldblum, Kasdan's film is slicker, better acted, and more dynamic—a great deal of neat and rhythmic crosscutting between characters, witty one-liners, and a rousing 1960s sound track (e.g., "I Heard It Through the Grapevine" and "You Can't Always Get What You Want")—than Sayles's work. Almost all the characters have achieved some semblance of upper-middle-class success—pop journalist, shoe store chain owner, real estate lawyer, and television actor. None of them works in social activist professions, and though they express some feeling about betraying their past ideals and a few pangs of conscience about their mainstream careers, there is little sign that these characters ever had any real politics to betray, except smoking dope, wearing long hair, and attending the odd antiwar rally. In fact, the malaise most of them feel has more to do with their own psychic make up than with conflicting values and ideals

In fact, the film basically affirms yuppie values and rejects holding on to the ideals of the past. It's their generous weekend host, Harold (Kevin Kline), the owner of a chain of shoe stores, who is the most sympathetic and dominant character. Harold is lean, athletic, a loving father, and the only one of the group who is happily married. He is at home in the 1980s—an investor and moneymaker, an integral part of his small town, and utterly realistic about what it takes to survive in the present. His antithesis is Nick (William Hurt), a bitter insomniac, a graduate school dropout, and, for good measure, a Vietnam vet who was wounded and, as a result, became impotent during the war. Nick sells drugs out of his run-down sports car, feels totally adrift, and hates his life. He inherits Alex's cabin and girl, but clearly there is nothing in his fragmented life that offers an alternative vision to Harold's complacent sense of well-being.

The Big Chill is an intellectually thin, well-crafted film that gives little sense of what the 1960s were all about. The politics and culture of the period are reduced to fashionable tag lines, and the only 1960s legacy they have kept seems to be a capacity for greater emotional and sexual spontaneity and ease. That easy, bantering style separates them from the stiff, dull, workaholic ad man who is unhappily married to one of the group. It provides them with a feeling of superiority based on their hipness, but these feelings are based more on matters of personal style and sensibility than on some ultimate difference of values.

The Reaganite 1980s were really the wrong historic moment for Hollywood to revive the politics of the 1960s. But *The Big Chill's* embrace of yuppie realism had strong links with aspects of the 1960s counterculture, which emphasized "doing your own thing" and giving all one's energies to developing the self, with little consciousness that a society needed some idea of social interdependence to be at all cohesive and whole. In fact, *The Big Chill* was a perfect expression of the "temporary truce between bourgeois and bohemian individualism as they joined together in a celebration of private life"[19] during the 1980s.

If it was difficult to make films that projected the political critique and culture of the 1960s in the period, still films critical of American politics were produced. *Missing* (1982), a box office hit, was the first American film made by French director Costa-Gavras (e.g., *The Confession*, 1970, and *State of Siege*, 1972). The political thriller plot centers around the disappearance of a young

American writer Charlie Horman (John Shea) and the arrival of his naive, apolitical, conservative businessman father, Ed (Jack Lemmon). The purpose of the narrative is to indict the United States for the CIA's collusion in the right-wing military coup of 1973, which overthrew the elected Marxist government of Salvador Allende in Chile. And that end is achieved here by personalizing the experience for an American audience by having them identify with the pain of an American Everyman, Ed Horman. He undergoes a political transformation and becomes enraged with American policies after discovering that the government was involved in his son's execution.

The film's power does not lie in its political critique, which neither illuminates what the Allende regime stood for or what the particular political dynamics of the coup were. Nor is Costa-Gavras particularly gifted at creating complex characters—the reasons for innocent Charles Horman and his wife Beth's presence in Chile (though Sissy Spacek gives an extremely natural performance) are never made clear. What is most striking is Costa-Gavras's gift for creating the terrifying atmosphere of a night city under martial law. It's a city where the sound of sirens and volleys of gunfire pierce the eerie silence, where pedestrians beg strangers for sanctuary, and where a stadium's bleachers are filled with people rounded up because of suspected leftist connections.

Costa-Gavras embeds his unambiguous political critique within the conventions of the thriller, but a film like Mike Nichols's *Silkwood* (1983) eschews melodrama for a muted, ambiguous account of the dangers of nuclear power. Based on a true story about a woman who had become a political heroine, Karen Silkwood, the film uses very different aesthetic strategies from both *Missing* and the earlier nail-biting, Oscar-winning entertainment about a demonic nuclear power industry, *The China Syndrome* (1979).

Silkwood avoids turning the problem of nuclear power into a schematic conflict between people of goodwill and a profit-hungry industry. Its heroine, Karen Silkwood (Meryl Streep in a natural, unselfconscious performance), is a tranquilizer-swallowing, chain-smoking, sexually promiscuous blue-collar worker whose three children are being raised by her husband. This tense, crass, unsophisticated protagonist can alternately be both abrasive and deeply feeling. And the film spends more time, using long takes and medium two-shots, to capture atmospheric detail—the clutter of her collapsing house—and realistically limn her difficult relationships (there are tedious moments as well as evocative ones) with her lover Drew (Kurt Russell) and her lesbian roommate Dolly (Cher) than in conveying the machinations of the nuclear power industry.

Silkwood's focus is on the feelings of ordinary people rather than on issues, and most of the workers are either too unaware or too frightened about the possible loss of their well-paying jobs to speak out about the plant's disregard for their safety. The workers are no heroic mass out of Eisenstein, the local union is ineffective, and the workers don't suddenly turn into angry, articulate critics of nuclear power. It's Karen who courageously and heedlessly takes the main role in agitating against the company and trying to bring to the *New York Times* evidence of falsified safety records—activity that is not simply aimed at changing company policy but also motivated by an unstated desire to realize a greater sense of self. The corporation itself is conceived not as a group of avaricious, stock villains but rather as an impersonal, opaque, and ultimately more insidious organization. *Silkwood* is a restrained work that leaves the cause of Karen's death in an auto wreck an open-ended question—it's either an accident or a cold-blooded murder by the company. And the fact that the company is ultimately shut down is seen only in a postscript without any inflated theatrics about the triumph of individual courage and virtue over the evil corporation.

Besides nuclear power, other 1980s political and economic problems were touched on by Hollywood. During the early 1980s, there was a run of farm bankruptcies, resulting in some suicides and even in the murder of a few mortgage-holding bankers by angry, frustrated farmers. A cycle of films like Robert Benton's *Places in the Heart*, Mark Rydell's *The River*, and Richard Pearce's *Country* (all in 1984) reacted to these events by focusing on small farmers—all of them strong women—struggling against the elements and the banks.

Places in the Heart was the most popular of the three films and won Academy Awards for its star Sally Field and scriptwriter Robert Benton. Set in rural Texas during the Depression—the world of Benton's youth—the film has a wonderful feel for the Texas landscape, climate, and the church services and dances that are at the heart of small town life. The film's narrative, however, is a thoroughly soft and sentimental fable, Sally Field playing a gutsy widow with two children who must make a profit on her cotton crop to save her farm. She is magically aided by two outsiders—a bitter, blind veteran, Will (John Malkovich), and a kind, black drifter, Moze (Danny Glover). It's soft-spoken, heroic Moze whose knowledge of the land helps save the farm, though the local Ku Klux Klan drives him off the land right before the film's conclusion. Benton's childhood memories are essentially sweet ones, and though racism pervades town life and the local banker is unctuous and manipulative, the communal ethic remains strong and even a defensive Will becomes less bristly and more emotionally open. The film concludes on a moving, phantasmagoric grace note with a church service where all the film's characters—living and dead, black and white—gather to affirm Christian and communal love.

Places in the Heart was basically an affirmation of the human spirit's capacity to triumph over adversity, but the other two farm films did make a stab at a political statement. The more interesting of the two was *Country*—a muted, unsentimental film about a farm family whose husband (Sam Shepard) collapses when their government loan is called in. The determined wife (Jessica Lange) maintains the family and organizes a group of small farmers to resist the government, resulting in her winning a temporary stay of foreclosure. The film's strength is its fidelity to the reality of farm life, and it uses few close-ups or dramatic scenes to distort the daily texture of that experience. However, though it attacked Reagan farm policy, the film blurred the nature of the political enemy by portraying it nebulously as "monolithic bureaucracy" and apathetic government.[20]

Besides making films like *Silkwood* and *Country*, whose liberal values were at odds with Reagan policies, Hollywood also began to make films that projected right-wing political views. It was a trend that gained momentum only after Reagan's landslide victory over Mondale in 1984. The first of these films was John Milius's *Red Dawn* (1984), a paranoid action movie about the invasion of the United States by a combined Russo-Cuban force and the defense of the country left in the hands of a group of young patriots. It revived the specter of the Soviet threat and demonstrated that anticommunism fused with exciting, reconstructed tank battles could sell.

Following *Red Dawn's* lead, Hollywood indulged in some Vietnam War revisionism with a series of films that exploited the remaining cause célèbre—the 2,500 purported MIAs left behind in Vietnam. In the process, Hollywood did nothing less than rewrite history and gave America a second opportunity to win the war, at least on the screen.

Of the reported 2,500 MIAs, many were presumed dead, but others were considered to be alive and held captive by the North Vietnamese. Anguished relatives and supporters initiated a campaign to obtain their release. And one former Green Beret colonel, James B. Gritz, was not satisfied with lobbying and led an abortive raid into Laos whose most notable accomplishment was that Hollywood could turn it into a film, *Uncommon Valor* (1983).

In its us-against-them portrait of a powerfully linked group of Vietnam vets against a craven government, *Uncommon Valor* reflected a pessimistic right-wing populism sharply critical of an uncaring society and government. In addition, the film provided a retrospective affirmation of Vietnam as a noble cause, whose only seeming limitation was that we didn't win the war. The narrative structure of *Uncommon Valor* also provided a model for other revisionist Vietnam works.

Uncommon Valor leaned heavily on one of America's most enduring archetypical forms, the captivity myth, which originally evolved from the Puritan fear that the American wilderness would corrupt them spiritually. The myth was built around a tale of pure white men and women taken prisoner by barbaric Indians who tempted them into sins of the flesh and spirit. The Indians don't succeed in subverting their piety, and, in fact, the prisoners rediscover God's will.

As these tales were modified in the 19th century, there emerged a fearless, stoic hunter-hero—Davy Crockett and Hawkeye—whose intimacy with Indian and wilderness lore gave him the skill to wrest the land away from the Indians and projected into the future the vision of a white man's agrarian Arcadia as the nation's destiny. That destiny helped justify our expropriation of the wilderness through methods that historian Richard Slotkin called a "regeneration through violence."

In films like *Uncommon Valor*, the Indians became the Vietnamese and the MIAs the prisoners of the captivity myth, but the central figure in the film, Marine Colonel Jason Rhodes (Gene Hackman), was too much the dignified, stoic professional soldier to become a hunter-hero. Hollywood, however, had other aspirants for the role, the first being half-Indian karate champ Chuck Norris, who had already established a screen persona of a mild-mannered, taciturn loner who puts to rout hosts of sleazy villains (e.g., *Force of One*, 1978).

In films, constructed in the captivity narrative tradition like *Missing in Action* (1984) and *Missing in Action 2: The Beginning* (1985), Norris (Colonel Braddock) plays an inexpressive, solitary hunter-hero who liberates MIAs at the expense of literally hundreds of Vietnamese soldiers. This hunter-hero is indomitable in the superman mode of a Michael Vronsky and is able to use the enemy's own guerrilla combat tactics, like wearing a camouflage suit, to triumph over them. And the films were extremely successful with the public because they guaranteed a great deal of bloody action, little extraneous dialogue, and, for the politically unconscious, even the illusion of final victory in Vietnam.

The *Missing in Action* films served as a warm-up for the apotheosis of this developing cycle, *Rambo: First Blood Part II* (1985)—a sequel to *First Blood* (1982), an extremely popular film about the bloody visit of John Rambo (Sylvester Stallone), an alienated Vietnam vet and Congressional Medal of Honor recipient—to a small town in the Pacific Northwest. *Rambo II* not only was a box office success—$57 million in the first two weeks—but also became a political byword after President Reagan referred to it in a number of his speeches. For Reagan, Rambo was a symbol of American machismo and patriotism, and the film's crude Russophobia and narcissistic camera worship of its star Sylvester Stallone's glistening, Nautilus-crafted body provided perfect fodder for Reagan's Hollywood brand of populism.

The film opens with Rambo being freed from a prison stockade, where he was incarcerated after his *First Blood* rampage, so that he can be sent on a secret mission into Vietnam to prove the existence of MIAs by photographing them. From that moment on, the film becomes a rant against the U.S.

government, embodied by an opportunistic bureaucrat, Murdock (Charles Napier), who both inspires the MIA mission and wants it to fail so that he can bury the embarrassing political issue for good. Murdock is seen by the film as Rambo's prime enemy and a cartoon symbol of a soulless and impotent American government that ostensibly betrayed its own troops because it lacked the will to win. And Rambo's uncontrolled Luddite-style outburst at the film's conclusion—using a machine gun to destroy Murdock's computers—supposedly spoke for all the ordinary GIs who suffered the callous manipulations and rationalizations of these government experts in Vietnam.

Coupled with this populist, superpatriotic backlash was a revival of the Soviet menace. The real enemy in the film are the Russians, not the North Vietnamese—the Soviets acting like an update of the Nazi SS, even to the point of being racists who view the Vietnamese as "yellow scum." And Rambo here is both a working-class echo of Colonel Kurtz, mumbling such aphorisms like "to survive a war you must become a war," and a hunter-hero who moves through the jungle, stripped to the waist, looking like an Indian brave or a scowling noble savage.

There is an undercurrent in the film suggesting that the Rambos of the world will never receive justice from the American government and that the only possible alternative is destructive rage. The film's dominant strain, however, is one of an America truly regenerated through violence—a resurrected nation bursting with pride, power, and unabashed aggression that can humble any enemy.

Nevertheless, by providing a touch of primitivism to the archetypes of the superman and hunter-hero, Stallone linked the character so close to his inarticulate persona that there was little possibility left for other films to work out new variations on the character. As a result, though Stallone succeeded in adding another mythic hero, along with Rocky, to his personal pantheon of America redux, he helped bring the MIA cycle to a standstill. Of course, desiring better economic and diplomatic relations, the North Vietnamese themselves began to permit U.S. inspection teams to search for the remains of the missing—the kind of pragmatic behavior that made it difficult even for Hollywood to go on constructing aggressively patriotic fantasies.[21]

Still, there were other films that fueled America's military buildup and Reagan's patriotic rhetoric. In 1986, Tony Scott's revved-up *Top Gun*—a film exulting in the military and in macho heroics—became one of the top box office hits. Its arrogant, adolescent hero, Maverick (a grinning Tom Cruise), is obsessed with becoming "top gun," the best of the best pilots, at the U.S. Navy Fighters Weapons School. The film's strength is its virtuosic and lengthy flying scenes and simulated dogfights shot from a variety of camera angles, but the rest is laughable dialogue, a contrived plot, and an unbelievable passionate romance between the narcissistic Maverick and his aeronautics instructor (Kelly McGillis). Still, the film would be only as disturbing as a glossy and banal navy recruiting ad if, at the film's climax, Maverick did not become a hero by engaging an unnamed enemy in a real war situation over the Indian Ocean. That narrative twist turns *Top Gun* into a film that is dangerously unable to distinguish war games from real war—reducing life-and-death situations into a plaything for male egos.

Films like *Top Gun* and Clint Eastwood's *Heartbreak Ridge* (1986), where a career gunnery sergeant (played by Eastwood) follows the tradition of old World War II movies turning raw rookies into men, readying them for a triumphant invasion of Grenada, may still have been produced in 1986. But that year also would see the first Hollywood film to really confront the concrete realities of the Vietnam War, Oliver Stone's Oscar-winning *Platoon*. Stone was a Vietnam War veteran whose film of remembrance and mourning had a cathartic effect for many Vietnam vets and nonvets alike. *Platoon* is most powerful and successful when it uses minimal dialogue and telling close-ups and medium shots to convey with great immediacy the war's everydayness: the stifling discomfort of the ants, heat, and mud of jungle and brush; the fatigue of patrols; the murderous cacophony and chaos of night firefights; and the boredom and sense of release of base camp. Stone also understood just how fear, fatigue, and rage could undermine some GIs' sense of moral restraint and balance and turn them into savages who massacre civilians and torch villages.

Stone's Vietnam is a bleak, horrific world where the GIs face an almost invisible, ubiquitous enemy. It's all seen through the eyes and voiceover narration (a number of self-consciously literary letters back home) of Chris Taylor (Charlie Sheen), an upper-middle-class, Yale dropout and patriot who, like Steven Crane's hero in *The Red Badge of Courage*, is initiated into manhood and transformed by the war. Taylor discovers not only Vietnam's terrors but also a gallery of working-class and underclass GIs who are given a bit more nuance than the norm for Hollywood war films. There is baby-faced, beer-can-crunching Bunny (Kevin Dillon), who loves war and killing; gum-chewing Sergeant O'Neill (John McGinley), whose obsequious attempts to find safety lead him only to greater danger; and a group of blacks of whom the earthy, wise King (Keith David) is balanced by the perpetually whining and malingering Junior (Reggie Johnson). The blacks are never turned into an anonymous mass, though the film's prime focus, as in most Vietnam films, is on the experience of white soldiers.

If the strength of *Platoon* is its ability to portray Vietnam as a world free of self-sacrificial heroics where mainly angry, disengaged, and divided GIs try to survive the madness in one piece and just get on the plane back home, its main weakness is its penchant for overblown literary conceits. Besides his

Platoon (1986). (Courtesy of Orion Pictures/Photofest.
Photographer: Ricky Francisco.)

ordinary GIs inhabiting a realist film, Stone created two mythic lifers: the
headband-wearing doper saint Sergeant Elias (Willem Dafoe) and the war-
loving, demonic Sergeant Barnes (Tom Berenger), whose Manichaean, melodramatic struggle tends to subvert the film's verisimilitude.

Both of them are constructed in larger-than-life terms: Elias is depicted as a
gentle, Christ figure, critical of the war that he has become weary of and given
far too many self-consciously significant close-ups by Stone, while Barnes, his

face crisscrossed with scars, is portrayed as a closet superman who asserts "I am reality" and is shot too often from a low angle to underline his forbidding character. On one level, these two portentous figures serve as symbolic fathers warring for the soul of Taylor (a somewhat bland character who doesn't have too vivid a soul); on another level, they supposedly reflect the political divisions within American society.

Platoon, however, lacked a genuine political perspective. It neither dealt with the mixture of nationalism and Marxist-Leninism that underlay the North Vietnamese military effort nor explored the political culture and specific policies involved in American intervention. When Stone ventures to make a political point, as he does in the film's final moments, it's as vaporous as the physical world he conjures up is grittily alive. He has Taylor indulge in a sermonizing voice-over that projects the facile, ethnocentric notion that the "enemy was in us" (as if America had fought the war to purge its own destructive impulses) and adds the harmless, banal sentiment that we must try "to find a goodness and meaning to this life."

Although *Platoon* was clearly not the final word on the war, it was an antidote to mindless political cartoons like *Rambo* and metaphysically confused works like *Apocalypse Now*. If Stone had little gift for capturing the political and social meanings of the war, he had at least echoed the dominant public feeling about Vietnam, that it was a self-destructive march into some kind of purgatory. Stone's authentic depiction of the mad and murderous world of combat was also so powerful an achievement that one could say that he had taken the first real cinematic step in Hollywood's coming to terms with Vietnam.

Platoon marked, after years of avoidance, wavering, and regression, Hollywood's total acceptance of Vietnam as a serious subject for film. In 1987, three films dealing with different aspects of the war were produced—*Hanoi Hilton*, Coppola's *Gardens of Stone*, and the only one worthy of a critical stir, Stanley Kubrick's *Full Metal Jacket*. Kubrick's work had grander aspirations than *Platoon*, dealing less with the concrete reality of Vietnam than with the military as an institution that breeds killers and projecting a vision of an innately brutal and corrupt human condition.

That vision of all human beings as potential destroyers and lovers of death, coupled with an Olympian, detached style, pervades almost all of Kubrick's work, notably *Clockwork Orange* (1968), where a futuristic, delinquent gang engages in orgies of destruction. In *Full Metal Jacket*, Kubrick brilliantly uses his unique style—overbearing close-ups, drained colors, harsh white and cold blue lighting, minimal dialogue, and an unnaturally severe barracks set—to choreograph the transformation of unformed recruits into trained marine killers.

Directing this dehumanization process is an obscenity-spouting, bullying drill instructor, Sergeant Hartman (Lee Ermey), whose relentless, sardonic barrage is so oppressively effective that it strips the men of their past identities and provides them all with new ones, naming one of them Private Joker (Matthew Modine) and still another Cowboy. Hartman's harangues often attain the imagistic richness of a poet of the profane, and they are permeated with a sense of menace. Kubrick has never been clearer about the links between sex, aggression, and death—in this case, cocks and rifles.

Unfortunately, the compressed power of the 45-minute prologue makes the film's second half—the Vietnam section—pale in comparison. Kubrick still dreams up inspired visual images and aural effects—a desolate, lunar landscaped Hue constructed out of an abandoned gasworks outside London and, after killing a female sniper, the chilling image of the marines marching into a blazing sunset singing "The Mickey Mouse Club Song"—sardonically fusing the carnage of war with the synthetic innocence of the popular culture that shaped the young marines. However, much of *Full Metal Jacket*'s second half is either conventional—a sniper sequence where one marine after another dies in blood-cascading slow motion is merely a more idiosyncratic variation on World War II films battle action—or given over to heavy-handed ironies. The central, choruslike figure Private Joker is a wry, ironic, less defined character than Sergeant Hartman. Joker's detachment is a projection of Kubrick's, but his exercise of irony feels too often like an overly literal cataloguing of the war's absurdities—the army newspaper *Stars and Stripes* attempt to provide happy news by calling search-and-destroy missions "sweep and clear" expeditions—than the kind of Brechtian mordancy that could get to the heart of the war's madness.

The ultimate and most striking irony implicit in Kubrick's version of Vietnam is that the film's most vital figures are its most lethal and brutal. Though Kubrick may not endorse the world of a Sergeant Hartman, he clearly has sympathy for characters who are at home in a nihilistic world. For Kubrick, it's the misanthropic who dominate and often triumph amidst the war's barbarism.

The most problematic element in *Full Metal Jacket* is Kubrick's Hobbesian view of human nature. Blaming it all on the savage nature of human beings may aptly describe some of the behavior on all sides in the war, but it is an evasion of its historical context. There was all too much anguish present in the Vietnam abattoir to totally conceive it in terms of pitiless irony and black humor. It was a war whose intense torment demanded more than Kubrick's cool genius.[22]

At the end of the decade, Oliver Stone returned to the subject of Vietnam and made a film that centered more on the cultural roots of the war effort than on the horrors of battle combat. *Born on the Fourth of July* (1989) was based on the autobiography of Ron Kovic, a paraplegic veteran who the war transformed from a macho, working-class patriot into an articulate antiwar activist.

The film's opening scenes sketch in bold, underlined strokes how Kovic's (Tom Cruise) values were formed in the Long Island suburbs by a mixture of repressive Catholicism, John Wayne films, patriotic parades, and the American obsession with competition and victory. In depicting Kovic's coming of age, Stone eschews subtlety both for images that are almost operatic, even vulgar, in their intensity and a swelling musical score to accompany them. Nevertheless, despite its sledgehammer style, the film captures with great poignancy and power Kovic's horrific experiences in a slum of a Bronx veterans' hospital; his uneasy, angry return to his forbidding mother-dominated, conservative, pro-war home; and his descent into alcoholism and self-degradation, which reaches its apotheosis in a wild fight with another vet Charlie (Willem Dafoe) while sitting in their wheelchairs in the middle of the Mexican desert. Stone is also much more adept at orchestrating emotional fireworks than in delineating the psychic and intellectual changes that Kovic goes through before he appears as a full-blown radical spokesman at the 1976 Democratic convention. The transformation is too abrupt, but *Born on the Fourth of July* marks the public's acceptance of the fact that it was more than just a mindless, suicidal war. That, at least in Vietnam, America's intervention was a consequence of our need to assert our national will and demonstrate to the world our imperial power.[23]

Vietnam was clearly not the prime subject of 1980s film. Hollywood also spawned a flood of teen comedies like Amy Heckerling's successful and sometimes funny and fresh *Fast Times at Ridgemont High* (1982) about a group of high school students who spend their time surfing, hanging around the local mall, and obsessing about sex, which is never treated as a real problem. Another was Paul Brickman's *Risky Business* (1983) starring Tom Cruise (Joel Goodson) as a straight, careful suburban high school senior who lives in a comfortable, white Chicago suburb with the usual foolish and unseeing parents who populate teen films. Most of his time seems spent indulging in elaborate masturbatory fantasies and worrying about what college he'll attend. Joel's parents leave on vacation, and he decides to take a risk for the first time in his life—to say, "what the fuck." He gets involved with a pretty, shrewd hooker who provides sex and solace and then, to make money, hosts a party that provides hookers for all his friends and even for a Princeton recruiter who is there to interview him. Insecure, guilt-ridden Joel has overnight become a daredevil-driving, smooth-talking middle-class pimp with shades, and the film cynically affirms this sleazy persona and his newfound talent for making the quick buck.

Risky Business is a perfect film for budding Reaganites. There is no danger here of Joel's risk taking to lead him to question or break from his upper-middle-class world; it actually helps him get into Princeton—where he'll major in business—and gives him a good start at learning what it takes to become a "future enterpriser." The hooker-girlfriend is a sharp, tough business-woman who will clearly be of help to Joel in acquiring a Porsche of his own and, after graduation, organizing hostile takeovers on Wall Street. *Risky Business* evokes a morally bankrupt world[24] where any action is justified if it will help you get ahead. It romanticizes both prostitution and cynical opportunism and endorses the success ethos—without a hint of irony.

The master of the teen picture, John Hughes, produced and directed a whole slew of films during the 1980s (e.g., *Sixteen Candles*, 1984; *The Break-fast Club*, 1985; *Weird Science*, 1985; and *Ferris Bueller's Day Off*, 1986) that conveyed some feeling for the social tensions and frustrations created by high school clique and lifestyle divisions—nerds, jocks, preppies, druggies, and val-ley girls. Sometimes even class barriers are alluded to—someone coming from "the wrong side of the tracks"—but in 1980s America, despite the continuing reality of class, that idea had little emotional or social resonance for adoles-cent moviegoers.

Hughes's films were cute, decent, and relatively innocent—none of them as hedonistic or cynical as *Risky Business*. The only culture that exists in his films is a white, suburban adolescent one—the films treat with contempt an absurd adult and parental world—and Hughes seems to be able to enter totally and unselfconsciously into a world of teenage mating rites, dress codes, and argot (e.g., "asswipe" and "geek"). Rebellion in a Hughes film is rarely anything more than a brash and spoiled kid hero like Ferris Bueller (Matthew Broderick) ingeniously and successfully flaunting school and other institutional rules but without ever deviating from a world that keeps him living a comfortable, possession-filled existence. All Hughes's films end neatly and happily, and in Elaine Rapping's words, Hughes's "kids are sui generis members of a self-sufficient, mysterious universe which operates not by the laws of capital but by magic, good Magic."[25]

One of the most popular teen films of the mid-1980s was Robert Zemeckis's *Back to the Future* (1985) (there have been two sequels so far), which combined teen comedy with science fiction. Starring television sitcom star Michael J. Fox (Marty McFly), the film combines time travel, a wild-eyed scientist (Chris-topher Lloyd) and his Rube Goldberg inventions, and nostalgia for the rela-tively innocent small town of the 1950s. Diminutive and clever Marty travels back 30 years to the time when his parents met in high school and inadver-tently alters his own and his parents' future. The film is inventive and has some charm, playing with the emotional-Oedipal problems involved in time travel. Marty's mother is at first attracted to him rather than to his spastic, timid father. But Marty succeeds in averting the danger of this incestuous connec-tion and pairs them off. In doing so, he leaves a legacy for the future, which transforms his seedy home and comic-pathetic 1980s parents—an overweight mother who is puritanical and drinks and a father with a lunatic laugh who allows himself to be mercilessly bullied—into a smooth, tennis-playing pair. The parents are now confident and successful and have moved up a couple of steps in class—the appropriate social background for a conventional teenage hero like clean-cut Marty. And though the film clearly endorses this Reaganite success story—Marty's time-traveling intervention aside—his father's ability to painfully assert his own will is the main reason he is able to create a new persona for himself; the parents are much more interesting as ineffectual, shambling failures than as stereotypical success stories.

During the Reagan years, many black economic and social gains of the 1960s and 1970s, ranging from the rate of college attendance to the proportion of two-parent families to relative income levels, began to decline while poverty and crime rates escalated. Hollywood, of course, was interested not in depicting these harsh, ominous realities but rather in finding black performers who assert their black identity, like Richard Pryor (*Stir Crazy*, 1980) and Eddie Murphy, who still would have crossover appeal.

In the 1980s, it was Murphy who was the big box office draw in films like Martin Brest's *Beverly Hills Cop* (1984). The film actually opens with a graphic montage of Detroit, evoking a predominantly black ghetto world of windowless bars, abandoned buildings, polluting smokestacks, and empty lots. The film, however, is not about the social reality of Detroit but about a rule-breaking, undercover cop, Axel Foley (Murphy), who sets out from its impoverished, violent urbanscape to find the murderers of a boyhood friend amidst the glitter and wealth of Beverly Hills.

The nonsensical plot, filled with soporific car crashes and shoot-outs, is merely a vehicle to provide the fast-talking, profane, homophobic Murphy a chance to do a number of routines and try out a number of voices. In his sweatshirt and sneakers, he plays the irrepressible bad boy who tweaks authority and convention but is, at the same time, utterly apolitical and safe. Murphy's Foley may coolly manipulate and dominate his fellow white cops, but the edge of his behavior is muted by the film projecting a vision of interracial camaraderie and ease between them. And when it comes to white women, Foley is utterly chaste. Murphy is an aggressive, hip, and funny comic, and *Beverly Hills Cop* is the perfect medium for him to reach a white audience—making them feel good so that they can root for a quick-witted black at the expense of dim whites (it also helps him hold a black audience) while preserving the racial status quo.

One of the rare films made during the early 1980s dealing with race was Norman Jewison's adaptation of Charles Fuller's prize-winning play *A Soldier's Story* (1984). The film stars a predominantly black cast and perceptively explores the question of racial identity—what it means to be a black in a world dominated by whites—but it is set back in time in the Deep South of 1944. Another, more popular and commercial work, directed again by a white, was Steven Spielberg's adaptation of Alice Walker's Pulitzer Prize–winning novel *The Color Purple* (1985)—a film about growing up a female victim in the Deep South.

Like the novel, the film is more about the oppression of black women by black men than about white racism. Celie (Whoopi Goldberg) is passive, sub-servient, and not very pretty. She is sexually and emotionally abused by al-most all the men in her life—brutal, callous males who express their own rage against being demeaned by viciously scapegoating women. But Celie ultimately gains self-respect, becomes independent, and achieves happiness by forming a communal house dominated by women. And the women are the powerful, luminous figures here—loving, supportive, nurturing and indomitable—while almost all the men are depicted as cruelly unseeing and uncaring.

The repressive, degrading nature of southern white racism is evoked, but the whites are peripheral to this feminist fable of female triumph. Spielberg's style tends to prettify, turning rural black poverty into a picturesque landscape filled with purple flowers, clear blue skies, green fields, and buzzing insects. There is also too much flashy editing, too many dramatic close-ups, and a couple of inflated musical sequences that look like they come from the MGM vault. Spielberg also played it safe politically, merely skimming over Celie's passionate lesbian love for a sensual, free-living, blues singer Shug (Margaret Avery). *The Color Purple* may be a sentimental, overdirected film, but the por-trayal of Celie's assertion of self and liberation from male domination leaves one emotionally stirred.

A more typical Hollywood treatment of racial issues was Alan Parker's *Mis-sissippi Burning* (1988), dealing with the 1964 disappearance of three civil rights activists during Mississippi's "Freedom Summer." Parker, a sincere, so-cially conscious director, decided that the only way he could make a viable commercial film about the black civil rights struggle was to invert reality and feature whites and the FBI as heroes (the FBI's role in the South was essen-tially antagonistic to the movement, often spying on rather than protecting activists) and turn blacks into mute victims—obliterating the basic fact that the movement was built on black collective action and courage.

Parker's film was "simply the latest in a long line of historical films which subordinate complex political and social processes to individual heroics and spectacular set pieces."[26] In this case, the civil rights movement is denuded of all political and social nuance and replaced by excitingly edited action se-quences and close-up confrontations between good FBI men—Anderson (Gene Hackman), a tough, local boy who is willing to bend the rules and Ward (Willem Dafoe), a by-the-book Yankee—and the ignorant rednecks who are

Klan members and unadulterated scum. That makes for a film that is strong on small-town atmosphere and the recycling of buddy film conventions and devoid of any feeling for historical fact or reality.

It was only in the last half of the decade that the films of a group of young black directors—Robert Townsend, Keenen Ivory Wayans, the Hudlin brothers, and the most original, Spike Lee—began to appear. Their works were rooted in black concerns and language and possibly signaled "the emergence of a new esthetic sensibility within Black America."[27] And despite the fact that they were centered in the specificity of black reality, they were able to appeal to white, mainstream audiences.

Spike Lee's films, the low-budget *She's Gotta Have It* (1986), *School Daze* (1988), and *Do the Right Thing* (1989), were personal works about complex aspects of black life that the larger public almost never saw before on the screen. The most politically controversial and formally imaginative of his films is *Do the Right Thing*, which both received a great deal of critical praise and was virulently attacked by some black and white critics. There were white critics who saw the film as stirring up race riots and as a black racist work, while a number of black critics saw it as being insufficiently militant or given to stereotyping black life. Lee's film elicited the kind of charged, extremely varied responses that clearly went beyond its mise-en-scène and touched a raw nerve in black–white relations.

Do the Right Thing was flawed: a bit too many film school tics (e.g., gratuitous oblique angles and tight close-ups), a tendency to sanitize some of the more destructive aspects of black inner-city life by eliminating both drugs and crime from the street, and a sexist depiction of its central female character, Tina (Rosie Perez)—Mookie's (Spike Lee as an underachieving, intelligent pizza deliveryman) undulating, nagging, foul-mouthed wife. Flaws aside, the more one views the film, the more its political complexity becomes apparent. One sees that Lee's film projects a genuine sense of political ambiguity, avoiding being either politically facile or polemical; he is a director genuinely groping for social answers—looking at Malcolm X and Martin Luther King as offering two alternative political visions and strategies. And the choice made by Lee's conflicted protagonist, Mookie, to hurl a garbage can through Sal's Pizzeria's window is seen not as a heroic act but as one that leaves him perplexed and saddened. The film's conclusion carries no answer to what it means to "do the right thing"—just more questions.

Do the Right Thing ultimately was a rarity among American films; it was a serious, dynamic work about something substantial—successfully fusing realism and stylization to evoke a kaleidoscope of black community life and problems on one Brooklyn street during a summer heat wave. And Lee truly loves and knows how to grant cinematic life to the physical texture and language of the street. Using an episodic narrative and a great deal of rapid cutting, point-of-view shots, talking heads, characters who skirt the edge of being cartoons, and other distancing devices like the disc jockey Love Daddy, who provides commentary and narration during the film, Lee touches on a number of prime social issues that face the black community. They range from police brutality and white racism to gentrification, black hostility toward white and Asian store owners, and the way black pride should be manifested. Lee's Brooklyn street, enveloped in artificial light, has clearly been sweetened and romanticized, but he doesn't totally avert the camera eye from some of the painful realities of black inner-city life. For example, Mookie continually evades his responsibility as a father, and many of the black characters lack a work ethic, spending a great deal of time merely jiving, hanging around, and indulging in the kind of race rhetoric and idle fantasy that become substitutes for any sort of coherent, decisive action—be it political or personal.

Given Lee's profound identification with the black community and culture, it was a sign of his skill that the character granted the most dimension in *Do the Right Thing* is Sal (Danny Aiello), the Italian American owner of the neighborhood pizzeria. Sal is depicted as an earthy, decent man whose life is his store. He has an amicable relationship with his black customers, who he treats, despite an undercurrent of paternalism, as individuals. But Sal is also a product of a subculture where the use of racist epithets like "nigger" are not unusual. Enraged, Sal spews out racist invective, but Lee never dismisses or calcifies him as just a bigot. He treats him sympathetically (even a bit sentimentally)—an honest, feeling man in a frightening situation whose dimensions he doesn't quite fully understand, responding the only way he knows how.

Lee's film may have heralded a breakthrough for black directors into the mainstream, but 1989 also saw a racially sensitive film like *Glory* evolve from more traditional and white Hollywood sources. Directed by Ed Zwick (creator of television's *thirtysomething*), the film dealt with the Civil War's 54th Massachusetts Infantry, an African American volunteer unit led by a white abolitionist Robert Gould Shaw (Matthew Broderick) who shed their lives in the cause of freedom. *Glory* would have likely been more profitable had it centered the action on the idealistic white officer. This time around, however, Hollywood gave more than equal time to the courageous members of the black regiment (e.g., Rawlins [Morgan Freeman] and Trip [Denzel Washington]), who, if not richly nuanced characters, are never reduced to stereotypes—racial or military genre film ones.

There was one other extremely popular mainstream 1989 film to touch on racial issues. Bruce Beresford's luminously acted, Oscar-winning *Driving Miss Daisy* (Jessica Tandy won an Oscar for best actress) deals with the warm relationship of a crotchety, elderly Jewish lady and her gracious, wise, black chauffeur Hoke (Morgan Freeman again) who serves her. Set in the South of a couple of decades back, the film is a too neatly calibrated work that intelligently choreographs the nuances of their relationship without disturbing an audience either politically or psychologically. The relationship is an inequitable, mistress–servant one, but Daisy's power is muted by age and her dependency on Hoke. The friendship permits a white audience to feel emotionally and socially at ease because Hoke is a courtly and restrained man whom they like and who almost never directly challenges the social status quo. The audience's sympathetic identification with this nostalgic, safe relationship makes them feel virtuous and liberal without their ever having to confront the pain and tortuous complexity of present-day black–white relations.

Though the late 1980s saw the production of relatively sophisticated films about black life and black–white relationships, this heightened cinematic consciousness did not find a parallel in the society at large. General Colin Powell may have become the first black to head the Joint Chiefs of Staff under President Bush, Bill Cosby's sitcom one of the top-rated television shows of the period, and Spike Lee a popular director and pitchman for athletic shoes, but, in the main, white acceptance extended to talented, elite blacks, not to the vast majority of the black population. In fact, during the 1980s, the Reagan presidency signaled, by word and deed, that racism was acceptable; "decent," upper-class George Bush used coded racist appeals as part of his presidential campaign; and there was a marked increase in general racial tension and even a proliferation of racial incidents on college campuses. What films like *Glory* possibly signified for a white audience was an affirmation of those democratic ideals that represented their best selves on questions of race. It was much less painful for the public to connect with this moral vision on film than to try to actualize these ideals by wrestling with all the complex social variables surrounding everyday racial issues.

The 1980s not only saw several black directors finally get the chance to make films, but there was a minor renaissance of women directors as well. From its inception, male-owned and -controlled Hollywood had closed off the opportunity for women to play a significant role behind the camera. There were only a handful that were allowed to direct films—Alice Guy-Blache, Dorothy Arzner, Ida Lupino, and Elaine May—none of their work explicitly feminist. The feminist movement, however, changed the situation for younger women directors, and in the mid- and late 1970s, overtly feminist films, like Joan Micklin Silver's *Hester Street* (1975) and Claudia Weill's *Girlfriends* (1978), were made.[28]

After these films appeared, women directors could move away from expressly feminist content while rooting their work in the assumption that female characters no longer perceive themselves solely in terms of their relationships with men and, as a corollary, that they would live more independent lives based on their own individual choices. Some of the most interesting 1980s films made by women directors were commercial, mainstream works like Barbra Streisand's *Yentl* (1983) and Susan Seidelman's offbeat second feature, *Desperately Seeking Susan* (1985), about two very different women switching identities (Madonna and Rosanna Arquette), while others were low-budget films like Joyce Chopra's *Smooth Talk* (1986), an adaptation of Joyce Carol Oates's story about an adolescent girl's frightening sexual initiation, and Donna Deitch's film about a passionate lesbian love affair set in the middle America of 1959 Reno, Nevada, *Desert Hearts* (1986).

Yentl, the most mainstream, was the result of Streisand's 15-year dream to adapt an I. B. Singer story for the screen. Streisand, in the megalomaniacal mode of an Orson Welles, produced, directed, starred (she sings every song), and even cowrote this big-budget, overly orchestrated, and sometimes bathetic work about a rebellious, intellectually avid Jewish shtetl girl, Yentl, who dresses up as a boy in order to study the Talmud. (Women were excluded from the world of learning in the orthodox Jewish religious tradition of the shtetl.) Streisand loves to underline, using split mirrors to connote Yentl's split self and a bird as a symbol of her flight, panning to a chicken as a metaphor for gossiping women, and bathing every sacred object (e.g., a talis) in a golden light.

Nevertheless, despite its heavy-handed and bloated images, *Yentl* is an ambitious, sometimes suggestive work that raises questions about the role of women, and about female bonding. Yentl, in her male disguise, establishes a link with a beautiful, deferential, traditional woman Hadass (Amy Irving), which is more intimate and tender than any male–female relationship in the film. The relationship is open to a variety of interpretations: as a homoerotic passion; as a nonsexual affirmation of female bonding; as an appreciation of the role domestic, supportive women play that would appeal to Streisand's more conventional fans; and the underside of her appreciation of Hadass—an independent woman's revulsion with Hadass's passivity and capacity for shape changing.[29] The film also concludes on a feminist note. Yentl sacrifices the man she loves—the kindly, manly Talmudist Avigdor (Mandy Patinkin), who wants her to stay at home and be a traditional wife, maintaining that a wise woman knows everything without opening a book, and heads for America to try out her wings and find room to grow.

Besides Streisand, there were other women who had an impact on Hollywood as producers. Jane Fonda formed a production company and made *China Syndrome* and *Nine to Five* (1981), Jessica Lange produced *Country*, Sally Field produced *Places in the Heart*, and Goldie Hawn together with Anthea Sylbert produced shallow, pop feminist films like *Private Benjamin* (1980) and *Protocol*

(1984). Though there is no guarantee that the fact of some women achieving power in Hollywood meant that a more profound feminist perspective would inform its product, the bottom line is still profit, and risk taking is usually left to filmmakers outside the system.

The 1980s saw a minor breakthrough for women directors and producers and for films not only projecting a feminist perspective but also dealing with gay and lesbian sexuality. Until the 1960s, most Hollywood films submerged, displaced, or hid any mention of homosexuality. Then, with the relaxation of the Production Code, films like *The Boys in the Band* (1970) and *The Killing of Sister George* (1968) were made that dealt with openly gay and lesbian characters but tended to perpetuate the most blatant, negative stereotypes—hysterically effeminate men and muscular and sadistic male hustlers and angry butch or sleek predatory lesbians. In these films, gay or lesbian characters were also rarely given the chance to have a happy, full life. However, in 1980s films like Bill Sherwood's *Parting Glances* (1985) and the previously mentioned *Desert Hearts*, a gay and lesbian cinema that defined itself in its own terms and voice made its appearance (e.g., best exemplified by the openly lesbian Cay's [Patricia Charbonneau] remark in *Desert Hearts*, "I don't act that way to change the world, I act that way so that the world doesn't change me.")

The films were a hopeful augur of future works that would authentically portray gay and lesbian life and consciousness and neither romanticize nor denigrate it.[30]

Despite the clear shift in Hollywood's attitude toward women and greater openness to unstereotyped images of gay life, the last years of the decade saw films that evoked strains of an antifeminist backlash. In very different ways, films like *Baby Boom* (1987), *Fatal Attraction* (1987), *Broadcast News* (1987), and *Working Girl* (1988) affirmed marriage and often projected negative images of independent career women. *Baby Boom* reverses the pattern of feminist films, centering on an ad executive, played by Diane Keaton, who leaves her high-powered job in Manhattan for a fulfilling life as mother and apron-clad housewife in small-town Vermont. Adrian Lyne's slick, overheated, manipulative *Fatal Attraction* skillfully creates frissons of suspense and fear while constructing an implicitly regressive, antifeminist vision. In *Fatal Attraction*, Dan (Michael Douglas), a New York attorney with a loving home and happy marriage to a beautiful, thoroughly domestic wife, has an intensely sexual weekend affair with a seductive, single book editor, Alex (Glenn Close). Afterward, he tries to brush her off, but the career woman, who lives in an inferno-like apartment, becomes vindictive and turns out to be a wild, murderous figure. Though basically a well-made, predictable thriller, the image it conveys of the unmarried, professional woman as pathetic and mad reaffirms the value of marriage and home as havens of warmth and stability and acts as a warning to women of the unnaturalness of living independent, solitary lives.

The backlash elements in writer-director James L. Brooks's (creator of the *Mary Tyler Moore Show*) *Broadcast News* are more subtle. This briskly paced film is filled with witty one-liners and has an insider's knowledge of how television deals with the news and newscasters. However, *Broadcast News* is much less a critique of the content, role, and value of television news than an updated portrait of a love triangle whose emotional life is no deeper than the wisecracks and the well-honed set pieces that permeate the film. The romance is salvaged a bit by extremely strong performances by the film's leads: Albert Brooks as Aaron, a knowledgeable, committed reporter who was born with Woody Allen's whine, insecurity, and self-deflective humor; William Hurt as Tom, a handsome, decent, intellectually limited anchorman whose pleasing and natural television persona make him the darling of the media executives; and Holly Hunter as Jane (an Oscar-winning performance), an extremely effective, bright, bossy news producer who has an unhappy private life. Implicit in the film is the notion that any woman like Jane who is a driven, successful, morally serious professional would, by necessity, live a tearful and solitary existence—that for a professional woman to have a happy personal life, she would have to submerge some part of herself into a conventional female persona.

Even Mike Nichols's glossy, populist fable *Working Girl* projected an anti-feminist strain. Nichols's slight fairy tale about a sweet, working-class Staten Island secretary, Tess (Melanie Griffith), whose financial wizardry both wins the heart of a Wall Street broker and turns her into an executive with a secretary and office of her own, is, on one level, a scenario for Reaganism—creating a world where overnight success and the big money (especially of the Wall Street variety) are available for anyone who has confidence and drive and can appropriate the style and accent of the upper-middle class. On another level, the film is a put-down of the type of cold, manipulative superwoman—Tess's boss Katharine (Sigourney Weaver), whose lack of softness and femininity help lead to her fall.[31] *Working Girl* is not interested in engaging in a serious critique of the corporate world or of feminist claims, but in Tess it found a heroine who combines ambition, shrewdness, and female vulnerability—a perfect alternative to all those hard, threatening women whose supposed female virtues and characteristics disappeared with success in the public world.

Films containing strains of antifeminism were just one of a number of cinematic currents during the last years of the decade. A popular, Capraesque fable like *Field of Dreams* (1989) sees the film's hero, Ray Kinsella (Kevin Costner)—a 1960s activist turned Iowa corn farmer—resurrect what the film sees as the purity of the past by following the instructions of a heavenly voice and transforming a cornfield into a baseball diamond filled with old ballplayers like

Shoeless Joe Jackson. Kinsella does this not only to recover an idyllic America but also to ease the pain of a disenchanted writer so that he can rediscover his muse and to bring about his own reconciliation with the father he once rejected—baseball becoming both a social and a psychological panacea.

Field of Dreams provides a great many simplistic soliloquies about the need both to dream and to re-create the innocence of childhood—a mixture of 1960s counterculture spirituality combined with the myth of the American rural past. It also attacks the utilitarian money culture and small-town censorship (an easy target), but its alternative vision is apolitical and nebulous, consisting of little more than a set of greeting card platitudes.

The soft-minded, nostalgic *Field of Dreams* was just one of the popular successes of 1989 that included a disparate group of films. Among them were the previously discussed *Do the Right Thing, Driving Miss Daisy,* and *Born on the Fourth of July,* a relentlessly middle-brow and pop homage to poetry and freedom like the *Dead Poets Society,* and big-budget, summer films like the imaginatively designed (influenced by Fritz Lang's expressionist *Metropolis* and Reginald Marsh's painting) and totally impersonal comic book epic *Batman* and Spielberg's *Indiana Jones and the Last Crusade*—the third and most human (which is not saying much) of the playful boy's adventure trilogy. Clearly, no single political and social trend could be gleaned from such radically different works, but the variety itself was a sign that Hollywood had become a touch less dependent on a teenage and action-oriented audience and could make a few films that would appeal to literate adults, albeit most of these films took few formal or intellectual risks.

NOTES

1. Lou Cannon, *Ronald Reagan* (New York: G. P. Putnam's Sons, 1982), pp. 329–413.

2. Nicolaus Mills, "Culture in an Age of Money," *Dissent* (Winter 1990): pp. 11–17.

3. Ibid., p. 13.

4. Gregg Kilday, "The Eighties," *Film Comment* (November–December 1989), p. 65.

5. Ibid., p. 66.

6. Budd Schulberg, "What Makes Hollywood Run Now?," *New York Times Magazine* (April 27, 1980), pp. 52–88. See also Leslie Wayne, "Hollywood Sequels Are Just the Ticket," *New York Times* (July 18, 1982), pp. 1–17.

7. Veronica Geng, "Pearls Before Swine: Review of Ordinary People," *Soho Weekly News* (September 17, 1980), pp. 58–59.

8. Barbara Quart, "Tootsie," *Cineaste* 12, no. 4 (Summer 1983), pp. 40–42.

9. Richard Schickel, "Slam! Bang! A Movie Movie," *Time* (June 15, 1981), pp. 74–76.

10. Michiko Kakutani, "The Two Faces of Spielberg—Horrors vs. Hope," *New York Times* (May 30, 1982), pp. 1, 30. See also Pauline Kael, "The Pure and the Impure," *The New Yorker* (June 14, 1982), pp. 119–22.

11. Richard Schickel, "At Last, Kate and Hank!," *Time* (November 18, 1981), pp. 112–13.

12. Aaron Latham, "Warren Beatty, Seriously," *Rolling Stone* (April 1, 1982), p. 19.

13. Belle Gale Chevigny, Kate Ellis, Ann Kaplan, and Leonard Quart, "Talking 'Reds,'" *Socialist Review* 12, no. 2 (March–April 1982), pp. 109–24.

14. Ibid.

15. Robert A. Rosenstone, *Romantic Revolutionary: A Biography of John Reed* (New York: Alfred A. Knopf, 1975), p. 4.

16. Richard Grenier, "Bolshevism for the 80's," *Commentary* (March 1982), pp. 56–63.

17. Joy Gould Boyum, "'Reds': Love and Revolution," *Wall Street Journal* (December 4, 1981), p. 35.

18. Al Auster and Leonard Quart, "Counterculture Revisited: An Interview with John Sayles," *Cineaste* 11, no. 1 (Winter 1980–81), pp. 16–19.

19. Fred Siegel, "Blissed Out and Loving It," *Commonweal* (February 9, 1990), p. 76.

20. Terry Christensen, *Reel Politics: American Movies from "Birth of a Nation" to "Platoon"* (New York: Basil Blackwell, 1987), pp. 165–66.

21. Albert Auster and Leonard Quart, *How the War Was Remembered: Hollywood and Vietnam* (New York: Praeger, 1988), pp. 99–112.

22. Ibid., pp. 131–45.

23. Christopher Sharrett, "Born on the Fourth of July," *Cineaste* 17, no. 4 (Spring 1990), pp. 48–50.

24. Elayne Rapping, "Hollywood's Youth Cult Films," *Cineaste* 16, no. 1–2 (Winter, 1987–88), pp. 14–19.

25. Ibid., p. 18.

26. Editorial, *Cineaste* 17, no. 2 (Fall 1989), p. 2.

27. Eric Perkins, "Renewing the African-American Cinema: The Films of Spike Lee," *Cineaste* 17, no. 4 (Spring 1990), p. 8.

28. Barbara Koenig Quart, *Women Directors: The Emergence of a New Cinema* (New York: Praeger, 1988), pp. 37–38.

29. Ibid., pp. 83–85.

30. Andrea Weiss, "From the Margins: New Image of Gays in the Cinema," *Cineaste* 15, no. 1 (Fall 1986), pp. 4–8.

31. Caryn James, "Are Feminist Heroines an Endangered Species?," *New York Times: Sunday Arts and Leisure* (July 16, 1989), p. 15.

7

THE 1990s

In his magisterial historical study of the 20th century, *The Age of Extremes*, the British historian E. J. Hobsbawm refers to the period between 1914 and 1991 as the short 20th century—the decades from the beginning of World War I to the fall of the Soviet Union. From this chronology, one can assume that Hobsbawm considered two key landmarks of that period to be the rise of communism in Russia and its ultimate disintegration.[1] Consequently, our chronology of the 1990s in American film begins on November 9, 1989, the day the Berlin Wall fell. On that date, irrevocable changes occurred for Americans and for people throughout the world, and the old Cold War certainties passed into history and a new post–Cold War era began.

Hardly anyone could foresee the end of communism in Russia and in Eastern Europe. Throughout the whole Cold War era, there had been rumblings of discontent in Eastern Europe from the Berlin riots of 1954 to the Hungarian uprising in 1956 to the Prague spring and its suppression in 1968 and the rise of Solidarity in Poland in the 1980s. Nonetheless, Soviet tanks had little trouble in repressing these acts of rebellion.

With hindsight, there was even evidence of increasing discontent in the Soviet Union. Nikita Khrushchev's 1954 denunciation of Stalin's crimes may be said to have been the first step in what would ultimately lead to the demise of communism. But along the way, there had been an increasing vociferous if not very powerful band of Jewish refuseniks and dissidents, led until his death by the physicist Andrei Sakharov. There was also a small but very brave underground movement of literary, political, and philosophical *samzidat*, which, if they hadn't shaken Soviet power, at least gave evidence a real opposition existed.

However, when the Soviet Union collapsed, there were those who quickly took credit for its demise. In America, one theory held that it was President Ronald Reagan's defense strategy, which practically tripled defense spending and encouraged surrogate wars against the Soviets in places like Afghanistan, that forced the Soviet Union into economic and then political bankruptcy. While this hypothesis could serve as a potent campaign slogan, it was far from the truth.[2]

A far more important reason for the breakup of the Soviet Union was the unwillingness of the moribund Communist Party to carry out economic and political reform. Reform was necessitated by decreasing economic productivity during the so-called years of stagnation under Leonid Brezhnev's gerontocracy and the need to combat the overweening power and privilege of a corrupt bureaucracy—the "nomenklatura."

Reform was initiated under the leadership of Mikhail Gorbachev. After he came to power in 1985, Gorbachev began a campaign of glasnost and perestroika. The former was an opening to the intellectual and cultural expression that had been suppressed throughout the entire history of the Soviet Union, and the latter was an attempt to restructure both the economy and the political culture.

Unfortunately for Gorbachev, his reforms opened a Pandora's box of previously repressed demands among the Eastern European countries and Soviet Union nationalities. This resulted in pressure from nationalities like the Latvians and Georgians for independence and Eastern European satellites demanding freedom from Soviet domination. The response by communist hardliners to these demands and to Gorbachev's policies was the ineffectual 1991 coup attempt, easily resisted by liberals led by Russian president Boris Yeltsin and ultimately resulting in the end of Soviet power.[3]

The demise of the Soviet Union left the United States the sole remaining superpower, a position that carried its own risks and problems. Nationalism, which had ironically been so long repressed in Eastern Europe by communism, reared its tribal and savage head. In the 1990s, the United States watched, at times impotently, as the former Yugoslavia descended into a series of chaotic and bloody wars of secession in Croatia, Bosnia, and Kosovo. The latter forcing the United States and its NATO allies into a 78-day air war to coerce the increasingly genocidal Serbs to retreat back to their homeland.

Europe wasn't the sole venue for the rising tide of nationalism. In the Middle East, Iraq, under the ruthless, quixotic, and cunning leadership of President Saddam Hussein, invaded the oil-rich kingdom of Kuwait, only to be turned back by a 42-day air and ground campaign led by an outraged United States and a large contingent of its European and Middle Eastern allies.

Far more threatening in the Middle East than the increasingly isolated Saddam Hussein was the dramatic rise of Islamic fundamentalism and its weapon of choice: terrorism. The United States had already been badly hurt by that weapon in 1983 when 241 U.S. Marines were killed when Islamic terrorists drove their explosive laden truck into the marines' billet in Lebanon. But at home, Americans had the illusion that they were immune to attacks—that is, until the February 1993 bombing of New York City's World Trade Center, in which six people were killed as a result of bombs set by a group of Islamic terrorists from a number of Arab countries. By the end of the decade, Americans trembled far more at the name of Osama bin Laden, an Islamic fundamentalist terrorist whose fanatic followers had bombed two American embassies in Africa in 1998, than they ever had at the military power of Saddam Hussein.

Although Saddam Hussein and Osama bin Laden might give Americans nightmares of bomb plots and poison gas attacks, a far more potent threat to American stability came from the quickening pace of financial and business globalization. With companies like McDonald's and Nike represented all over the world and foreign companies buying American ones (DaimlerChrysler) as well as American companies merging with and taking over foreign ones (Merrill-Lynch), business was becoming far more international than it had ever been—so much so that a dip on the Hong Kong stock market or the Japanese Nikkei securities index was almost certain to cause trouble the next day on the American financial markets. In fact, in 1998, America's almost decadelong prosperity was placed in serious jeopardy by the domino fall of Thailand's currency, followed in swift succession by the collapse of the Indonesian and South Korean economies and a deep Japanese recession. Were it not for the efforts of the American Federal Reserve quickly lowering interest rates in the United States and the International Monetary Fund pumping funds into these bankrupt economies, there might have been a worldwide financial collapse rivaling that of 1929.[4]

Prosperity and an almost decade's long soaring of the stock market (the Dow Jones stood at 3,500 in 1993 and was at 11,000 by 2000) was one of the hallmarks of the eight years of Bill Clinton's presidency. Clinton, then the virtually unknown governor of Arkansas, seemed to come out of nowhere in 1992 to challenge a popular incumbent president. He skillfully used the slogan "It's the economy, stupid," with its explicit message that the economy is in decline as a brickbat to defeat President George H. W. Bush in the 1992 election.[5]

More important, Clinton staked a claim as a New Democrat, moving away from the politically and economically untenable New Deal consensus that emphasized expanding the welfare state and increasing social spending and recasting the party's appeal after years of Republican dominance. He embraced free markets and the balanced budget and committed himself to the shrinking of government programs. He also took away all sorts of wedge issues from the Republicans, like crime and welfare, by providing Democratic alternatives that spoke of greater individual responsibility for one's life without obliterating the notion that government had some obligation to create a more equitable and just society. Clinton's creed could be best summed up in this statement when he began his campaign for the presidency in 1992: "Government's responsibility is to create more opportunity. The people's responsibility is to make the most of it."[6]

Consequently, Clinton committed himself to a limited social contract that offered social reforms like national service, school construction, the assault weapons ban, a higher minimum wage, earned income tax credits for the working poor, and welfare reform, whose meanest provisions Clinton has tried to modify. (On the whole, welfare reform was a necessary though flawed move away from traditional liberalism that has so far worked somewhat better than expected.) He also carried out his campaign promise to choose "an administration that looks like America" with the appointment of unprecedented numbers of minorities to major administrative positions, including the first black commerce secretary (the consummate political insider Ron Brown), the first female attorney general and secretary of state, and a second woman to the Supreme Court.[7]

Of course, there were failures, like the FBI siege of the Branch Davidian compound in Waco, Texas, and the defeat of the highly touted but unwieldy attempt at health care reform presided over by First Lady Hillary Clinton. And the 1994 election saw the Democrats lose control of both houses of Congress and the president seemingly being pushed into irrelevancy. Clinton, however, was blessed with enemies like Congressman Newt Gingrich, who became Speaker of the House in 1994. Gingrich, a plump, silver-haired, demi-intellectual conservative, devised a strategy (the Contract with America) where business groups would work closely with social conservatives like the Christian Coalition to build a common agenda of deregulation, privatization, tax cuts, school prayer, and opposition to abortion and gun control. Gingrich and his band of House conservatives (many of them from the South) overreached themselves, and soon the strategy began to break down. Voters may have felt a distrust for government, but they didn't want to turn the clock back to the 1950s, and they didn't share Gingrich's antipathy toward Medicare, the Environmental Protection Agency, and the Department of Education. In addition, when the Republicans tried to pass a budget bill over presidential vetoes and allowed the government to shut down, they went too far and gave Clinton a weapon to beat them with in the 1996 election. The ultraconservative wing of the Republicans did not disappear, but the party in the 1996 election, by choosing a traditional Republican—Bob Dole—to run against Clinton, opted for a less ideological form of conservatism.[8]

Though Clinton may be remembered primarily for his domestic achievements, he also helped broker and stage the signing of an interim Middle East settlement (including the handshake between Palestine Liberation Organization Chairman Arafat and Israeli Prime Minister Rabin) and played a role in settling the conflict between the eternally warring parties in Northern Ireland, the negotiation of the Dayton Accords (which ended the Bosnian War), and the successful conclusion of the Kosovo air attacks. Though none of these conflicts can be said to have been fully resolved and can blow up again, still the United States successfully exerted its power in all these conflagrations.

Domestic and foreign policy achievements aside, it was Clinton, the complex personality, who dominated the politics of the 1990s. Clinton was a charismatic man of preternatural political gifts, impressive intellect, and policy expertise with a talent for public empathy possessed by few other American politicians. Talents that were marred by a flawed character that seemed to lack a genuine emotional or moral center. One often felt when listening to him that feelings and political arguments and positions, even if he believed in them, came too easily and that more reflection, introspection, and social commitment were in order. In addition, Clinton's inability to tell the truth went beyond the professional politician's normal prevarications, and he had a sexual appetite that led him into politically irresponsible and self-destructive actions.

Perhaps nothing illuminates his personality than these two statements made by Clinton, one during his first presidential campaign and the other during his presidency. The first was a memorable moment in Dover, New Hampshire, in February 1992 just before election day of the New Hampshire primary. It was a period when Clinton's candidacy seemed about to unravel as a result of the Gennifer Flowers sex scandal and the controversy over his Vietnam-era draft status. Talking to the audience about their problems and not mentioning his own, Clinton said in closing, "I'll be with you till the last dog dies."[9] It's the kind of comment that was emblematic of Clinton's empathetic form of populism.

The second was the humiliating moment almost six years later in January 1998 when a red-faced Clinton told a press conference, "I did not have sex with that woman—Miss Lewinsky." He was forced to retract that comment seven months later when he acknowledged that he did have the infamously "inappropriate relationship" with her. The confession revealed Clinton at his worst—hiding his adulterous conduct behind euphemisms like "inappropriate relationship" just as he had tried to cloak his extramarital affairs with nebulous remarks like "problems in our marriage" in his appearance with his wife Hillary on 60 Minutes in 1992 at the time of the Gennifer Flowers scandal.[10]

For a president whose fondest desire was to leave a brilliant and noble legacy, it is especially galling that perhaps the one thing that the Clinton presidency would be remembered for most was that he was the third president in American history ever to be impeached. Again Clinton was saved by the booming economy, a shift in the public's attitudes toward sexual transgressions, and the nature of his enemies. The economy's unprecedented success caused many Americans, who might otherwise have disapproved of his moral conduct, to nevertheless give him high marks for his presidential leadership and refuse to support his removal from office. In addition, the 1990s public consumed vast quantities of celebrity gossip, confessional entertainment, and self-help advice that blurred the distinction between fame and notoriety and also made them more forgiving of misbehavior. The other element was the grim self-righteousness and clear political motivation and ineptitude of his gang of impeachment stalkers led by the implacable special prosecutor Kenneth Starr.

Clinton's struggle against impeachment was also helped by the tin-eared House Managers of impeachment. These die-hard conservatives, led by avuncular Henry Hyde, chairman of the House Judiciary Committee, refused to listen to the American people, who had indicated repeatedly by public opinion polls and in the 1998 elections (where the Republicans lost seats in the House and Senate) that they did not want Clinton impeached. The committee Republicans were obsessed with ousting a Clinton who they abhorred as a baby-boomer representative of the 1960s draft-dodging, pot-smoking culture of permissiveness and, more important, as the man who helped prevent the triumph of conservatism.[11]

Impeachment aside, any final evaluation of the Clinton years was sure to note that its most significant political characteristic was a skillful shunning of radical change and bold solutions. Clinton's Third Way political perspective became a model for European Social Democrats like Tony Blair and Gerhard Schröder in their ascent to power. Nonetheless, there was one area where radical change had occurred, and this was just as likely to have been spurred by the Clinton administration as it was to have occurred despite it. Never before had the United States had as long a period of economic expansion as under Clinton. In addition, that expansion included low unemployment (the lowest in 30 years) with virtually no inflation and increasing productivity. In addition, an economy was taking shape that was more and more reliant on the computer and cyberspace-related e-commerce. No further evidence of this is needed than the fact that when Clinton took office in 1993 there were 50 websites on the Internet and that, by 2000, there were 50 million. Economists and entrepreneurs more and more referred to this economic state of affairs as the "New Economy."[12]

The Clinton administration had helped this New Economy come into being because of its economic plan to reduce the deficit and by spurring free trade
with agreements such as the North American Free Trade Agreement. But it
had also helped it by removing the last vestiges of government regulation in
many sectors of the economy. Among these were the Telecommunications Act
of 1996, which leveled the economic playing field for television, cable, and
telephone companies, and in the waning days of the century the repeal of the
Glass-Steagall Act, a piece of Depression-era legislation that had erected an
impenetrable firewall between the financial activities of banks, stock market
companies, and insurance businesses.

The film industry was enormously affected by some of these economic
changes. One little noticed change was the expiration of the Federal Communications Commission's financial interest and syndication rule in 1995. This rule
had prevented networks from having any financial stake in programs produced
in prime time. With the rule gone, the old studios that had made television production a mainstay of their profits suddenly felt these profits threatened. Similarly, the Telecommunications Act of 1996 removed the prohibition against
owning more than 12 television stations.

As a result, a series of megamergers began to convulse Hollywood. The first
of these in 1995 was the Disney studio's merger with Capitol Cities/ABC,
which owned the ABC-TV network. The following year, Time Warner, which
owned Warner's movie studio, saw its holdings greatly expanded by the addition of Turner Broadcast Networks, which owned cable television and sports
franchises and the Castle Rock movie production company. In 1999, Viacom,
which owned Paramount studios along with the Blockbuster Video store chain,
MTV, Nickelodeon cable networks, and the publisher Simon and Schuster,
merged with CBS. These mergers created synergistic companies that could
conceivably buy books from their publishing arms, produce movies from the
scripts, advertise them over their networks, and then turn the more successful
ones into miniseries or sitcoms.

While the influence of these mergers was undoubtedly profound on an economic level, on an artistic one, Hollywood was dramatically transformed by
the growing significance of the independent cinema movement. Though always a factor in American film as a training ground for new talent or as a
medium for directorial experimentation and political and social criticism by
idiosyncratic and original artists like John Cassavetes and John Sayles, the
independent movement had never been able to gain the attention of large
audiences.[13]

However, after Robert Redford's founding of the Sundance Film Festival in
1984—a festival devoted almost exclusively to independent documentary and
fiction films—the movement blossomed. The independent American cinema's breakthrough moment, however, didn't come until 1989, when Steven

Soderbergh's independent film *Sex, Lies and Videotape* signed up with an aggressive distribution company (Miramax), won a best-film prize at the Cannes Film Festival, and then went on to rack up large box office grosses in America. Suddenly, studio executives who had long ignored the independent cinema descended on the Sundance Film Festival with open checkbooks and long-term development deals for recent graduates of film schools or precocious filmmakers who had maxed out their credit cards trying to make their dream film. When they got there, they found that a number of small companies like Miramax, New Line, and October had already monopolized the situation by creating relationships that assured them the pick of the independents. The response of the studios was to buy these companies and let them function in a boutique arrangement within the larger studios (e.g., Disney/Miramax and Warner/New Line), an arrangement that was sometimes referred to as "Indiewood."

Nonetheless, these smaller companies did have a bracing effect on Hollywood. They funded movies that dealt with issues (e.g., lesbianism, AIDS, suburban life, and racial and ethnic minorities) that Hollywood had long since ignored in favor of romantic comedies, high-concept works about ghosts and children inhabiting adult's bodies, and action films with lots of car chases, explosions, and special effects. The defining moment for independent cinema came at the Academy Awards ceremony of 1996, when four of the five nominees for best picture were produced by independents (*The English Patient*, *Shine*, *Secrets and Lies*, and *Fargo*). However, perhaps the most striking achievement of the independents came in 1998, when Miramax studio's stylishly light period piece *Shakespeare in Love* beat out the highly acclaimed favorite, Steven Spielberg's patriotic epic *Saving Private Ryan*, receiving the Academy Award for best picture.[14]

It was a victory that undoubtedly owed as much to the marketing genius and chutzpah of Miramax's reigning minimogul Harvey Weinstein as to the movie's quality, demonstrating how much the independents had come to resemble the studios. The independent success story was achieved as much by deal making, media manipulation, and playing hardball as by talent. Many of the directors had less interest in creating original works—expressing something they can't say within the system—than in using their films as a path to fame and the big dollars of the Hollywood mainstream. Still, with the advent of digital video—a format that will permit anybody with $50,000 to make high-production-value films—there will be no diminution of fledgling directors making independent films. The quality of them, not their quantity, is the question.

The Hollywood mainstream, however, still had to churn out film in accord with its traditional, audience-pleasing formulae. Like everyone else, Hollywood was ill prepared for the end of the Cold War and the post–Cold War era. Even a year after the fall of the Berlin Wall, the film industry was still producing films that reeked of the Cold War, albeit with faint hints of the coming collapse of communism. The most popular of these was action-film director John McTiernan's (e.g., *Die Hard*, 1988) *The Hunt for Red October* (1990). The film is based on a Tom Clancy techno-thriller that remained on best-seller lists for over two years and sold as many as 5 million copies. *The Hunt for Red October*'s narrative revolves around the Soviet Union's highest-ranking submarine commander, a gruff, authoritarian Marko Alexandrovich Ramius (Sean Connery) and his officers who plot to defect. Their plan is to take with them the most sophisticated high-tech Soviet submarine ever built—one with such speed and undetectability that it could hover near the coast of the United States without ever being discovered.

When a patrolling U.S. sub discovers the *Red October*, the reflexive response of American leaders is that this is the beginning of a Soviet first strike. This notion is successfully challenged by a bright CIA analyst, Jack Ryan (Alec Baldwin), who believes that the commander wants to defect. Predictably, he joins Ramius and a U.S. sub commander and helps thwart the best efforts of the Soviet sub fleet to destroy the *Red October*. The film is all crosscutting between sub interiors, close-ups of advanced technical equipment, intercuts of the immense *Jaws*-looking *Red October*, and reaction shots of anxious Soviet and American naval personnel. The film's emphasis on submarine technology dwarfs its utterly flat characters and perfunctory, banal dialogue.

What is most interesting about a mechanical film like *The Hunt for Red October*, especially in light of the Cold War's end, are its political assumptions, not its aesthetics. The most striking was that Soviet naval officers, certainly among the most privileged group in their society, had become so disillusioned with their country and its ideology (the sub's political officer, who mouths the party's line, is killed by Ramius) that they felt compelled to defect. (Ramius's background as a Lithuanian provides added resonance with its reference to the disgruntled Baltic nations and their desire for independence from Russian domination.)

Of course, these assumptions are Clancy's responsibility since he always took a tough line on the Cold War. They point to the widely held belief, even before the fall of the Berlin Wall (the book appeared before the collapse), that faith in the Soviet system had almost disappeared. They also implicitly acknowledge the fact that despite this, the Cold War left such a dangerous residue of mistrust that one mistake might still lead to catastrophe and that there was a need for reasonable men like Jack Ryan and Marko Ramius to overcome the last vestiges of Cold War paranoia.

The intensity with which American cinema still pursued Cold War narratives and scenarios is in sharp contrast with the lack of interest in constructing stories that dealt with post–Cold War events such as the Gulf War. Since the war in 1991, only two studio-produced films specifically dealt with it: *Courage Under Fire* (1996) and *Three Kings* (1999). This is especially odd in view of the tremendous hoopla that greeted the victorious end of the war, especially the declarations that the so-called Vietnam syndrome was finally dead and buried. Perhaps the reason was that Americans took little pride in defeating a country with the gross national product of Kentucky and that the victory remained tarnished by the fact that after all the smart bombs and stupid politicians, Saddam Hussein still remained in power in Baghdad, outmaneuvering all the international weapons inspectors sent to Iraq to try to enforce UN sanctions.

Courage Under Fire, though an earnest attempt at dealing with the Gulf War, was hardly the kind of film to strike many imitative sparks. Directed by Edward Zwick (*Glory*, 1989) and starring Denzel Washington and Meg Ryan, it depicts Lieutenant Colonel Nathaniel Serling's (Washington) search for the truth about Captain Karen Walden's (Ryan) possible Medal of Honor Award–winning heroism during the war. Beside the introduction of certain contemporary politically correct tropes—like a black officer investigating the battlefield field actions of a white woman officer—the film used an old-fashioned *Rashamon*-like structure as the basis of the narrative (some of Captain Walden's troops claiming she was a coward, others affirming her courage). *Courage Under Fire*, however, offered very little insight into the nature of the war itself except for Serling's own guilt and remorse over a "friendly-fire" accident where he killed American soldiers during it (the majority of U.S. casualties in the war having been killed by friendly fire). Ultimately, *Courage Under Fire* doesn't go much further than the liberal problem film of the 1940s—personalizing the social problem and settling for an angry sexist villain and leaving out any sense that the military as an institution may have its own difficulties in dealing with women officers.

Three Kings, directed by an independent film director David Russell (e.g., *Flirting with Disaster*, 1996), is a hybrid work—on the one hand an imaginative absurdist take on the war and on the other a conventional action film. Three reservists—solid, straight family man Sergeant Troy Barlow (Mark Wahlberg); glowering, Jesus-loving Chief Eldin (Ice Cube); and a sweet comic redneck Conrad Vig (Spike Jonze)—find the map to Saddam's hidden stash of stolen Kuwaiti gold bullion. Led by Special Forces Major Archie Gates (George Clooney), they go on a postwar expedition to steal it for themselves and on the way become involved in their own miniwar against the Iraqi army units. Russell shoots the war with a handheld camera, and it chaotically explodes on the screen with scenes popping out of other scenes and with stark close-ups of what bullets can do to a soldier's guts. It's a media war, the film keeps

reminding us, where the army totally collaborates with the media and ubiquitous television reporters build their careers by frantically racing around com-
peting for stories. It's a war where most of the American soldiers never see
combat and learn most of what they know about the war from CNN.

The film's political perspective is conveyed by the heroic Clooney character, playing a variation on his macho, antiauthoritarian, unbelievably adept
television doctor. He lectures his American cohorts on how the war was for
nothing since the United States encouraged the uprising against Saddam but
then refused to support it when we defeated Iraq. It's a war that American
troops engaged in, presumably to help a nation, Kuwait, preserve its independence but also to protect America's oil sources. Russell depicts it also as a war
whose legacy is not freedom but a country of mines and car hulks littering the
desert, innocent Iraqi children killed in bombing attacks, Shiite rebels being
shot, and cranes black with oil from the burning wells. The film is most incisive when it satirizes the power of globalization exemplified by an Iraqi army
torturer, trained by the U.S. military, having a discussion with the imprisoned
Troy on the pros and cons of Michael Jackson's cosmetic surgery. In fact, everybody in the film—Americans, rebels, and the Iraqi army—is obsessed with
brand names, opening businesses, and American mass culture. In one scene
when the Americans descend on an Iraqi bunker, they discover rooms filled
with goods stolen from Kuwait, including everything from jeans to Cuisinarts
to cell phones and television sets playing the Rodney King video.

Three Kings alternates between scenes of derring-do—the Americans blowing
up Iraqi helicopters and storming bunkers—and sometimes trenchant black
comedy about a senseless war. It ends like any conventional action film with
the likable Americans eschewing their avarice for discovering a conscience.
They jettison their load of booty to help the Shiite rebels get safely across the
border to Iran. The final message of the film, despite all the absurdities and
contradictions of the war (the final one being that Iran, for at least a decade
America's greatest antagonist in the Middle East, serves as safe haven for the
refugees), is that the Americans are the good guys.

With the collapse of the Soviet Union and the ambiguous victory in the
Gulf War offering very little comfort, Hollywood faced a dearth of credible
foreign adversaries who could be utilized to build conflict and fear into its
films. One option that existed was a holdover from 1950s cinema, namely, to
look to the skies and other planets for fictional enemies from space as possible
antagonists. *Independence Day* (1996) provided just such an enemy. The space
invaders depicted in *Independence Day* aren't the messianic Giacometti-like
aliens depicted in films such as *Close Encounters of the Third Kind* (1977) or the
cuddly little *E.T.* (1982). They are repellent-looking space meanies who are
reminiscent of the Mars invaders in *War of the Worlds* (1953).

Independence Day is a combination of 1950s alien invasion film and 1970s disaster film—much of the film a pastiche of other works (e.g., *Star Wars*, 1977, and *The Towering Inferno*, 1974). The aim of these fiends from outer space is to destroy civilization. So they quickly lay waste to most of New York (including the Statue of Liberty and the Empire State Building), Washington, and Los Angeles. And if anyone still doubted their malevolence, they also obliterate a bunch of Los Angeles New Agers who foolishly welcome them as saviors.

Everything looks bleak until the president, Thomas J. Whitmore (Bill Pullman), a former Gulf War veteran pilot who until then has been perceived as a Clintonian waffler, joins forces with brash, quick-witted, top-gun fighter pilot Captain Steve Hiller (Will Smith) and environmentalist and computer genius David Levinson (Jeff Goldblum) to deal these alien invaders their comeuppance.

Thrown in for comic relief is Judd Hirsch as David's unshaven, sneaker-wearing Yiddish-accented father and a wild-haired, mad scientist played by *Star Trek: The Next Generation*'s Brent Spiner.

It hardly matters that all this is utterly derivative. What is significant is that in this cheery cartoon of a film, the brotherhood of man, symbolized by the world forces, combines to oppose the aliens. And a quartet that contains a white Protestant president, a former black rapper, an intellectual Jew, and an alcoholic ex-pilot Russell Casse (Randy Quaid) right out of *Dr. Strangelove* defeat the forces of intergalactic evil accompanied by a final montage of people all over the world rejoicing.

It was this sort of patriotic rainbow coalition—unifying the world under American command—that prompted Senator Bob Dole (no movie critic or fan), the 1996 Republican candidate for president, to laud it by saying, "Bring your family. You'll be proud of it. Diversity. America. Leadership."[15] This extravaganza of special effects soon became one of the highest-grossing films of all time, proving that for Hollywood affirming American patriotism by saving the human race from alien extermination would prove an apt substitute for fighting communists.

If intergalactic fiends weren't sufficient, there was always the patriotic trump card of World War II. Interestingly enough, it was in the Soviet Union that World War II had first become known as "The Great Patriotic War." In the United States, not only was it the war that everyone could agree was the last "Good War" (given the ambiguities and dark side of the Korean War, Vietnam War, and Gulf War), but it was also fast becoming the American equivalent of the "Great Patriotic War." It was seen as a war fought against powerful, purely evil enemies that threatened our very existence as a nation; required a total national commitment; and ended in unambiguous victory. So on the roster of Hollywood's international evildoers (now that the Red Menace was out of the way), the Nazis and the Japanese could still be relied on to invoke a frisson of fear and a patriotic surge of pride from the American public.

There was no one better to arouse these feelings of fear and pride than Hollywood's most successful director, Steven Spielberg. With the completion of *Saving Private Ryan*, Spielberg had already directed six of the top 20 box of-fice grossing films of all time. Furthermore, ever since 1993 and his Academy Award–winning *Schindler's List* (to be discussed later in the chapter), he had aspired to make films with moral and social content that, at the same time, would appeal to wide audiences. Spielberg was a master of film technique and Hollywood genre conventions and often brought great stylistic inventive-ness to his films—leaving audiences with a sense of visceral excitement as well as nostalgia for older forms of cinematic storytelling.

Spielberg's *Saving Private Ryan* strikes a patriotic note right from the start, with a giant American flag rippling in the breeze accompanied by John Williams's mournful score in the background. The camera then slowly tracks after an aged veteran and his family on his return to the battlefields and cem-eteries of Normandy and then in flashback dissolve from the veteran at a grave site to a squad of wet, vomiting, and frightened soldiers landing at Dog sector of Omaha Beach on June 6, 1944. What follows is what one military historian, John Keegan (*The Face of Battle*), has called, "the most terrifying, realistic thing ever done in the cinema."[16]

The first 25 minutes of the film are probably the most brilliant evocation of war's horrors ever filmed. Shooting with his camera low to the ground like a combat photographer so that blood and water frequently splatter the lens and seen from the points of view of a German machine gunner and from the soldiers themselves and using diffused light and unsaturated colors, Spielberg presents a staggering portrait of the randomness and chaos of D-Day's vio-lence. He fills the screen with terrifying moments, such as a wounded soldier searching for his arm, another whose face is blown apart, a GI screaming for his mother as his intestines spill out onto the beach, others engulfed in flames, and the blood of the wounded and dying turning the ocean red. Spiel-berg shoots much of the horror in close-up and jagged tracking shots and concludes the sequence with a long overhead shot of the beach littered with bodies and body parts. In this sequence, the soldiers are anonymous, and there are no facile heroics—Spielberg evoking just the image of war as abattoir.

However, after providing the audience with this sort of startling real-ism, Spielberg then aims for patriotic transcendence. He strikes that note when the chief of staff of the armed forces, General George C. Marshall (Harve Presnell), on learning that three of Ryan's brothers had died in com-bat just that week, orders that the surviving Ryan brother be rescued from com-bat. To justify his decision, he reads a passage from Abraham Lincoln's famous

Civil War letter to Mrs. Bixby, a mother who had lost five sons in that war. Sanctified by Lincoln's eloquent rhetoric, *Saving Private Ryan* takes on new meaning. As a result, from the ultimate in combat realism, it becomes a brilliantly directed—every off-angle tilt and every shot-reverse-shot is artfully chosen—relatively conventional combat mission war film.

Before we know it, we are following in color the journey of that archetypal World War II squad consisting of a cynical, wise guy from Brooklyn, Private Reiban (Ed Burns); a Bible-quoting southern sharpshooter, Private Jackson (Barry Pepper); a tense, Nazi-hating Jewish kid, Private Melish (Adam Goldberg); a passionate Italian, Private Caparzo (Vin Diesel); a sensitive medic Wade (Giovanni Ribisi); and the loyal, battle-hardened Sergeant Horvath (Tom Sizemore). If you remember these guys from somewhere else, it's because they've already appeared in such World War II classics as *A Walk in the Sun* (1945) and *The Story of G.I. Joe* (1945). To augment this feeling of déjà vu, there is the battle-weary, vulnerable Captain John Miller (Tom Hanks), who has seen too many beachheads and too many men die. Miller is a wise, small-town high school teacher out of Frank Capra—a heroic, Everyman leader free of bloodlust who just wants to finish the job and go home to his wife. And there is Corporal Upham (Jeremy Davies), the awkward, frightened intellectual translator who has never seen action before and whose rite of passage into war's murderousness Spielberg focuses on in the film's final battle. None of the eight men are complex creations, but, at the same time, they are sufficiently individuated to successfully serve the genre.

In their quest for Private Ryan, the squad has to destroy the occasional German machine gun nest and radar installation and have an angry argument over whether to kill a captured German soldier whose obsequious odiousness seems to have been culled from some of the worst of the World War II films. There are also moments of repose—a night in a destroyed cathedral—where they recall their pasts or contemplate the war. Much of their talk involves justifying to themselves the possible squandering of the lives of so many to save just one life. Indeed, it goes against the philosophy of Captain Miller, who believes that the 94 men who died under his command have perhaps saved the lives of thousands. However, in World War II films, it's not the philosophy but the mission and chain of command that matter. Consequently, when they finally find the callow Private Ryan (Matt Damon) and he refuses to leave his post "with the only brothers I have left," they all remain with him to do the good, brave thing and defend a vital bridge crossing against a furious German counterattack. They are vastly outnumbered, and the Germans have tanks, so Sergeant Horvath, Private Melish, Private Pepper, and Captain Miller die in the process. Lives must be lost so that the film would be seen as a serious work, not a juvenile action film. In addition, much too neatly, the cowardly

Corporal Upham must ironically learn about the brutal necessity of killing by shooting the German prisoner whose life he pleaded for in an earlier scene. The sequence's action is choreographed stunningly, but it's melodramatic and interminable, and the squad's fearlessness and courage against impossible odds is really not much different than the behavior of John Wayne and company in countless, less vaunted World War II films.

In the penultimate scene, the dying Captain Miller leaves Private Ryan with the moral injunction to "earn this"—to live a life that justifies their sacrifice. Those words seemed aimed less at Private Ryan—who has already demonstrated that he is a man of courage—than at future generations asking them to adhere to Miller's notions of decency and self-sacrifice. The film ends as it begins with a final image of the billowing American flag and Williams's mournful music. In *Saving Private Ryan*, Spielberg, as in many of his 1990s films, sought to confront large historical and moral themes, such as American racism and the Holocaust (e.g., *Amistad* and *Schindler's List*), bearing witness this time to the heroism of Americans who fought and died in World War II in Lincoln's words (quoted by General Marshall) on "the altar of freedom."

However, except for the film's opening 25 minutes, *Saving Private Ryan* often bears skillful witness more to Hollywood's World War II film genre than to the war. The soldiers may kill a few German prisoners after seeing their comrades slaughtered, but these are not the officers and enlisted men from *Platoon*—there are no psychopaths and rapists among them. These are good men fighting a virtuous war against an evil ideology. The war may be horrific, but it's neither meaningless nor futile. This is Spielberg's ahistorical valentine to America and Americans at their best—expunging almost all the contradictions, moral transgressions, and absurdities that exist in any war, even a good and necessary one like World War II.

Released six months after *Saving Private Ryan*, Terrence Malick's *The Thin Red Line* reinforced the return of World War II as a film subject. The two films and two directors, however, could hardly have been more different. Unlike Spielberg, who had been in the popular spotlight for more than two decades since his first success *Jaws* (1975), Malick had become reclusive after the release of his last film, *Days of Heaven* (1978). Nonetheless, that film and his earlier work, *Badlands* (1973), were critical favorites that turned Malick into a cult figure.

A further contrast is that Spielberg's film is heroic and patriotic, while Malick's is poetic and philosophical. Based on James Jones's 1962 novel of the same name, Malick, however, eschews Jones's naturalistic treatment of the American invasion and battle for control of Guadalcanal for an evocation of a glorious natural world where Melanesian islanders swim serenely in clear, azure ocean waters and tall green grass waves in the wind. This pastoral idyll is disrupted by the war's savagery, which in turn moves the soldiers to indulge in a great deal of sometimes insightful, other times vaporous and portentous, philosophical and poetic interior monologues about the character of war, nature, and death.

As he does in his previous films, Malick uses extensive voice-overs to portray the emotions and ideas of his protagonists, whose voices and faces often blur and rarely can be individuated. And his portrait of the defeated Japanese is very different than Hollywood's usual conception of them as anonymous cannon fodder or strutting barbarians. Malick humanizes the Japanese, portraying them after being defeated, screaming in fear, begging for mercy, or assuming the lotus position as they await their deaths or imprisonment. There are also conflicts that take place between the Americans. One of them depicts the struggle between the idealistic philosophy of Private Witt (Jim Caviezel) and the cynicism, even nihilism, of Sergeant Welsh (Sean Penn). They argue over whether the world of our senses ("this rock") is the ultimate reality or whether we are part of a single Emersonian oversoul ("the glory"). A more baleful struggle occurs between the railing, driven Lieutenant Colonel Tall (Nick Nolte) and the compassionate Captain Staros (Elias Koteas) over whether to storm, in a costly frontal assault, the heavily defended redoubts of the Japanese.

Though Nolte's ranting sometimes goes over the top, he successfully captures the desperation of the Homer-quoting, war-loving colonel, who, passed over for promotion, sees this battle as his last chance for vindication. Staros, on the other hand, may be too passive and sensitive—better suited to leading a college seminar than a combat infantry platoon. Malick, however, is less interested in character than in stunning images of light streaming through trees in the rain forest and close-ups of birds, crocodiles, and lush island vegetation—providing an almost pantheistic view of nature, one that grants life but is also bound by death. If Spielberg's film was the ultimate homage to the Hollywood war genre, Malick's film, though not opposed to our entry into World War II, gives no sense of the historical basis for Guadalcanal but provides a truly original visual and oral meditation on war.

If enemies from the Cold War, from World War II, and galaxies far, far away didn't suffice, there was always an internal enemy. As a result, the 1990s were also notorious for their internecine culture wars. And the enemy here was just as likely as not to be the cultural legacy of the 1960s. To liberals, the radical impulses of the 1960s had given way to more traditional politics and more structured, conventional lives as the 1990s and middle age closed in on them. For some liberals their newfound moderation caused them to wonder if they had betrayed the best of themselves and perhaps in so doing the future of America.

In the minds of conservative Americans, the 1960s challenge to traditional bourgeois ideas about family, sexual relations, and for a brief moment even capitalism itself was seen as responsible for the climbing divorce rate, the rising number of teenage pregnancies, and soaring drug use. The 1960s were viewed as the enemy—an anarchic decade responsible for our collective moral decay as well as the failure of our national will. Consequently, whatever the political perspective, perhaps the most significant though generally unacknowledged legacy of the 1960s was a pervasive anxiety about America's destiny.

Oddly enough, a glimpse of that anxiety, though not generated by fear of the 1960s, is evoked in *Star Wars: Episode I—The Phantom Menace*—the 1999 prequel to one of the great Hollywood successes, George Lucas's *Star Wars Trilogy* (*Star Wars*, 1977; *The Empire Strikes Back*, 1980; and *Return of the Jedi*, 1983)—a film usually numbered in the top 10 box office grossing films of all time and a special favorite of Gen X Americans.

However, despite the fact that the film's narrative revolves around a dispute about the taxation of trade routes in the Galactic Republic, *The Phantom Menace*'s main preoccupation are its special effects. Still, there is frequent reference made to the Galactic Republic's ineffectuality in this crisis, which is alternately assigned to the fact that "the bureaucrats are in charge" and that "there is no civility only politics, no interest in the common good." Of course, one wonders if this is Lucas's way of revealing his anxieties about the state of contemporary affairs or if it is just some nebulous intellectual scaffolding he has constructed after reading too much of Gibbon's *Decline and Fall of the Roman Empire*.

The answer is an obvious one; what really matters to Lucas, as it has since his first film, *THX 1138* (1971), is neither politics, character, nor even mythology but rather special effects. Unfortunately, those used in *The Phantom Menace* lost their power to excite us as they had in the 1970s and 1980s. Twenty years of video games, the Internet, and a whole series of the rival *Star Trek* films had dimmed the wonder that once greeted the brilliant effects of the earlier *Star Wars* films. Lucas, also, seemed to be repeating himself with the rocket-ship race with its swooping camera that is reminiscent of the rocket-fighter attacks in *Star Wars*. Furthermore, although one shouldn't expect political correctness in galaxies far, far away, there is some tin-eared indifference to minorities with bumbling Stepin Fetchit–like characters, such as the Jedi knight's valet, Jar Jar Binks, who also speaks with a Jamaican accent.

Despite this, *The Phantom Menace* was virtually critic-proof and grossed a record-breaking $28.5 million in the first weekend after its release. Consequently, if George Lucas was betraying some small measure of anxiety about the fate of the American republic in *The Phantom Menace*, he obviously didn't have any at all about the operations of American capitalism.

A much more serious inquiry and response to what had gone wrong with America since the 1960s was offered by director Oliver Stone in his presidential films *JFK* (1991) and *Nixon* (1995). Stone's ambitious, brilliantly edited films (flash-forwards, flashbacks, flash cuts, jump cuts, a mix of newsreels, still photos, fiction, black and white and color, and so on) touched a nerve, and even before their release, journalists, politicians, and assorted literati weighed in with denunciations and critiques of the films. Tom Wicker, the former op-ed columnist of the *New York Times*, called *JFK* "paranoid and fantastic, filled with wild assertions, that if widely accepted would be contemptuous of the very constitutional government Stone purports to uphold."[17] Smug conservative pundit George Will anathemized *JFK* as an "act of execrable history and contemptible citizenship, by a man of technical skill, scant education, and negligible conscience."[18] The Nixon family's comment on *Nixon* was the less eloquent but certainly more succinct description, calling the film "character assassination."[19]

Stone certainly was not without his defenders too. In an article in *The Atlantic*, political and cultural polymath Garry Wills referred to Stone's body of work, saying that "great novels are being written with the camera—at least when Stone is behind the camera."[20] Norman Mailer, no stranger to the pungent metaphor, said that Stone "has the integrity of a brute"[21] and in an especially insightful afterthought commented that *JFK* "should be seen not as history but myth, the story of a huge and hideous act in which the gods warred and a god fell."[22]

Stone would have readily agreed with at least part of Mailer's estimate. In interview after interview following the release of *JFK*, he consistently argued that "I'm presenting what I call a countermyth to the myth of the Warren Commission."[23] What was missing in all the controversy over Stone's presidential films was any references to connections between the two films beside the obvious historical links. Nevertheless, there were two essential links between the two films. The first was that in an important sense, both were mysteries, or, more precisely, one was a murder mystery (*JFK*) and the other a moral mystery (*Nixon*). The second was that, taken together, they presented Stone's mythic interpretation of American history and politics since the 1960s.

JFK's status as a murder mystery is most clearly evoked by soft-spoken New Orleans District Attorney Jim Garrison (Kevin Costner) in his summation to the jury (one that in actuality Garrison never delivered) in the Clay Shaw trial, in which he refers to the Kennedy assassination as "the murder at the heart of the American dream." The image, however, of District Attorney Garrison heroically walking the mean streets of New Orleans in search of the real Kennedy assassins is one that gave critics of the film the most pause, especially when even die-hard conspiracy theorists considered Garrison's investigation and subsequent indictments "a grotesque misdirected shambles."[24]

However, for Stone, Garrison's record as a thrice-elected New Orleans district attorney, his more than 20 years of service in the military, and his later career as an appellate judge marked him as a patriot and a Capraesque uncommon common man. Just as significant for Stone was the fact that Garrison was the only American law enforcement official ever to bring indictments in the Kennedy assassination. This allowed Stone to enter the surreal world of the Warren Commission report, giving him the opportunity to present a grand unified conspiracy theory of his own.

In *JFK*, Garrison's initial suspicions are aroused by the summer that Lee Harvey Oswald (Gary Oldman) spent in New Orleans just before the Kennedy assassination, presumably working for "The Fair Play for Cuba" committee. This inspires Garrison's descent into the lower depths of New Orleans society. Among those he meets among the city's demimonde are the jittery, gay, defrocked priest and anti-Castro mercenary David Ferrie (Joe Pesci), and the crudely direct, former homosexual prostitute and prison inmate Willie O'Keefe (Kevin Bacon). The latter implicates the smooth, elegant Clay Shaw (also known as Clay Bertrand [Tommy Lee Jones]) and also regales Garrison with his racist Aryan nation philosophy.

In Stone's version, Garrison's life is one of utter bourgeois respectability. There are frequent cloying, clichéd domestic scenes between Garrison and his nagging wife, Liz (Sissy Spacek), and their clamorous children. And the mixture of his conventionality and his commitment to the rule of law have left him poorly equipped to confront the dark side of American life. Still, Garrison's persistence and unwavering courage and integrity bring him more and more into conflict with the immense power of that side of American life, especially its political and economic incarnation—the military-industrial complex.

At the very beginning of the film, Stone refers to this colossus in newsreel footage of President Eisenhower's 1960 farewell address warning of its power. However, it isn't until Garrison's meeting with the shadowy former black-ops agent Colonel X (Donald Sutherland) that Garrison really begins to fully understand the forces he is confronting: a supposed cabal of high-level military men, Mafia dons, oil millionaires, Cuban exile leaders, and CIA agents whom Colonel X convinces him carried out a "coup d'état."

Using Colonel X as his Virgil, Stone also reveals the political subtext of his film. According to Stone's dubious historical scenario, Kennedy was killed because he wanted to end the Cold War and begin withdrawing American troops from Vietnam. In Stone's view, had Kennedy lived, we would have been spared the trauma of Vietnam—an assertion that obviously cannot be proven. So for Stone, Kennedy's assassination not only resulted in the loss of a beloved prince but also embodied an end of an era of American innocence and idealism.

This loss of idealism so central to *JFK* is also referred to time and again in *Nixon*. Idealism is, of course, the last thing one associates with Richard Nixon. Yet for Stone, Nixon is a complex figure, at once a gifted Machiavellian who had a great deal of political hubris and a man who was equally paranoid, self-pitying, and guilt ridden. The mystery that Stone tries to solve in *Nixon* is the question of what were the personal and moral sources of such a tragic and intricate character. Here, Stone is aided by actor Anthony Hopkins, who, though bearing scant physical resemblance to Nixon, nonetheless stunningly conveys his physical awkwardness, lack of charm, tight smile, furtive look, and, most important, his combination of self-conscious, compensatory machismo, and embarrassing mawkishness without ever turning him into a cartoon. In addition, Joan Allen's solitary, long-suffering, sometimes tough-minded Pat Nixon grants her a complicated humanity that all the media images of the smiling, supportive wife never provided.

Hopkins's and Allen's performances are the most striking aspects of *Nixon*. Stone also uses frequent visual references (e.g., newsreels, oblique angles, and dark rooms) to *Citizen Kane* to get to the heart of Nixon's character. His appropriation of this classic film as a central metaphor for understanding Nixon was logical given Welles's efforts to penetrate the mysteries of Kane. Indeed, this time, instead of one "rosebud," there are a host of possible rosebuds that offer clues to the enigma that was Richard Milhous Nixon.

The primary one is Nixon's mother, Hannah (Mary Steenburgen), whom he described as a "saint" but whose severity, self-righteous moralizing, and unintentional rejections would have eviscerated the soul of an even more self-confident child than little Richard Nixon, who once referred to himself in a letter to her as "your good dog."[25] Stone also offers tantalizing clues, such as the "four deaths" that Nixon refers to as stepping-stones to his presidency. These included most prominently the deaths of John and Robert Kennedy and more personally the deaths of Nixon's two brothers (Arthur and Harold), the latter enabling him to attend law school and leaving him with a legacy of guilt.

Stone also allows us to ponder whether it could have been psychological and class resentment that motivated Nixon. As John Ehrlichman (J. T. Walsh) says to H. R. Haldeman (James Woods), "You've got people dying because he didn't make the varsity football team. You've got the constitution hanging by a thread because the old man went to Whittier and not Yale." Finally, there is a double-dealing, hypocritical Henry Kissinger's (Paul Sorvino) portentous judgment: "Imagine, if this man had been loved."

Beside providing a somewhat facile psychological explanation for Nixon's political behavior, Stone also provides an intellectual-ideological rationale for some, albeit not all, of Nixon's political failings. By the time of Nixon, the cancer that Stone had diagnosed in *JFK* had evolved into an invincible all-powerful government, an almost mythic creature that Stone refers to as the "beast"—a creature that no individual, no matter how powerful, can control.

The power of the beast, the hidden government that Nixon hints at, is the penultimate metaphor in Stone's conspiracy-driven vision of American politics embodied in both *JFK* and *Nixon*. It is quite simply, according to Stone, that had Kennedy lived, he would have withdrawn from Vietnam and ended the Cold War. However, the threat of that caused such consternation in the lethal Leviathan/Beast—the military-industrial, CIA–Mafia–Wall Street complex—that they passed a death sentence on him. In the wake of his death, there occurred a period of political demoralization that Richard Nixon, with his combination of relentless political ambition, ruthless pragmatism, and self-destructive vindictiveness, brought to its tragic culmination. Or, as an anguished Nixon himself puts it one night as he passes before the portrait of Kennedy (the political figure who obsesses him) during the Watergate scandal, "When they see you, they see what they want to be. When they see me, they see what they are."

Oliver Stone's presidential films were certainly not the last word in Hollywood's attempt to come to grips with the past 30 years of American history. Vastly different in style and content was Robert Zemeckis's (*Who Killed Roger Rabbit?*) Academy Award–winning *Forrest Gump* (1994). The center of the film is a low-IQ (75), Zelig-like hero, Forrest Gump (Tom Hanks), with an odd, stiff-legged walk and utterly flat voice, whose life provides a superficial, magic realist tour of American society from the 1950s to the 1990s. A dim Forrest moves effortlessly and almost unconsciously from all-American football star, Vietnam War hero, international ping-pong champion, and seafood mogul to New Age guru while also participating in key historical moments, like inadvertently joining the black students who defy Governor George Wallace and integrate the University of Alabama (the scene using digital computer effects to merge Forrest with real newsreel footage). Forrest makes this journey armed only with the truisms of his spunky, loving mamma (Sally Field): "Life is like a box of chocolates" and "You never know what you're going to get."

Forrest Gump is a film whose commitment to patriotism, family values, and entrepreneurial spirit endeared itself to right-wingers. Forrest is devoted to his suicidal, drug-addicted childhood sweetheart, Jenny (Robin Wright); is a loving father to their son; and starts a seafood business as an homage to his black army buddy, Bubba (Mykelti Williamson)—becoming a millionaire. This led the Reverend Pat Robertson to observe that the film proves the existence of "tiny cells of conservatism burrowing deep inside the Hollywood elite."

Still, Forrest, like Peter Sellers's Chauncey Gardiner in *Being There* (1979), was the kind of blank slate that anyone could project their values on and claim for their side. If he embodied some conservative values, he also, though named after the founder of the Ku Klux Klan, Nathan Bedford Forrest, is the only white in a black gospel choir and maintains a deep link to Bubba. And though a Vietnam War hero, he ends up, by accident, addressing an antiwar rally and is praised by its Abbie Hoffman look-alike leader.

Obviously, the film is no affirmation of the 1960s—both the Black Panthers and the Students for a Democratic Society are seen as radicals who bully, posture, and talk jargon. However, the film's ultimate concern is more philosophical than political. The embittered, legless Lieutenant Dan (Gary Sinise), whose life Forrest saved in Vietnam, rants that "nothing just happens, it's part of a plan." The response to his fatalism comes from Mamma Gump, who says that "you make your own destiny." Forrest, in turn, synthesizes the two positions, holding that we both have a destiny and float "around accidental like on a breeze."

Forrest's folksy synthesis is another example of the film's sentimental governing notion that he is a holy fool, blessed with great sympathy and an artless simplicity that makes him a fount of wisdom, capable of moving some of the despairing characters—Jenny and Lieutenant Dan—to ultimately affirm their lives. Zemeckis, with the help of Hanks's virtuoso performance, has made a skillful, manipulative film that substitutes greeting card treacle for real ideas and emotions.

Unlike Stone's docudramas and Zemeckis's holy fool fable, the western has always been a barometer of the nation's culture. From the classic westerns of the 1920s and 1930s (*The Iron Horse* and *Stagecoach*) to the revisionism of the late 1960s (*Little Big Man* and *McCabe and Mrs. Miller*), the genre has often illuminated the concerns of American society and culture. And though by the 1980s and 1990s Hollywood made few westerns, two of those made in the 1990s—*Dances with Wolves* (1990) and *Unforgiven* (1992)—were ambitious, serious works that won Academy Awards for best film.

Dances with Wolves, directed by and starring Kevin Costner, who plays the somber, understated, gentle Lieutenant John Dunbar, whose suicidal heroics in the Civil War allow him, by his own choice (he wants to see the frontier and remove himself from civilization), to be posted out West. Dunbar is transferred to an isolated outpost in Lakota territory, where he comes into contact with Sioux, who, after initial wariness, accept him as one of their own and name him Dances-with-Wolves.

Dunbar, an observant man, keeps a journal where he writes, "I had never known a people so eager to laugh, so devoted to family, so dedicated to each other." Costner's Sioux are mythicized—they are in harmony with nature and their sexuality and blessed with an intuitive wisdom that makes them totally superior to most of the vulgar, murderous, rapacious, and mad whites in the film. There are bad Indians—the feral Pawnees—but the film's real primitives are the whites.

Dances with Wolves' celebration of noble Indians touched an anxious chord among many Americans who felt that in our pursuit of wealth and disregard for our environment, we had lost touch with our spirituality. However, this handsome, epic film, filled with long shots of prairies, hills, sunsets, snows-capes, and buffalo grazing, is emotionally undeveloped and sentimental and as mythic in its depiction of the Indians as the old Hollywood was in its ste-reotyping them as bloodthirsty savages. Modern anthropological studies have shown that the Indians were just as wanton as the whites in their annihilation of the buffalo and that they almost succeeded in wiping out the continent's deer population.[26] In fact, in contemporary America, while some whites at-tend Indian "sweats" to connect with their spiritual being, many Indian tribes are opening gambling casinos to gain access to wealth.

A more subtle revision of the classic western was Clint Eastwood's noir-ish western *Unforgiven*. The film is dominated by black, rain-swept prairie nights; morally corrupt characters; and the use of a rich chiaroscuro for in-terior scenes. Eastwood begins the film with a feminist twist, shooting from the point of view of the prostitutes of a frontier town (Big Whisky), who, after one of their number is scarred by a cowboy, offer a reward to anybody who will kill him. From that point on, the prostitutes become merely observ-ers (though we are made conscious of their feelings and humanity—a rarity in a western) rather than central figures in a film that centers on William Munny (Clint Eastwood), an aging ex-outlaw turned failed pig farmer who has moved away from a life of murderous crime.

Nevertheless, Munny joins forces with a serene former partner, Ned Logan (Morgan Freeman), and a callow, blustery, myopic gunman, the "Schofield Kid" (Jaimz Woolvett), to get the reward. Their journey turns into an ironic view of the American West's cult of violence and a saga of a redeemed man's momentary resurrection of his past, monstrous self so that he can avenge a friend's killing.

Big Whisky is dominated by a sadistic sheriff, "Little Bill" Baggett (Gene Hackman), who indulges in beatings and summary justice in order to keep the peace. When "English Bob" (Richard Harris), a droll, bullying paid killer, accompanied by his craven, obsequious amanuensis, dime novelist, W. W. Beauchamp (Saul Rubinek), comes to claim the prostitute's reward, "Little

Bill" beats and humiliates him—debunking the novels written about Bob's supposed heroic reputation.

The film's power lies in its subverting the romanticization of violence in the western: English Bob is all empty bravado and afraid of Baggett's intimidating games; the inept Schofield Kid, who after killing his first man, begins to understand the nature of death and wants no part of killing (e.g., "I'd rather be blind and ragged than dead."); and even Munny, while delirious and feverish, speaks about his fear of dying. And in avenging the killing of Logan, the reformed Munny murders Little Bill and five of his deputies, vowing to come back and kill every man, woman, and child in Big Whiskey if they follow him. The supposedly exhausted Munny, who at the film's beginning is too inept to hit a can that he practices shooting at, has now turned into a coolly, indomitable murderer who exemplifies D. H. Lawrence's judgment that the basic American soul consists of being "cold, isolate and a killer."[27] Unfortunately, Eastwood's practically unrivaled contemporary status as a heroic masculine icon undermined the film's critique of the western's usual romanticization of outlawry—leaving the audience identifying with rather than being repelled by his bloody actions.

One thing missing from all these attempts at evoking American culture's condition was any mention of social class. That, oddly enough, came from an unexpected source—the Academy Award–winning blockbuster *Titanic* (1997). Almost all the discussion about the film prior to its winning of the Oscar for best picture usually centered on its decor and outstanding special effects, such as submersible cameras and the remarkable depiction of the sinking of the supposedly unsinkable luxury ship. Further buzz came from the prepubescent girls who flocked to the film numerous times just to drool over young heartthrob Leonardo DiCaprio, who starred as the tragic, androgynously handsome Jack Dawson.

One who did mention the film's class content was Chinese communist president and party leader Jiang Zemin, who pronounced the film "Marxist"[28] (undoubtedly a surprise to media moguls Sumner Redstone of Paramount and archconservative Rupert Murdoch of Twentieth Century Fox, who between them invested a record-breaking $200 million in the epic tale). The Chinese leader was clearly focusing on the fact that within the flash of the film's dazzling special effects was the tiny germ of a story of love between the classes—the brief but indelible love affair between the voluptuous, rebellious Rose (Kate Winslet) and the impetuous bohemian artist Jack.

This first-class-steerage romance begins when genteelly impoverished Rose, engaged, out of economic necessity, to a brutally controlling, sneering, wealthy Cal (Billy Zane), decides that her future as a bird in a gilded cage is more than she can bear and attempts a rather picturesque suicide plunge from the prow of the doomed ship. Jack, of course, stops her, and they begin a whirlwind love affair that incurs the wrath of both Cal and his villainous bodyguard, Spicer (David Warner), who try to murder Jack. In all this nonsensical, melodramatic derring-do, the rich, with a few exceptions, are depicted as snobbish, greedy, cold, and generally cowardly (Cal survives by getting into the lifeboats with the women and children, while Jack dies saving Rose), while most of the ship's vitality, honesty, and decency seem to reside belowdecks. Is it any wonder, then, that Jiang Zemin would applaud this movie?

One cinematic genre that went through a small renaissance was political satire. Possibly because Bill Clinton's behavior as president provided so much comic material for Jay Leno and David Letterman, a number of sophisticated political comedies were made in the 1990s. They ranged from a roman à clef of Clinton's 1992 campaign, *Primary Colors* (1998), an almost prophetic anticipation of strategy employed by Clinton to divert attention from the White House scandals; *Wag the Dog* (1997); a radical, hip-hop inspired farce, *Bulworth* (1998); and a film about a high school class election that becomes a sly metaphor for adult political campaigns, *Election* (1999).

Based on political journalist Joe Klein's pseudonymous novel, *Primary Colors* went over much of the same ground that Chris Hegedus and D. A. Pennebaker's documentary *The War Room* covered back in 1993, with two particularly notable additions. The first was that the witty, politically incisive script was written by Elaine May and directed by Mike Nichols, who as a comedy team in the late 1950s and early 1960s built a reputation as brilliant satirists of contemporary manners and morals. The other was that *Primary Colors* places Bill and Hillary Clinton (also known as Jack and Susan Stanton [John Travolta and Emma Thompson]) at the film's center.

Travolta is almost perfect as the Clinton double—Jack Stanton—the governor of a southern state running for the presidency. His politically ruthless and seductive Stanton has the raspy accent, the body language, the empathetic handshake, the populist touch, and the gift for self-destruction that his real-life counterpart has. In a similar fashion, Thompson captures Hillary's seriousness, efficiency, aggressiveness, and willingness to turn a blind eye to her husband's inability to keep his fly zippered. They operate with a single will when it comes to electing Jack Stanton president. It's that overarching ambition and Stanton's lack of discipline that touches and sometimes destroys all the people who surround them.

It includes Henry Burton (Adrian Lester), the "black George Stephanopoulos," a polite, idealistic grandson of a legendary civil rights leader who signs on as their deputy campaign director. Henry's perspective is the dominant one in the film, but the character is too pallid to make his moral quandary and consciousness (should he quit or stay with a dirty, negative campaign that has good intentions?) of much dramatic interest.

Primary Colors, like the novel it is based on, is most effective when dealing with political strategies. It has a particularly astute understanding of how idealism gets compromised in the quest for political power, and though critical of the Stanton's squalid tactics, it accepts that the political arena is not a place for moralists or those who refuse to be corrupted. Largely passed over by the public, *Primary Colors* may not have the psychological complexity of an *All the King's Men* (1949), but it's a lively, often wittily, incisive portrait of contemporary American politics.

Barry Levinson's (*Rain Man*) *Wag the Dog*, written by David Mamet and Hilary Henkin, moves into the black-comic, *Strangelove* realm. Its premise is that a sex scandal in the midst of a presidential campaign sends all his aides scurrying to provide damage control. They come up with a sardonic, self-assured, understated spinmeister, Conrad Brean (Robert De Niro), who decides to stage a war to divert attention from the president's problems. To aid him, he reaches out to archetypal, narcissistic Hollywood producer Stanley Motss (Dustin Hoffman gives a scene-stealing performance) because, as Brean says, "war is show business."

The notion that there is no difference between political and media manipulation is not an original one. However, Stanley Motss's unflappable staging of the war with its special patriotic anthem; demonic, arch-terrorist enemy ("Albania"); and psychotic war hero, Sergeant William "old shoe" Schumann (Woody Harrelson at his most wild-eyed), is truly inspired. The whole production is augmented by songs, a made-for-television-funeral, and an eye for merchandizing tie-ins and back-end deals (movies, T-shirts, and a memorial clock).

About two-thirds through, the film begins to lose momentum, and its comic conceit wears thin. Still, there is a clear-eyed view of political spin control and of Hollywood's gift for manipulating the popular imagination and the public's willingness to be seduced by it. It is also prophetic about what occurred during the impeachment process when Clinton ordered the bombing of Iraq for defying the United Nations and was denounced by a number of congressional Republicans for using a "wag the dog" strategy.[29]

If *Wag the Dog* can be viewed as a synonym for spin control, Warren Beatty's political farce, *Bulworth*, is a model for Hollywood-style radicalism. When we first see California senator J. Billington Bulworth, Beatty's hero (Beatty directed, co-wrote, and starred in the film), he is unshaven, sleepless, surrounded by discarded junk food cartons, compulsively watching himself on television campaign commercials, and breaking down. Bulworth was a 1960s left-liberal (there are photos of him with Bobby Kennedy and Martin Luther King Jr.) and has recently begun to give platitudinous speeches attacking "welfare cheats" and doing obeisance to "family values." In absolute despair, he takes out a $10 million life insurance policy and hires a hit man to kill him.

Freed from the necessity of political caution, Bulworth attacks the Democratic Party's most loyal constituencies, telling blacks that the party won't take you seriously until you drop O.J. and Hollywood Jews that "it's funny how lousy your stuff is. I guess the money turns everything to crap." However, after a night at a black after-hours club—dancing, listening to rap, snorting cocaine, and becoming infatuated with a beautiful black hit woman, Nina (Halle Berry)—Bulworth is transformed into a comic version of Mailer's White Negro. He then turns into a rap politician, awkwardly using hip-hop rhythms and rhymes to attack corporate dominance of politics and the media and even advocating socialism.

Ironically, this sudden attack on mainstream politics turns Bulworth into a popular hero, an election winner, and, echoing the 1960s, an assassination victim. Beatty's homily that a popular politician speaks truth to power at one's peril is undeniable. What is dubious in *Bulworth* is the sentimental thesis that the only source of authenticity, vitality, and salvation in America lies within the black inner city since every other strata is tarnished by the money culture. The inner-city ethos transforms Bulworth from a buttoned-down, cynical, political opportunist into a socially committed South Central Los Angeles home boy complete with knit cap, shades, and short pants who can convince a drug-dealing thug, L.J. (Don Cheadle), to magically become a community activist.

The inner city also produces a Nina who, when she stops strutting and scowling, sounds like a Marxist Harvard professor eloquently describing the deindustrialization of the ghetto and the destructive power of a consumer culture built on self-gratification as the reasons for dysfunction in the black community. It is precisely the community's self-destructiveness and fragmentation and the basis in reality of those ominous black street stereotypes that Beatty uses for their comic value (and to sometimes provide a glimpse of the humanity underneath the posturing) that make his vision seem simplistic. Beatty has trotted out the tattered, absurd notion that life on the bottom is intrinsically more decent and more meaningful than the lives of the more comfortable and privileged.

Beatty's banal solution to the racial divide is no better. His idea that we've "all got to keep fuckin each other until we are the same color" is at best simplistic. As a radical solution, it sounds remarkably like the one offered by neoconservative critic Norman Podhoretz's 1960s essay (in his liberal phase) "My Negro Problem and Ours." Similarly, the homeless Rastaman's (the Marxist poet Amiri Baraka) repeated admonition to Bulworth, "Don't be a ghost! you got to be a spirit," though supposedly a call to action, sounds more like nostalgia for a more confrontational era.

Given Hollywood's usual bland political perspective, a film like *Bulworth* that attacks capitalism can be seen, by comparison, as an ambitious, politically radical work. It is also graced with one of Beatty's strongest performances as the vulnerable, despairing Jay Bulworth, and it is alive with farcical humor and truly imaginative moments. Still, its attempt to build tension with a murder plot is lame and intrusive. And, more important, its critique of American politics degenerates into ultraleft, 1960s romanticism.

The political satire *Election*, by not taking clear sides, avoids moving in an ideological direction. The film was directed by Alexander Payne, whose previous, much less subtle film *Citizen Ruth* (1996) provided a satiric look at both right-to-life and abortion rights advocates. Set once again in Payne's hometown of Omaha, Nebraska, the film centers on the election of a class president at the almost all-white, ironically named George Washington Carver High.

The chief and initially unopposed contender is Tracy Flick (Reese Witherspoon), a Liddy Dole clone, all ferocious ambition and self-righteousness. Tracy diligently plans her campaign for class president down to the smallest detail, including how many sticks of gum she can give to each student as a campaign gift. What she doesn't count on is the antipathy of her teacher and the film's prime narrator, Jim McAllister (Matthew Broderick). For McAllister, though he keeps an outwardly controlled demeanor around Tracy, her constant attempts to gain his attention and approval in class are as grating as chalk scratching on a blackboard. So, in order to thwart Tracy, McAllister convinces the sweet, dim jock Paul Metzler (Chris Klein) to run against her.

Although the film initially seems to tilt against the comically monstrous Tracy, especially given her blatant drive for success, there is also a strain of pathos in her solipsism and isolation. Payne's gift is to contrast Tracy's blind ambition with the intelligent McAllister's own lack of self-awareness. Trapped in a dead marriage and a dead-end job, McAllister doesn't recognize that some of his malice toward Tracy is also motivated by jealousy of her youth, energy, and promising future—qualities so lacking in his own life. *Election* became more than a just film that uses a high school political campaign as a satiric metaphor for the ego-driven emptiness of American politics—it also turns into an understated, sly depiction of human frailty. The ambiguity of Payne's film derives from his empathy for all his characters' flawed natures.

Though political films like *Primary Colors*, *Wag the Dog*, and *Election* dealt with an important issue—the cynical degradation of our political culture and discourse—it was only *Bulworth* that touched on the most troubling and seemingly intractable problem of all—race. The race question was exacerbated in the early 1990s by conditions in the African American community that found at least 56 percent of black families headed by a woman, 45 percent of black children living below the poverty line,[30] and black unemployment generally tripling the rate of white unemployment. This also had a profound effect on crime levels, which saw more than 1 million black males in prison in the 1990s and the likelihood that 1 black male in 21 would be murdered in his lifetime, most likely by another black man.[31]

These appalling statistics and the culture of social fragmentation and despair they conveyed inspired the most significant wave of films about blacks that had come out of Hollywood since the blaxploitation films of the 1970s. Indeed, one of the curtain-raising films of this trend, John Singleton's *Boyz 'N the Hood* (1991), begins with a screen credit that announces the fact the 1 in 21 black males is likely to die as a result of homicide. The film follows up that proclamation with an unsubtle, didactic tale of three young Boyz—Tre (Cuba Gooding Jr.), Doughboy (Ice Cube), and Ricky (Morris Chestnut)—growing up on the blood-soaked streets of South Central Los Angeles. The film interweaves their rites of passage with the message that the black male's salvation lies in the embrace of patriarchal authority—a strong single mother being insufficient. *Boyz* drives that point home by having the guidance and discipline of Tre's father, the righteous, Afrocentric Furious Styles (Larry Fishburne), saving him from the seductions of street culture and the fate of the promising athlete Ricky, who is murdered, and Doughboy's equally doomed gangstadom.

What was disturbing about the film was that its depiction of drive-by shootings and use of crosscut chase sequences had the most appeal for the young black males in the audience rather than the film's deftly textured evocation of street and neighborhood life and exhortations on black history, neighborhood control, safe sex, the white conspiracy, and the need for black enterprise. In fact, there were numerous incidents of reported gang violence that occurred throughout the country in the wake of the film's theatrical release, a pattern repeated by the Hughes Brothers in *Menace II Society* (1993)—a film with somewhat similar themes and characters.

Menace II Society, however, was as apolitical, dark, and nihilistic as *Boyz 'N the Hood* was hortatory. Neither of the two films was as socially critical and evocative as Spike Lee's *Clockers* (1995), both a powerful lament and an attack against the pathology of inner-city life that was much less commercially successful. The Hughes Brothers may have seen their frightening and cold *Menace II Society* as avoiding glorifying inner-city violence and depicting it as repellent and oppressive. However, the film's casual drug dealing, ripping people off, and arbitrary killing and the boys' brutal victimization of women elicited cheers and catcalls from inner-city and suburban adolescent audiences.

Not only does blood flow as freely as malt liquor in *Menace II Society*, but there is hardly even a trace of hope to be found in the story of the antiheroic Caine (Tyrin Turner) and his friends, as there was for the sweet Tre in *Boyz*. *Menace II* does include an authoritative black teacher, Mr. Butler (Charles Dutton), who talks to the young men about responsibility and community and a few other characters struggling to get out of the inner city (through playing football or becoming a Muslim), but it is the directionless lives and gratuitous violence ("you are never going to know what's going to happen and when") accompanied by a heavy rap score that dominates the film. In fact, Caine's description of his friend, the uncontrolled, murderous O Dog (Larenz Tate), that "he was America's nightmare, young, black and didn't give a fuck" seems to have been meant to apply to a whole generation of poor black males.

In contrast to Tre's loving parents (his mother is caring and educated and has a good job), Caine's were drug users, dealers, and murderers, and his mentor, Pernell (Glenn Plummer), was serving a life sentence. Nothing can save Caine—the love of a good woman, the Christian faith of his grandparents, or the black nationalism of one of his friends. Caine's fate seems inevitable, for, as Mr. Butler says, "The hunt is on, and you're the prey."

Some of the harshest criticisms of these films came from blacks who felt that films like these projected a distorted image of black life. One black writer wrote, "The tragedy of the present black film revival is that too many films concentrate on these lost souls at the expense of the truly fascinating stories of thousands of young black people who are succeeding beyond the wildest dreams of my generation."[32]

These critics undoubtedly spoke for a new generation of black men and women who had managed to become middle class. By 1995, aided by affirmative action and the Clinton prosperity that increased black home ownership and wages, at least 50 percent of African Americans considered themselves middle class. In addition, whereas in 1960 only 7 percent of blacks had ever been to college, by the 1990s that figure was more than 21 percent.[33] A group this large, however nebulous and uneasy the reality of their middle-class status was, provided a sizable audience that was attractive to Hollywood producers. It moved them to make more films in the mid- and late 1990s directed by both white and black filmmakers and committed to black family values and centering on mobile, middle-class black characters rather than continuing to produce films focusing on inner-city violence and gangbangers.

Many of the films were romantic comedies. They ranged from Forest Whitaker's *Waiting to Exhale* (1995) to Kevin Sullivan's *How Stella Got Her Groove Back* (1998) to Malcolm Lee's *The Best Man* (1999). *Waiting to Exhale* was a commercial hit, based on Terry McMillan's best-selling novel that equally appealed to both a black middle-class female and white female audiences. The film deals with four black women friends—Savannah (Whitney Houston), a television producer; Bernadine (Angela Bassett), a divorced corporate executive; Robin (Lila Rochon), an insurance company executive; and Gloria (Loretta Devine), the owner of a beauty salon—and their man problems. The film is a paean to beautiful, successful black women while suggesting that most black men are too insensitive and exploitative to be worth pursuing. *Waiting to Exhale* obviously was meant to appeal to a new black middle-class woman attracted more to the lyrics of a romantic ballad than to the nihilism of a rap song and more likely to be found turning the pages of *Essence* and *Glamour* than the Moynihan Report.

Another film, George Tillman Jr.'s *Soul Food* (1997), eschews romantic comedy for an extended homily on the need for black family solidarity and black male pride. When family matriarch, Big Mama Jo (Irma P. Hall), an earthy, wise character whom anyone familiar with Lorraine Hansberry's *A Raisin in the Sun* would recognize, goes into a coma and dies, her family, consisting of her three beautiful daughters—Maxine (Vivien Fox), Terry (Vanessa Williams), and Lady Bird (Nia Long)—and their husbands, begins to self-destruct. However, little Ahmed (Brandon Hammond), Big Mama Jo's doting grandson, cannily brings the feuding sisters and their husbands together by reviving the family's 40-year-old tradition of a Sunday soul food dinner. *Soul Food's* aims are salutary, and it touches perceptively on some aspects of black middle-class life, but the film is essentially no more than sentimental soap opera centering on black rather than white characters.

Fortunately, all black films weren't either hood films or mediocre homages to the new black middle class. Black independent filmmakers such as Julia Dash's stylized *Daughters of the Dust* (1991) explored the Gullah heritage of blacks, evoking the oral tradition of the sea islands that lie off the coast of South Carolina and Georgia. Similarly, Charles Burnett's fresh *To Sleep with Anger* (1990) combined black folk material and a touch of mysticism and prose poetry with a realistic depiction of Los Angeles black middle-class life in the tale of a friend from their rural southern past, the charming, devilish Harry (Danny Glover), who insinuates himself into the family and nearly destroys it. Later in the decade, a film like Kasi Lemmons's *Eve's Bayou* (1997) dealt with a child's-eye view of her parents' troubled marriage in a self-enclosed black enclave in 1960s Louisiana. Although these films achieved deserved critical acclaim and even some international festival awards, none of these films captured the imagination of a wider audience, either black or white.

What was equally surprising was the failure of two highly touted films about the African American experience from two of the most successful entertainers of the 1990s: Oprah Winfrey and Steven Spielberg. Winfrey, whose syndicated television talk show was virtually the television bible of legions of

American women, seemed practically a shoo-in to attract a large crossover audience. However, her production of Nobel Laureate Toni Morrison's poetic and bleak *Beloved* was a failure both with audiences and with critics. Part of the problem was due to the difficulties in translating Morrison's metaphor and symbol-clogged novel to the screen. One may also attribute its failure to the bleakness of a film dealing with a former slave Sethe's (Winfrey) memories of the child she killed to gain her freedom being resurrected by the appearance of a mysterious black woman (Thandie Newton), who embodies the spirit of that child. Unfortunately, it was probably too much of an emotional stretch for an audience that associated the positive-thinking talk show hostess with the hugs of absolution and tears of renewal that were regular features of her highly rated television show.

In the same way, Spielberg, who succeeded with almost everything he touched in the 1990s, failed with his attempt to tell the story of the *Amistad* (1997), the Spanish slave ship that was taken over by a slave mutiny and that became a symbolic battle ground for abolitionists and slaveholders in the antebellum United States. Spielberg's film was graced by two impressive performances from Djimon Hounsou, as Cinque, the acknowledged leader of the revolt, and Anthony Hopkins, as former president John Quincy Adams, who defended the slaves before the Supreme Court. However, with its repetitious courtroom scenes, its demonization of the proslavery forces, and its inability to have the slaves and their defenders really communicate with one another, the film lacked dramatic energy, preventing it from rising beyond the level of an interesting historical tableau.

Though a critical and box office failure, *Amistad* was only a modest blemish on the directorial reputation of Spielberg, who had risen to a point somewhere between genius and sainthood as a result of his 1993 film *Schindler's List*. Adapted from Thomas Keneally's semidocumentary novel about Oskar Schindler, a Nazi Party member and wartime profiteer who became a "righteous gentile" by saving the lives of more than 1,100 Jews in Poland during World War II, *Schindler's List* not only won Spielberg an Academy Award for best director but also established him in Hollywood as a morally serious artist who at same time demonstrated that he could be perfectly at home with the bottom line.

Grappling with the theme of the Holocaust presented problems for any artist, even one as talented and singularly knowledgeable about the cinematic and dramatic potential of film as Spielberg. First and foremost of these was the terrible fear of possibly trivializing and vulgarizing such an apocalyptic and horrific event. There were critics like George Steiner who had written that "the world of Auschwitz lies outside of speech as it lies outside of reason."[34] Still, there was the compelling need, despite the utter desolation

Schindler's List (1993). (Courtesy of Universal Pictures/Photofest.)

and hopelessness of the experience, to bear witness to these crimes, which had inspired such stylistically and intellectually different documentaries as Alain Resnais's elegant, understated *Night and Fog* (1955) and Claude Lanzmann's much harsher, more trenchant and unadorned *Shoah* (1985) and Joseph Losey's hauntingly ambiguous fictional film *Mr. Klein* (1976). Even Hollywood had produced credible Holocaust works, such as Sidney Lumet's powerful evocation of the Holocaust survivor in *The Pawnbroker* (1965) and Alan J. Pakula's earnest but melodramatic version of William Styron's novel *Sophie's Choice* (1982).

Spielberg succeeded in walking a tightrope between what might have become crass exploitation and what is a heightened realistic representation, shot in a formally virtuosic and self-conscious manner—dramatic lighting, a voluptuous black-and-white mise-en-scène, crosscutting, fluid montage, handheld camera shooting, and Yiddish folk songs on the sound track. Most of these formal elements are artfully used in the powerful sequences depicting the destruction of the Krakow ghetto and the selection process (the apotheosis of Nazi objectification), where the Nazis made everybody undress and decide who was able bodied enough to become slave laborers and shipped off the others to die in the death camps. There are emotionally stirring touches, such as the little girl in the red coat (seen from Schindler's point of view)—a vivid contrast to the film's black-and-white footage—who wanders innocently amidst the ferocious clearing of the Krakow ghetto, only to wind up later as a limp, crumpled tiny body on a pile of corpses. Spielberg turns her into a striking symbol for all the innocents that the Nazis annihilated.

Despite Spielberg's skill at classical narrative construction and genius for emotionally moving an audience, the film is not free of problems. A central difficulty is the mystery of Schindler's character. Liam Neeson may have star looks and, shot from a low angle, tends to overwhelm all the other characters, like the heroic protagonists of many Hollywood films, but he is utterly convincing as the womanizing, hedonistic con man turned courageous humanitarian. Nonetheless, the film grants no real insight to what moves Schindler to do what he did, nor does it shed much light on a character who, before the war, was almost arrested on his wedding day and who, after the war ended, appropriated charitable contributions meant to help his wife. The film never gets inside his psyche, and beyond Schindler's suggested moral revulsion with Nazi genocide, we never truly learn what inspired his selfless humanity and often reckless heroism.

Perhaps Spielberg and his co-screenwriter Steve Zaillian felt that an explanation might emerge in the contrast between Schindler's mere roguery and the demonic murderousness of German SS officer Amon Goeth (Ralph Fiennes). The psychopathic Goeth, who is placed in charge of the Plaszow concentration camp (created as a slave labor camp after the clearing of the Krakow ghetto), is practically Schindler's double in his corruption and his love of wine and women. However, in contrast to Schindler, who as his connection with the Jews increases, so does his commitment and protectiveness of them, Goeth brutally revels in his power of life and death over the camp inmates and treats the Jews as vermin whom he can kill on a whim. One difficulty with Fiennes's performance and Spielberg's conception of Goeth is that, however depraved he is, he emanates a romantic, larger-than-life aura along with his monstrous villainy.

Since Spielberg focuses so intensely on the German characters, the Jewish ones, with the exception of the shrewd, disciplined Itzhak Stern (Ben Kingsley), are less individuated and depicted mainly as characters in swiftly moving anecdotal vignettes in order to personalize the Holocaust for the movie audience. Their presence provides the audience with virtuous victims to identify with, but they remain basically opaque figures who look more like Hollywood actors than like people living close to the abyss. On the other hand, Stern is portrayed as a man of great self-control whose business skill is necessary and complements Schindler's talent for making contacts and his more imaginative personality. At first, Stern is wary and resentful of Schindler, but as Schindler's plans become clear to him, his feelings blossom into respect and finally warmth. Stern is the one Jewish hero in the film, for it's his mastery of detail and quiet courage that keeps the factory going and helps save the lives of the 1,100 Jews.

What's more troubling about *Schindler's List* were the moments of Hollywood kitsch that run through the film. There is the heavily ironic scene (civilization merged with barbarism) during the liquidation of the Krakow ghetto where an SS officer plays classical piano as the roundup and murder of the Jews continue. And there are cliff-hanging moments where a heroic Schindler rides to rescue a trainload of his Jews who have been wrongly sent to Auschwitz-Birkenau. Another scene melodramatically builds audience tension and fear (in a quasi-Hitchcock mode) by having Schindler's terrified women workers think that they are entering an Auschwitz gas chamber but then finding themselves in a shower room. Finally, there are the crass moments of Schindler's lachrymose farewell speech (much of it shot in close-up and theatrically lit) to his rescued workers just before their liberation and his teary guilt-stricken breakdown over the fact that he didn't save more of them. It's almost as if the Holocaust occurred so that Schindler could be morally redeemed. All these scenes—and others where music is used on the sound track to heighten feeling—are rendered to wring the most sorrow and tears out of events that could be shot in a less manipulative, artificial manner and still arouse profound emotion.

One can go on picking holes in a film that sacrifices character for visual power and beauty and narrative excitement and the creation of a world of good and evil for a meditation on the complex nature of the Holocaust. Though given Spielberg's penchant for using the whole arsenal of film technique, *Schindler's List* is, in comparison to his other films, a work of social realism. It is also one of the most optimistic films made about the Holocaust—centering on survivors rather than the millions who went to their deaths. However, the fact is that it is Spielberg, working in the mainstream Hollywood tradition, not Lanzmann's great interview-based *Shoah* (Lanzmann refused to use any direct representation of the past), who has made the larger public conscious of the horrors of the Holocaust. If we view *Schindler's List* as a work of popular culture, not documentary realism or high art, Spielberg's achievement is a considerable one.

The film also did raise the whole issue of the Holocaust and its use in American life. For one thing, many critics objected to what they perceived as an "Americanization of the Holocaust,"[35] the film emphasizing American cultural values, such as the need of our popular culture to create heroes, especially in an event that was noteworthy not so much for its heroes as for its victims. Others objected to the film's suggesting that the emergence of the state of Israel was in some way the logical outcome of the Holocaust—a theme that Spielberg repeats in the final moments of the film when the surviving

Schindlerjuden, accompanied by actors and extras in the movie, place stones on Schindler's gravestone in Israel. Many also saw the symbol of the Holocaust being used as a means of perpetuating the image of Jewish "victimhood" when the reality is that they are one of America's most successful minorities. In addition, the memory of the Holocaust helped sustain a group consciousness for a generation of Jews whose religious and ethnic ties were generally weakening because of both intermarriage and the general prosperity, opportunity, and power that Jews enjoy in America.

There were those who even challenged the right of Jews to monopolize the use of the term "holocaust" and that the notion of genocide applied exclusively to the murderous behavior that had occurred in Europe between 1939 and 1945. For example, some African American scholars have referred to the millions of blacks who died in the "middle passage" or who were worked to death on American plantations as a "black holocaust."[36] And the 1.5 million Armenians massacred by the Turks during World War I generally perceived themselves as the first victims of 20th-century genocide. As a result, the words "genocide" and "holocaust" seemed above all to take on an expanded meaning and became part of the sacralization of victimhood in the 1990s. No better place was this on display than in the use of the word "genocide" that some gay activists appropriated to describe the effect of the AIDS plague on the gay community.

For most of its history, Hollywood's relation to gays and lesbians was best described by critic Vito Russo (himself a victim of AIDS) as the "celluloid closet."[37] However, though overt depictions of gay characters or gay themes in films were taboo, they often appeared in covert fashion in dialogue, double entendres, and characters whose physical and personal characteristics were so blatant that only the dimmest audience members would miss what was being suggested. Being closeted extended from screen depictions to the lives of a long list of homosexual actors, directors, and producers who were forced to live double lives to survive professionally.

In the 1980s, Hollywood, confronted by the more open evidence of homosexual lifestyles produced by the growth of the gay and lesbian movement, responded with tepid films such as *Making Love* (1982), about the coming out of a repressed gay doctor. However, the AIDS epidemic (known as the "gay cancer") that started in the early 1980s presented filmmakers with a challenge. On the one hand, it was a headline story with almost daily casualty counts, including famous Hollywood names such as Rock Hudson publicly succumbing to the disease. Consequently, films that made people aware of the disease almost constituted a public service. It was also a topic filled with just the kinds of dramatic emotions and triumphs over adversity that was stock in trade for Hollywood filmmakers. On the other hand, there was the fear that these films would repel the more religious and homophobic members of the audience, and it would show up in what Hollywood revered more than topicality, public service, or sentiment—their profit margins.

One of the early films dealing with AIDS was the generally critically well-received *Long Time Companions* (1990) (it even garnered an Academy Award nomination for one of its leads, Bruce Davison). The film sympathetically traced the lives of a group of upper-middle-class gay friends from their first hearing about AIDS until it tragically alters all their lives. It was a small-budget, straightforward film—a touch too sanitized—that didn't receive the audience response it deserved. In contrast, Jonathan Demme's—an idiosyncratic director whose best work (e.g., *Something Wild* and *Citizens Band*) identified with individuals at odds with the social system—$25 million production of *Philadelphia* (1993) reached into the mainstream. His film gained for Tom Hanks, who played the AIDS-stricken lawyer Andrew Beckett, his first Academy Award for best actor. However, *Philadelphia* is much less about AIDS or homosexual lifestyles than it is about homophobia. Denzel Washington, playing Joe Miller, a macho, quick-witted, ambulance-chasing lawyer, is hired by Beckett to take his case against his White/Anglo-Saxon/Protestant, white-shoe law firm for wrongful termination and is the movie's real center.

Beckett, a personable, up-and-coming star at his firm, had been summarily dismissed when evidence of his AIDS became unmistakable. While Miller takes the case, perhaps because as a black man he can sympathize with the kind of discrimination that Beckett is confronted with, he's unprepared for the scrutiny that his own homophobic attitudes soon come under. From taking jibes about his own sexual preferences to even another black gay man trying to pick him up as well as fears that contact with Beckett might place his own family in jeopardy, Miller has to confront his own ignorance and prejudices about homosexuals and AIDS. Miller is the surrogate for the movie audience, which is supposed to identify with him exorcising his homophobic demons and achieving some form of liberal tolerance and understanding.

Throughout it all, the even-tempered Beckett maintains a strangely imperturbable stoicism quite at odds with his scene-by-scene physical deterioration. There is one scene in the film, however, where Beckett conveys intense feeling, and the film rises to high art. When Beckett and Miller meet to discuss the former's upcoming testimony, the film's frames go red with a passionate glare, and seen from a high overhead angle, Beckett glides around his loft with an IV in his arm ecstatically listening to Maria Callas's aria "O Mamma Morta" from Giordano's *Andrea Chenier*. He translates the words for Joe, especially its brilliant chorus, "I am oblivion. . . . Ah! I am love." In that moment, Joe, moved by Beckett's sensitivity and heartache, starts to transcend his own discomfort with gayness and begins to grasp their shared humanity.

Unfortunately, not everything in *Philadelphia* is quite as brilliant as that moment. For example, Beckett's old law firm colleagues are portrayed as kind of patrician devils, especially its gay-loathing senior partner (Jason Robards). In contrast, Andrew's suburban family, with Joanne Woodward as his mother, is practically a hallmark card of unconditional support and love, as is his non-sexual relationship (the film carefully avoids dealing with gay sex) with his nurturing partner, Miguel (Antonio Banderas). Demme has made a simplified, conventional (a great many courtroom confrontations) thesis film that is both moving and extremely safe. Andy Beckett is merely a nice man who happens to be gay and is suffering from a deadly disease. The film never goes any deeper than that in characterizing him or in evoking the gay social world. It's the type of skillful, emotionally manipulative, self-congratulatory film that Hollywood often makes so that it can display its liberalism while simultaneously leaving the audience emotionally and intellectually undisturbed.

The antithesis of being a safe and simplified film was Kimberly Peirce's gender-bending *Boys Don't Cry* (1999). The film is based on the 1993 murder of Brandon Teena, a cross-dresser who was killed because she/he had stolen the affections of the girlfriend of a Nebraska ex-con. *Boys Don't Cry* is a direct, emotionally honest film, and Hilary Swank, who won a 1999 Academy Award for best actress for her performance as Brandon Teena/Teena Brandon, captured the recklessness, eroticism, and pathos of Brandon Teena, who could no longer bear her life as a woman and decided to pass as a man.

At first, Brandon seemingly lives out her dream by linking up with two young thuggish sociopaths, John Lotter (Peter Sarsgaard) and Tom Nissen (Brendan Sexton III), and Lotter's girlfriend, the tough, deadpan, but dreamy Lana (Chloe Sevigny), who works in a spinach factory. Ironically, it is Brandon's feminine characteristics, especially her/his gentleness, that stand in such marked contrast to the cruelty of Lotter and Nissen and that first gain Lana's attention and then her love. It is this tenderness that also marks their love-making scenes in which Brandon somehow manages to get away with his masquerade.

When Brandon/Teena's impersonation is revealed, Lotter and Nissen's subsequent brutal rape and murder of her is almost too difficult to watch. In the process, Brandon/Teena is turned into an almost sainted victim, albeit one that is a petty criminal and whose pitiable fantasy life consists of wanting to go to Graceland with Lana. Furthermore, not since Richard Brooks's production of Truman Capote's *In Cold Blood* (1967) has a film captured, in its depiction of Lana's dysfunctional family life and its portrait of a social world consisting of shabby homes and trailers, cheerless roadhouses, and roads stretching out to nowhere, the bleakness of middle-American life (though there are times when the characters talk hopefully about the future where Peirce by using striking lighting, grants the barren landscape an eerie beauty). *Boys Don't Cry* is an unsentimental film that avoids condescending to its intellectually limited, socially marginal characters and feels both psychologically and socially true.

Images of victimization were hardly the exclusive province of gays and blacks in the 1990s. While the images of women projected by Hollywood were decidedly more positive, they were nonetheless permeated with ambiguity. On the one hand, Hollywood recognized the commercial potential of films that presented a positive image of women; on the other, it all too frequently presented those images in traditional genre packages that could subtly undermine that positive image. Two films, *A League of Their Own* (1992) and *Thelma and Louise* (1991), illustrate this paradox.

Penny Marshall's *A League of Their Own* depicts a neglected chapter in American sports history—the women's baseball league that was founded during World War II to help satisfy Americans' craving for the national pastime while many of the male ballplayers were away at war. The film centers on the creation and rise of the Rockford Peaches, one of the premier teams in that league. At the center of this contrived, sentimental story is the tension between the Hinson sisters. There is Dottie (Geena Davis), the married, totally professional, and highly talented catcher for the Peaches, and her angry younger pitcher sister, Kit (Lori Petty), who is petulant and clearly jealous of her sister's superior athletic ability. However, this film's only real virtue is capturing the bonding that went on among these female ballplayers who had to confront all sorts of male condescension and contempt because they just wanted to play ball. For example, the league had the players take charm lessons, and a number were recruited more for how they looked in short skirts than for their baseball skills. They also had to endure the sexist jeering of male fans and promotional slogans such as "Catch a foul ball, and get a kiss."

Despite its feminist perspective, the film all too frequently lapses into stereotypes (the team's owner is a miser, the chief scout a boor, and the manager [Tom Hanks] a sexist drunk who predictably is transformed into a proponent of women's baseball). Ugly-girl jokes abound, and the film even has Madonna playing a promiscuous character called "All the Way May." The film is well intentioned but permeated with clichés and patronizing stereotypes that subvert its supposed purpose.

It was controversy rather than condescension that surrounded flashy, high-concept director Ridley Scott (*Alien* and *Blade Runner*) and first-time scriptwriter Callie Khouri's *Thelma and Louise*. The film revolves around two women whose weekend getaway turns into a violent chase through an endless highway of motels, diners, and gas stations and a stunningly shot American Southwest landscape of plains, deserts, and John Ford's Monument Valley. Some critics charged that the adventures of the initially dizzy, guileless, and oppressed housewife Thelma (Geena Davis) and the tough, wary, independent waitress Louise (Susan Sarandon), whose violent response to an attempted rape send them on a cross-country crime-and male-chauvinist-pig-bashing spree, were examples of "toxic feminism," "a paean to transformative violence," and female "fascism."[38]

Much of the angry critical response to *Thelma and Louise* was engendered by the violence committed by the two women. However, it really exemplified the double standard at work from critics who barely raised an eyebrow when Arnold Schwarzenegger blew away dozens of people in *Total Recall* (1990) or who seemed to prefer women depicted as prostitutes transformed by a man into a Cinderella in the romantic comedy hit *Pretty Woman* (1990).

Critical outbursts aside, *Thelma and Louise* was a shrewd, entertaining, seamlessly constructed work of pop feminism. Both Thelma and Louise free themselves of the constraints of home, husband, and society and turn themselves into tough female outlaws. Feckless, sloppy, and a passive doormat for her idiotic, philandering husband Daryl (Christopher McDonald), Thelma is magically transformed (by a man) from bimbo into an erotically charged desperado who takes charge of her own destiny. Louise, a bit less stereotyped and more self-aware, is at first rigid and controlling but learns to loosen up and take life on its own terms.

The most frequently raised criticism of the film was its male bashing. The film contains a multitude of female revenge fantasies involving punishing would-be rapists, crude truck drivers, and Gestapo-like state troopers. The other male characters are also simplistic and include Thelma's previously mentioned husband, a cartoonish male chauvinist, and handsome J. D. (Brad Pitt), the manipulative convenience store bandit-hitchhiker who steals Thelma and Louise's money (not, however, before he treats Thelma to her first orgasm). More interesting and a touch more complicated is the character of Jimmy (Michael Madsen), Louise's hard-drinking, flawed, commitment-shy musician boyfriend who loves her enough to let her go, even after he proposes. Finally, there is the one and only truly good male, the sympathetic detective Hal Slocumbe (Harvey Keitel), who develops a paternalistic affection for Thelma and Louise—whose lives he wants to save.

The most often criticized aspect of the film even by feminists was Thelma and Louise's suicidal ending. Cornered by a posse of state troopers and FBI agents, the outlaw pair affirm their friendship with a kiss and opt to drive off a cliff rather than surrender. While some feminists saw it as a symbolic liberating gesture—the only choice for women in a male-dominated, oppressive society—many others saw the finale as overdetermined and the notion that a woman's freedom is discovered in death as absurd.

However, Thelma and Louise were trapped by more than just society or a posse; most of their actions were determined by the conventions of the road movie. Like *Bonnie and Clyde* (1967), *Easy Rider* (1969), and *Butch Cassidy and the Sundance Kid* (1969), death was inevitably the outcome of the journeys taken by the films' protagonists. Still, *Thelma and Louise* is the kind of genre film that remains open to multiple and often contradictory interpretations. One could even see the film's objectification of men as a sly, ironic comment on how countless Hollywood action films have treated women.

Thelma and Louise is open to manifold interpretations—it's a film without much intellectual or emotional depth. What is significant about the film, however, is not its complex treatment of feminist consciousness but rather its gift for creating powerful pop images of female independence.

That the genre conventions didn't always have to act as a straitjacket was demonstrated by Quentin Tarantino's *Pulp Fiction* (1994). Tarantino, a movie autodidact whose film school was a southern California local video store, directed the relentlessly energetic, heist-gone-bad film, *Reservoir Dogs* (1992), whose virtuoso profanity and multitude of pop-cultural references vaulted it almost overnight into an independent film cult classic. His less linear, larger-scale *Pulp Fiction* was an ironic, postmodernist reworking of familiar film noir clichés, such as the boxer who refuses to take a dive in a fixed fight, the gangster's moll with a roving eye, and the camaraderie of two professional killers.

Tarantino's postmodernist style was characterized by putting aside the traditional linear story line in favor of four overlapping stories that contain characters from each story as well as moving back and forward in time. His self-conscious dialogue was filled with comic riffs, such as hit man Vincent Vega (John Travolta) explaining to his volatile, born-again partner Jules Winnfield (Samuel L. Jackson wearing an Afro wig) that the cheeseburger in the Paris McDonald's was called a "Royale with cheese." There are also scenes where grisly violence explodes, only to turn into moments of black humor, such as when Vincent accidentally and literally blows a victim's brains out and the duo have to turn to Jules's hen-pecked nervous friend Jimmie (Tarantino) and the avuncular, ultrafastidious fixer Wolf (Harvey Keitel) to help them clean up the mess. Playing Jimmie, who's married to a black woman, Tarantino self-consciously demonstrates how hip and beyond conventional liberalism he is by tossing the word "nigger" around every chance he can get.

Nor does the film stint on pop-cultural references. For instance, Vincent takes his boss's glamorous, coke-sniffing wife, Mia (Uma Thurman), to Jack Rabbit Slim's, a 1950s retro restaurant that features Douglas Sirk steaks and a Buddy Holly martini, served by a waiter who looks like James Dean, and includes a twist concert introduced by an Ed Sullivan impersonator. There are also clear narrative references to films like *Kiss Me Deadly* (1955) and *Deliverance* (1972) and television shows like *Charlie's Angels*. In addition, to the delight of postmodernist theorists, Vincent dances a self-reflexive twist with Mia that resurrects memories of Travolta's greatest hit, his star-making role as Tony Manero in *Saturday Night Fever* (1977).

Tarantino's film is smart, entertaining, stylish (striking camera angles and 360-degree pans), and permeated with macho posturing. There are also moments where Tarantino's gothic, horror comic touches, such as the sadomasochism and male rape scenes where Butch and the black mob boss Marcellus Wallace (Ving Rhames) are imprisoned by a couple of redneck neo-Nazis, go over the top. What is most disturbing about Tarantino's films are their rejection of the real world and their lack of moral center. His films are about nothing more than words and images that, with originality and wit, parody Hollywood and television genres for audiences who are so insulated from the world that they desire nothing more.

In contrast to Tarantino's work, there were films, particularly in the early and late 1990s, that tried to consciously say something about American culture and society and about the emotional state of angry white males. Whether that white male anger stemmed from the loss of economic and social status as a consequence of the economic downturn that hit middle-class, mid-level-management males particularly hard in the beginning of the decade or the existential malaise that entrapped some middle-class suburban males in the more prosperous second half of the 1990s, the results were usually the same—self-destruction.

In Joel Schumacher's *Falling Down* (1993), Michael Douglas plays a laid-off defense worker, William Foster, an exasperated and volatile man just waiting to explode. On an extremely hot day in Los Angeles, he takes a murderous journey across a sun-baked nightmare city violently acting out what the director views as the fantasies of many ordinary urban dwellers. Confronted with a compendium of irritating to profound urban ills—from traffic jams, graffiti, jostling crowds, and general boorishness to smog, gangbangers, homelessness, and the omnipresence of guns—the film's brush-cutted Everyman strikes out at a variety of urban stereotypes, including dour Korean grocers and Latino thugs. (It is interesting that blacks and gays, who make up significant portions of the population of Los Angeles, are left untouched by his rampage.)

Falling Down is an exploitative, cartoonlike film that tries to have it both ways. Foster, or D-FENS (his moniker), is enough of an abusive father and trigger-happy sociopath to repel audiences with his behavior but also someone whose confusion over his loss of economic viability and social marginality and his desire for revenge they can identify with. The film makes D-FENS more sympathetic by juxtaposing him with a neo-Nazi, homophobic manager of an army-navy surplus store (played by Frederick Forrest) who he rejects as "a sick asshole." The film also suggests that D-FENS's fury is clearly more justifiable than the white-trash racist's. Schumacher's film ultimately illuminates little about the condition of American cities or the resentment and rage of an economically displaced Everyman—sacrificing social meaning for a fast-paced narrative and kinetic violence.

English theater director Sam Mendes's first film, the Oscar-winning *American Beauty* (1999), also focuses on an angry white man who wants out—the sour, ironic Lester Burnham (Kevin Spacey, who delivers every line with dazzling and subtle mockery). He's the sardonic center of a dysfunctional suburban family that includes his self-hating, uptight, materialistic wife Carolyn (Annette Bening does a nice bitchy turn) and their sullen teenage daughter Jane (Thora Birch). There is nothing left to their marriage but contempt and recriminations, and Lester, who has lost his odious job and his place in the family, finds solace only in salivating daydreams (rose petals floating out of her open sweater) about Jane's absurdly vain, nymphet friend, Angela (Mena Suvari). There is also a family of new neighbors, even more disturbed and alienated than the Burnhams. It consists of a rigid, homophobic, brutal ex–marine colonel father (who turns out predictably to be gay); his catatonic, servile wife; and their son Ricky (Wes Bentley)—an eerily perceptive drug dealer and voyeuristic loner who becomes involved with Jane.

American Beauty provides the blackest of comic portraits of American suburban life. There is nothing nuanced about this film—over-the-top caricatures being the rule and the social reality of the suburbs reduced to a few motifs, such as cheerleaders, selling real estate, jogging, and growing roses. There is also no reason to believe that the film's characters were ever happy and empathetic and that the distorted and disconnected lives they now lead are a consequence of America's destructive values.

The film is witty and contains striking and sometimes haunting imagery (the product of cinematographer Conrad Hall's keen eye)—like a plastic bag floating in the wind or Rick and Lester standing, a distance from each other against a blank wall, smoking pot. At the same time, it doesn't feel that different in its heavy-handed, melodramatic skewering of suburban lives than another black comedy permeated with loathing for a similar milieu, Todd Solondz's *Happiness* (1999).

What is most distinctive about *American Beauty* is Kevin Spacey's Lester, who is the one complex character in a gallery of basically one-dimensional figures. The cynical man who feels he's dead already renews himself as an aggressive adolescent—smoking dope, building up his body, blackmailing his boss, and becoming sexually turned on. Spacey's discovery of some personal peace before being killed may be self-consciously poeticized, but it's much more imaginative than Mendes's social satire of suburban life.

The world of Mendes's *American Beauty* is a bitingly comic mirror of Stanley Kubrick's final film (he died at age 70 before its release), *Eyes Wide Shut* (1999). It's a film that provides a fitting movie coda to American cinema's fin de siècle.

Kubrick had already peeked across the millennial divide in his mystical and socially critical *2001: A Space Odyssey* (1968) and the violent, nihilistic *A Clockwork Orange* (1971). Kubrick's coldly cerebral, ironic, formally imaginative films were always eagerly awaited. This was the case with *Eyes Wide Shut*, his first feature since the Vietnam War film *Full Metal Jacket* (1987). The expectations of the film were accentuated by rumors flying about dozens of takes, continuous reshooting, and the absolute secrecy required by Kubrick of all its participants. None of these production problems and personal tics were new for a perfectionist like Kubrick. Nevertheless, the usual anticipation was heightened by his death and the advanced hype that began to build up around the film, which now also took on something of the weight and significance of a last testament.

Disappointment was bound to result from such high expectations. Stanley Kauffmann, in *The New Republic*, titled his review of *Eyes Wide Shut* "Kubrick: A Sadness"[39] and said that the film was "a catastrophe." Other critics attacked Tom Cruise's performance and Kubrick's inability to convincingly capture the relationship between a man and woman. There were, however, a few critics who differed. For example, Janet Maslin wrote a rave review in the *New York Times*, stating, "This astonishing film is a spellbinding addition to the Kubrick canon."

The fact that *Eyes Wide Shut* evoked such widespread condemnation and such passionate praise is less a sign of failure than the film touching on some profound critical nerve.[40] Perhaps it was Kubrick's treatment of sexuality in this film—a mixture of cold, voyeuristic interest (a great many shots of female nudes) and utter revulsion—connected, on a deeper level, to the linkage of sex and death in so many of his works. For example, it was a repeated motif in *Dr. Strangelove*'s scene of airplanes copulating and in *Full Metal Jacket*'s drill sergeant urging his men to treat their rifles like their mistresses. The film also projected a view of bourgeois marriage that saw it as a mixture of tenderness, loyalty, boredom, spite, and alienation.

The inspiration for *Eyes Wide Shut* was Arthur Schnitzler's 1926 novella *Traumnovelle*. Schnitzler's work, though rarely read or staged today, was highly regarded in his day. Sigmund Freud, who was his contemporary in Vienna, considered Schnitzler his equal in the understanding and acknowledgment of sexuality as a singular force in the human condition. Though Kubrick was probably aware of Freud's high regard for Schnitzler, it could hardly have been the deciding factor in his attempt to adapt the novel to the screen. His use of the novella probably had more to do with its investigations of sex and the dissection of the ways in which dreams and the irrational erupted into reality.

Actually, Kubrick's attempt to do a film about sex and sexuality went back to the 1960s, when he tried to adapt Terry Southern's novel *Blue Movie* to the screen. Ironically, *Blue Movie* dealt with a highbrow director's efforts to make a big-budget porn movie with famous stars. With Tom Cruise and Nicole Kidman as his stars in *Eyes Wide Shut*, Kubrick seemed to be turning Southern's fiction into a reality.

Of course, *Eyes Wide Shut* is not porn (Warner Bros. made absolutely sure of that by digitally censoring some graphic sexual imagery in the film's orgy scenes). It is, however, a string of dreamlike sequences—all of them beautifully shot with a stately tracking camera, strikingly eerie lighting, and emotionally resonant long shots of the protagonist walking down abandoned streets and long, empty halls and corridors—of a man who has lost his moorings. However, the few scenes that are psychologically incisive alternate with scenes so labored and self-conscious that they made one wonder if someone other than the driven perfectionist Kubrick was responsible for its final cut.

Eyes Wide Shut focuses on a young, beautiful, moneyed, upper-middle-class New York couple, Dr. Bill Harford (Tom Cruise) and his wife Alice (Nicole Kidman), who are invited to a Christmas Eve party at the home of a millionaire friend (whose conventional, easygoing persona belies his corrupt nature) where they both engage in sexual flirtations. After smoking some pot, Alice cruelly confesses having had, the previous summer, a wild sexual fantasy about a young naval officer. This admission and the midnight summons to the home of a dying patient sends Bill out on a long night's journey where he has a series of sexual encounters that range from the mysterious to the absurd and finally to the dangerous and forbidding.

What links Bill's encounters is their heavy coupling of sex and death and their dreamlike quality. Thus, Marion (Marie Richardson), the tremulous daughter of his dead patient whom Bill has hardly ever spoken to, peremptorily confesses her passionate love for him at her father's deathbed. The scene is exquisitely lit, and the two of them, seen in two-shot, seem like characters in a powerful, soft-focused dream. Then the friendly prostitute (Vinessa Shaw), with whom Bill has a casual and interrupted encounter and whom Bill attempts to visit the next day, turns out to be HIV positive. Finally, the mysterious naked hooker who saves Bill's life at an orgy he contrives to attend is found dead of an overdose.

The linkage of sex, danger, and death is harnessed to Kubrick's theme of the ways in which the irrational erupts into and disrupts life, as in *The Shining* (1980), where a writer's inner demons prompt him to murder. In *Eyes Wide Shut*, it is Alice's recounting of her sexual fantasy and then later of a nymphomaniacal nightmare that disrupt the complacency of their supposedly harmonious marriage and are replayed compulsively like black-and-white pornographic films in Bill's mind. Later, Bill visits the costume shop of a sly, bearded Milich (Rade Sherbedgia [Serbedzija]), who self-righteously excoriates the Japanese tourists playing sex games with his daughter, only later to sell her sexual services to them as well as offering them to Bill.

It is the lengthy orgy scene that aroused the most intense criticism. With its masked and costumed participants, almost naked models in masks and thongs, ominous music, and couples engaged in sex, the sequence is stiff, nonsensical, and overly solemn and, despite its bizarre surface, lacking in sexual and emotional energy. Nonetheless, it provides a dramatic denouement for what otherwise might have been a loosely connected series of sexual misadventures. More important, the orgy scene, with its combination of pagan mystery and Black Mass, is in keeping with Kubrick's sexual vision, where sex has almost nothing to do with erotic pleasure and everything to do with chilling cynicism about the human condition. For example, Alex, the Droogie, in *Clockwork Orange* refers to sex as a sterile, mechanical act—the "old in and out." In *Eyes Wide Shut*, Kubrick connects sex with almost everything that seems corrupt and frightening.

It is this collision with the nightmarish world of their sexual fantasies and decadent sex that send Bill and Alice scurrying back to the safety and complacency of their bourgeois marriage. In the film's final moments, they speak of their desire to start over, but first, in Alice's words, they have to do something important: "fuck." For Kubrick, this is a relatively happy ending. Kubrick makes it clear that their once-shut eyes have opened a bit. They have awakened to the complex longings and darker undercurrents of marriage—to the existence, in symbolic terms, of the orgy mask (that in one scene lies on a pillow next to the sleeping Alice) in their lives.

Despite most critics viewing *Eyes Wide Shut* as an abject failure, it is an ambitious, deeply problematic film that despite its profound flaws is a memorial to a filmmaker's lifetime obsessions and themes. One might point to it as evidence that Kubrick was still capable of change even at this late stage of his career since *Eyes Wide Shut* is the first film in which he ever really attempted to deal with human intimacy (though Cruise's character remains a cipher and the relationship between him and Kidman lacks any heat or depth). More significant, Kubrick's *Eyes Wide Shut* stands as a fitting monument to the cinema, which reached its hundredth anniversary in the 1990s. Indeed, *Eyes*

Wide Shut, with its evocation of dreams and fantasies and the role they play in our everyday lives, provides a parallel to the impact of film illusion and fantasies on our own psychic landscapes. American films have allowed us to roam far and wide in time and space. They have also permitted us, as we have argued throughout this book, some consciousness and understanding of the spirit of the times and the culture. One has little reason to doubt that that American film will continue to supply the same opportunity for entertainment, escape, and even insight in the millennium to come.

NOTES

1. Eric Hobsbawm, *The Age of Extremes: A History of the World, 1914–1991* (New York: Vintage Books, 1996), pp. 1–17.

2. Michael R. Beschloss and Strobe Talbott, *At the Highest Levels: The Inside Story of the End of the Cold War* (New York: Little, Brown, 1994), pp. 475–93.

3. Hobsbawm, *The Age of Extremes*, pp. 461–99.

4. Thomas L. Friedman, *The Lexus and the Olive Tree* (New York: Anchor Books, 2000), pp. xi–xxii.

5. George Stephanopoulos, *All Too Human: A Political Education* (New York: Little, Brown, 1999), pp. 81–107.

6. Martin Walker, *The President We Deserve: Bill Clinton: His Rise, Falls and Comeback* (New York: Crown, 1996), p. 347.

7. Jonathan Chait, "The Slippery Center," *The New Republic* (November 16, 1998), pp. 19–21.

8. Lars-Erik Nelson, "Clinton and His Enemies," *New York Review of Books* (January 20, 2000), pp. 18–22.

9. Stephanopoulos, *All Too Human*, pp. 51–80.

10. Ibid., pp. 64–67.

11. Jeffrey Toobin, *A Vast Conspiracy: The Real Story of the Sex Scandal That Nearly Brought Down a President* (New York: Touchstone, 1999).

12. Friedman, *The Lexus and the Olive Tree*, pp. 3–28.

13. John Pierson, *Spike, Mike, Slackers and Dykes: A Guided Tour across a Decade of American Independent Cinema* (New York: Hyperion, 1997), pp. 6–20.

14. Peter Bart, *Who Killed Hollywood? . . . and Put the Tarnish on Tinseltown* (Los Angeles: Renaissance Books, 1999), pp. 64–65.

15. Louis Menand, "Independence Day," *New York Review of Books* (September 19, 1996), pp. 14–16.

16. Mel Gussow, "A Child (and an Adult) of War: A Military Historian Puts a Vivid Cast on World War I," *New York Times* (July 3, 1999), p. B11.

17. Tom Wicker, "Does 'JFK' Conspire against Reason?," *New York Times: Sunday Arts and Leisure* (December 15, 1991), pp. 1, 18.

18. James Petras, "The Discrediting of the Fifth Estate: The Press Attacks on JFK," *Cineaste* 19 (Winter 1992), p. 15.

19. Bernard Weinraub, "Nixon Family Assails Stone Film as Distortion," *New York Times* (December 19, 1995), p. C18.

20. Garry Wills, "Dostoyevsky behind a Camera: Oliver Stone Is Making Great American Novels on Film," *The Atlantic Monthly* (July 1997), pp. 96–101.

21. William Grimes, "What Debt Does Hollywood Owe to Truth?," *New York Times* (March 5, 1992), pp. C15, 22.

22. Norman Mailer, "Footfalls in the Crypt," *Vanity Fair* (February 1992), pp. 124–29, 171.

23. Lance Morrow and Martha Smilgis, "Plunging into the Labyrinth," *Time* (December 23, 1991), pp. 74–76.

24. Anthony Summers, *Conspiracy* (New York: Paragon, 1989), p. 11. This book has been reissued with the new title, *Not in Your Lifetime: The Definitive Book on the JFK Assassination* (New York: McGraw-Hill, 1998).

25. Fawn Brodie, *Richard Nixon: The Shaping of His Character* (Cambridge, MA: Harvard University Press, 1983), p. 76.

26. Nicholas Lemann, "Buffaloed: Was the Native American Always Nature's Friend?," *The New Yorker* (September 1, 1999), pp. 98–101.

27. D. H. Lawrence, *Studies in Classic American Literature* (New York: Doubleday and Co., 1951), pp. 43–73.

28. "Titanic Praised by Chinese President Jiang Zemin as Politically Correct Class Warfare," *Wall Street Journal* (May 15, 1998), p. 11.

29. Frank Bruni, "Wagging Tongues in 'Incredibly Cynical Times'," *New York Times* (August 21, 1998), p. C19.

30. Andrew Hacker, *Two Nations: Black and White, Separate, Hostile, Unequal* (New York: Charles Scribner's Son, 1992), pp. 67–92.

31. Ibid., pp. 179–98.

32. Playthell Benjamin, "These Boyz Lives: Let Us Now Praise (or Pan) Menace: Six Critics Speak," *Village Voice* (May 25, 1993), p. 23.

33. Stephan and Abigail Thernstrom, *America in Black and White: One Nation Indivisible* (New York: Touchstone, 1997), pp. 183–202.

34. Berel Lang, *Act and Idea in the Nazi Genocide* (Chicago: University of Chicago Press, 1990), p. 151.

35. Norman Finkelstein, *The Holocaust Industry: Reflections on the Exploitation of Jewish Suffering* (New York: Verso, 2000).

36. Randall Robinson, *The Debt: What America Owes to Blacks* (New York: Dutton, 2000), p. 216.

37. Vito Russo, *The Celluloid Closet: Homosexuality in the Movies* (New York: Harper and Row, 1987).

38. "Why Thelma and Louise Strike a Nerve," *Time* (June 24, 1991), pp. 52–56.

39. Stanley Kauffmann, "Kubrick: A Sadness," *The New Republic* (August 16, 1999), pp. 30–31.

40. Graham Fuller, "Is *Eyes Wide Shut* a Genius's Final Erotic Masterpiece? Over to the U.S. Critics," *The Observer* (July 18, 1999), p. 6.

8

2000–2009

The lamps are going out all over Europe; we shall not see them lit again in our lifetime.
                        —Lord Edward Grey (1862–1933), August 3, 1914

That memorable comment could have been uttered about what occurred on September 11, 2001, in New York. On that horrific, apocalyptic day, two jetliners crashed into the World Trade Center in New York City, killing almost 3,000 people, as well as another that dove into the Pentagon in Washington, D.C., murdering another 300 people. A fourth crashed into a field in Pennsylvania, destroying all aboard. The bombing was an assault on civilization and an act of war that created chaos, terror, and despair in New York; overwhelmed the area's hospitals and blood supply; and exposed recovery workers to dust laden with cancer-causing asbestos. Americans all live now with the foreboding that another bombing attack will likely take place, especially given the emergence of incidents involving homegrown terrorists seeking to collaborate with al-Qaeda.

The events of September 11 were perhaps the most violently catastrophic in a decade, which *Time* magazine, in its December 7, 2009, cover story called "The Decade from Hell." It was a decade that began with a disputed election and ended with the severest economic downturn since 1929, one that economists and journalists began referring to as "The Great Recession."[1]

The irony of it all was that it was preceded by a decade in which peace and prosperity were preeminent. The end of the Cold War and the breaking down of the Iron Curtain had ushered in a decade in which some overly sanguine historians spoke of "The End of History,"[2] and economists saw the American budget turn deficits into surpluses, as the nation seemed to be moving toward full employment.

But this decade had a forbidding beginning. It opened with a constitutional crisis where the fate of the nation hung for 36 days on some "hanging chads" (bits of ballot) in Florida that would show whether voters had preferred Vice President Al Gore or Texas governor George Bush in the 2000 presidential election. Though Gore received more than 500,000 more popular votes than Bush nationwide, victory hung on which candidate would win Florida's electoral vote. Ultimately, the courts were called in to decide whether to halt the recounting of the Florida ballots with Governor Bush ahead by fewer than 300 votes. And only after a politically biased, majority Republican Supreme Court, by a slim five-to-four margin, weighed in to stop the recount did Vice President Al Gore concede and Governor Bush declared the winner.

In Bush's first year in office, his achievements proved to be meager. He pushed through Congress regressive tax cuts that served mainly the wealthy and helped create giant deficits and an underfunded "No Child Left Behind" education bill (an example of Bush's "compassionate conservatism") that was supposed to raise educational standards. In a startling reversal of previous foreign policy, he killed the adherence of the United States to the internationally agreed-on 1997 Kyoto proposals on climate change as well as uncritically backing Israeli positions in the Middle East rather than attempting to be a mediator and honest broker in the manner of previous administrations, such as those of Bill Clinton and Bush's own father—not that any of them succeeded in making much of a dent in that endless conflict.

As a result, September 10, 2001, found him with the lowest favorable rating ever recorded of any president in his first year in office.[3] However, after Bush's initial stunned response and disappearance during the first terrifying, agonizing days after 9/11 and despite the failure of government intelligence agencies and the administration to deal with the domestic terrorist threat before and on that day, he ultimately found his footing as a war president.

Within a few weeks after 9/11, he initiated a bipartisan-supported international "War on Terror," launching bomb attacks in Afghanistan that led al-Qaeda, the terrorist group who planned and carried out the World Trade Center attacks, and their Taliban allies to flee the capital of Kabul. Unfortunately, in the aftermath of those quick victories, the United States and its Afghan allies failed to capture the leadership of al-Qaeda and the Taliban (Osama bin Laden, Ayman al-Zawahiri, and Mullah Omar), permitting them to continue their armed struggle against the United States and its Afghan and NATO allies.

The attacks in Afghanistan were a prelude to the Bush administration's much grander ambitions in the Middle East. Encouraged by a group of neo conservatives (who were committed to aggressively spreading American power and democracy abroad) whom he had appointed to office in the Defense Department and National Security Council, such as Paul Wolfowitz, Douglas Feith, John Bolton, and hawkish Republican holdovers from the Nixon, Ford, and Reagan administrations, like his vice president, Dick Cheney, and Secretary of Defense Donald Rumsfeld, Bush used the crisis to promote a final reckoning with Iraqi dictator Saddam Hussein.

Under the guise of protecting the world from the weapons of mass destruction that they claimed Saddam Hussein possessed and the reported shadowy links between the Iraqi regime and al-Qaeda, the Bush administration prepared to invade Iraq. They were undeterred by UN investigators who couldn't find any evidence of weapons of mass destruction, and the decision to go to war was spurred with comments like their refusal to permit "the smoking gun to be a mushroom cloud."[4] The administration's commitment was buttressed by using the enormous prestige of Secretary of State Colin Powell, who gullibly accepted misguided and erroneous information fed by the CIA to make a convincing argument at the United Nations for an invasion.

Within a month of a bombing campaign that was arrogantly dubbed "shock and awe," the forces invading Iraq, which also included the British, succeeded in toppling the Hussein regime. And on May 1, 2003, on the aircraft carrier *Abraham Lincoln*, President George W. Bush grandiloquently declared, "Mission accomplished."

Bush, of course, couldn't have been more wrong. Not only was the mission not accomplished, but what it ushered in was an insurgency that has lasted to this very day. Not only were no weapons of mass destruction discovered after the invasion, but the United States made a series of mistakes that encouraged the horrendous violence that followed the invasion.

Cautioned early on by a former chief of staff of the armed forces, General Eric Shinseki, that the invasion force was not large enough to succeed in pacifying Iraq after the invasion and the lack of any real postinvasion planning, Iraq quickly became the scene of deadly chaos. In addition to constant attacks on Allied forces by al-Qaeda and Sunni insurgents, there was disastrous looting subsequent to the invasion and the rise of militias beholden to radical Shiite Islamic clerics like Muktada el-Sadr, who openly defied and waged war against the "occupation." Even more potentially disastrous was the open warfare that developed between Sunni and Shia Muslim communities in Iraq that verged on civil war.

In addition, the insurgency was fueled by the misguided policies of the Coalition Provisional Authority (as the American-led government was called), policies that dismantled the Iraqi army, resulting in thousands of trained and armed men ready to battle the Americans. Further exacerbating the anger at the Americans, not only in Iraq but also throughout the world, were the reports and pictures in the press in April 2004 of the barbaric conduct of American guards at Abu Ghraib prison, where Iraqi prisoners were routinely abused, humiliated, and tortured.

Nor were abuses and questionable policies and practices confined to Iraq. Using the threats to national security as their rationale, the Bush administration, backed up by Justice Department attorney John Yoo's dubious legal formulations, engaged in actions that at the very least bordered on the unconstitutional and at worst as violations of human rights. These policies included illegal wiretaps by the National Security Administration and the rendition (sending terrorist suspects abroad) to black sites (foreign countries that permitted torture), where they were often subjected to so-called enhanced interrogation methods that included the forbidden practice known as "waterboarding."

The Bush administration also espoused and practiced a theory of executive power ("unitary executive") that greatly expanded the power of the presidency. Our mean-spirited Darth Vader of a vice president, Dick Cheney, refused to turn over to sanctioned congressional committees documents regarding consultations he had involving energy issues. They also overreacted to a critical op-ed article by Ambassador Joseph Wilson casting further doubts on the need for the invasion. In order to punish him, they "outed" his wife, Valerie Plame, a CIA agent. Frank Rich wrote that this action against Wilson "was a replay of the gangster tactics of the Watergate felon, Charles Colson,"[5] who sought to smear Daniel Ellsberg after he had leaked the Pentagon Papers to the *New York Times*. And the president himself routinely issued "signing statements" that permitted him to ignore portions of laws passed by Congress that he did not agree with—a systematic attempt to take power from the legislative branch. Furthermore, ensuring that these kinds of conservative practices might be enshrined in American politics for decades to come, the president appointed, with some Democrats voting against them, ultraconservative justices to the Supreme Court—Chief Justice John Roberts and Associate Justice Samuel Alito Jr.

The failures in Iraq, where casualties mounted, appeared to make President Bush vulnerable in the 2004 election. However, a compound of clever election tactics that emphasized fears over national security with anxieties about social issues such as gay marriage proved to be a winning strategy—this, coupled with the mistakes of his opponent, the solemn, stiff, but knowledgeable Senator John Kerry, a Massachusetts Democrat. Despite exhibiting a mastery over the complexities of foreign policy, Kerry had embarrassingly waffled on some key issues, such as funding for the Iraq War ("He was for it before he was against it"). He had also allowed himself—a Vietnam medal winner—to be "swift-boated" by a group of pro-Bush Vietnam veterans questioning his war record in Vietnam. This allowed the much less informed, sometimes oblivious Bush, who projected an affable, regular-guy persona, to gain a narrow election victory.

Riding the crest of his 2004 election victory, President Bush seemed poised to enact a right wing agenda that undermined hallowed social programs, such as Social Security, which he planned to privatize. However, the first blow that undermined the second Bush term was struck by nature.

In August 2005, Hurricane Katrina, a category 5 storm, hit the city of New Orleans—one of the poorest metropolitan areas in the country. The city weathered the hurricane but not the subsequent storm surge, which breached a number of the already weak levees that were supposed to protect the city. In the wake of the storm, more than 2,000 people died—the majority poor and black—and the damage to property was in the billions of dollars. Television footage powerfully evoked a city filled with dead bodies decaying for days on its streets and in its yards, amid mounds of debris and abandoned and pulverized homes. The federal and state response to this tragedy was incompetent at best and indifferent at worst—a monument to the failure of the idea of limited government.

The president reacted to the catastrophe very slowly. Instead, he delegated his response to the head of the Federal Emergency Management Agency, Michael Brown, whose previous experience as head of the International Arabian Horse Association hardly qualified him to deal with such an extensive disaster. In addition, the president's public praise for Brown ("heck of a job, Brownie") ranked with his "mission accomplished" speech as a major blunder and a symptom of his administration's utter lack of awareness of the calamity's extent.

The appointment of Brown—a striking illustration of the Bush administration's cronyism—was linked to a culture of corruption that seemed to permeate the Republican Party (not that the Democrats were free of the taint of corruption). Fed by the belief that there would be a permanent Republican majority and control of all branches of government, hard-line conservative Republican Majority Leader Tom DeLay of Texas allowed a lobbyist, Jack Abramoff, to influence legislation in return for huge campaign donations and perks such as golf vacations abroad. Nor was the corruption involved solely with money. The Republican Party, which prided itself as the upholder of family values, saw that image badly tarnished when Republican Congressman Mark Foley of Florida was revealed to have sent sexually inappropriate e-mails to congressional interns.

Cronyism and corruption were hardly the only things undoing the Bush presidency; there was also the lingering disaster of the Iraqi occupation that was resulting in rising casualty rates as well as calls for U.S. withdrawal. And all these factors led to a reversal of the Republican hopes for a permanent Republican majority when the Democrats gained control of Congress after the 2006 election. Those hopes were further undercut by the symptoms of economic collapse that were coursing through the financial system. Spurred by the bursting of a housing bubble that had been fueled by subprime lending (giving mortgages to people with less-than-ample credit or collateral) and further aggravated by the bundling of those mortgages into so-called derivatives that were then traded among banks and investment houses, a number of venerable but avaricious financial institutions found themselves in ruinous economic situations. The first sign of the coming financial disaster occurred in March 2008, when the investment house of Bear Stearns, which had even weathered the Great Depression, collapsed and was merged with JP Morgan Chase. The shock waves from this failure reverberated through the economy as mortgage foreclosures increased and financial institutions showed an increasing reluctance to extend credit to businesses, leading to layoffs of employees.

Finally, in September 2008, the respected financial services firm of Lehman Brothers was forced into bankruptcy. This sent a further chill throughout the financial world, in turn resulting in a freezing of credit because banks that were wary of the solvency of other banks refused to lend money to those banks. The unraveling of the credit market produced a downward spiral that brought the entire economy to the brink of collapse and an economic depression that might have eclipsed that of 1929.

Only the infusion of federal funds with a more than $700 billion "bailout" (the Troubled Asset Relief Program) saved mortgage companies like Freddie Mac and Fannie Mae from collapse as well as private companies like the giant insurer AIG and a number of megabanks such as Citibank, Bank of America, and Wells Fargo from going under. The bailout was seen as a necessity but was criticized for not placing strict controls on what the banks and AIG did with the money.

All this occurred as the United States was going through one of the most historically momentous presidential elections in its history. On the Democratic Party side, along with Senator Joe Biden of Delaware, former senator and 2004 vice-presidential candidate John Edwards of South Carolina, and Governor Bill Richardson of New Mexico, it pitted two outstanding untraditional candidates: a woman, Senator Hillary Clinton of New York, and a barely known African American, Senator Barack Obama of Illinois, both of whom had a real chance of becoming the nominee and the first of their sex and race to become president.

For the Republican Party, burdened with the Bush record and loss of political capital, its nominees included Bush's foremost challenger in the 2000 presidential primary campaign, Senator John McCain of Arizona; Rudolph Giuliani, the former mayor of New York City who was touted as and continually promoted himself a hero for his leadership of the city after 9/11; Mitt Romney, the former moderate governor of Massachusetts; and some dark-horse candidates, such as Libertarian Congressman Ron Paul of Texas, the Bible-thumping ex-governor Mike Huckabee, and the bland ex-senator turned television actor Fred Thompson of Tennessee.

For the Democratic Party, the race quickly boiled down to an intense and often bitter struggle between Obama and Clinton. Initially, the vaunted Clinton machine was expected to steer the senator smoothly toward the nomination. However, Senator Obama's surprise win in Iowa narrowed the race down to three candidates and, after Clinton pulled a comeback in New Hampshire, to two candidates. Then both candidates slogged through a number of primaries and at the end of the process the most delegates.

Obama gained the nomination because of his campaign's discipline and superior fund-raising ability—using untraditional means of raising campaign financing through the Internet—and because of the enthusiasm he generated among Hispanics and black voters and especially among young voters with his message of change. Finally, the campaign's imaginative organizing, which focused on caucus states where a few votes made the difference, was ignored by the Clinton campaign, a strategic mistake that was a significant cause of her defeat.

Obama's campaign contained the usual gaffes and crises that dog almost any presidential campaign. There were his seemingly offhand comments about "bitter people"[6] in small-town America that allowed the Clinton campaign to label him an elitist and out of touch with the working class (a tag that the Republicans continued to use against him). Foremost of these difficulties, however, was dealing with Obama's bitter, self-aggrandizing former pastor, the Reverend Jeremiah Wright's vitriolic video diatribes against America as a white supremacist country. Wright's tirades made it necessary for Obama to address the issue of race in a speech that was next to his 2004 Democratic Party keynote address, the best of his career. Obama evoked the complexities of the racial situation in this country, stating that for the African American community, the "path [to a more perfect union] means embracing the burdens of our past without becoming victims of our past."[7] And "in the white community, the path to a more perfect union means acknowledging that what ails the African-American community does not just exist in the minds of black people"[8] but is a legacy of discrimination. It was an eloquent, subtle, and conciliatory address that set the tone for the rest of the Obama's civil, intelligent, and graceful issue-based campaign against the Republican defamation machine.

Despite these stumbles, by June 2008 Obama had sealed his victory. And in a convention that was more like a coronation, culminating in an outdoor acceptance speech rally attended by thousands, Obama accepted the nomination along with his veteran and more populist vice-presidential ticket mate, Senator Joe Biden. Initially, the Republican nomination was equally hard fought. After the Iowa caucuses, won surprisingly by Governor Mike Huckabee of Arkansas, based on his appeal to religious fundamentalists, who played a large role in the Iowa caucuses, the campaign of Senator McCain seemed moribund. But McCain's maverick appeal to New Hampshire voters breathed new life into his campaign. This, coupled with his embrace of fundamentalists in the ensuing South Carolina primary, propelled him into the lead. On the other hand, the campaigns of his chief adversaries seemed to implode. Giuliani's strategy of ignoring the early primaries and waiting for the Florida primary, where he stood some chance of winning, never succeeded. Huckabee, despite strong support from conservative Christian fundamentalists, never gained any traction with moderates or the party elite and suffered from a lack of funds. Governor Romney experienced no such lack, but, dogged by questions from the party's base over his Mormon beliefs and his changes of position on social issues such as abortion and gay marriage, he won a few primaries but trailed McCain badly. By March 2008, McCain was universally acknowledged as the nominee.

The one wild-card note injected into the coming election was McCain's surprise choice of Governor Sarah Palin of Alaska as his running mate. McCain chose the little-known governor in order to gain fresh political support for his underwhelming campaign; take the spotlight off his opponent, who had before the Democratic Convention made a triumphal tour of Asia and Europe; and thought he could elicit the support of a number of women Democrats who were disaffected by the Democrats' rejection of their favorite, Hillary Clinton.

Initially, it seemed a compelling and brilliant move. Palin wowed the convention with her populist "hockey mom"[9] attacks on Obama. This, coupled with her good looks and a carefully crafted personal narrative as an activist who fought the big-money interests in Alaska, even if they were fellow Republicans, complemented by a telegenic family, was bought by and served to energize the Republican base that had been wary of McCain. The base saw the charismatic Palin as an Everywoman who they felt represented their feelings and beliefs in the best way possible. However, what she was a tough, sharp-tongued political pro with a talent for facile demagoguery. She worked hard at turning white-working class voters against Obama—treating him as a symbol of Ivy League elitism and intellectuality; as well as in a more veiled manner exploiting his unusual family history and his being black.

McCain's gamble, however, was undermined by Palin's lack of preparedness for the media scrutiny that follows any national candidate. Palin was undone by a series of television interviews with a low-key network anchorman, ABC's Charles Gibson, where she seemed unsure and uncertain of even some of the basic policy issues of the past decade. And in a subsequent interview with CBS's Katie Couric, she displayed an abysmal lack of knowledge about some of the most important aspects of American political culture. Added to this was the ongoing satire of Palin, where some of her comments, like believing that she had foreign policy expertise because she could see Russia from her window, became instant fodder for late-night comedians and a hilarious on-target imitation by Tina Fey on *Saturday Night Live*.

Yes, Palin's performance may have exhilarated the Republican base, but it was a drag on the McCain candidacy and with the larger voting public, especially independent voters. In addition, the once-upon-a-time man of honor John McCain desperately descended into the Nixonian depths in the campaign and engineered a venomous attack on Obama as a "socialist." That didn't help him, and neither did his own uncertain actions as the financial crisis deepened. President Bush had called both candidates to the White House to participate in meetings about the bank bailout bill that was having trouble passing Congress. McCain initially said he was going to suspend his campaign and even pull out of the first presidential debate because of the crisis. Then, after suffering criticism for his actions, he suddenly reversed himself.

In those debates, a grim-looking McCain hardly distinguished himself, barely looking at his opponent and in one debate and referring to Obama as "that one."[10] And Obama's election campaign, with the help of experienced political operatives such as David Axelrod and David Plouffe, was as disciplined and well financed as the primary one. Eschewing public funding and raising $750 million in campaign contributions, Obama was able to mount campaigns in every state, even ones that were considered Republican strongholds, such as Indiana. Accompanying this were legions of well-organized volunteers who rang doorbells, manned phone banks, and brought out the vote on Election Day.

Obama won the election with 53 percent of the vote, and on election night, November 4, 2008, in Chicago's Grant Park, there was a tumultuous celebration of his victory. President-elect Obama addressed cheering crowds (included among them were a teary Jesse Jackson and Oprah Winfrey), black and white, young and old. For black men and women, this was a moment few thought they would see in their lifetime. The great civil rights warrior John Lewis said that he had few tears left after witnessing that moment. Obama, more eloquent and self-possessed than ever in this transcendent moment, made a plea for unity that would help the nation deal with the dangerous multiple crises it faces.

A similar reaction occurred when Obama was inaugurated on January 20, 2009, in Washington, D.C. A crowd estimated at approximately 2 million showed up for the ceremonies. Many of them expected all sorts of rhetorical fireworks from the gifted orator Obama. However, he was unusually solemn as he took the oath of office in a time of two ferocious wars and an economic downturn that had already destroyed the lives of many millions of Americans and threatened even more. Obama spelled out some of the errors of the previous years. And implicitly criticizing the Bush administration, he stated that "for our common defense, we reject as false the choice between our safety and our ideals." He called for a new "era of responsibility" and told them that the challenges would be met.[11]

We would be suspending our critical faculties and be overly sanguine if we could say that Obama had met most of these challenges in the two years he's been in office. Obviously, the jury is still out on the Obama presidency. Obama had succeeded in getting an economic stimulus bill through Congress with the help of a minimum of Republican support (only three Republican senators voted for it). It was a bill that was criticized by some liberal economists as not going far enough in the amount of money pumped into the economy and for containing too much tax relief. There were other positive actions by the administration. These include lifting the Bush restrictions on federally funded embryonic stem cell research, appointing the first Latina to the U.S. Supreme Court, signing a law committed to improving the ability of women who allege pay discrimination to sue their employer, and committing the United States to reducing nuclear proliferation. And, of course, the most significant act, the health reform bill, which some Republicans predicted would be Obama's "Waterloo," proved to be his greatest triumph in his first year and a half in office. After enduring a long string of crises and modifications during its seemingly endless 14-month passage through Congress, where the administration had to deal with a shrewdly manipulated, vitriolic backlash from all the usual interest groups—medical practitioners, insurance and pharmaceutical companies, and the added opposition of a number of moderate/conservative Blue Dog Democrats (frightened of voter backlash)—the bill became law in March 2010. Overnight, Obama, whose presidency was beginning to be compared to that of Jimmy Carter, suddenly seemed, at least hyperbolically, a new Franklin Roosevelt.

In foreign policy, Obama signaled a new era of American engagement, especially in the Middle East. In a speech in Cairo, he acknowledged the grievances of the Palestinians and balanced it with the needs of the Israelis. He also moved to "reset" U.S.-Russian relations by revising American plans to deploy a missile shield in Eastern Europe, presumably aimed at Iran but thought by the Russians to be targeted against them. By the same token, carrying out a campaign promise, Obama began winding down the U.S. occupation of Iraq by bringing American troops home though without a clear sign that Iraq would ever function as a relatively unified democracy. And there is the quagmire of Afghanistan, where U.S. troops have been for nine years. After a great deal of discussion and military pressure, Obama escalated the commitment by approving a troop surge of 30,000, which will cost more than $36 billion over the next three years. So far, there has been little return for American efforts both on the ground and in building the capacity for Afghani self-governance. The United States continues to be dependent on the support of the frustrating, untrustworthy, and utterly corrupt Afghan president Hamid Karzai, the Taliban controls large portions of southern and eastern Afghanistan, and there is little sign that the United States can turn an ethnically divided and tribally based Afghanistan into a viable state that could deal with the Taliban without American support.

Ironically enough, given that the war still rages, Obama was awarded the 2009 Nobel Peace Prize. It was given to him not for his actual accomplishments but for his promise (something Obama readily acknowledged) and the fact that he was the opposite, stylistically and as a speechmaker, from an inarticulate, arrogant, chauvinistic Bush, whom the Western Europeans generally despised. But peace was also the last thing he was able to achieve on Capitol Hill. The Republicans, pursuing a bloc-voting strategy, with not one member willing to vote with the Democrats, opposed almost every Obama initiative, often without offering any alternative.

A new right-wing populist movement, the "Tea Party," intensified the Republican hostility to Obama by holding a number of heated protest meetings and rallies. They condemned him as "a tyrant" and "socialist" because of the stimulus package, and, though it would be hard to find a political program they were united behind, they were clearly committed to small government and reduced taxes and opposed to environmental and gun controls. The movement was fostered by the ultraconservative 24-hour news network Fox News; and right-wing talk show ranters like Rush Limbaugh, Glenn Beck, and Sean Hannity; and think tanks like the Freedomworks Foundation of former House Majority Leader Dick Armey, who seemingly had taken the Republican Party over from mainstream conservatives. On the fringes of the almost all-white movement were outright racists and the so-called birthers, who didn't even believe Obama was an American citizen.

Despite the powerful opposition and its often defamatory content and the torturous journey of much of his legislative agenda through Congress, Obama maintained, at least in public, a puzzling equanimity, even detachment. He also clung far too long and unrealistically to his belief that he could act as a mediator and acquire bipartisan support for his political agenda from a party dedicated to undermining him. Obama's behavior and political strategy were in keeping with who he was. Anyone bothering to read his best-selling, gracefully written and acutely perceptive autobiography *Dreams of My Father*[12] would have known that.

The book's emphasis is on the multiracial Obama's quest to make sense of his racial identity and inheritance, and though Obama embraced his links to the black community, he always avoided being prescriptive. He believed that the truth, in all its ambiguity, took precedence over cultural and racial loyalty. And his early years as a community organizer in Chicago and as both a participant and an observer of the Chicago political machine, in all its cutthroat maneuvering and favor trading, helped deepen his commitment to a pragmatic liberal politics. Obama was clearly never on the left or even a full-blown progressive and remained wary of operating as an angry black politician—an image that he understood would play right into racist stereotypes and undermine his agenda.

Finally, as Obama stated in his inaugural address, the challenges the nation faces are extraordinary: he must try to get the economy back on track and deliver jobs to the almost 15 million people who are currently unemployed, and he belatedly understands that there is a need to put the nation's financial system under much more stringent regulation—it is hoped that the modest new financial reform bill will make at least a start at doing just that. It's what Obama failed to do when he came to power, bringing in as his economic team two men close to Wall Street, Tim Geithner and Larry Summers, who opposed attaching strings on the bank bailouts. There are other situations he must deal with. Will he be able to finally withdraw the troops from Iraq and end the war in a fragmented Afghanistan in a manner that neutralizes the threat from al-Qaeda (very dubious)? Can the United States reduce its dependency on fossil fuels like coal and oil and reduce the potential for the despoliation of the environment and disastrous climate change? And it's imperative to finally pass a comprehensive immigration bill that is effective, just, and humane—both making U.S. borders less permeable without indulging in witch hunts of illegal aliens who already reside in the United States. Any one of these tasks would be an enormous hurdle for any administration to accomplish. Among the positive things that one can say of the Obama administration is that it has recognized these challenges and has begun to confront some of them. Solving these problems will be an onerous task given that Obama must deal with a divided Congress and a public that is wary of government intervention and spending.

In the first seven months of 2010, Obama met his campaign promise by withdrawing combat troops from Iraq, passed a landmark bill overhauling financial regulations, and reformed student loans, and, by any fair measure, the past couple of years have seen more progressive legislative change (despite the compromises involved) than any two-year period since the 1930s. He also passed a major stimulus package that, according to the Congressional Budget Office, may have saved up to 3.3 million jobs and lowered the unemployment rate by 1.8 percent.[13]

But going in to the 2010 midterm elections, none of Obama's achievements seemed to matter to the public. And though he has both weathered the horrific BP oil spill (despite being characteristically slow to react) and the General Stanley McChrystal affair (where the military officer charged with executing President Obama's war plan for Afghanistan cracked wise in a magazine interview about Obama, Biden, and the men in charge of Afghan policy), he had lost the message war.

Obama had been forced to convince the public, over the din of vicious Republican Party attacks and Tea Party rallies, that his policies have accomplished something. But his difficulty didn't lie only with finding a successful narrative to promote his presidency. Obama couldn't escape the depressing reality that property foreclosures this year were expected to be more than 3 million (30 percent greater than two years ago), unemployment remained persistent at more than 9 percent, and the public generally felt that the economy was not improving. As a result, in the midterm elections, the Democrats were demolished in the House—losing more than 60 seats—and barely clung to their majority in the Senate by six votes

The film industry faced a different sort of challenge. Proving the old adage that Hollywood was depression-proof, in 2009, the worst year of the "Great Recession," the film industry had its most profitable year ever, garnering more than $10 billion at the box office. In addition, the global movie market swelled as movies became ever more international and ever more oriented to worldwide reach and to pleasing its public. Good box office did not mean that the industry did not face major changes, especially in the realm of technology. In that area, the film industry had to deal with the issues of digitalization and the rise of the Internet. On the one hand, digitalization (the switch from analog to a digital format) allowed for the creation of stunning special effects and computer-generated characters that were increasing lifelike. It also held out the promise, once theaters were converted to receive digital transmissions, of saving millions of dollars in production and distribution costs. And it permitted the production of many films in 3D, and if the success of *Avatar* (2009)—one of the highest-grossing films of all time—is any indication, that changeover was likely to occur more swiftly than previously assumed.

Perhaps the most immediate effect of the advent of digital technology was its effect on independent production. Though the studio-linked independent divisions of the 1990s had begun to break down—with even Miramax (which had broken with Disney in 2005) staff reduced by 70 percent and the number of its releases limited to just three films per year. However, using lightweight digital cameras and desktop editing systems like Final-Cut-Pro, films could be made for a few thousand dollars by novice filmmakers. An example of this was the independent horror film *Paranormal Activity* (2009), which was made in the spirit of *The Blair Witch Project* (1999) for less than $15,000 with digital equipment and went on to become a huge box office hit. In fact, by 2006, it was the norm for independent directors to use digital cameras. Digitalization also provided independent producers with access to a distribution network that existed on Internet sites such as YouTube.

The Internet provided the film industry with great potential and possibly a genuine threat (though it hasn't yet happened). Films could now be streamed via the Internet into people's home televisions, their computers, and even their iPhones. Aware of this, NBC Universal, New Corp (Twentieth Century Fox), and the Disney Company created Hulu. This Internet site features full episodes and clips from hundreds of television shows and movies.

Even more revolutionary on a day-to-day level is the onset of what many have called "convergence" with old forms of media, such as music, films, and newspapers appearing in new media, such as the Internet. This latter trend has caused concern in the film industry, where piracy fears are ever present. And the example of Napster, which caused an enormous fall in income and legal issues for the music industry, is in the forefront of movie executives' minds as an illustration of what impact the Internet could have on the industry.

However, independent films, despite smaller budgets and declining and aging audiences, continue to be made. Still, according to *New York Times* film critic Manohla Dargis, "Any future alternative film culture will depend on the cultivation of younger patrons who are used to receiving much if not all of their entertainment at home and on hand-held devices."[14] But through the decade, directors like Anna Boden and Ryan Fleck (*Half Nelson*, 2006, and *Sugar*, 2008), Kelly Reichardt (*Old Joy*, 2006, and *Wendy and Lucy*, 2009), and Ramin Bahrani (*Man Push Cart*, 2005; *Chop Shop*, 2007; and *Goodbye Solo*, 2009) have made low-budget, realist films without special effects or striking editing and camera angles that were powerful works of art. Here were films with greater emotional and social resonance than most star-dominated mainstream works.

Then there are the "Mumblecore" films (an imposed rubric that the directors shy away from) made by a group of indie American filmmakers who are committed to an ethic of self-help and collaboration. Their intimate, small, stripped-down films are performance-based open-ended narratives and focus usually on the relationships of young, middle-class college grads whose days are spent in conversation. The majority of the characters are smart, slightly adrift, somewhat faltering in speech (a great many unfinished sentences and uncomfortable silences), and generally unsure of themselves. The films are made on tiny budgets and eschew stylistic virtuosity, and many of the actors are nonprofessionals. Few of the films have had theatrical exposure.

The elder statesman—and arguably the most gifted among this group of directors—is Andrew Bujalski, who has made three films: *Funny Ha Ha* (2002), *Mutual Appreciation* (2005), and his latest, *Beeswax* (2009). The films may lack a breathless pace and a conventional narrative, but at their best they are psychologically subtle and evoke a feeling for quotidian humanity. It's hard to predict what will happen to the Mumblecore group—some of the directors and actors are already doing mainstream film work (e.g., the Duplass Brothers' *Cyrus*, 2010). But the Mumblecore films provide a possible model for the survival of independent film.[15]

The politics and culture of the era were, as always, reflected in the films of the decade, including a number of the previously mentioned independents. This was noteworthy in both the films that won awards and those that gained large box office returns as well as films that may not have gained widespread attention. One of the latter films, perhaps because it was produced and released too soon, was Oliver Stone's *W* (2008). *W* may have been flawed, but it was the only narrative film that attempted to construct a portrait of a man whose personality and policies dominated the decade—George W. Bush.

Unlike Stone's previous meditations on the presidency *JFK* (1991) and *Nixon* (1995), which in the former case appeared almost 30 years after the events they depict and in the latter something like two decades after its protagonist resigned from office, *W* neither was dominated by conspiracy theories like *JFK* nor captured the personal and moral sources of a tragic, self-destructive character like *Nixon*. Instead, *W* presented the public with the story of a hollow, permanently adolescent frat boy who never should have been president and who lacked a tragic dimension.

Perhaps Stone would have been better off treating George W. Bush as purely an object of *Saturday Night Live*–type satire. And indeed, there are moments in the film with W talking about being "misunderestimated" and wondering if our children "is learning" or comparing "enhanced interrogation techniques" to the bullying, drunken hazing of his fraternity days that would be successful as skits on that program. Instead, Stone seems to treat George W. both satirically and with a certain amount of tenderness. Bush's policies are critically hammered, but Stone never views the swaggering, crude, ex-alcoholic, callow, self-doubting, and, most important, intellectually unequipped for office (he based his disastrous political decisions on his "gut") George W. as anything less than sincere. Josh Brolin's strong performance captures much of the affable, energetic Bush's natural gift for politics and, at the same time, his capacity for fatuousness but skillfully avoids turning him into a mere buffoon.

W portrays some of the other cabinet members, advisers, and family members who surrounded the forty-third president with some insight, though none of them are explored in any depth. However, the more fully realized ones go beyond stereotyping. "Poppy" Bush (James Cromwell) is viewed respectfully as an emotionally tight mainstream Republican and American aristocrat proud of his family tradition who is constantly upset by the George W.'s carousing and floundering, though, at the same time, he keeps bailing him out of trouble and helping him win the presidency. And Richard Dreyfuss captures the sullen Dick Cheney's odiousness in his slithering around the Oval Office and the halls of the West Wing, putting down his rival, Colin Powell (Jeffrey Wright), and asserting that the need to control oil production is the prime reason for going to war.

Less defined are Secretary of State Colin Powell as the only skeptical and critical cabinet officer, who is loyal to a fault and ultimately acquiesces to going to war; the carefully made-up and toadying and opportunistic Condoleezza Rice (Thandie Newton); and Toby Jones as the unctuous, insidious political "brain" Karl Rove, who gives George W. the words he lacks. Scott Glenn's Donald Rumsfeld is too broad a caricature, announcing, "You know Mr. President I don't do nuance," and ostentatiously gulping down a piece of pecan pie after the president has solemnly announced that he has given up desserts for the course of the Iraq War. Rumsfeld is portrayed as a man without a clue who provides little sense how much power he carried in the first years of the Iraq War.

The film continually cuts between the rise of W from his frat boy, reveling days to his first forays into politics as an inept, losing congressional candidate to the planning and debate within the administration about going to war in Iraq and back again. In a striking scene in the war room, Cheney accuses Powell of being "Neville Chamberlain" and then goes on to present the neoconservative dream of a plan for the domination of the Middle East, concluding with his vow that "they'll never fuck with us again."

Nonetheless, in Stone's version, the most profound battle that George W. faces is his Oedipal struggle with "Poppy" Bush. During his early years, Poppy is constantly critical of George W. He shifts from mild disapproval, "You disappoint me Junior," to expressions of true outrage when he chastises W with the comment, "What are you cut out for? Partying? Chasing tail? Driving drunk? Who do you think you are, a Kennedy?" It's the disciplined Jeb, not George, who is Poppy's favored son, and George feels the rejection viscerally. George W.'s dissatisfaction even extends into his presidency, when he dreams of himself and Poppy going *mano y mano* and Poppy denouncing him with the comment, "You've ruined it, the Bush name, it took 200 years to build it, and you ruined it." Obviously, despite winning the presidency, Stone's George W.

remains a permanent adolescent—continually hungering for his father's approval.

While Stone avoids exploring the full range of issues and crises that the Bush Jr. presidency confronted—the Florida recount, 9/11, Hurricane Katrina, and the economic meltdown that started in 2006—and does little to make us understand (Stone has never shown a gift for capturing the relationships of men and women) the nature of W's relationship with his wife, the supportive, quietly intelligent Laura (Elizabeth Banks)—the impact of the evangelicals on Bush Jr. hits the mark. Stone shows us W being "born again" after a serious night of drinking and becoming part of an evangelical prayer group that propels him into advising his father in his 1988 presidential election bid. Finally, in 1999, George W. then governor of Texas, can announce to his fundamentalist mentor that "I believe that God wants me to run for president." And unlike Ronald Reagan, who first used the "Moral Majority" in his electoral coalition and then for the most part ignored them when he was in office, W not only accepts their support but also attempts in many instances to implement policies they favored, such as limiting stem cell research, involving the federal government in the Terri Schiavo case, and forbidding the use of federal funds for abortion internationally. In fact, according to Stone, Bush Jr. felt that he was doing God's work as president.

W is in the Stone mode, meaning that it lacks subtlety—it's repetitive and reductive in its explanation of Bush Jr.'s political motivation, as if all that he does politically is based on his need for his father's affirmation of him. Still, it does recognize the full force of the evangelical movement in American politics and culture. One sign of its vigor was confirmed by the huge success of Mel Gibson's Catholic fundamentalist film *The Passion of the Christ* (2004), which earned at least $370 million in its worldwide distribution, making it the fifteenth-highest-grossing film of all time, but which also generated fierce debate among those who saw it as a "primitive, pornographic, bloodbath"[16] and others who argued that it was an expression of Gibson's "Traditionalist Catholic faith."[17]

That faith included Gibson's rejection of the reforms of Vatican II (1962–1965), which included the decree *Nostra Aetate*, absolving the Jews of the bloodguilt for Jesus's crucifixion. Nor did it deter Gibson's father from denying the Holocaust.[18] Gibson, of course, denied any anti-Semitic intent, though it's not absurd to see the strains of it in the film.

Unlike previous much more beatific Hollywood New Testament epics like Nick Ray's *King of Kings* (1961), George Stevens's *The Greatest Story Ever Told* (1965), or even Martin Scorsese's controversial *The Last Temptation of Christ* (1988), which concentrated on the Christian narrative emphasizing Jesus's life and his spiritual teachings. Scorsese's Jesus, however, while free from sin, is subject to every form of temptation that ordinary human beings face, including fear, doubt, depression, reluctance, and lust. Gibson's approach is totally different—though his Jesus is shown, in passing, to have doubts, the film concentrates on the last 12 agonizing hours of Jesus's life. In addition, in attempting to give the film authenticity, Gibson had his characters speaking in subtitled Aramaic and "street" Latin.

In Gibson's single-minded, overwrought version, those 12 hours begin with Jesus's (James Caviezel) blue-tinted moments of anguish in the Garden of Gethsemane, where he is tempted by an androgynous Satan (Rosalina Celentano) and betrayed by Judas (Luca Lionello), who has his 30 pieces of silver flung at him in slow motion by the high priest Caiphas (Mattia Sbragia).

The core of this somewhat stylized film (e.g., point of view and bird's-eye shots) is the brutalization of Jesus that Gibson seems to exult in—depicting it in all its bloody detail. Those familiar with Gibson's career will remember the intensity of his portrayal of William Wallace's being drawn and quartered in his Academy Award–winning *Braveheart* (1995). But that moment of violence, extreme though it was, did not compare to the barbaric torments inflicted on Gibson's Jesus. In fact, most of the film deals with the graphically depicted torture of Jesus and his death on the cross.

Jesus's face is beaten almost to a pulp after his arrest by Temple guards, then he is whipped by a laughing group of brutal Roman legionnaires; then, still being able to stand, he is flayed by a cat-o'-nine-tails with hooks at their ends. All of this Gibson depicts with rivulets of blood coursing across Jesus's body. But the end is hardly in sight in Gibson's account, as we are then treated to the savage way Jesus is treated on the path to Golgotha, complete with additional whippings and his hauling the crushing burden of the cross on which he is ultimately to die. Nor is this an end to Jesus's physical suffering since we are then treated in excruciating detail to each spike that is driven into Jesus body on the cross.

The film's only relief from this incessant violence is through brief flashbacks to the Last Supper and to moments when Jesus was still a carpenter in Nazareth. Beside this, the only other quieter, human moments in the film are the Roman prefect Pontius Pilate's (Hristo Naumov Shopov) contemplating passing sentence on Jesus. Gibson's Hamlet-like Pilate can find no wrong in Jesus, but bowing to pressure from the high priest and fearing rebellion in Judea, Pilate allows him to be crucified. (The historical Pilate was actually seen as a cruel and insensitive man—a savage ruler who came close to causing insurrections among the Jews.)

As far as the charge of anti-Semitism goes, the film provides a mixed picture. Yes, the Jewish establishment—the high priest and his entourage—clamor for Jesus "the blasphemer's" blood, as does the crowd that chooses to release the criminal Barabbas rather than Jesus. The film, however, also leaves out the fact that Caiphas, like Pilate, had similar doubts about the crucifixion but felt that he was politically dangerous and wanted to keep the political lid on.

As a result, those scenes may offer anti-Semites unintentional (or is it intentional?) comfort, but along the route to Golgotha, an ordinary Jew, Simon, comes to aid and comfort Jesus. This controversy aside, the film is still a monument not to spirituality or faith but to sadomasochism. It essentially reduces Christ's life and his beliefs to his willingness to bear the burden of and be punished for humanity's sins. The film's final moment confirms this as the resurrected Jesus (face bathed in a divine light), cleansed of his wounds, prepares to march forward with a heavenly choir on the sound track.

If Christian fundamentalism provided an underpinning to the politics of the Bush years, the Middle East was the central focus of its foreign policy. In this film, it was the Israeli-Palestinian conflict—that profoundly tragic and seemingly irremediable and endless struggle that served as the basis of Steven Spielberg's 2005 film *Munich*.

Spielberg, as a filmmaker, has had something of a split personality. On the one hand, he has skillfully directed big-hit entertainments such as *Jaws* (1975) and *Raiders of the Lost Ark* (1981). On the other, he has attempted films of moral and social seriousness, such as the *Schindler's List* (1993), *Amistad* (1997), and, reportedly President Bush's favorite film, *Saving Private Ryan* (1998). Spielberg's divided self is evident from the odd couple of writers he chose to work with in Munich, Eric Roth (*Forrest Gump*), and the brilliant Pulitzer Prize–winning playwright Tony Kushner (*Angels in America*, 1993–1994), the latter who has taken a publicly critical stance toward Israel.

Munich, based on a 1984 book, *Vengeance*, by George Jonas, begins with a quasi-documentary-like depiction of the 1972 massacre of 11 Israelis by the Palestinian terrorist group Black September at the Munich Olympic games. As these events unfold, we hear the voices from the Olympic television coverage of ABC broadcast journalist Peter Jennings and the final mournful report by sportscaster Jim McKay that "they're all gone."

This traumatic event is extended through the film, as Spielberg doles out through flashbacks—emotionally laden fragments of the massacre—that haunt the mind and dreams/nightmares of the film's central character, Avner (Eric Bana). Avner is the young Sabra chosen by Prime Minister Golda Meir (Lynn Cohen) and the Israeli Mossad to seek vengeance against 11 Palestinians who they believe planned and carried out the Munich rampage. Indeed, the film might have borne the title "Golda's List," as she sets its moral tone by justifying the plan with the rueful comment that "every civilization finds it necessary to negotiate compromises with its own values" and the even harsher sentiment that "the world must see that killing Jews is an expensive proposition."

Avner, the son of an independence war hero, is put in charge of a team of specialists consisting of the bomb maker Robert (Matthieu Kassovitz), the forger Hans (Hanns Zischler), the gunman/driver Steve (Daniel Craig), and the self-styled skeptic and cleaner-up of the crime scene Carl (Ciaran Hinds), who asserts that Jews have not been free of destructive actions from 1948 on. Except for the sensitive but quietly lethal Avner, who we learn had an unhappy childhood and passionately loves his wife and baby daughter, the other members of the team are given almost no backstories and just a couple of lines to superficially define who they are. Clearly, this is not a film where the exploration of character plays a central role.

Munich is most striking in constructing tension-ridden set pieces that depict in rich procedural detail the assassinations, from surveillance to the explosive deaths of the masterminds. The film is also sufficiently nuanced to view the assassinated terrorist planners not as stock villains but as civilized poets, loving fathers, and fierce idealists. These are real people with feelings who are killed, not some anonymous or monstrous enemy. There is also an exhilarating, fluidly edited commando-style attack in Lebanon that is carried out by the group and some other Israelis, including the future prime minister Ehud Barak, who is disguised in pearls and a wig.[19] *Munich* is always more successful in its action thriller aspects than in its attempt to explore the ideas behind the interminable struggle between Israelis and Palestinians.

The film's political conversation and ideas always seem self-consciously and theatrically inserted rather than organically connected to the action, though, if the ideas are too calibrated and sometimes pedestrian, they are never mere empty platitudes. For example, in a scene where there is an exchange of ideas between a Palestinian terrorist and Avner, they encounter each other when they share a safe house by accident, with the Palestinian mistakenly believing that Avner is a "Red Army" member. The Palestinian passionately argues with Avner that the struggle will go on for centuries if necessary and that the justification for it is that "home is everything." The scene may feel contrived, but the Palestinian's words concisely convey one powerful motive why Hamas today is able to garner support of the majority of the population in Gaza.

In a similar manner, Spielberg can't resist alluding to the Holocaust when Avner's mother tells him, "Whatever it took, whatever it takes, we have a place on earth." It's a not so different sentiment than the one held by the Palestinian terrorist—believing that the ends justify the means—and one reason, among many, that the two sides in the conflict find themselves in an irreconcilable situation.

The talk occurs as Avner (whose commitment to killing has always been touched by a little wariness) becomes more and more disillusioned and despairing about what he is doing. Signs of his growing disaffection can be seen when he bursts into tears on hearing the voice of his infant daughter in Brooklyn over the phone. He also must deal with the deaths of three of his team members (all of them disenchanted as well with their murderous assignment). That includes the death of Carl, who is killed by a beautiful Mata Hari (Marie-Josee Croze)–type assassin on whom the team exacts swift, extremely violent, almost orgiastic revenge. It leads one the team to exclaim, "We're supposed to be righteous. We're Jewish."

Soon Avner's dissatisfaction descends into paranoia—he feels that he inhabits a world permeated with murder with bombs planted everywhere and begins to suffer from insomnia. He decides that his only option is to give up his role as head of the assassination team and also to take a more extreme step and opt out of his allegiance to Israel entirely. He chooses love for his wife and daughter and living in New York over his commitment to Israel.

Avner's choice is dramatically depicted in the film's final moment, when he meets with his cold, unsympathetic case officer, Ephraim (Geoffrey Rush), who urges him to return to Israel and argues that group's assassinations were committed to achieve a peaceful future. Avner, however, wants to stop the whole cycle of retribution and refuses to return. Each then turns and goes his separate way in the shadows of the Twin Towers—an all-too-obvious portent of things to come.

His decision is in some way similar though much less cynical and amoral than the choice made by the mysterious extended French family, who are in business with death and who provide Avner with information (for immense sums of money) about the whereabouts of the Palestinian assassins they are targeting. The family patriarch and expert cook, Papa (Michael Lonsdale), was once a fighter in the French Resistance but then becomes totally alienated from all political groupings and chooses as his credo "a plague on all their houses." The group's oddness is heightened in a way that makes them seem to belong to a more generic espionage film than to this basically realistic work.

Munich is a mainstream film that avoids trying to lighten the grim, tragic situation it portrays and makes an ambitious and rare attempt to shed some light on the Israeli-Palestinian struggle. Spielberg may not have illuminated all the complexities of the conflict, but the film succeeds in conveying that in the name of the good, evil can be committed and that a piece of a nation's soul and moral power is destroyed in the process. In essence, it questions the whole notion of engaging in violent retaliation, which has been the norm in the Arab-Israeli conflict.

However, the film also provides scant historical background for the terrorism that both sides committed. There is the record of the Jewish Irgun and the Stern gang in the era leading up to and including the 1948 Arab-Israeli War and the long and increasingly bloody record of the Palestinian terrorist groups after Munich. In addition, Abu Mazen, or, as we currently know him, Mahmoud Abbas, the current president of the Palestinian Authority, was the person who financed the Black September operation at Munich. But that's demanding too much from a film that at least begins to pose incisive questions about the whole cycle of terrorism and counterterrorism that has permeated Israeli-Palestinian history.

Though the Arab-Israeli struggle might be the most contentious issue facing the United States in the Middle East, the most vitally significant issue for Americans was the problem of oil. Americans, who constituted only 5 percent of the world's population, used 20 percent of the world's petroleum. And with domestic oil production dwindling, control of Mideast oil was essential to the economic and national security of the United States.

Stephen Gaghan, the writer/director of *Syriana* (2005) and no stranger to the issue of drugs since his script for *Traffic* (2000) (discussed later), referred to the addiction of the United States to oil as America's "crack."[20] In *Syriana*, Gaghan created a geopolitical thriller centered on the issue of the control of Mideast oil. The film's multiple story lines mesh avaricious corporate honchos and corrupt lawyers brokering backroom deals in Washington, Pakistani immigrants working in the Persian Gulf oil fields, a struggle for power in an oil-producing Gulf state, and a callous and murderous CIA supposedly pursuing this country's interests in the Middle East. The film's narrative strands may be convoluted, but it matters little in this solemn, politically provocative, exhilaratingly edited film about the moral rot at the center of American power.

Syriana focuses on four distinct and loosely connected major characters. One of them is Bob Barnes, played by an overweight, bearded, and depressed George Clooney in an understated, striking performance as a veteran CIA ground operative with language skills whose covert activities take him from Tehran to Beirut. Barnes has been hung out to dry by the agency after criticizing U.S. policy in Iran. Another is Bennett Holiday (Jeffrey Wright), a quietly observant, uptight, careerist black lawyer delegated by his white-shoe law firm to provide due diligence on a merger between the oil giant Connex and the smaller Texas oil company Killen, a merger that would clearly expose some criminal activity on the part of Killen. There is Bryan Woodman (Matt Damon), an ambitious but decent oil consultant whose son's tragic death at a party at the home of a Mideast emir allows him to become economic adviser to one of the heirs to the throne, the Western-oriented reformer Prince Nasir (Alexander Siddig). And finally, there's Wasim Khan (Mazhar Munir), a Pakistani laborer who loses his job after the Connex-Killen merger and then in quick succession becomes a Muslim extremist and then a suicide bomber after he attends a local madrassa. Wasim's transformation and the scene with the imam lecturing students in the madrassa may be too schematic. But it's a clear illustration of how Islamic fundamentalism—in offering a community and the certitude of the true, divine path—can be seductive to people with little hope.

Despite the juggling of so many narratives, the film provides a convincing portrait of the insidious machinations of U.S. power wielders. For instance, in Holiday's efforts to, in the old hard-boiled detective vernacular, find someone "to take the fall" for the criminal activities that allowed Killen to get its pipeline, he meets with one of the chosen victims, the company's chief financial officer, Danny Dalton (Tim Blake Nelson), who tells him, "Corruption is our protection. Corruption keeps us safe and warm. Corruption is why we win." Dalton's statement strikingly encapsulates *Syriana*'s damning vision of U.S. government agencies and the nation's powerful oil companies.

To grant the characters some kind of human dimension, Gaghan provides each of his major characters with a bit of personal backstory. The solitary Holiday has to contend with a bitter alcoholic father (William C. Mitchell), Woodman, with a wife (Amanda Peet) from whom he is estranged after the death of their child, but none of it goes very deep. This is a film where personal relations are secondary to impersonal political forces that are best symbolized by the CIA's drone missile that is used to assassinate Prince Nasir and dominate the film.

There is nothing subtle about *Syriana*. Political thrillers tend to go in for conspiracies, and sometimes one feels that there is something too neat about the construction of a world where a nefarious collusion between oil companies, lawyers, politicians, and Mideast monarchs controls the global oil supply. But if *Syriana* makes the truth a bit less ambiguous than it probably is, the general thrust of its attack feels powerfully on target. Gaghan and Clooney have made an intelligent and politically resonant and uncompromising work that, with its worldwide sweep from Washington to Texas to Tehran to Beirut and an anonymous oil-rich desert kingdom, becomes nothing less than a powerful macroeconomic morality play. It's one that depicts a thoroughly corrupt world dominated by oil served by governments and corporations that care only about power and profit.

Much less ambitious but certainly revelatory about later developments in the Middle East is Mike Nichols's and scriptwriter Aaron Sorkin's *Charlie Wilson's War* (2007). In it, Charlie Wilson (Tom Hanks) goes from a boozy, priapic liberal Texas congressman to a driven crusader for greater American involvement in the struggle of the Afghan mujahideen against the Soviets after they unwisely invaded Afghanistan in 1980. Wilson's transformation and his campaign for greater aid to the Afghans is initially inspired by a sexual dalliance with a right-wing, born-again militantly anticommunist Houston socialite, Joanne Herring (a strained Julia Roberts), and is aided by an angry, foul-mouthed, extremely intelligent, equally anticommunist CIA operative, Gust Avrakotos (Philip Seymour Hoffman). So ultimately successful was Wilson's campaign that he got American aid to the Afghans increased from $10 million to $1 billion.

The problem with *Charlie Wilson's War* is that it never decides whether it's a broad Feydeau sex farce or a serious political film. As a result, in one scene, Wilson tries to juggle a serious conversation about Afghanistan aid with Avrakotos with an attempt to deflect a serious sex and cocaine scandal by continuously rushing from room to room and from door to door. They also riff off each other with great comic timing and dexterity. The film juxtaposes the farcical scenes with interminable montages of Afghans shooting down Soviet planes and helicopters and other scenes where Wilson is maneuvering to get more arms to the mujahideen.

Charlie Wilson's War, however, does end on a seriously critical note with a quote from Wilson (who left Congress in 1996), "We fucked up the end game," referring to the fact that after the Soviets left in 1989, the United States effectively ignored Afghanistan, leaving it to the designs of the Taliban and al-Qaeda. Not much of a triumph for Wilson, given the quagmire we confront there now. And even the belief that there was an "end game" that would have made a political difference in Afghanistan is far from certain.

A similar though much briefer and more limited type of failure is featured in the events depicted in Ridley Scott's (*Gladiator*, 2000) *Black Hawk Down* (2001). Scott's film recounts the notorious battle on October 3, 1993, when a combined force of elite U.S. Rangers and Delta Force attempted the capture of Somali warlord Mohammed Farah Aidid and some of his key lieutenants.

Instead of the contemplated simple surgical strike, the attack turns into murderous chaos—sniper fire from every roof, helicopter crashes, and street-by-street firefights—lasting for more than 15 hours and resulting in the deaths of 18 Americans and more than 500 Somalis. Most significant, it provided devastating photos of a dead American soldier being dragged through the streets of Mogadishu and kicked and spat on. It was these casualties and the photos that prompted the Clinton administration to withdraw from what was viewed as a humanitarian mission (delivering UN food shipments to starving Somalis) in Somalia. America's precipitous withdrawal emboldened terrorists like Osama bin Laden, who believed that it showed the "weakness, frailty and cowardice of U.S. Troops."[21]

Though the events depicted in *Black Hawk Down* may have inspired bin Laden, the film does nothing to give the audience a clear picture of the historical/political context for the turmoil in Somalia—a failed state without a government that functions. The fog of war in this case extends not only to the historical background of what precipitated the street warfare (as an afterthought, the film provides some opening and closing titles to give us an utterly superficial sense of the battle's political significance) but to the character of the participants in the raid as well, for, besides some perfunctory opening dialogue that provides just a hint of personality to some of the soldiers involved in the raid, the film relies almost exclusively on images of combat. The U.S. soldiers are predictably courageous and tough, and one of them is even an idealist who is fighting to make a difference, but they are basically anonymous. Scott choreographs the bloody spectacle with consummate skill and maximum excitement—his cinematic flair in depicting the carnage being the centerpiece of the film. Action is its own justification in *Black Hawk Down*, and Scott barely gives a thought to the emotional and political consequences of the raid.

The events of the Russo-Afghan War (1980–1989) and the Somali civil wars were distant enough in both time and space to make it relatively easy for Hollywood to produce films about them. An entirely different dilemma confronted filmmakers about the events of September 11, 2001. It was difficult to make a film about an event whose apocalyptic images left a legacy of silent weeping, emotional ache, and sense of dread for many Americans. For months, it was hard to escape the haunting and traumatic nature and, at times, accompanying nightmares of September 11. This was especially true for New Yorkers, who bore the brunt of 9/11.

Nonetheless, within one year of those events, the film industry produced two films about 9/11: Oliver Stone's *World Trade Center* (2002) and Paul Greengrass's *United 93* (2002). Of the two films, Stone's is the more conventional and less interesting. It centers around two first responders, Port Authority Police Sergeant John McLoughlin (Nicolas Cage) and Officer Will Jimeno (Michael Pena), and their respective, deeply caring families who experience 9/11 firsthand. The film is directed in a much less flashier and more solemn style then the usual Stone film.

World Trade Center is a well-meaning, solemn, and apolitical film—Stone suspending his usual critical take on American society. The film does a good job at reconstructing some of the overwhelming terror and shock (a body falls from one tower) that the collapse of the emblematic buildings into an inferno brought on. Though it can't quite convey the fevered reality of a day that felt like the end of the world was near, Stone's aim is to offer a tribute to the ordinary men—police and firefighters—who acted with great bravery and selflessness on that fatal day. In his sentimental, uplifting version, almost every character does the right thing, the disaster bringing out decency and compassion in most people affected. And though it's true that most of the responders did transcend themselves on that day and the days that followed, a depiction of heroism demands something richer than a one-dimensional portrait to make it come dramatically alive.

Paul Greengrass, who directed the brilliant docudrama *Bloody Sunday* (2002) about the massacre of innocent civilians by British troops in Derry, Northern Ireland, in 1972, directs the documentary-style film depicting the fatal flight of United 93. That's the plane that terrorists were planning to crash into the Capitol building in Washington, D.C. It went down in a field near Shanksville, Pennsylvania, killing all aboard after a group of passengers attempted to overpower the hijackers.

In contrast to the Stone film's stars, like Nick Cage and Maggie Gyllenhaal, the actors in *United 93* are nearly anonymous. It also includes actual participants in the day's events, such as Ben Sliney, the head of the central command center of the Federal Aviation Administration (FAA) in Herndon, Virginia, who tried heroically to keep some kind of control over the day's terrible events.

United 93 piles agonizing, tension-filled detail on detail as early morning passengers arrive at Newark Airport, where United 93 originated. They talk on their cell phones, read morning newspapers, or doze as the flight crew assemble, chatter about pending days off, check the aircraft, and get ready for takeoff. Greengrass restlessly cuts between these actions and, more ominously, a group of young Muslim men who look like students, led by Ziad Jarrah (Khalid Abdalla), engaged in their morning prayers and then readying to embark on their suicidal mission.

Nothing seems out of the ordinary until American Airlines Flight 11 (the aircraft that will crash into the Pentagon) disappears from the screens of the air controllers centers in New York and at the FAA headquarters. Then frantic questions are raised and indecision seems to reign supreme until, disastrously, the television screens in the headquarters are filled with CNN's tragic images of the smoldering World Trade Center towers. Then air traffic controllers leap into action, but all their attempts are futile (e.g., getting military planes in the air)—they are left with no recourse.

The sense that nothing can be done to save the plane makes the hijacking of United 93 even more terrifying for the film's audience as the frightened but adrenaline-stoked terrorists take over the plane and kill the pilots, one of the crew, and a passenger. Greengrass avoids turning a group of passengers' last-ditch attempt to retake United 93 into some kind of superpatriotic action. Their behavior is not heightened (no John Wayne gestures or sense of invulnerability); rather, their reactions are based simply on their primal fear and their survival instinct. Even Todd Beamer's (David Alan Bashe) posthumously famous "Let's roll" is uttered as an almost soft aside rather than as the patriotic call that it later was transformed into.

Greengrass's harrowing tale, made with the support of the 9/11 families, is a fitting tribute and memorial for the victims of that terrible event. It keeps everything unadorned—no humor to mute the torment and no human-interest stories about passengers on the way to see their grandchildren for possibly the last time—and the film neither personalizes nor caricatures its characters. Greengrass's very powerful and controlled docudrama stays linked to the actual events and leaves all the dramatic frills, heroics, and emotional manipulation out of the film.

If there is one disturbing note in this honest, stirring film, it lies in one of its final titles, which announced, "America's war on terror had begun." It was a war that would result in a number of films that raised important moral and strategic questions for movie audiences about American policy. One of the issues that went to the very core of American values was what became known as "extraordinary rendition"—the practice of sending captured and suspected terrorists for questioning and imprisonment to countries that practiced torture.

Rendition (2007), directed by Gavin Hood (*Tsotsi*, 2005), is a star-filled melodrama with Jake Gyllenhaal and Reese Witherspoon playing characters with a conscience in a world that has little use for it. The film grapples with the issue of torture—by constructing three interlocking stories—that begin to clutter the film. The first deals with the kidnapping of Egyptian engineer Anwar El-Ibrahami (Omar Metwally) by the CIA because he is suspected of aiding terrorists who had killed a CIA operative. After being kidnapped, he is transferred to an unnamed North African country where he is imprisoned and tortured. The second is an attempt by his very pregnant and blond American wife Isabella (a perkily resolute Reese Witherspoon) to find out what happened to him and to have him released. Finally, there is the forgettable Romeo-and-Juliet romance of the upper-class daughter of El-Ibrahami's chief torturer and a poor Muslim militant.

Though *Rendition* is sincere, the film contains little energy or dramatic tension. The little that exists comes from the debates that Isabella's former boyfriend—Alan Smith (Peter Sarsgaard), the chief of staff for a ranking senator (Alan Arkin) whom she enlists in helping to find her husband—has with the senator, who waffles on the issue of torture. And those he has with the icy, smug southern CIA chief Corrine Whitman (Meryl Streep), who follows the Bush/Cheney line that "Americans don't torture" and that torture may potentially save the lives of thousands of innocents.

In this film, technically the Americans do not engage in torture since the actual torture is carried out with relish by an odious foreign police operative, Abasi Fawel (Igal Naor), in some unnamed North African country. It's observed firsthand by an inexperienced CIA analyst, Douglas Freeman (Jake Gyllenhaal), who is sickened by the horror of a man being hung up on chains and given electric shocks ("This is my first torture," he ingenuously says).

Rendition does make the case that America's outsourcing of torture is indefensible, but it never succeeds in becoming more than a civics lesson.

If *Rendition* was unlikely to generate much outrage in its audience, neither was Robert Redford's equally star-studded, static, talky *Lions for Lambs* (2007). Redford's seventh directorial effort might have been better off as an idealistic PowerPoint presentation calling for public engagement to bring an end to the Afghan War. Like *Rendition* but more awkwardly, *Lion for Lambs* is constructed as a multilayered plot consisting of the attempt of brashly self-confident, ambitious and shallow neoconservative presidential hopeful Senator Jasper Irving (Tom Cruise) to manipulate a liberal television journalist, Janine Roth (Meryl Streep), to promote his slightly more eloquent version of the Bush/Cheney line about bringing victory to Afghanistan. Along the way, they debate the necessity of the war in Afghanistan—each one scoring points—but the film is clearly on the side of the hesitant but tough-minded Streep, who adds a touch of internality to characters who are, in the main, nothing more than their political positions. In fact, Streep seems to be doing a lot of acting—a great many tics and gestures—in a film that doesn't call for it.

The film's others segments concern the attempt of an idealistic ex-Vietnam vet and political science professor Stephen Malley (Robert Redford) to arouse a brilliant but cynical and callow student (Andrew Garfield) to become engaged in the issues, and the final part is about two Malley-inspired students—one black and one Hispanic who volunteer for Special Forces operation in Afghanistan (obviously, learning the wrong lesson about making a difference) and are surrounded and destroyed by the Taliban. These are men that the film views as merely cannon fodder for those who wield power.

But with dialogue like Malley's angry comment when he tries to get a rise from the spoiled student that "Rome is burning" and Irving's equally banal "America is a force of righteousness," one gets the impression that the film seems to be operating on automatic albeit liberal pilot. Being on the side of the angels in both *Rendition* and *Lions for Lambs* clearly isn't sufficient to make for good art. And as for good politics, one needs more of a critical intelligence, not a pastiche of liberal editorials to make the film more interesting than reading the daily paper.

As the wars in Iraq and Afghanistan continued into their fifth and sixth years, an increasing number of films began to deal with the GIs who served in the wars. These films, much like the early Vietnam films that preceded them by almost three decades, focused more on returning soldiers and their families on the home front than on the war itself. In *Grace Is Gone* (2007), Stanley Phillips (John Cusack), a devoted husband and loving but emotionally awkward and dour father who has been discharged from the service because of bad eyesight, has to cope with the death of his wife, who was serving in Iraq. Too disconsolate to break the news immediately to his two daughters, he takes them on a cross-country trip to an amusement park so as to give them one last moment of pleasure before having to convey to them the devastating information. In the process of traveling through an America of undistinguishable motels and highway eating places, he predictably strengthens his bond to the girls and begins to cope with his tragic loss.

Grace Is Gone is a thin and sentimental work—we never really learn much about Stan beyond his being inarticulately pro-war (e.g., he's loyal to the powers that be) and emotionally bottled up. The film contains a strong performance by Shelan O'Keefe, who plays his older daughter Heidi—a depressed, perceptive, knowing 12-year-old on the threshold of adolescence. And Stan's brother John (Alessandro Nivola), a drifting, scruffy professional student, is allowed to make telling criticisms of the war. *Grace Is Gone* is a sincere film, but decency doesn't make for art, nor is it sufficient to evoke the complexity of the home-front experience.

In a similar manner, another road movie, *The Lucky Ones* (2008), traces the cross-country journey of three returning Iraq GIs, who team up to confront the perils of the home front: Fred Cheaver (Tim Robbins), a 50-ish career army sergeant, heading for an encounter with a wife who, barely moments after greeting him, announces that she wants a divorce; T. K. Poole (Michael Pena), a cocky macho who must deal with fears about his sexual adequacy after being wounded in the genitals; and a sunny, hobbling Colee Dunn (Rachel MacAdams), who wants to deliver her dead boyfriend's guitar to his parents. The film is apolitical and dominated by broad comedy, contrivance, and the formulaic—just another piece of Hollywood hackwork.

The inadequacy of these films didn't mean that there weren't films produced about the war that didn't have merit. For example, *Stop-Loss* (2008), directed by Kimberly Peirce (*Boys Don't Cry*, 1999), the title deriving from a clause in military contracts that allowed the armed forces to extend service even when an enlistment is over, is a generally effective and moving evocation of the kinds of wounds that a war can cause even for those who came back physically unscathed.

Stop-Loss begins horrifically with a digital camera depiction of a deadly ambush of American troops in Tikrit, Iraq—in a scene permeated with grievous wounds and death. Almost immediately, it shifts to the return of three ordinary American men to the small Texas town of Brazos. The film provides a richly textured slice of a red-state homecoming—the military and American patriotism are celebrated—as the buddies get drunk, fight, and womanize. (Clearly, there is the basis for another, more complex film inherent in the homecoming scenes.) However, there is a raging dark side to this return home replete with post-traumatic stress (flashbacks and flash cuts to the Iraq ambush and constantly hearing the sound of bombs bursting), alcoholism, domestic abuse, and profound depression.

The inarticulate, totally physical Steve Shriver (Channing Tatum) is out of control—he can't sleep in his bed and digs a foxhole in his yard thinking that he's on a mission, and a suicidal, depressed Tommy Burgess (Joseph Gordon-Levitt) beats up his fiancée and then uses their wedding presents for target practice (the army suicide rate is above the civilian rate for the first time since the Vietnam War).[22] After Iraq, a return to domesticity is impossible for him. For all the soldiers portrayed here, it's male friendship that is primary over every other commitment. The most stable and principled and the leader of the three (though beset with guilt about leading his men into the ambush), Staff Sergeant Brandon King (Ryan Phillippe), finds out that he has been stop-lossed, a fate he shared with nearly 81,000 other GIs—basically a backdoor draft. With the words "fuck the president," barely out of his mouth, he angrily sets off on a cross-country trip with an empathetic female friend/girlfriend, Michelle (Abbie Cornish)—whose character the film barely limns—to find a senator who emptily promised, as politicians do, that he would help Brandon the war hero if he ever needed it. There is no escaping the war's legacy on the journey, as Brandon calls on the parents of one of his men who died and runs into a black AWOL soldier hiding out with his family in a fleabag motel—part of an underworld that the war has created. There is also a powerful scene of Brandon's visit to a badly maimed and blinded comrade, Rico Rodriguez (Victor Rosak), who through his ordeal has managed to keep up a cheery patter about feeling "lucky." The scene's one flaw is that the lingering close-up of Rico's face begins to manipulate his pathos for audience sympathy.

Brandon has the chance to escape to Canada or Mexico but fears the loss of self and his world and, in a too contrived and Hollywood-style manner, decides to rejoin the army with the military-loving Steve. Brandon's loyalty to and intimacy with Steve, built on brawling rather than words, is stronger than any antagonism he has toward the Iraq War. Peirce avoids weighing Brandon down with any well-defined antiwar sentiments that go beyond his rage toward his commanding officer about being called back to the war.

The film is utterly attuned to the experiences of its characters whose sense of patriotism and anguish are utterly merged. Peirce knows that the soldiers are mere fodder and is clearly critical of the war. However, though her characters can express pain and resentment about what they have been through, they themselves are rarely antiwar. *Stop-Loss* is a good film that is finally too conventional—too bound to external behavior and incident—to go deep into the heart of its characters' emotional lives.

The wounds of American soldiers are reflected in an emotionally deeper much more tragic manner in *The Messenger* (2009). Subtly directed and co-written by first-time director Oren Moverman, himself a veteran of the Israeli army, the film deals with Staff Sergeant Will Montgomery (a riveting Ben Foster), a highly decorated and wounded veteran of the Iraq War who, with three months left in his enlistment, is assigned to work for the Casualty Notification Office. A tension-ridden, angry Montgomery carries all sorts of scars from Iraq: shrapnel in his body, a girlfriend who is marrying someone else, and a heavy dose of survivor's guilt.

His unit has the onerous task of notifying families that their sons or daughters were killed in action. Montgomery's mentor and partner on the job is Captain Tony Stone (Woody Harrelson). Harrelson, breaking from his usual affable wild-man roles, is an officer whose stoic, efficient professionalism and commitment to the rules of his job (e.g., no touching and no offering help or compassion to the families) hides profound loneliness, insecurity, and insomnia. For Stone, who has never faced the enemy, adhering to the rules seems to help keep him together.

The vulnerable Montgomery treats the job with obvious distaste, his face silently registering every one of both his troubled and his empathetic feelings when he delivers the standardized spiel to family members about the death of loved ones. They react with rage, hysteria, denial, collapse, and quiet despair, and he can do nothing more than stand there.

The film also uses silence to great effect in other scenes. The bond—violating every army rule—between Will and a widow (played with great restraint by Samantha Morton, one of the people who he delivers death notices to) is delicately handled without the need for much talk. Both are wounded people in a guilt-ridden situation who are hesitant about stepping over the line romantically. Still, their erotically charged yearning for each other is powerfully conveyed (despite or because they barely touch each other), and the film aptly avoids taking their relationship to a simple resolution.

The Messenger contains no images of military combat or war horrors. And though the army, for the macho, womanizing, recovering alcoholic Stone, is his whole life, he holds off from endorsing its patriotic rhetoric. Neither officer is, however, antiwar, but the film stirringly conveys the pernicious effect of the war on those who see combat. The film suggests that those who experience battle have survived a world so painful that it's beyond the understanding of their friends and families back home—that the war is so monstrous that it's beyond justification.

For the most part (except for a drunken wedding sequence where they play at war in the parking lot), *The Messenger* also eschews the predictable scenes that are usually an integral part of recent films that deal with the return home of war vets—alcohol-fueled fights and berserk, murderous rages. Instead, it uses the more understated and sensitive effects of unsentimental close-ups that give us images of vets that have been indelibly marked by war.

An equally mournful but much more elegiac film about what the Iraq War did to American soldiers was Paul Haggis's *In the Valley of Elah* (2007). The Valley of Elah refers to the place in the Bible where David slew Goliath. Inspired by real events, Haggis's film was based on an article by Mark Boal about the murder of Specialist Richard Davis that appeared in *Playboy* magazine in May 2004.

The film begins with a blank-screen voice-over of a GI calling for a buddy to get back into a humvee. In the very next moment, we hear a telephone ringing to inform Hank Deerfield (played with seamless and powerful emotional minimalism by Tommy Lee Jones) that his son Mike (Jonathan Tucker), just returned from Iraq, has gone AWOL. Hank is an austere, retired army military police sergeant who served in Vietnam and whose creased, pitted, and furrowed face suggests a depth of experience and weariness with life. After leaving his wife Joan (Susan Sarandon in a nondescript role), the stoical, taciturn Hank sets off to search for his son. On his arrival in Fort Rudd, New Mexico, he discovers that his son has been murdered and his body viciously stabbed and dismembered.

In attempting to find out who murdered his son, Hank works out a wary partnership with a local police detective, Emily Sanders (a deglamorized but still beautiful Charlize Theron), a stressed single mom struggling to overcome her lack of experience as a detective and the crude sexism of her fellow officers. Sanders becomes impressed with Hank's forensic skill (he's a much better detective than the pros) and then, at first hesitantly and then full throttle, joins him in investigating and unraveling the mystery of Mike's death.

Of course, as in all police procedurals, there are the requisite red herrings. The one that reveals something about an aspect of Hanks's nature involves a Mexican American buddy of Mike's, Private Ortiz (Victor Wolf), a former member of a drug gang who is initially suspected of killing Mike. Ortiz's capture moves Hank to explode in a redneck racist tirade that is the one emotionally uncontrolled moment in the film for this inexpressive, repressed man.

But luckily, this spare film is also about another set of more profound issues than just solving this awkwardly constructed, not particularly interesting murder mystery. Haggis sees the film as "asking questions about where we are in America right now and what's happening."[23] So he places a moral mystery at the film's center, best reflected in the metaphor of the Valley of Elah, and its suggestion of fighting monsters. Who the monsters are is not clear at first. Is it the army that tries to engage in a cover-up of Mike's murder, or is it his buddies who stonewall Hank? Or is it Mike himself whose cell phone carries a set of difficult to decipher, frightening digital video images from his tossing a football to Iraqi kids who steal it to the committing of war crimes, like torturing prisoners? Or is it the war itself with its roadside bombs and orders to regard every civilian, even children, as a potential threat that is the monster? For that's what the war does—shredding the souls of the soldiers who go to fight there. What makes the movie a morally resonant work is the growing revelation of how the war in Iraq has devastated and dehumanized the soldiers fighting it. All the other questions about moral culpability are secondary to the Iraq War—an incarnation of hell itself.

At the film's conclusion, Mike's murderer is found. But Haggis cares much less about finding the killer than about how the patriotic, lifelong military man Hank has changed. Hank, who had no sympathy for a broken Mike's tears when his son called asking him to help him get out of the army, remains committed to the troops but is finally aware what the war has done to them and to the country. So Haggis closes on a mournful note that, despite seemingly heavy-handed, is somehow quite powerful. Returning home, Hank passes a school and runs up an American flag upside down that his son had sent him. It's the internationally recognized distress signal—his acknowledgment of the dreadful state that the nation has found itself in because of a war that eviscerates the psyches of the young men who enlist and fight in the Iraq quagmire.

This loss of moral compass is further underlined in Brian De Palma's low-budget, experimental *Redacted* (2007), an antiwar film whose formal innovations include a mixture of fictional visuals: a video diary made by one of the soldiers, a pretentious French-produced war documentary, online testimonials and news pieces, and a terrorist website showing the murder of the platoon's master sergeant (the plethora of Iraq War images suggesting that seeing all this seems to make barely an iota of difference in how the war is conducted). In a fragmented, self-reflexive manner, De Palma produces a story much like his 1989 Vietnam War film *Casualties of War* (1989). Like *Casualties* (though that film has a beautifully shaped narrative), *Redacted*'s central focus is a fictionalized account of the rape and murder of a teenage Iraqi girl and the remorseless killing of her family by barbaric, racist American soldiers who view the Iraqi as "sand niggers." Other soldiers in the platoon know about the rape but either voyeuristically watch or are too intimidated to report what happened. The film's grand ambitions can't quite overcome the overly theatrical acting (the villains are conceived as cartoons), a use of music to oppressively underline events, and a self-consciousness about how innovative the film is. De Palma also adds a heavy-handed but powerful final photo montage that is both gut wrenching and exploitative. The photos are mostly of women and children killed in the war, and the final shot is of the fictional teenager killed in the film, her mouth gaping, eye turned to camera, lying in a puddle of blood.

A very different kind of response to the Iraq War is depicted in gifted action-film director Kathryn Bigelow's (e.g., *Blue Steel*, 1989, and *Point Break*, 1991) Academy Award–winning and visceral *The Hurt Locker* (2009). Instead of the moral morass of the Iraq War, we explore the character of a war lover defined in an opening-title quote by former *New York Times* journalist Chris Hedges as someone for whom the rush of battle is often a potent and murderous addiction.

The war lover or artist of demolition in this film is Staff Sergeant William James (Jeremy Renner), who joins an explosive disposal unit after the unit's former leader, Sergeant Matt Thompson (Guy Pearce), is killed. For this unit, every time they go out, it's a matter of life and death. James embraces the adrenaline rush that comes from disarming the improvised explosive devices that have been carefully planted by the Iraqi insurgents. In his first action with the squad, he calmly sets the tone by dramatically disposing of his SCUBA-diving-looking protective helmet and declaring, "If I'm going to die, I'm going to die comfortable."

James is relentless and expert in his pursuit of disarming the bombs that are often set in daisy-chain patterns on the perilous streets of Baghdad, which, though not shot there, feel authentically ominous—streets where every person looking out of a window or passing on the street can be the enemy who will turn into a sniper or detonate a bomb. James is so caught up in a job that he revels in the lethal artistry of the Iraqi bomb makers, keeping as trophies a whole set of their detonators in a box.

His two squad mates—the by-the-book professional Sergeant J. T. Sanborn (Anthony Mackie) and the jumpy, anxiety-ridden Specialist Owen Eldridge (Brian Geraghty), who is seeing an emptily glib base psychiatrist—feel resentment toward his seemingly foolhardy recklessness (though in this chaotic war, where death is everywhere, he is usually too professional to needlessly gamble their lives). The two men have 38 days left in their deployment and don't want to take unnecessary risks. Nevertheless, their sharing a deadly task forms a bond among these utterly physical men that is sealed by a drunken display of brutal pummeling of each other after a particularly violent encounter with a band of Iraqi snipers.

Bigelow's cinematographer, Barry Ackroyd, keeps the heightened momentum of the film moving flawlessly with his darting handheld camera and his extreme close-ups of three men's reactions to danger. In addition, scenes are edited so skillfully that tension is maximized, as in the scene that depicts the wounding of Eldridge after James insists that the group pursue through dark, narrow alleys some insurgents in the wake of a massively destructive, scorched-earth nighttime suicide bombing attack.

The Iraqis in the film are treated as curious and possibly dangerous specta-tors of the squad's efforts or as a shadowy and lethal other. The sole exception to this is James's fondness for a soccer-loving, bootleg DVD hawker—a boy he nicknames Beckham (Christopher Sayegh). But the film is too realistic—too aware of how ambiguous relationships with the Iraqis are—to turn him into a cute mascot like the old John Wayne war films would have done.

Sanborn is looking forward to returning home after his tour is up—feeling that "nobody gives a shit" about the war. But for James, war remains a drug he can't get enough of. It's underscored when James returns home to his wife and child and can't adjust to domesticity. This is hammered home, in a not-too-subtle scene, when a disgruntled James, confronted by a cornucopia of brands in a supermarket, can only toss one at random into his shopping cart. It follows then that all that's left for him is to return to Iraq, his only real home. *Hurt Locker*'s final scene shows James striding down a street in some city in Iraq in his full bomb-disposal regalia doing what he really loves.

By focusing on the troops and the sensation of combat, *Hurt Locker* chooses to avoid any more expansive discussion of the war. Bigelow chose to enter the psyches of these men but asked nothing about the meaning of the war. In fact, the film is neither antiwar nor pro-war but simply portrays men taking part in a conflict that has great human cost. Perhaps Bigelow and her scriptwriter, the ubiquitous Mark Boal, might have been better served if, rather than build-ing the film around Chris Hedges's statement about war as a drug, they had paid some attention to his 2003 commencement address at Rockford College, where he said, "We are embarked on an occupation that if history is any guide will be as damaging to our souls as it will be to our prestige and security."[24]

However, the absence of explicit politics and the breathless tension and vivid and thrilling action probably best explain why *Hurt Locker* was the most successful of the Iraq films. There were the usual conservative objections about these films demoralizing the troops and indulging in antiwar propaganda, but they did not stir much controversy. The reality is that most of these films have not been able to command either liberal or conservative audiences. Though the Iraq War produced giant protests in the early years, the fact that no draft was instituted became a prime factor in allowing the public's passions to be-come generally inured to Iraq's everyday violence as it endlessly stretched on. Thus, the films played to empty houses, until a striking apolitical film like *Hurt Locker* evoked the reality of the war, without ever passing judgment on why we were there.

Hollywood's depiction of the soldiers who fought in Iraq wasn't its only re-sponse to the war. Clint Eastwood's *Flags of Our Fathers* (2006) might first ap-pear as an homage to the greatest generation and their taking part in World

War II. But on another level, in portraying the gap between the heroic myth and the reality of war, it could serve as a critique of all the "mission-accomplished" hype and the manufactured bogus heroism involved in the rescue of Jessica Lynch that marked the Iraq War.

Eastwood's film, co-written by William Broyles Jr. and Paul Haggis, was taken from James Bradley's 2000 best-seller about the Iwo Jima campaign and Joe Rosenthal's iconic photo of six American GIs raising the American flag on the island, probably the most memorable moment of that battle and perhaps of the war. The bloody Iwo Jima battle was no simple victory. It was a 35-day struggle that took the lives of 6,821 Americans and saw 20,000 wounded and more than 21,000 Japanese killed.[25]

World War II was not Iraq—it was seen as the "Good War." Nevertheless, in a voice-over at the film's outset, the tone of the film is set. A character states, "Every jackass thinks they know what war is." And Eastwood demonstrates here the gap between the mythology of war and reality, or, as John Ford taught us, when "the legend becomes a fact, print the legend."

In this case, it is the supposed heroism of the three surviving GIs who raised the flag: John "Doc" Bradley (Ryan Phillippe), a navy corpsman, and two marines, Rene Gagnon (Jesse Bradford) and Ira Hayes (Adam Beach). Ironically, as Eastwood shows us, the flag in the famous photo was actually the second flag raised over Mount Suribachi—the original one was kept by an officer who didn't want it to fall into the hands of a visiting dignitary.

Because of their participation in that indelible photo, the three GIs are sent home to participate in war bond drives to raise money and lift morale for the war effort. Eastwood cuts back and forth between scenes of the actual battle shot in denatured colors, except for thick, red stains of blood, and in striking black and white with graphic shots of GIs with their guts oozing out or decapitated and home-front moments of the three forced to reenact their heroic moment on papier-mâché mountains before 50,000 cheering citizens at Soldier Field in Chicago or seeing it represented in kitsch ice cream sculptures.

Of the three, the handsome Gagnon is the only one to revel in his new-found celebrity and the career opportunities it seems to present (predictably, he ends up a janitor). He's also accompanied by a silly, shallow fiancée who gushes over all the fuss and ceremony. Bradley and Hayes feel the most pain, guilt, and even nausea at having seen their buddies die and being turned into symbols and war bond salesmen—no war loving heroes here. A self-lacerating Hayes, especially, seems the most haunted by the war and rages at himself and at the role he's forced to play. He's also alternately lionized for his heroism and at the same time condescended to by being called "Chief" (Hayes was a Pima Indian)—even barred from being served in certain restaurants. Drinking heavily, Hayes finally leaves the bond tour and is sent back to the front.

Bradley is decent, caring, and the most levelheaded of the group but in later years never wants to talk to anyone about his years in the service or Iwo Jima. The three seem to embody F. Scott Fitzgerald's famous comment, "Show me a hero and I will write you a tragedy."[26] They may not quite have been heroes, but clearly their lives were damaged if not turned into tragic figures by being celebrated as heroes and then spit out after they served their function. Of the three, Hayes is the most lost and tragic. He ends his life doing odd jobs, drifting around the country, and sleeping off drunken binges in jail, all of it famously evoked in Johnny Cash's song "The Ballad of Ira Hayes."

Eastwood repeats too often his main theme that these were ordinary soldiers who felt they had done nothing special and were repelled by being used and packaged by public relations men. The point is incisively made, but the repetition and the fact that the three men's emotional reactions (except for Hayes) are not particularly interesting diminish its effect. And unfortunately, by concentrating the film's final moments on the fictional version of the author James Bradley's (Tom McCarthy) relationship with his father—a man who never talked to his son about the war or the flag raising—mires the film in sentimentality, for to balance his years of silence, his father's last days are spent calling out for a buddy who had died on Iwo Jima and even apologizing to his son for not being a good father. Thus, rather than the powerful, somber scenes of war's abattoir and desolation that marks its best moments, the film seems to peter out without a fitting denouement.

In addition, though we hardly ever glimpse the tens of thousands of Japanese hidden in pillboxes and tunnels in that mountain, their loss of lives is barely touched on. However, in a bold move, Eastwood simultaneously shot *Letters from Iwo Jima* (2007) from the Japanese perspective on the battle and succeeded making a war film that uniquely explored the enemies' military and national culture.

A more direct use of the past to comment on the events of the present, especially the often supine relationship of today's media to government and the irresponsible use of the airwaves by pundits and provocateurs, was George Clooney's concise and elegantly shot (all claustrophobic interiors) *Good Night, and Good Luck* (2005). Clooney, whose father was a television anchorman in Cincinnati, Ohio, and Lexington, Kentucky, who idolized Edward R. Murrow, used the story of Murrow's confrontation with Senator Joseph R. McCarthy to reflect on contemporary abuses of civil liberties by the Bush/Cheney axis in response to terrorist threats.

Clooney begins his biopic with Murrow's famous 1958 speech to the Radio-Television News Directors Association in which he decried the medium's decadence and escapism and told the assembled newspeople that unless television changed, it would become merely "wires and lights in a box." Clooney's perfect pitch use of black and white to reflect the era as well as his use of Mc-Carthy in newsreels and kinescopes rather than using an actor to play him lend an aura of authenticity to the film it might otherwise not have had. The only problematic note in the film is the strained use of Dianne Reeves as a jazz singer whose songs are intended as a kind of Greek chorus to the film's narrative.

Adding another strong dimension to the film is the performance of David Strathairn as Murrow. Strathairn, a fine actor who almost never gets to play a lead, provides a powerful imitation of Murrow. He gets just right the tilt of the head, the hand holding the omnipresent cigarette (smoke curling into the frame), and the Saville Row suavity of Murrow as well as his dour glances; his crisp, clipped diction; and his wry sense of humor. The film stays with the public Murrow—the private one remains outside its scope. The solemn, serious Murrow's job meant being part of show biz as well (purity was impossible), so he had to interview camp entertainers like Liberace for the banal *Person to Person*—where his only way of maintaining a bit of integrity was displaying off camera a grimace of revulsion after prostituting himself. That was the program people often referred to as "Lower Murrow," or, as Murrow said, "To do the show I want to do, I have to do the show I don't want to do."[27]

The show that Murrow wanted to do was *See It Now*, which between 1951 and 1957 was the pioneer in broadcast journalism and documentary. The "golden age" of *See It Now* was its conflict with Senator Joseph R. McCarthy, who was then in the heyday of his anticommunist witch hunts.

See It Now's confrontation with Senator McCarthy began innocently enough when the series took up the cudgels for Lieutenant Milo Radulovich, a young air force officer who had been cashiered because he consorted with his father and sister who presumably read Serbian communist newspapers. *See It Now*'s attack on McCarthy didn't go unnoticed, and shortly thereafter Don Surine (Robert Knepper), one of McCarthy's henchman, counterattacked by handing one of Murrow's gang of CBS journalists a packet of documents linking Murrow to communism—the usual charge during those red scare years.

See It Now's March 1954 show on Senator McCarthy is justly famous and is often pointed to as one of the high-water marks of television journalism. Clooney captures the tension and exhilaration of that program and the attack on the show for editorializing, at a time when television was forbidden to do so by the "fairness doctrine," which required television to air both sides of controversial issues. However, as Murrow says at one point, "I've searched my conscience and I cannot accept that there are two equivalent sides to every story."

The world depicted in *Good Night, and Good Luck* consists almost totally of the television studio and CBS headquarters. Clooney has a real feeling for the intense and sometimes exhilarating atmosphere of the newsroom and for detailing the studio technology of that era—control boards, microphones, and unwieldy cameras. It's also a hard-drinking, heavy-smoking, and patriarchal world. Staff producers Joe and Shirley Wershba (Robert Downey Jr. and Patricia Clarkson) are secretly married in defiance of company policy, and when discovered, it's Shirley who gets the pink slip. (She is the only woman in that milieu who has more responsibility than a secretary in the newsroom.)

Within that world, Murrow has to deal not only with the onslaught of McCarthy but also with pressure from executives like CBS's founder and board chairman William S. Paley (Frank Langella), who gives a silky performance that is both threatening and supportive. There are a couple of tense scenes where Paley, after supporting Murrow for years, dresses him down because he feels he's alienating the sponsors. For Murrow there is no escaping the fact that television is a commercial medium whose bottom line is always profit, and that's the smooth, power-wielding Paley's prime commitment.

The film charts the downfall of the demagogic, bullying, and self-pitying Senator McCarthy. His decline begins with the absurd investigation of Annie Lee Moss—a seemingly modest black Washington, D.C., communications clerk who is accused of being a communist spy (without corroborative evidence) and loses her job. That was followed up by that memorable coup de grâce—a rhetorical question delivered by attorney Joseph Welch during the Army-McCarthy hearing: "Have you left no decency, senator?"

Nonetheless, despite Murrow's courage in dealing with Senator McCarthy, the film ends on a melancholy note. First, there is the suicide of an emotionally troubled Don Hollenback (Ray Wise)—a CBS reporter who idolized Murrow. Hollenback was hounded to his death by accusations of communist sympathies made by a vicious Hearst columnist Jack O'Brian, then by Paley's abrupt cancellation of *See It Now* and its replacement by a less frequent documentary series *CBS Reports*, or, as critics referred to it, *See It Now and Then*.

Perhaps if Clooney had widened his lens, the film would have been even more touched with pathos. For in less than three years, Murrow was forced out of CBS and took a job in government as head of the U.S. Information Agency. Also Fred Friendly, who is played by a low-key George Clooney, is depicted in the film as a complaisant and muted second banana to Murrow and not the "Brilliant Monster"[28] he was known as at CBS. Friendly ultimately resigned in 1965 as news president when CBS refused to broadcast George Kennan's testimony to the Senate Foreign Relations Committee on the Vietnam War. Finally, there is the questionable use of newsreel footage at the end of the film of President Dwight D. Eisenhower decrying the unconstitutional denial of civil liberties in the era—the very same Dwight D. Eisenhower who refused to attack Senator McCarthy during his 1952 presidential campaign for impugning the honor of Eisenhower's mentor and one of the most important secretary of states of the 20th century, General George C. Marshall.

Good Night, and Good Luck provides a compressed version of history; so much is left out, including the many factors that led to McCarthy's downfall, that had nothing to do with Ed Murrow or CBS. But it succeeds well is demonstrating to this generation's often compromised and conglomerate-controlled media what it means to be a journalist who can defend liberty and risk alienating his own bosses and undermining his career to take on the liars, opportunists, and moral monsters that hold power.

If Murrow made integrity stylish, Edward Wilson (Matt Damon), the protagonist in Robert De Niro's consistently intelligent, intricately plotted, and methodical second directorial effort (*A Bronx Tale*, 1993), *The Good Shepherd* (2006), makes devotion to duty and loyalty to country absolutely soulless.

Through the character of Wilson, De Niro and the screenwriter Eric Roth (*Munich*) trace the evolution of the CIA from its days as the Office of Strategic Services (OSS) in World War II to the Bay of Pigs. That fiasco frames the film as Wilson attempts to discover what went wrong and to protect his own place in the agency from internal attack. The film flashes back to Wilson as a poetry-loving intellectual at Yale, where he is initiated in to the supersecretive, ritual-bound White/Anglo-Saxon Protestant (WASP) fraternity Skull and Bones, the home of former presidents, Supreme Court justices, and other members of the power elite—an organization not so different than the CIA. He is then urged to spy on an intellectually sinuous professor of poetry, Dr. Fredericks (played by the great Michael Gambon), who is revealed to be a double agent. His spying on Fredericks leads to his recruitment into the OSS by General Bill Sullivan (Robert De Niro), who is modeled after "Wild Bill" Donovan—an aggressive non-WASP during a time when East Coast WASP aristocrats—Dean Acheson, George Kennan, and John J. McCloy—appointed themselves as guardians of the nation and the dominant force in the CIA, which the OSS turns into.

At the same time he enters—after dropping a romance with the one woman he ever truly cares for, the hearing-impaired Laura (Tammy Blanchard)—into a loveless marriage with Margaret "Clover" Russell (Angelina Jolie), a senator's daughter whom he has gotten pregnant. Clover is beautiful, neurotic, and repelled by his world—but her opaque presence has little function in the film except to illustrate how emotionally empty Wilson's personal life is. The remote, stony Wilson leaves his family for six years to London and postwar Berlin, where he is totally enmeshed in the machinations of his agency. The CIA may call for loyalty from its operatives and a commitment to the country's interests, but it's a universe of dark rooms, murmurs, whispers, surreptitious phone calls, and, of course, secrets—one where nobody can be trusted and betrayal is the norm. As Dr. Fredericks says about poetry, "You have to look behind the words to understand the meaning." In the espionage universe, nothing is what it seems.

Wilson is no James Bond superhero or one of John le Carré's ambivalent cloak-and-dagger operatives. He is a precise man who carries out his assignments faithfully without much hesitation, and Damon perfectly captures his uptight meticulousness. At first, however, he is still merely the patriotic idealist, but with his first betrayal—the murder of Dr. Fredericks by British intelligence because he talks too loosely about his work to the rough trade he picks up—everything changes. Before being murdered, he warns Wilson, "Get out while you can, while you still believe, while you still have a soul."

The work becomes dirtier—a Mata Hari from the other side has to be dispatched, and in England, Wilson is mentored by and works with a British agent, Arch Cummings (Billy Crudup), modeled on the infamous Kim Philby—a man of immense charm and stunning duplicity who has been spying for the Russians.

Wilson, on his return to the United States, seems to withdraw even further inward and become more and more the gray bureaucrat who takes suburban buses to work and oversees the brutal torture of presumed double agents. In addition, Wilson's relationships seem to be pared away; first his wife leaves him, then his boss is revealed to have embezzled funds from the CIA, and then his son struggles to make a connection with the emotionally frozen Wilson. Ultimately, the closest relation Wilson seems to have is with his Soviet counterpart code-named "Ulysses" (Oleg Stefan), a wily superficially humane agent with whom he seems to share a kind of professional cordiality often involving quid pro quo exchanges.

Wilson's ultimate act of betrayal is of his son Edward Jr. (Edward Redmayne). His son who loves him has followed in his father's footsteps and joined the CIA, only to be compromised by falling in love and planning to marry a black woman who is secretly a KGB agent. It is Edward Sr. who agrees to have the son's pregnant fiancée thrown from a plane. The whole episode feels much too melodramatic for a film generally free of histrionics and excess. In the film's final moment, Edward plods on rewarded for his efforts by becoming head of the CIA's counterintelligence unit as the strains of *Poor Little Buttercup* from Gilbert and Sullivan, the song he once sang in drag at Yale. The drag performance can be seen as prefiguring the world of professional pretense he has spent his working life in.

The Good Shepherd is a serious film—treating espionage not as a world of derring-do and adventure but as one dominated by careful, prosaic work. For example, the agency expands a great deal of time analyzing a tape recording and photograph of a man and a woman having sex that may explain what happened at the Bay of Pigs. The film's narrative can be unwieldy, and it becomes a bit too neat when it suggests that one reason for Wilson's total commitment to the agency is to make up for his father's committing suicide because he had compromised his honor.

What is most compelling about the film is the portrait it creates of a man who loses his soul because he does work that is morally odious and how a government agency whose aim is to protect American democracy loses its way in murderous games that have little to do with national interest. The film doesn't directly ask if the whole espionage/counterespionage apparatus is necessary at all, but on the evidence presented here, the wisest course would be to limit the CIA's future activities to intelligence gathering.

Though a film like *Good Night, and Good Luck* constructed a vivid portrait of moral and political courage, what was in short supply in American film was the depiction of actual bravery in the face of almost overwhelming violence and intimidation by a man who will not flee his responsibilities. It is this kind of heroism that is depicted in Terry George's (*Some Mother's Son*, 1996) *Hotel Rwanda* (2004).

Hotel Rwanda, built on real-life events, centers around Paul Rusesabagina (Don Cheadle), the shrewd manager of the Belgium-owned luxury Hotel Milles Collines in Kigali, the capital of Rwanda, who rescued 1,268 Tutsis and moderate Hutus during the genocidal slaughter of more than 800,000 Tutsi's and others in 100 days in Rwanda in 1994. For his efforts, Rusesabagina, an Everyman turned hero, has been called the "African Schindler."

Hotel Rwanda takes place not in the romantic, colonial Africa of *Out of Africa* (1985) but rather in the world of power politics where the world's superpowers did nothing while the barbaric slaughter in Rwanda raged unabated (they didn't see it as their issue, having little economic or geopolitical significance), a policy for which President Clinton issued a public apology.[29] This failure was perhaps best summed up by a raspy-voiced, world-weary Nick Nolte as Colonel Oliver, a commander of the UN peacekeepers who only had 300 unarmed troops under him and was ordered to withdraw from Rwanda during the genocide but not before they save the Europeans at the hotel. Oliver says to Paul, "You should spit in my face. . . . The West, all the superpowers they think you are dirt. They think you are dung. You're not even a nigger. You're African." Paul—apolitical, immersed in his work, and a bit naive—has believed there is no real crisis. And given that he identifies himself with Europe and European culture, he is stunned by the news that to the Europeans he's nothing more than a nonentity.

What distinguishes *Hotel Rwanda*, which is more a well-paced, competently directed political melodrama filled with almost incomprehensible carnage than a complex reflection on politics and history, is the outstanding performance of

Cheadle as Rusesabagina. Cheadle's Rusesabagina is an unfailingly polite man who runs his upscale hotel according to the highest standards of service and who adapts the cunning, strategic obsequiousness, and bribery that helps him serve his clientele to aid him in saving the lives of people, including a group of orphans who have taken refuge in his hotel.

The only moment when Rusesabagina's mask of competence and control breaks down is when, returning from a warehouse where he has gone to get supplies for the hotel, his truck literally rides over a highway strewn with corpses. Paul weeps uncontrollably but then, realizing his responsibilities, straightens his tie and goes on with his duty to the refugees and his family.

Paul is a Hutu who is married and deeply in love with his wife Tatiana (Sophie Okonedo), a Tutsi—this puts him in a difficult position in a country where the hatred that exists between these two groups is at the root for the rampant destruction that is let loose there. (Ironically, the two groups have become almost physically indistinguishable.) The film does sketch a few lines of historical background about the origins of their conflict: when it was a Belgian colony, the Belgians historically favored the Tutsi over the Hutus—having them run the country—but when they exited, the Hutus took control and began to violently pay back the Tutsis for the abuse of their power. But the film needs a deeper exploration of African and Rwandan history to provide a proper context for the madness of the genocide. Focusing on one man's heroic story is insufficient.

The film's conclusion has a Hollywood touch with the arrival of the Tutsi rebel forces and Paul and family on the way out of the country. And given that Paul and his family's fate is at the center of the film, it almost passes for a happy ending. But this is a stirring film that can't help but move one. It succeeds in depicting another moment in the 20th century that was replete with what one writer has referred to as the "Problem from Hell."

While it isn't surprising that after 9/11 the public and filmmakers paid so much attention to the "war on terror," another war was taking place—the "war on drugs." That war was an ongoing dilemma for Americans that cost thousands of lives and billions of dollars. That war and the problems that accompany it were the focus of Steven Soderbergh's (*Sex, Lies, and Videotape*, 1989) film *Traffic* (2000).

Traffic was an American remake of a more complex five-hour 1989 British miniseries titled *Traffick*. Soderbergh's version uses three at times interlocking plots to trace the drugs from Mexico to the streets of American cities. Among the cast of characters are cops, thugs, drug bosses, politicians, and the American drug czar. Its multilayered structure begins with Tijuana state policeman Javier Rodriguez (a laconic Benicio Del Toro, the film's most layered character) and his partner Manolo caught in a murderous web of political corruption centered on the Mexican drug trade.

In bleached-out sepia tones with Spanish subtitles and handheld camera, the soulful, idealistic Rodriquez turns the tables on the plotters but not before seeing his partner killed and his own values compromised.

From Mexico, the film moves north and in cool bluish tints deals with a reserved, single-minded Ohio Supreme Court Justice Robert Wakefield (Michael Douglas), who is the newly appointed American "drug czar," who aggressively sets out to win this war. He has an A student, spoiled and neglected daughter Caroline (Erika Christensen), who develops a drug problem that turns from occasional use to severe addiction, including turning tricks in black inner-city Cincinnati. The family does all the right things in dealing with her, but their interaction is totally devoid of emotional depth, and the Wakefields' marital problems are skimmed over. The point heavily made by this narrative is that nobody is immune to drug addiction, including the privileged children of powerful drug warriors.

Finally, in bold colors, there is the story of Helena Ayala (Catherine Zeta-Jones), who in order to save her arrested drug lord husband (Steven Bauer) from conviction unconvincingly goes from pampered, pregnant, country club housewife to a hard-nosed crime boss who orders hits without the least hesitation and fends off extortion from a Mexican cartel. It's as if one of the women on television's innumerable housewives reality shows suddenly turned into Tony Soprano.

Traffic doesn't offer any facile solutions to the drug problem. In fact, for all the billions spent, the film sees the drug war as unwinnable. As Wakefield, fully chastened by his family's experience, says in press conference before he walks away from his job, "How can you make war on your own family?" Another complication is the fact that in Mexico and other Latin American countries, law enforcement is permeated with corruption.

Traffic is an ambitious film that succeeds in shedding light on the nation's drug problems and authoritatively depicting the nature of the drug culture. In addition, Soderbergh uses the texture of locations evocatively (e.g., Tijuana and inner-city Cincinnati), but *Traffic*'s characters are subordinated to the film's didacticism—everything has to be articulated. The film contains too many lectures—Caroline's preppy, insufferable boyfriend lectures Wakefield on racist politics, and a midlevel drug dealer engages in a tirade about the futility about stopping the drug trade in the age of the North American Free Trade Agreement. And the film's bitter conclusion has to be slightly sugarcoated to grant the audience a drop of hope—a bug placed by the Drug Enforcement Administration in the drug lord's house when he is released from prison and Rodriguez beatifically watching kids play baseball on a field that he has paid for.

The financial depredations of the American corporate chief executive officer (CEO) was just sleeker and more respectable looking but equally destructive as the pernicious activities of the drug lords. Our homegrown corporate criminals, like Dennis Kozlowski (Tyco), Bernie Ebbers (World Com), Ken Lay and Jeffrey Skilling (Enron), and Bernie Madoff, made the robber barons of the 19th century seem almost like choirboys.

Tony Gilroy's directorial debut film, the darkly entertaining (he skillfully uses New York's night streets to build tension), marvelously performed *Michael Clayton* (2007), turned to the world of corporate corruption from that of international espionage. Gilroy had written the scripts for the hyperkinetic Bourne Trilogy.

The center of the film is the eponymous Michael Clayton (George Clooney)—a weary, lined, 45-year-old loyal son of a clan of Irish Americans and an ex–assistant district attorney who is divorced with an eight-year-old son (his family relations are merely sketched). He's also a gambling addict—in hock to loan sharks for $75,000—and, most important, does morally squalid work as a "fixer," or, as he would have it, "janitor" ("the smaller the mess the easier to clean up") for a powerful, successful New York law factory that employs 600 lawyers. A duplicitous, dangerously avuncular Marty Bach (Sydney Pollack) heads the firm—Kenner, Bach, and Ladeen—whose only principle is profit. For the firm, the law is there to be manipulated, and Michael's most important custodial task is to get their star bipolar litigator, Arthur Edens (Tom Wilkinson in a ranting, striking turn), back into the fold after a sensational meltdown at a deposition of a lawsuit that has had six years of court delays. Arthur is repelled by it all and wants to reveal that the firm's client and the target of a huge class-action suit, the giant agribusiness U/North, has been systematically pouring lethal, carcinogenic pesticides into soil, costing the lives of more than 450 people. He may be a manic-depressive, but he has become a truth teller who won't, in his words, "aid the sickness any longer."

The person most immediately threatened by Arthur's disclosures is Karen Crowder (Tilda Swinton), U/North's chief legal counsel and in line to become it's CEO. Swinton's Crowder is a combination of vulnerability and steely murderous ambition who tremulously hires a private security firm to observe and ultimately murder Edens. Swinton is the kind of actress who can add complexity to any role. Her preparation for a corporate presentation by rehearsing her spiel in front of a mirror, inspecting her sweaty underarms, and straightening her hems tells us all we want to know about this anxious, driven woman.

Michael Clayton is ultimately a tale of moral redemption. Michael is aware how compromised his life has become, that he is part of a Darwinian world where everybody is out for himself. And gradually he develops a conscience. At the film's climax, he gets Crowder to confess her crimes and has her arrested. However, Michael's regeneration is a bit too facile—the film offers little of his internal conflict, though the scene where he watches horses in a pastoral setting presents the possibility of an alternate life touched by calm and light. But *Michael Clayton* is primarily a traditional thriller augmented by a social critique. And *Michael Clayton* permitted the charismatic Clooney, following his performance in *Syriana* and direction and performance in *Good Night, and Good Luck*, to lay serious claim to the mantle that Warren Beatty and Robert Redford, established in the 1970s and 1980s as Hollywood's liberal conscience.

Clooney's liberal credentials shouldn't have been but were bolstered by his role as Ryan Bingham in the slick, well-crafted Jason Reitman's (*Juno*) comedy/romance *Up in the Air* (2009). Smooth as it was, Reitman's film did hit a particular nerve since on one level it deals with layoffs and firings in corporate America. We are living in country hit by the worst economic crisis since the 1930s—with official unemployment statistics in the double digits and unofficial estimates of close to 17 million Americans being out of work. In the film's opening montage of recently actually laid-off workers (with a couple of well-known character actors thrown in), Reitman captured their confusion, rage, and despair about the economic and psychological state that they had, without warning, been plummeted into.

Ryan Bingham is no liberal. In fact, he seems to have no politics or moral center at all. He works for a company euphemistically called Corporate Transitional Counseling (CTC), whose repellent job it is to lay off workers whom their bosses are too cowardly to fire themselves. Ryan is one of CTC's ablest road warriors who spends 322 days on the road and "43 miserable days at home." Footloose and fancy free hardly describes Ryan, whose motto is, "to know me is to fly with me," and whose shallow philosophy is summed up to the motivational seminars he sometimes is a speaker at: "Moving is living." And as far as relationships are concerned, the disconnected, family- and relationship-averse Ryan urges his audiences to unpack them as easily as he symbolically unpacks a knapsack he brings with him as a prop to these events.

Ryan's well-oiled world is suddenly threatened by Natalie Keener (Anna Kendrick), a recently graduated (Stanford), callow, PowerPoint princess who has convinced the bosses at CTC that the Internet promises the most cost-efficient means of firing workers. Ryan defends his job and way of life by inviting the ambitious, smart Natalie on a cross-country expedition to see what the real world of firing people is really like. As they move from one anonymous middle-American city to another and sometimes one deserted office to another—Natalie's self-assured, almost robotic persona begins to break. She turns out to be predictably more human and vulnerable to the pain she has to dole out and to romantic failure than her perky, cool surface has conveyed.

Ryan's serene isolation is also gradually undermined when he meets the sophisticated, sexually liberated Alex Goren (Vera Farmiga), who seems to lead a life just like Ryan's ("I'm the woman you never have to worry about. Think of me as yourself, only with a vagina."). Not since *The Graduate* has plastic seemed so sexy, as Alex and Ryan compare plastic and privilege cards in a modern-day version of foreplay and share postcoital interludes on their laptops planning trysts that match their peripatetic schedules.

The coup de grâce to Ryan's lifestyle, however, is when he and Alex travel to Ryan's kid sister's wedding in small-town Wisconsin. Ironically, Ryan suddenly finds himself giving marital advice to a groom with cold feet and begins to yearn for a different kind of life. He is ready to move from an uncommitted pleasurable relationship with Alex to a romantic one. But the move is brought short when he makes a surprise visit to Chicago and discovers Alex's real life—one committed to a husband and children. The shocker is more narrative contrivance than something we can believe about Alex, who seems to have genuine feeling for Ryan and is not just treating him as an escape from her domestic life.

What is most interesting about *Up in the Air* is the virtual world that Ryan inhabits. He is a man who revels in the recycled air of airports and airplanes and whose vision of domesticity is based on bare, identical hotel rooms in different cities. Ryan may retrace his school days with Alex, but he is a man without genuine roots or links. However, *Up in the Air* is primarily a witty entertainment and doesn't look to get to the heart of this sterile brave new world bounded by Blackberrys, My Space, Skype, and Twitter—one where social networking has replaced intimacy.

And when dealing with callous and contemptuous way the corporations deal with their employees, the film opts for the traditional Hollywood bromide about family values triumphing over marketplace values. It's underlined by the same laid-off workers who sketch out the terrors of unemployment so vividly in the opening montage, now describing how family and friends have meant so much to them during their crisis—odd, given that the marriages and relationships we see in the film are problematic or broken and the fact that long-term unemployment often leaves one too disconsolate to be saved by family love and can result in the destruction of the family as well. If Reitman had made a genuine critique of the corporate world, he would have avoided softening the savagery of its ethos.

However, the unemployed are no more than an engaging device rather than the center of this watchable, one-liner-filled film. Clooney as always is charming, intelligent, and extremely cool. The film feels as calibrated as Ryan's travel plans. There is no happy ending—Ryan return to flying incessantly bringing bad news to countless employees. It should be a terribly dark ending, but we never feel Ryan's pain or pathos—Clooney just can't stop himself from being alluring. And if the film had ended in true pathos, it would have become a much less crowd-pleasing film.

"I want the fairy tale," so says Vivian Ward the character played by Julia
Roberts in her breakthrough film *Pretty Woman* (1990). In *Erin Brockovich*, directed by Steven Soderbergh (*Traffic*), the eponymous title character played
by Julia Roberts has the fairy tale wrapped in the true story of a twice-divorced,
working-class mother of three young children with a double-digit bank account who takes on a multi-billion-dollar California utility and wins the largest
settlement ($333 million) in U.S. history.

Watching the film one might instinctively think of *Norma Rae* (1979) or
Silkwood (1983), but the ex–beauty queen Erin is not just a spunky, earnest
trade unionist or a disillusioned whistle-blower. In her push-up bras, tight-
fitting short skirts, stiletto heels that force her to teeter while walking, and a
potty mouth that would shame a stevedore, she is a tough-talking, formidable
opponent to petty bureaucrats; uptight, condescending corporate lawyers; or
anyone else who has the temerity to get in her way.

Though Erin's struggles are primarily with PG&E, the faceless giant California utility that has slowly been leaking cancerous toxins into the lives of
the working people of the desert town of Hinkley, California, she also storms
around the office of her gruff but lovable boss, Ed Masry (a thick-bodied,
Albert Finney—no longer the handsome working-class protagonist of the
early 1960s *Saturday Night, Sunday Morning*)—a hack lawyer whose idealism
and competitive zest is revived by a driven, socially committed Erin. There is
also George (Aaron Eckhart), her gentle, bearded, tattooed biker next-door
neighbor (inevitably more sensitive and vulnerable than Erin) who becomes
her lover and a nurturing Mr. Mom to her kids but is disaffected by her workaholic ways and leaves her.

Erin Brockovich's character conveys the desperation inherent in the life of
a single working-class mother and carries feminist overtones—Erin's sense of
self-worth is predicated on her winning this class-action lawsuit and realizing
herself. She also classically struggles, rather unsuccessfully, with the dilemma
of creating some sort of balance between work, her children, and the man she
is with—she is a woman who won't bend to a man's needs. However, the film
is essentially a star vehicle for Julia Roberts, who won an Academy Award for
her performance. She is practically in every scene, and despite not being conventionally beautiful, her wide full mouth, radiant smile, full mane of hair, and
lithe body grant life to every frame.

In lesser hands, this film could have come close to treacle, but Roberts is
utterly convincing as a perceptive, resourceful working-class heroine. We believe in her capacity to empathetically reach out to Hinkley's inhabitants and
in garnering their support without alienating them. Her life may have been
dominated by failure, but in this situation all her instincts and experience

work for her—the triumph of working-class intuition and earthiness over elitist expertise. Erin will never be underestimated again.

The denouement of the case comes too quickly, and, of course, George returns to Erin. Happy Hollywood ending and all, this is a first-rate entertainment with a working-class heroine one can believe in, who remains true to herself at the film's conclusion.

If Erin Brockovich is the archetypical working-class heroine, then, though further down the class scale, her male movie counterpart is Jimmy "Bunny Rabbit" Smith Jr. Smith, played by Eminem (Marshall Mathers), in Curtis Hanson's (*LA Confidential*) *8 Mile* (2002) is a white rapper from Detroit totally enmeshed in a black world (a model for whites who like to adopt black inner-city vernacular and style), hitherto known primarily for rap lyrics that featured a scatological wit liberally laced with large doses of misogyny and homophobia.

The street 8 Mile is literally the border between the blue-lit, burnt-out, graffiti- and trash-ridden devastated neighborhoods of urban black Detroit and its leafy white suburbs. It's the home of Smith and his interracial crew made up of the dim "Cheddar Bob" (Evan Jones), the gentle giant Sol George (Omar Benson), the absurdly self-serious and comically political DJ Iz (De'Angelo Wilson), and the dreadlocked, sharp, and entrepreneurial "Future" (Mekhi Phifer), who believes in Smith and his talent. They are not thugs, but street fighting and gratuitous violence are an integral part of their life.

Unlike earlier cinematic working-class heroes who often fought their way out of poverty with their fists (*Body and Soul*, 1946, and *Rocky*, 1975), Jimmy Smith's weapon is his profane imagination and the words he jots down on scraps of paper. By means of his words, he seeks out his opponents' vulnerabilities and verbally opens gaping wounds with powerful hip-hop lyrics at the local rap battleground a club known as "The Shelter."

Initially, an insecure Smith can't seem to find his voice and literally chokes up in his first battle at the Shelter before a sneering black crowd who taunt and call him "Vanilla Ice." However, propelled by a dead-end job in a stamping plant; a sexually aggressive, ambitious new girlfriend; and his ultraloyal crew, Smith ultimately does find his voice and in classic Hollywood style reduces the reigning hip-hop champion at the Shelter, "Papa Doc" (Anthony Mackie), to speechlessness and then predictably leaves Detroit to set out on the road to success.

With its echoes of James Dean and the young Brando, the hoodie-wearing Eminem is convincing as the up-and-coming rapper, who is nothing else but a realist about his life ("I am white trash."). He's more personally gentle and soulful than his lyrics, and though Eminem as an actor gives off little affect, one can believe that he's a complex mixture of softness and hardness, both genuinely sympathetic and shaped by the defiance of the street. His sensitivity is manifested most strongly in is tenderness toward his little sister Lily (Chloe Greenfield), who lives in a trailer with his alcoholic, unemployed, self-pitying mother Stephanie (Kim Basinger), a woman who perfectly embodies the word "slattern."

In addition, though the film hardly focuses on what brought on the city's breakdown, Hanson's camera provides a real sense of the postapocalyptic scene that is contemporary Detroit. And he refuses to temper or sentimentalize the harsh world that his characters inhabit—offering them no quick fixes. What the film doesn't explain is why rap has captured the imaginations of inner-city youth and become a path for some to affirm their sense of self. Is the choice of rap a way to express anger with bows to some ghetto traditions, such as the "dozens," or musical forms, such as jazz "cutting" contests? Why profane wit and imagination has succeeded boxing as a means of working-class mobility will remain a mystery to anyone who sees 8 Mile.

While 8 Mile depicts a new vibrant, creative, if poorly understood aspect of youth/popular culture, the Palme d'Or–winning film at Cannes, Elephant (2003), directed and written by Gus Van Sant (e.g., My Own Private Idaho, 1991, and Good Will Hunting, 1997), probes a more tragic and violent side in the lives of young people.

Elephant is Van Sant's fictional version of the 1999 Columbine High School massacre in which 15 students died and 23 were wounded. Unlike Michael Moore's polemical and simplistic documentary Bowling for Columbine (2002), Van Sant's film doesn't assign blame or really provide explanations. It's more a nonjudgmental meditation on what occurred that day rather than an attempt to analyze the nature of the massacre. What it does is track, without being linear, a number of high school students through their day until its fateful conclusion.

The film spends much of its time in the often-silent halls of the immense, well-appointed, suburban Watt High School (a school outside Portland, Oregon), except for cutaways to beautiful cloud formations. It uses a handheld camera, verité style, to provide long, meandering takes that capture the daily flow of the students' school life and snatches of their desultory conversation. At other times, the same scene is shot from several different perspectives and doubles back on itself—though never suggesting the truth is Rashomon-like. One of the students the camera observes is blond, laid-back John (John Robinson)—all the students in the film were nonprofessionals who improvised their own dialogue—who must deal with the disarray of his alcoholic father (Timothy Bottoms) before he goes to class. There is also an assortment of your usual middle-class, mostly white suburban high school cast of characters: Nathan

(Nathan Tyson) and Carrie (Carrie Finklea), a handsome jock and his jealous girlfriend; Elias (Elias McConnell), a budding young photographer who talks knowingly about the use of contrast and is serious about his art; three chattering, bulimic, cute girls, Nicole (Nicole George), Brittany (Brittany Mountain), and Jordan (Jordan Taylor); and the plain-looking, gawky, alienated-from-her-peers-and-her-body Michelle (Kristen Hicks), who is reprimanded by her physical education teacher for not wearing gym shorts. None of the students' personalities are defined; they are just ordinary adolescents going about their day. In fact, Van Sant is more interested in evoking the atmosphere of the high school day than in providing a penetrating take on high school culture.

Van Sant devotes the last half of the film to the two sociopathic killers, Alex (Alex Frost) and Eric (Eric Deulen), who smoke pot, play violent video games, buy a mail-order automatic weapon, watch a Hitler documentary, and share a homosexual embrace and kiss in the shower (utterly gratuitous given that the film does nothing with this) before they go on their murderous rampage. Van Sant avoids offering any clear causal factor or factors for their actions.

There are some possibilities thrown out. Was it bullying, for in one scene a student throws paper at Alex? Was it lack of parental involvement? Was it an obsession with Hitler for the Columbine massacre took place on April 20, Hitler's birthday? Or was it confusion over their sexual identity and fear of homophobia? Given what we see, all these explanations feel lame and irrelevant, for Van Sant doesn't acknowledge or emphasize any one of them.

Van Sant's film is disturbing without being exploitative—most of the violence occurs offscreen, but the chaos that erupts of shouted warnings, tears, wild dashes, and point-blank killings remains terrifying. The transformation from the buzz of an ordinary school day to cacophony and bodies littering the hallways is strikingly done. Van Sant has made a unique and audacious film.

Still, Alex's last remark to Eric before they go on their killing spree—"The most important thing is to just have fun"—doesn't leave us with much. We don't need an explanation that ties everything up in a neat box, but it's not enough to depict what takes place with consummate cinematic fluency. Some sort of hypothesis about why this massacre might have occurred would have given this film more of a moral and social grounding, even if no simple answers exist.

Though eyebrows might have been raised over the homoerotic hints in *Elephant*, it hardly compared to the furor that surrounded director Ang Lee's (*Crouching Tiger, Hidden Dragon*, 2000) so-called gay cowboy movie *Brokeback Mountain* (2005). Lee's film was inspired by Annie Proulx's 1997 *New Yorker* short story. Clearly, Proulx's short story and Lee's film of it are not only stories of a couple of Marlboro men in love but also tragic tales of romantic longing and loss.

Brokeback Mountain (2005). (Courtesy of Focus Features/Photofest.)

The film begins in 1963 as two cowboys, a relatively confident and aggressive rodeo rider Jack Twist (Jake Gyllenhaal) and an impoverished, inarticulate ranch hand Ennis Del Mar (Heath Ledger), are hired to tend to a flock of sheep one summer in the stunning green-blue Grand Teton Mountains of Wyoming. One night after drinking and wishing to ward off the cold and loneliness, they share a tent and have passionate sex. Stunned by what they have done, they can barely acknowledge it. Ennis says, "This is a one-shot thing we got goin' on here," and Jack mumbles back, "Ain't nobody's business but ours." But they continue to have sex the rest of the time they work there. The romantic/bucolic idyll on the mountain—isolated from societal pressures—is the apogee of their lives.

Four years later, both are married and have children: Ennis to an earnest, caring woman Alma (Michele Williams) and Jack to an entrepreneurial ex–rodeo queen Lureen (Anne Hathaway) and to her odious father's money—he owns a thriving farm machinery business. However, a card from Jack renews their relationship, which continues as yearly "fishing trips" where all sexual restraint is dropped and little fishing takes place. Jack, being the more adventurous, expressive, and comfortable with his sexual nature, proposes that they go off and live together. But Ennis, exposed in early adolescence to the object lesson of a gay ranch hand beaten to death, can't do it and says stoically, "If you can't fix it, you gotta stand it." He accepts the fact that he lives in a world where being closeted is the rule, and both are unable to ever admit that they are gay. They also never use the word "love"—it's a relationship that can never speak its name and is doomed to frustration. Every time Jack leaves, Ennis is filled with a sense of longing, loss, and guilt.

Ennis's wife feels utterly rejected, becoming totally wary of their relationship after she sees him sharing a fervent kiss with Jack. They ultimately and painfully divorce, and Ennis ends up alone living minimally in a mobile home with a television as his companion—becoming even more laconic and quietly despairing. And Jack, who has gay relationships and does a fair amount of cruising, is murdered. All that is left of their relationship is a postcard of Brokeback Mountain, though, Ennis, a tender and loving father, has a bit of consolation of his daughter's infrequent visits and love.

The world outside their relationship is merely sketched, but the film convincingly conveys that it's a time and place where relationships like theirs are taboo and dangerous. The relationship between the two men is at the center of the film, and both actors give striking performances, especially the late Heath Ledger. On one level, Ledger's performance seems almost a tribute to legendary western stars like the mumbling, taciturn Gary Cooper, but there is nothing conventionally heroic about the role he plays. Ennis is a cowboy who falls from his horse and does not engage in any derring-do. On a more significant level, Ledger's Ennis is an uneasy, uneducated man of few words but a character who communicates profound, tragic, and even eloquent feelings that few of the past stars of westerns ever realized or even attempted to convey.

In the film's most emotionally stirring and haunting scenes, Ennis visits the isolated farmhouse of Jack's parents—a bitter, angry father and a soft, sympathetic mother. He looks around at Jack's bare, neat bedroom; stares at his boots; and caresses his shirt. The scene carries a great deal of emotional weight without the use of words: capturing the narrow world that shaped and oppressed Jack and Ennis's moving sense of permanent bereavement and defeat.

A question arises why critics should have been so surprised at what some crudely referred this story of thwarted love to as a "gay cowboy" movie. There were westerns made long before, like Howard Hawks's *Red River* (1948), that contained obvious homoerotic content. And in 1948, critic Leslie Fiedler had exposed the homoerotic content of American literature going back to Natty Bumppo and Chingachgook.[30] However, in *Brokeback Mountain*, the homoerotic is not submerged but acted out, without it turning into a social problem film. Obviously, there were critics who still had difficulty accepting that a tragic romance between men was as worthy a subject as a heartbreaking heterosexual love affair.

Further proof, if any were really necessary, that the era of the celluloid closet was a thing of the past and that films about gays had come of age is offered by the first biopic of a gay political hero, *Milk* (2008), directed in a more linear and accessible style than Gus Van Sant used in *Elephant*.

Harvey Milk, whose career had been amply depicted in the 1984 Academy Award–winning documentary *The Times of Harvey Milk*, was an openly gay man (the first elected to political office) who was voted on to the San Francisco Board of Supervisors in 1977 and then assassinated, along with Mayor George Moscone, by a former supervisor, Dan White, in 1978.

Milk begins with a foreboding of the tragedy to come as Harvey (Sean Penn), speaking into a tape recorder, details the events of his life. Van Sant then cuts to a fateful meeting in a subway station between Harvey—then a closeted, suit-and-tie-wearing, sexually ravenous insurance agent and the young, handsome, curly-haired hippie Scott (James Franco)—on the afternoon of Harvey's 40th birthday. Afterward in bed, Harvey complains to Scott, "I'm 40 years old, and I haven't done anything I'm proud of." It sets the stage for the film's depiction of Harvey's re-creation of himself into a gay activist and leader.

Harvey and Scott begin a relationship, move to San Francisco, and become part of that city's golden age of gay culture. Milk starts a camera shop in the Castro that is beginning to transform itself into a gay neighborhood. Though the San Francisco police hated homosexuals and it was still not safe being an openly gay man in the city, within a few years, by virtue of his extrovert charm, self-deprecating humor and irony, and leadership qualities, Harvey becomes the so-called Mayor of Castro Street. It's a title well earned because of his being a shrewd political tactician—exemplified by his ability to forge alliances with unlikely allies such as the Teamsters, his charismatic gift for reaching his own constituency, as well as his willingness to defy San Francisco's gay elite, who counsel going slow and being more subtle and less direct in his political advocacy. They are old-time liberals who lack Harvey's capacity to garner support from the street.

It takes time and hard work for Milk to achieve political success—he is elected to the San Francisco Board of Supervisors only on his third try. The film focuses on the nature of Harvey's political commitments that define his essence. His devotion to politics ends up being too obsessive for Scott, who leaves him. But Harvey attracts others to his cause like Cleve Jones (Emile Hirsch), a street kid who he transforms into a skilled political organizer/activist, and a variety of others whose names we learn but the film barely sketches. His choice of lover after Scott, the apolitical, hysterical, pathological Jack (Diego Luna), leads to tragedy. The only explanation the film provides for why Milk got so intimately involved with somebody so emotionally unstable and unsuitable is Harvey's throwaway line that "his private life is a mess."

The film's most clearly evoked and disastrous relationship is Harvey's with another Board of Supervisors member, Dan White (a strong performance by Josh Brolin). White, an Irish American Catholic and former cop and firefighter, is a tortured soul whom Harvey with a touch of condescension and a wink and a nod believes is "One of Us." Closeted or not, Harvey is slightly repelled and wary of White, who is filled with rage and resentment. But White is needy and seeks Harvey's approval, just as Harvey, in turn, with a bit too much self-assurance, thinks he can turn him into an ally. It all ends tragically with White (enraged that he can't get his job back after resigning or out of homophobic rage) murdering Harvey and Mayor Moscone (Victor Garber) and White's infamous rationale for his actions, which became known as the "Twinkie defense."[31]

However, the center of *Milk* is not his relationship with White but Harvey as a political hero and martyr. We see him courageously and eloquently challenging such homophobes as the orange juice queen Anita Bryant (shown in newsreels) and California State Senator John Driggs (Denis O'Hare), who sponsors a referendum, Proposition 6, which would have forbidden gays and lesbians to teach in the public schools (shades of South Carolina's right-wing ideologue, Senator Jim DeMint). Harvey plays an instrumental role in having the initiative defeated by more than a million votes. And in his brief 11 months as supervisor, he is responsible for passing a stringent gay rights ordinance for the city.

Milk is not mere hagiography. Sean Penn's striking, Academy Award–winning performance as Harvey may dominate, but the film is more than a biopic. It vividly captures the justified anger and evolving power of the gay movement that has begun to demand its rights. Penn is able to inhabit Harvey's body with a prosthetic nose that mimics Harvey's rather large one. However, more than grasping Milk's body movement and voice, Penn conveys Harvey's unrestrained and humorous quality as a political speaker—picking up a bullhorn and shouting, "My fellow degenerates . . . my name is Harvey Milk, and I'm here to recruit you." He also convincingly projects Harvey's basic decency, gift for empathy, and selfless commitment to the movement without turning him into a secular saint and making the film seem saccharine.

After Milk is murdered, Van Sant beautifully constructs in long shot a stirring scene of a candlelit night memorial march of 30,000 people to San Francisco's City Hall—his friends walking in front with tears in their eyes. They are marching in accord with Harvey's motto that is frequently recited by him, "You gotta give them hope." Harvey's sense of hope is inclusive and richly rendered—extending to straight people as well as gays and lesbians—and helps make *Milk* an emotionally resonant, truly first-rate political film.

Harvey Milk's mantra that "You gotta give them hope" is surprisingly close to the 2008 Obama campaign's slogan, "Yes we can." And in the wake of his victory, there were those who believed (or hoped) that a postracial America would be ushered in with Barack Obama's election. These were people we thought were either pollyannaish or conservatives who just wanted to deny America's continuing racial inequalities and tensions. In subsequent years, that hope faded quickly, as the buoyant feelings of Obama's election night began to disappear. Plainly, Obama's waning popularity should not be arrogated primarily to race, but a significant minority exists (though few own up to their racism) who are incensed by the fact that a black man is president. The fact is that race has remained a powerful factor in our lives. It may not have been "the issue," but profound structural racism and inequality exist and remain generally unaddressed—race remaining the most profound divide in America.

Hollywood once fled from the issue of race, but since it realized that there was a large black film audience, it has, since the 1960s, consciously used black stars and at least touched on the subject. Though one would have a hard time coming up with more than a handful of mainstream films that treated the subject seriously. However, in the 21st century, it did provide a number of award-winning films. One was the 2004 surprise Academy Award winner for best film, *Crash*, directed by first-time filmmaker Paul Haggis, whose previous work had been as a scriptwriter for Clint Eastwood's award-winning *Million Dollar Baby* (2004).

Crash is an ambitious, ensemble work that wrestles with the theme of racism and its impact on a number of characters from a variety of class, ethnic, and racial backgrounds. It takes place in Los Angeles—a sprawling city viewed as a rigidly class and racially divided urban turf where the car rules and, as one character says, "nobody touches you, so we miss it so much we crash into each other just so we can feel something." The only exception is when the film's characters break out of their isolation to express racist venom. Given the number of characters, the film needs the kind of fluid editing that seamlessly cuts from one group of characters' story to another narrative—granting them all sufficient time to develop.

The film takes place in a feverish 36-hour period that encompasses car crashes, a carjacking, and a volatile encounter between a racist white policeman and an upper-middle-class African American couple whose dignity he robs. In addition, illegal aliens are smuggled, an Iranian immigrant small store owner, feeling continually victimized, spins out of control and attempts to kill an innocent Hispanic locksmith, and a politician manipulates the facts about a murder involving a black and a white cop in order to get reelected. In sum, an overheated film with too many melodramatic incidents and coincidences, an inflated, intrusive sound track, and a too-schematic quality where every interaction turns out to have racial connotations.

But *Crash* does contain a number of striking performances, including Don Cheadle as a decent, soft-spoken, despairing detective who is trapped by his own ambivalent feelings toward both the compromises of his job and his loyalty to his street criminal brother; Sandra Bullock (playing against her girl next door movie persona) as a well-off, neurotic, bitchy wife of the Los Angeles district attorney who is filled with anger toward and fear of Hispanics and African Americans; and Matt Dillon as racist cop who is also the caring son of a disabled father and the kind of professional who will risk his life to rescue from an overturned car the wife of the black couple he had so viciously harassed.

What's disturbing about *Crash* is not only its penchant for revving up the action and emotion but also Haggis's need to try to balance its dark, almost apocalyptic portrait of Los Angeles with some contrived scenes where some of the characters discover a sudden capacity for understanding "the other." Haggis's attempt to offer some redemptive magic, however, never takes hold.

What resonates in this flawed, suggestive, and ambitious film is the feeling of an American city profoundly driven by stated and unstated racist feelings and stereotyping, though in this film many of the characters express feelings about race and ethnicity that people usually don't articulate or express in code. *Crash* achieves this without simplistically defining the city's population as one consisting merely of oppressors and victims. In fact, most of *Crash*'s characters are capable of being extremely flawed and prejudiced and of defying expectations. *Crash* is far from a subtle work, but it captures something of the racial and ethnic hostility that often exists on and beneath the surface in large American cities.

But one of the few films made by a black director, Lee Daniels (*Shadowboxer*, 2006), that had crossover appeal, *Precious*, is not about racial hostility or discrimination but rather deals with the dysfunction and degradation of one black family. A poster child for that dysfunction is Claireece "Precious" Jones (Gabourey "Gabby" Sidibe), the heroine of this film, based on the novel *Push* by Sapphire. Precious is a depressed, morbidly obese, functionally illiterate 16-year-old who was sexually abused and impregnated twice by her drug-addicted father. She is now pregnant with her second child by him; the first, whom she calls Mongo, is a Down syndrome child. Her world goes beyond the Dickensian in its sordidness and squalor—making *Oliver Twist* (1948) seem like *The Sound of Music* (1965).

So relentlessly dreadful is Precious's life that, at moments, such as a flashback scene of her mother kicking her in the face as she goes into labor at the age of 12, one is tempted to look away. The sadistic, profane mother, Mary, is played by the comedian Mo'Nique, in a powerful Academy Award–winning performance. Her sole occupations seem to be sitting in her fetid apartment, watching television game shows, eating fast food, ripping off the welfare system, and emotionally tormenting and physically brutalizing Precious—turning her into a virtual slave. Since the film takes place in 1987, Mary is the embodiment of Ronald Reagan's hyperbolic welfare queen—a one-time politically winning symbol for the Republicans among white voters that evoked the ex-cesses of the welfare state and promoted crude racial stereotypes. However, though Mary's behavior is so outsized and extreme, the film rarely feels like it's merely indulging in the grotesque for its own sake.

Though *Precious* may be on one level an unsentimental and raw inner-city horror story (a Harlem enveloped in graffiti and garbage), on another it is an almost Cinderella-style fairy tale of a pathetic, barely verbal victim, though one with a vulnerable and soft inner voice, moving from a living hell to some-thing that resembles redemption, albeit as a jobless, HIV-positive mother The only thing Claireece has to console her are Hollywood and television-style fantasies where she whirls around in silk and feather boas, adored by the world. For her, there is no life beyond the fantasies (that are more than a touch heavy-handed), which provide the one bit of ephemeral self-esteem in a life where hatred and self-hatred are the norm. What the film doesn't purport to be is a work dealing with inner-city social problems. It's Precious's evolution that is at its center, and the film avoids making any grand statement about the plight of those who live in the inner city.

Precious's life begins to change when she is forced to leave her mainstream junior high school because she is pregnant for an alternative school for at-risk students. For the first time in her beaten-down life, an enormous well of em-pathy and support awaits her at the school, which becomes her too-good-to-be-true refuge. Enrolled in the "Each One, Teach One" academy (Did anyone notice that the name of this school was the slogan of Castro's campaign to eradicate illiteracy in Cuba?), she is taught to read by a beautiful, lesbian, no-nonsense teacher named, appropriately enough for a fairy tale, Ms. Blu Rain (Paula Patton). She also establishes a real connection with her rowdy but car-ing classmates, who are given a bit of individuality, and with a tough and com-passionate social worker Ms. Weiss (an unadorned Mariah Carey). It is also to Ms. Weiss that Mary gives vent to her frustrations, anger, jealousy, and despair in a soliloquy that doesn't as much justify her actions as add a dimension and depth to her that undermines the image of simple monstrousness.

There may be an overload of abusive and destructive behavior in *Precious*, and some black writers and critics felt it misrepresented African American life in depicting it in such a pathological manner.[32] But the film contains a number of black characters who live responsible, socially committed lives and just tries to capture what is painfully wrong with one black family, not condemn the whole black experience as barbaric and diseased. In addition, the film's rough honesty lifts it out of the realm of well-constructed melodrama or the manipu-lative exploitation film. At its conclusion, the film permits Claireece a ray of hope, for through an act of will she has created a new self that may be able to survive the difficult life ahead. Hard to believe, but the film succeeds in convincing us that it is within the realm of possibility.

The most subtle and least sensational film dealing with urban life was the previously mentioned indie, Ryan Fleck and Anna Boden's *Half Nelson* (2006), set in a derelict Brooklyn of abandoned lots, ominous night streets, and claustrophobic apartments. The film centers on the relationship between a drug-addicted, politically left-leaning, over-30 junior high school history teacher, Dan Dunne (the gifted Ryan Gosling), and a clear-eyed, independent, basically innocent African American 13-year-old student, Drey (Shareeka Epps).

The chain-smoking, haunted-looking Dan teaches history to a class of African Americans and Hispanics. He's a passionate and hip teacher who instructs the students on the civil rights movement, Attica, and America's role in the destruction of Salvatore Allende. *Half Nelson*, however, avoids the facile optimism of so many Hollywood inspirational films about teachers who save their students from the perniciousness of the streets like *Stand and Deliver* (1988) and *Lean on Me* (1989). Dan's pupils don't suddenly become infused with political idealism, but his teaching makes some of them more conscious of politics and history, while the others remain asleep or incapable of hearing anything. And for all Dan's passion, one senses that the students don't exist for him as individuals until he gets to know Drey.

Half Nelson, however, is a film that almost always chooses moral complexity rather than the simple dichotomy between good and evil that defines *Precious*. The uneasy bond built between Drey and Dan (and race is never made an issue) is the only hopeful note the film leaves us with. In Fleck and Boden's view, though the state of our politics is rotten and the school system barely functions, there are no social transformations or utopias in the offing. The dreams of the 1960s are over, and there are just individuals struggling to make sense of their lives and trying to connect to each other. The film's quiet realism is outside the Hollywood norm, and in Dan, *Half Nelson* has created a memorable figure—intelligent, disordered, self-destructive, and trapped.

But it's not the *Half Nelson*s and other small films like Noah Baumbach's psychologically sophisticated, pathetic/comic *The Squid and the Whale* (2005) that reach a mass audience. It's blockbuster franchises like *Spiderman*, *Batman*, *X-Men*, and *Harry Potter* and an animated film like *Shrek* (2001)—all of them followed by a number of sequels—that garner the large audiences and the big money. All the latter are big-budget versions of comic books, children's books, and animated works. They are also escapist entertainments, usually released during the summer, appealing primarily to the young and loaded with special effects and nonstop action, leaving an audience suffused in sensation and little else—almost nothing to contemplate and too shallow to feel deeply about.

It is disturbing that the studios, during the past decade, seem to have, with rare exceptions, abandoned the adult audience. It's not only the action block-busters that make immense profits; even a clamorous, graceless musical, *Mamma Mia* (2008), with Meryl Streep—giving an atypically embarrass-ing performance—made over $600 million. Other films that do well are low-budget horror films and Judd Apatow's sentimental, lecherous comedies aimed at male adolescents of all ages, like *Knocked Up* (2007) and *Superbad* (2007).

But it's the blockbusters that interest us most. That's where the triumph of style over substance can be seen most vividly. The best of these films, like the first *Harry Potter* and the first *Spider-Man*, are films that on one level can be beguiling. *Harry Potter and the Sorcerer's Stone* (2001) is the first of a series of fantasy adventures, based on novels by J. K. Rowling. The film ingeniously constructs a parallel world of witchcraft and magic whose focus is a young he-roic wizard, Harry Potter, who does battle with the forces of evil at the Hog-warts School. One gets weary watching unicorns, satyrs, ghosts, monster dogs, moving staircases, talking portraits, and so on, but a Quidditch tournament, played in the air with broomsticks, fusing elements of soccer and hockey, uses inventive special effects. And an enchanted shopping tour of a bustling Hogwarts London is stunningly designed—Harry getting ready for school pick-ing up wands and other school paraphernalia at uniquely eccentric and de-signed shops. The film can become tedious, but there are moments when it can feel fresh and imaginative.

Spider-Man (2002), based on the 1962 Marvel comic, features no Super-man or Batman but an ordinary, vulnerable, dissatisfied New York adolescent who gets bitten by a radioactive spider and develops superpowers like flying and climbing and somersaulting up tall buildings. The film contains the usual special effects and mind-numbing explosions, chase, and fight scenes. How-ever, though *Spider-Man* predictably defeats the supervillain, Toby McGuire's likable, wry superhero gives the film an aura of sweetness.

And then there is *Avatar* (2009), James Cameron's (*Titanic*, 1997) world-wide box office champ and 3D extravaganza that, costing $230 million, has made so far more than $2 two billion. *Avatar* is a science-fiction film filled with thrilling special effects and digital animation and built around a pulp narrative—a boy's adventure and heroics and conventional romance—that has political overtones.

Avatar is critical of American capitalist greed, militarism, and colonial-ism (there are echoes of the Iraq War). The film is pro-environment and anti-privatization (the enemy is an evil corporation like Halliburton or Blackwater) and embraces an alternative world. It's a world that believes in a form of pan-theism and is inhabited by graceful, nine-foot-tall, blue-skinned Na'vi, who the American corporation's private army engages in a preemptive attack on. *Avatar* also includes memorable themes from *Dances with Wolves* (2000) and *The Last Samurai* (2003) of the American who goes native. But what is memorable about *Avatar* is not its politics but Cameron's creation of a stunning-looking, lush paradise filled with inspired flora and fauna that is spiritually connected at its roots.

Still, even at their most imaginative, these films do little more than provide wish fantasies for the young. The dreams here are rooted less in the unconscious or consciousness of the director (though Cameron's film carries a personal vision of a sort) and more in the fantasies of heroes who confront and defeat evil that have always inhabited American popular culture, from the 19th-century dime novels through John Ford westerns through *Superman* and *Batman*. Thus, the popularity of these films is not bound to a particular need of the public to flee the reality of a decade characterized by two endless wars, a skyrocketing unemployment rate, and the politics of resentment. The times may play a role in their allure, but the appeal of the blockbusters is basically timeless.

In the beginning of this chapter, we referred to the *Time* magazine cover story that called the decade "The Decade from Hell." If there is a hound from hell—an indestructible killer who talks in riddles and embodies monstrous evil—it is Anton Chigurh (Javier Bardem) in Joel and Ethan Coen's 2007 Academy Award–winning film *No Country for Old Men*.

No Country for Old Men takes place in 1980 and is based on Cormac McCarthy's exhilaratingly written, nihilistic genre novel. The film is part melancholy elegy for a culture that is fast disappearing and part contemporary western thriller that contrasts the values of the Old West of rough justice and personal integrity with a new world whose values are dominated by greed and relentless, passionless evil. The voice of these older values is the stoical, weary sheriff, Ed Tom Bell (Tommy Lee Jones). Jones, who himself is from Texas, where the film takes place and whose arid, wind-swept landscape is beautifully evoked in the film, does not so much play the role of the craggy, decent, slow-moving Sheriff Bell as inhabit it. Bell decries this new age of encroaching darkness where drug and money rule with comments like, "It starts when you begin to overlook bad manners. Anytime you quit hearing 'sir' and 'madam' the end is pretty much in sight."

Llewelyn Moss (Josh Brolin) embodies the new era. He's a cowboy, a welder, and Vietnam vet who lives in a trailer and treats his wife badly. Out antelope hunting one day, he stumbles across a drug deal gone sour with the ground littered with abandoned vehicles and bodies. He also discovers $2 million in cash, which he decides to keep, resulting in his being pursued by a number of drug gangs and Chigurh. Moss is in some ways a bad, avaricious guy but has some residual decency, and the rest of the film sees unambiguously bad guys chasing him to his inevitable death.

Anton Chigurh is obviously the film's most striking figure, though less of a person than an emblem of evil. With his Prince Valiant haircut, strange accent, and idiosyncratic weapon of choice—a murderously effective pneumatic stun gun—his pursuit of Llewelyn is the most relentless. In Chigurh's world, there are no rules just randomness. A flip of a coin can determine whether Chigurh will kill you. And nothing can stop him—neither gunshot wounds nor cars crashing into him—as he inexorably moves through the world like a remorseless killing machine. And Bell feels overmatched dealing with Chigurh, walking away from confronting him.

For the Coens, whose often-violent films pay tribute to classic American movie genres, albeit with sardonic humor and irony (*Blood Simple*, 1984, and *Miller's Crossing*, 1990), it's hard to take at face value that they are fully in accord with the kind of pitiless bloody inhumanity—a belief that you can't stop the brutal and barbaric from triumphing—that both the film and the novel project. The Coens have always had a cool and comically dark view of the human condition, but the film seems less like one of their rare personal works (*A Serious Man*, 2009) than a triumph of virtuoso filmmaking—dynamic crosscutting—and craft.

The vision is McCarthy's not theirs, but whether Chigurh is an apt symbol for the values of the first decade of the new century is certainly debatable. The film offers no economic or social explanation for the nature of the world it depicts—just a metaphysical belief in the triumph of evil.

However, America clearly does confront concrete and real challenges at the end of the first decade of the new century: Will we be able to return to some semblance of economic prosperity, or does the future hold a generation of economic stagnation and low growth, with high unemployment and concomitant social disruption and despair? Will the United States be able to confront the issue of globalization and compete with rising, low-wage economic giants, such as India and China, that have shaken off centuries of being economically moribund to become our rivals for economic dominance? Will our society be able to withstand the specter of Islamic terrorism, which, despite not being a real existential threat, still can disrupt our lives with selective terrorist actions and might cause us to overreact and subvert our own values and liberties in order to defeat them? And how do we deal with the new technologies that raise all sorts of legal questions, may threaten our privacy, and have changed our lives so dramatically?

Obviously, films do not offer answers to any of these questions, but film images are both indications of and bolsterers of popular feelings. And though there is never a simple one-to-one relationship between, for example, a film's critique of the Iraq War and popular sentiment, the films do suggest that some real public unease with the war exists.

McCarthy used a quote from a poem by William Butler Yeats as the source of the novel's title to encapsulate the essence of his vision. Thus, perhaps another Yeats poem might prove equally useful in summing up the questions and challenges we face and what films might be called on to illuminate in the first decades of the 21st century: "And what rough beast, its hour come round at last, slouches toward Bethlehem to be born?"[33]

NOTES

1. Courtney Schlisserman, "'Great Recession' Gets Recognition in A.P. Stylebook," *Bloomberg Online*, February 23, 2010. http://www.bloomberg.com.

2. Francis Fukuyama, *The End of History and the Last Man* (New York: Free Press, 1992).

3. Sean Wilentz, *The Age of Reagan: A History, 1974–2008* (New York: Harper-Collins, 2008), p. 435.

4. Thomas E. Ricks, *Fiasco: The American Military Adventure in Iraq* (New York: Penguin Press, 2006), p. 59.

5. Frank Rich, *The Greatest Story Ever Told: The Decline and Fall of Truth in Bush's America* (New York: Penguin Books, 2006), p. 181.

6. Dan Balz and Haynes Johnson, *The Battle for America, 2008: The Story of an Extraordinary Election* (New York: Viking, 2009), p. 206.

7. "Barack Obama's Speech on Race," *New York Times* (March 18, 2008). http://www.nytimes.com.

8. Ibid.

9. Balz and Johnson, *The Battle for America, 2008*, p. 342.

10. Ibid., p. 365.

11. Ibid., p. 389.

12. Barack Obama, *Dreams of My Father: A Story of Race and Inheritance* (New York: Three Rivers Press, 1995).

13. Shamin Adam, "Obama's Economic Stimulus Program Created Up to 3.3 Million Jobs CBO Says," *Bloomberg Online*, August 10, 2010. http://www.bloomberg.com.

14. Manohla Dargis, "Talking about a Revolution (for a Digital Age)," *New York Times* (January 29, 2010), section AR, p. 11.

15. J. Hoberman, "It's Mumblecore," *The Village Voice* (August 14, 2007). http://www.villagevoice.com.

16. Jonathan Rosenbaum, "The Passion of the Christ," *The Chicago Reader* (April 14, 2004). http://www.chicagoreader.com.

17. Ty Burr, "The Passion of the Christ is a Graphic Profession of Mel Gibson's Faith," *Boston Globe* (February 24, 2004). http://www.boston.com/bostonglobe.

18. James Ridgeway, "Out of Control: Mel's Dad May Think That 'Oscar' Is a Jewish Name," *The Village Voice* (February 17, 2004). http://www.villagevoice.com.

19. Benny Morris, *Righteous Victims: A History of the Zionist-Arab Conflict, 1881–2001* (New York: Vintage, 2001), p. 381.

20. J. Hoberman, "Spy Game: *Traffic* Writer's Slick Oil Thriller Oozes with Intrigue but Crams Too Much into Its Drum," *The Village Voice* (November 15, 2005). http://www.villagevoice.com.

21. Lawrence Wright, *The Looming Tower: Al-Qaeda and the Road to 9/11* (New York: Alfred A. Knopf, 2006), p. 189.

22. Elizabeth Bumiller, "As Military Suicides Hit Record High, Pentagon Faults Commanders," *New York Times* (July 30, 2010), section A, p. 10.

23. Sheila Roberts, "Paul Haggis Interview, in the Valley of Elah," *Movies Online* (September 15, 2007). http://www.moviesonline.ca.

24. Joanne Laurier, "*The Hurt Locker:* Part of a Deplorable Trend," *World Socialist Web Site* (August 10, 2009). http://www.wsws.org.

25. John Keegan, *The Second World War* (New York: Penguin Books, 1990), p. 566.

26. F. Scott Fitzgerald, *The Crack-Up* (New York: New Directions, 1993), p. 122.

27. Joseph E. Persico, *Edward R. Murrow: An American Original* (New York: Laurel, 1988), p. 352.

28. Ralph Engelman, *Friendlyvision: Fred Friendly and the Rise and Fall of Television Journalism* (New York: Columbia University Press, 2009), p. 6.

29. Samantha Power, *A Problem from Hell: America in the Age of Genocide* (New York: Basic Books, 2002), p. 386.

30. Leslie Fiedler, *Love and Death in the American Novel* (New York: Dell, 1967), pp. 211–14.

31. Carol Pogash, "Myth of the 'Twinkie Defense': The Verdict in the Dan White Case Wasn't Based on His Ingestion of Junk Food," *San Francisco Chronicle* (November 23, 2003), p. D1.

32. Ismael Reed, "Fade to White," *New York Times* (February 5, 2010), section A, p. 25.

33. W. B. Yeats, *The Collected Poems of W. B. Yeats* (New York: Macmillan, 1956), pp. 184–85.

9

THE 2010s

In the early morning hours of November 7, 2012, Mitt Romney conceded the presidential election to Barack Obama. The outcome of the election came as a shock to Romney and his team. After October 3, 2012, the first presidential debate in Denver with a frazzled, seemingly unprepared Obama, the media and polls declared Romney the debate winner. In the weeks that followed large and adoring crowds attended his rallies, and Republican Party internal polling showed him ahead in a number of crucial swing states. Nevertheless, Obama won the election with 51 percent of the vote compared to Romney's 47 percent. Obama won every crucial swing state with the exception of North Carolina and the electoral vote by a large margin (332–206).

The Obama campaign's ability to portray Romney as a rapacious capitalist, when he was a director of Bain Capital, helped undermine his image as a socially responsible, moderate conservative. As did the slogan that Vice President Joe Biden repeated endlessly on the campaign trail that the accomplishments of the Obama administration included "GM is alive and Osama bin Laden is dead," reminding voters, especially in the crucial Midwest swing states, of how Romney had written an op-ed piece that argued the auto industry should be allowed to go into bankruptcy during the bleak early days of the 2008 "Great Recession." Romney also hadn't helped himself when he was secretly recorded telling a group of donors that 47 percent of the electorate would never support him because of all the government aid they received. (Still, the right wing of the party felt he wasn't sufficiently ideologically committed or inspirational as a conservative.)

These factors coupled with Obama's almost 93 percent support in the black community, 73 percent support among Latinos, and 53 percent among women led to Obama's victory. In the wake of that victory, Obama held out the hope that the political, and particularly the congressional, gridlock that had gripped the nation since 2010 might be over.[1] In an interview with *Rolling Stone*, he said, "My hope is that the American people send a message to Republicans that there's going to be some self-reflection going on—that it might break the fever." They might say to themselves, "You know, we've lost our way here. We need to refocus on trying to get things done for the American people."[2] Those words fit right into Obama's affirmation of the strength and endurance of democracy, and his optimism about the ultimate virtue of the American people. Optimism built on a focused effort that life will get better, even when we are bound by bleakness and tragedy. Obama's faith was not nebulous, but a feeling wrought from pain and tragedy.

Belief is obviously never sufficient, since Obama's wish was never realized as the Republicans continued to block every Democratic initiative from jobs to budget, to climate change, to immigration. Toward the end of Obama's tenure in office, they even refused to meet and vote on Obama's choice for the Supreme Court, the respected centrist Merrick Garland, after the sudden death of the smart, bullying, arch-conservative Justice Antonin Scalia—an adherent of judicial originalism.

One hypothesis is that the urbane, controlled Obama didn't help himself, because of his penchant for separating himself from the mass of politicians, and refusing to cultivate them—even exhibiting a quiet contempt. However, though he was clearly no Joe Biden like glad hander and schmoozer, it is doubtful that even a wheeler dealer like Lyndon Baines Johnson could have done much better with the obdurate Republican House, which had set out to destroy Obama. Also Obama didn't invoke as often the great rhetorical skill that had vaunted him into public consciousness and the presidency. Though there were moments during the second term such as the Newton school massacre and the Charleston murders of nine black parishioners and their minister, his 2016 State of the Union address showed that he could still be eloquent and riveting when he asserted that democracy needs a "willingness to compromise," and that public life diminishes when only the most extreme voices get attention.

He also rarely attempted to rally voters to his agenda with the use of his "Bully Pulpit." So except for executive orders that laid down new rules on environmental protection, federal pay, rights to same-sex couples, and the setting aside of huge tracts of land as landmark sites, there were relatively few domestic achievements in his second term that compared with the passage of the $800 billion stimulus bill that helped stabilize the economy in the very first days after he took office. Nor was there anything comparable to the Clean Power Act, the Affordable Care Act (anathematized as Obamacare) that provided medical coverage to close to 20 million uninsured Americans, or the Dodd-Frank financial regulation bill that placed tight controls on banks and even set up a consumer protection agency. Still, by the end of his presidency, unemployment had shrunk to 4.8 percent from the high of 7.8 percent at the beginning of his tenure in office, 11 million new jobs had been created, a bull market for stocks with The Dow and S&P 500 at record highs, and home prices recovering to their pre-crash (2005) highs.

Obama's record in foreign affairs was more mixed. Perhaps his most important achievement was an historic nuclear deal with Iran (despite Republican and Israeli opposition), which in exchange for the lifting of economic sanctions staved off any attempt by the Islamic Republic from gaining nuclear weapons. Another achievement was his ending the almost 60-year failed policy of the American isolation of Cuba by establishing diplomatic relations, and even making an historic visit to the island. In addition, he helped negotiate the Paris Climate accords, which set standards to keep global warming and climate change in check. By far, his biggest failures, however, were his inability to end the Afghanistan War, which after 15 years earned the title "the Forever War" with 2,356 U.S. soldiers having been killed and 19,950 wounded in Afghanistan. U.S. troops are now down to 9,000, but the war continues as bloody as in the past.

Obama was also unable create any workable policy or solution to the Syrian Civil War. A product of the Arab Spring (2010–2012), the Syrian conflict spiraled into a myriad of factions and militias and ethnic minorities all vying for power. The most brutal force by far was Bashar al-Assad's regime, which used poison gas and barrel bombs to try and subdue the rebels. These weapons, coupled with his alliance with Russia, Iran, and the Hezbollah of Lebanon, kept Assad in power. Nonetheless, large segments of his country fell out of his control, as over an estimated 400,000 people died in the conflict, and 10 million refugees were created, many of whom descended on a generally antagonistic Europe for asylum, creating the most unprecedented refugee crisis on that continent since the end of World War II.

Another by-product of that crisis, combined with the American withdrawal from Iraq in 2011, was the rise of ISIS (Islamic State). Declaring itself the Caliphate of the Muslim world, ISIS captured city after city in Iraq and came within miles of Baghdad before a reconstituted Iraqi army, Shiite militias, and U.S. Special Forces halted its momentum. Obama poured men and money into the fight against ISIS, and by the end of his tenure the forces of the Caliphate, held only a small portion of Iraq and was on the defensive in Syria as well.

Despite these reverses, ISIS remained a dangerous foe, particularly because of its use of social media, which gave it a hold on many young Muslims in the West, whom it inspired to terrorist attacks such as the murderous assault against the editors and writers of *Charlie Hebdo* magazine, the carnage at the Bataclan Music Hall in Paris (2015), and the truck mayhem in Nice (2016). Nor was the United States immune to ISIS-inspired terrorist attacks. For example, there were murderous assaults in San Bernardino, California (2015), and Orlando, Florida (2016), where scores were murdered and maimed.[3]

Still, if the scandal-free, socially committed Obama could not succeed in overhauling our politics, his eight years in office projected a luminous and transformative quality. That fact should never be forgotten.[4]

When the 2016 primary election campaign began, it seemed as if we had entered an alternate universe. The prime cause for this somewhat surreal state of affairs was the candidacy of Donald Trump—a man mostly known as a wealthy New York City real estate developer and as the star of the reality TV programs *The Apprentice* and *Celebrity Apprentice*. Trump's first direct foray into politics had been as a leader of the 2011 "birther" movement, which falsely claimed that President Obama was born in Kenya and not in the United States and therefore not eligible to be president.

That sort of racist demagoguery was the basis of Trump's initial entry into presidential politics. He made a splash by claiming that Mexican undocumented immigrants were criminals and rapists and that one of his first steps as president would be to build a wall to keep them out of the United States and make Mexico pay for it.

He followed that in a series of debates with his Republican primary opponents—more notable for invective and name-calling ("little Mario")—than any serious policy discussion. Trump was able to build a steady and finally insurmountable delegate lead that propelled him into becoming the Republican presidential candidate. In the process, he seemingly alienated many establishment Republicans, who considered him intellectually and temperamentally unfit to be their president.

The Democratic Party too complacently saw it as a forgone conclusion that former secretary of state Hillary Clinton would be their candidate. Initially, it was assumed that her principal rival would be Vice President Joseph Biden, who took himself out of the race after his son died. It turned out that Clinton's most persistent and popular adversary was the independent senator and former Socialist from Vermont, the populist and earnest Bernie Sanders, whose attacks on economic inequality and billionaire and corporate control of government and calls for free college tuition and a better health care system gained him a passionate following among the young and many progressive democrats. Despite Sanders's quixotic and tenacious struggle, Clinton's support by the party's leadership and a large portion of its base helped her become the first woman ever to run for president as the candidate of a major political party.

The presidential campaign was what those who remembered the phrase from the very original sitcom *Seinfeld* might have called "bizzaro world." It was highlighted by Trump's not-so-subtle embrace of the so-called alt-right (who were a small piece of his support), that took the form of embracing nationalism, misogyny, racism, and an hypocritical advocacy of law and order. He also had to deal with a scandal that would have destroyed a more conventional candidate—the release of a video from the TV program *Access Hollywood*, which caught him boasting of grabbing women's genitals. But Trump's supporters—his base—embraced him despite his sleazy, unconscionable behavior. They admired his macho authoritarianism, his simplistic certitudes, and his supposed gift for deal making that would magically bring them jobs. They saw him as a bluntly honest politician; a millionaire who's garish, nouveau riche style offered a life model to aspire to; and a member of the moneyed elite, whose style provided the illusion to his base of being one of them—his barroom bravado and populist manner being sufficient.

Trump may also have offered much more red meat rhetoric than clear policies, but his commitment to bring back jobs to America and redress unfair trade deals and revoke treaties that supposedly robbed Americans of employment struck a chord among white working-class voters.

Still, Hillary Clinton, more knowledgeable and cogent on the issues than the policy-ignorant Trump, and favored in most polls, was given to political blunders. The attacks were hypocritical, but still she shouldn't have picked up money giving speeches at Goldman-Sachs. More importantly, she had to continue fighting off charges that somehow a private e-mail server that she had maintained during her time as secretary of state had compromised the nation's security. Though the FBI initially cleared her of any criminal offense except carelessness, the charges dogged her throughout the campaign and heightened a sense of her being untrustworthy that many felt about her. In the very last days of the campaign, the FBI director, James Comey, resurrected the e-mail controversy when he said that additional e-mails of Mrs. Clinton had been found on a separate computer of one of her aides.

Clinton was also never a natural campaigner, seemingly packaged, and self-conscious in her public appearances, without a common touch. She was also almost as unpopular, for some reasonable and countless unjustifiable reasons (e.g., her gender), as her rival. All these problems combined with a sense of overconfidence in her campaign that had her politicking in states that had for decades been Republican strongholds, while they neglected key swing states that had gone for Obama in the previous two elections. In addition, picking a benign but bland establishment politico like Tim Kaine for vice president rather than someone from the Sanders wing didn't help. As a result, on election eve, November 8, 2016, to the shock of pollsters, pundits, and progressives, Donald Trump was elected president, when he won the Electoral College vote by 304–227, even though he lost the popular vote by almost 3 million votes. He achieved this by maintaining Republican control of the so-called red states and breaching Mrs. Clinton's firewall in the Midwest and Pennsylvania by a total of 77,740 votes.

But beyond these perfectly understandable reasons for Hillary's Electoral College loss to Trump, a fascinating intellectual and political debate developed on whether it was economic desperation or cultural grievance that drove the white working class voter to provide Trump's margin of victory. Numerous articles have been written exploring the subject, from the liberal Columbia University historian Mark Lilla's viewing Clinton's campaign as falling into the rhetoric of diversity, calling out explicitly to African American, Latino, LGBT, and women voters at every stop. Lilla saw this as dismissive of the "white working class" and as failing to "appeal to Americans as Americans."[5]

There is no question that Clinton and the Democrats should have been more aggressive about the needs of those who felt economically anxious and forgotten in a globalized economy. They probably could have more passionately defended the labor movement and promoted greater economic equality and job creation for those who didn't qualify for welfare. But we truly doubt that cost her the election.

It would be an understatement to call Trump's first days in office a chaotic mess. He constantly bragged about the size of the crowd at his inauguration: all evidence to the contrary. He promulgated a travel ban, aimed primarily against Muslims from seven countries that was vigorously protested by thousands and quickly overturned in the federal courts. His national security advisor was forced to resign because he had spoken to the Russian government about the lifting of sanctions even before the inauguration and then lied about it to Vice President-Elect Pence, who knowing nothing publicly defended him. (At this writing, the major scandal involving the Trump administration's ominously undefined relationship with Russia is still evolving.) And one of his cabinet choices—the anti-labor, proposed secretary of labor, Andrew Puzder, was forced to withdraw primarily because of a history of spousal abuse. Nonetheless, the cabinet members that were confirmed represented a cross section of ultraconservatives, Wall Street multibillionaires, and generals, whose goals, in the main, if their past statements and ideas were any guide, was to turn the clock back on any progressive policies that had been adopted in the previous eight years, possibly the past century. Indeed for all these missteps, and the foreboding and rage of many who marched against Trump carrying signs reading "Give the Man a Chance to Kill the Planet," "Putin's President is the Biggest Loser," and "Strong Women, Strong World," Trump still remains in power.

Hollywood, on the other hand, seemed almost impervious to the political world's volatility. In 2016, the film industry had its best box office year ever, clearing $11.37 billion, with Disney and Warner Brothers studios leading the way. Nevertheless, there were ominous trends confronting the industry. For example, attendance at theaters declined, in large part because technology now provided new platforms for the audiences to watch films. Overnight Netflix, Amazon, and iTunes, which had barely registered as competition for the studios, suddenly became competitors. They not only became venues to show the studio films but began producing films of their own, as well as providing a means for the audience to stream film on their computers or even their mobile phones. The fact that films could be streamed was most problematic for theaters, despite the fact that no home viewing can match the experience of viewing film in the darkness and silence of a theater. The competition forced them to try different alternatives to attract audiences. One alternative taken was turning themselves into expensive dinner theaters, where audiences could have meals and drinks as they watched a film. Another was opening theme parks like Universal Studios Hollywood, which is a film studio and theme park initially created to offer tours of the real Universal Studios sets, and now offers rides, shows, and restaurants around films like *Harry Potter*. Of course, this is all about marketing and profit making, not films.[6]

Finally, what has become clear is that global demand for Hollywood film has grown as the relative size of the United States domestic market has decreased. In addition, big-budget action films like the ones dealing with comic book superheroes do better at the box office across all countries, compared to other genres. China's box office ticket sales now surpasses that of the United States, so the major film studios are forming new partnerships with Chinese companies and building production studios in the country to gain better access to the world's fastest-growing film market. Obviously, a greater dependence on foreign markets most likely means Hollywood will produce more violent action movies, and more sequels that can be turned into mass merchandizing dollars like the Star Wars sequels.[7]

One issue that has haunted Hollywood for decades and captured national attention was the issue of diversity. The paucity of African Americans and women in leading roles in the industry was shameful. In 2015, a highly regarded film *Selma*, directed by Ava DuVernay with an outstanding performance by David Oyelowo as Martin Luther King Jr., was shut out except for an Oscar for best song. The issue finally came to a head at the 2016 Academy Awards ceremony when for the second year in a row no African American was nominated for any of the leading categories such as best male or female actor, or best picture. It prompted a boycott of the ceremonies by a number of leading black actors and directors (e.g., Will Smith, Spike Lee), and saw the hashtag #OscarsSoWhite appear all over the social media. Though it was hard to be definitive about the role of racism in the award ceremony, the fact was that for years Hollywood relegated black actors to the most stereo-typed roles, so the anger had a basis in reality. Ultimately it led to a degree of soul-searching in the industry, which resulted in an opening up and increase of the number of younger men and women, many of them African Ameri-can, eligible to vote on the awards. As a result, the 2017 awards had the most nominations of African Americans ever, and the Oscars for the best male and female supporting actors went to the African Americans as did the best picture award to a film directed by a black man (Barry Jenkins) *Moonlight*, a triptych of episodes about the life of a young gay black man. Though this was an important step forward, it was not a cause for celebration, since the vast majority of those who dominated the industry were still white males. Though there are a few women film directors (e.g., Kathryn Bigelow) and studio executives (e.g., Amy Pascal), the number, and that holds even more so for Latinos, Asians, and other minorities, in influential roles has hardly been addressed.

One of the *New York Times'* two main film critics, Manohla Dargis, wrote: "There isn't a back-room cabal of cigar-chomping male—and female—executives conspiring against female directors, at least that I know of. Rather, the reluctance to hire women seems symptomatic of a conservative, fear-driven industry that recycles the same genres, stereotypes and impoverished ideas year after year."[8]

One film that provided a model for a way out of political stalemate dur-ing the Obama years and a possible guide to political success was Steven Spielberg's masterful film *Lincoln* (2012). *Lincoln*, written by Tony Kushner (*Angels in America*), whose previous collaboration with Spielberg was the Israeli revenge drama *Munich* (2005), loosely based much of the historical context of the film on Doris Kearns Goodwin's *Team of Rivals: The Political Genius of Abraham Lincoln* and James McPherson's *History of the Civil War: The Battle Cry of Freedom*.

Daniel Day-Lewis in an Academy Award–winning indelible portrayal of our eloquent, haunted president depicts Lincoln here. Lewis's nuanced per-formance is complete with high-pitched voice and homely jokes and stories that hide political cunning and deeply felt idealism, behind a shrewd façade of folksiness. His Lincoln was jovial and approachable, would just as soon tell a ribald anecdote about the revolutionary hero Ethan Allen, and would listen to the latest bit of military information or military strategy from his indispensable secretary of war, Edward Stanton (Bruce McGill). However, at the same time, he is vitally and irrevocably committed to passing the Thirteenth Amendment to the Constitution, which would abolish slavery in the United States. In order to do this, Lincoln had to navigate the demands of conservative Republicans and somehow round up the necessary votes needed to pass the amendment in the House of Representatives (the Senate having ratified the amendment in a previous session).

In fact, what gives *Lincoln* its uniqueness is the smart and incisive depiction of the messy legislative process and devious political maneuvering. With the help of his secretary of state, William Seward (David Strathairn), Lincoln is not above hiring a trio of political hucksters to engage in persuasion, bargaining, and if necessary a bit of political arm-twisting in the form of patronage deals to garner the votes of some wavering or uncommitted congressmen.

Lincoln also had formidable adversaries in the House such as the Copperhead (anti-war Democrat) firebrand Fernando Wood (Lee Pace), as well the powerful support of the radical Pennsylvania Representative Thaddeus Stevens (an eccentrically entertaining Tommy Lee Jones). Stevens made his commitment to racial equality and abolition a moral crusade, and clutching his walking stick and with hairpiece slightly askew has a gift for silencing a pro-slavery Democrat by roaring, "sit down you ignorant nincompoop. You insult God."

Despite the fervency of his belief in the abolition of slavery, Lincoln, as the film portrays him, was no abolitionist. Indeed in a dramatic but contrived scene in the very first moments of the film, he is confronted by a black soldier, who is as articulate as Kushner, demands to know why black soldiers are paid less than white soldiers and why there are no black officers. This confrontation ends harmoniously and theatrically, as both white and black soldiers go marching off reciting portions of Lincoln's Gettysburg address. Much more revealing of Lincoln's attitude toward black people is in a scene with Elizabeth Keckley (Gloria Reuben), Mary Todd Lincoln's dressmaker, who, when asks Lincoln what he thinks of her and her people, he can only answer honestly, "I don't know you."

Still, if Lincoln is deft in his political life, his dealings with his family are less successful and assured. We see his melancholic side as he copes with his neurasthenic wife, Mary (Sally Field), whom he calls "Molly," who is still grieving over the death of their young son Willy in the very first year of the war. He also finds it difficult to cope with the demand of his eldest son, Robert (Joseph Gordon-Levitt), who wants desperately to join the army. Lincoln's only personal solace in the midst of these familial woes is his sweet, affectionate moments with his youngest son, Tad (Gulliver McGrath).

Lincoln (2012). Directed by Steven Spielberg. Shown: Daniel Day-Lewis
(as Abraham Lincoln). (Courtesy of Dreamworks/20th Century Fox/Photofest.
© Dreamworks/20th Century Fox.)

There are scenes where Spielberg's lighting and silhouetting may grant
Lincoln an iconic aura, but it's the flawed life-sized Lincoln who dominates
the film. Toward the end of the film, we can feel his profound weariness and
despair from presiding over a war that cost so many lives and tragically tore
the country asunder. And the scene where the Thirteenth Amendment
finally passes is a moving one—despite the film's awareness that it was just a
first step in the still agonizingly not quite finished road to racial equality.

There are also powerful wordless moments in the film: one that opens the
film with a potent reminder of the opening battle scenes of Spielberg's *Saving
Private Ryan* as Union and Confederate soldiers grappling fiercely in the mud
of battle; another when we watch as Lincoln rides silently through the carnage in the aftermath of the battle of Petersburg.

Of course since the legacy of the Civil War has always been a contentious
issue, there have been criticisms of the film. Most notably from historians
like Eric Foner (*The Fiery Trail: Abraham Lincoln and the Abolition of American
Slavery*[9]) criticized the film for failing to show that it was the abolitionists, not
Lincoln, who were the driving forces behind the Thirteenth Amendment.
Other historians have felt that the film leaves out the activities of slaves in
freeing themselves and the role of free blacks in the nation's capital. Still

others questioned the lack of accurate historical context in the film, since it left out the fact that Lincoln had gained a landslide victory in the election of 1864, gaining almost 80 percent of the Armies vote, and thus had tremendous leverage in the Congress to pass whatever he needed.[10]

But this is a work of art and does not purport to be a documentary, so the complexity of history is sometimes reduced for dramatic effect. *Lincoln* chose to put more emphasis on the role of the charismatic president (the "great man theory of history") rather than on the multiple and collective forces involved in bringing about change. Still, the essential fact is that Spielberg has undoubtedly created a cinematic monument to a great president—a president, whom, quite surprisingly, even Karl Marx once summed up as, "one of those rare men who succeeded in becoming great, without ceasing to be good."[11]

If *Lincoln* exalted the president's political cunning and idealism George Clooney's (he directed and co-wrote), *Ides of March* (2011) goes to the opposite extreme depicting political cynicism and corruption.

Clooney plays presidential hopeful Mike Morris. But the film focuses primarily on two political strategists Paul Zara (Philip Seymour Hoffman) and Tom Duffy (Paul Giamatti), who eat and sleep politics, and whose only political commitment is to win elections by any means necessary (Duffy's campaign maxim is, "We're going to get down in the mud with the fucking elephants"). Though Zara has only one rule—loyalty—that makes him a touch less cynical, he is no more sympathetic than his rival.

Morris says all the right things unwaveringly and intelligently affirming every liberal talking point. He smoothly brushes aside his opponent's religious challenge with "my religion is the U.S. Constitution." But the film's prime focus is on his handsome, young, gifted press secretary, Stephen Myers (Ryan Gosling), who adulates Morris—the man and his ideals—but is extremely ambitious. His idealism can't prevent him from being dragged into the mire of double-dealing and betrayal that is the norm in this film.

The Ides of March is filled with complicated plot turns—a suicide, firings and blackmail, which all feel a bit contrived and are probably better suited to a thriller and practically empty of political content. Indeed when Myers loses his faith in Morris, it's not because he's betrayed his political commitments but because he's fired him for an unseemly meeting with Duffy. By the film's conclusion, Myers has turned into a man who is nothing more than raw ambition, his face a somber mask without a touch of the charm he once exuded.

Both primary candidates seek support from the powerful Senator Thompson (Jeffrey Wright), a North Carolina senator who is cold, calculating, and black. But Clooney skirts the issue of race and depicts Morris as making a deal with Thompson—someone we are led to assume doesn't share his political ideals and treats it as a political commonplace, as if there is nothing unique about a black man in the South with Thompson's weighty power and status.

The Ides of March tells us that politics is a dirty business and it's hard to sustain one's ideals in the muck. A different less facile film might have explored the real political differences between the candidates and not just stylishly evoke only the squalid machinations involved in winning an election. The film's cynicism is much too easy. Morris's principles are mere window dressing for a film that believes that corruption and duplicity are the rule.

Besides the exaltation of political idealism in *Lincoln* and the opposite depiction of the muck and mire of politics in *The Ides of March*, another side of Hollywood's representation of politics and American history is its long tradition of hagiography, mostly notably of Abraham Lincoln, which Spielberg's film is the latest example of. Just think of D.W. Griffith's *Abraham Lincoln* (1930) and John Ford's more highly regarded *Young Mr. Lincoln* (1939). At least it took the film industry almost 50 years to get started on that bit of apotheosis. It comes as a bit of surprise that a more muted idealization process was already at work on President Obama even before he had left office.

First off was *Southside with You* (2016), which is a sweet, predictable chronicle of Barack and Michelle Obama's first date. The film skirts close to hagiography, but is too perceptive to be totally defined by it. Another more ambitious film was Vikram Gandhi's *Barry* (2016), a modest portrait of Barack's first term as a 20-year-old student at Columbia University in 1981,which offers an insight into his early years, when New York was a much more violence and graffiti-ridden city than it is today.

Barry (Devon Terrell), as he liked to be called then, is a smart, articulate, reflective, and controlled young man, who is still looking for a home in the world—a place where he can be understood. He struggles to define himself—he's biracial, raised in Hawaii, and without any experience of inner city life. This "invisible man" (the film heavy-handedly underlines this referring too often to Ellison's great novel) is somewhat anguished and confused about where he belongs. The estrangement from his Kenyan father (who left when he was two years old) adds to these feelings. He discovers in his encounters with the inner city, which includes time spent in the projects, complete with urine-soaked stairwells, shooting galleries, prostitutes, and elevators that are permanently out of order, that it will never be home.

He is also ill at ease at a mostly white Columbia—where a campus security guard treats him as a suspicious intruder and a white student obtusely demands to know why black people always have to make everything about slavery, when Barry invokes the subject in a class discussion.

Nevertheless, Columbia was a liberal institution, and no den of racism. Barry meets a lively, empathetic white upper-middle-class fellow student

Charlotte (Anya Taylor-Joy), who falls in love with him. She is from a family of privileged Connecticut liberals, who much too self-consciously display how much good they do for those less well-off. Barry can't abide their world and displays a touch of paranoia when walking with Charlotte in Harlem, believing that everybody is staring at them because they are an interracial couple.

Barry doesn't attempt to get at the heart of Obama's anguish, and a number of secondary characters barely make an impact—though his beloved, intellectual, bohemian, somewhat disassociated mother, Ann Dunham (Ashley Judd), is presented very sympathetically. Still a president is not judged by the nature of his soul or sensibility, but what he accomplishes in office.

One can only wonder if this is just the beginning of a series of films treating Obama with great care, or merely a pale farewell to a presidency much admired by liberals. The danger is that it will fade as the memories of his years in office grow dim and the reality of the Trump ascendency sinks in.

In the years after the 2008 "Great Recession," the number one issue facing the country was the economy. If anything summed up the film industry's representation of those conditions, it was the words of Michael Douglas's Academy Award–winning performance as the corporate raider Gordon Gekko in *Wall Street* (1987)—not his famous credo that "Greed is good," but his less widely remembered but equally revealing comment that "It's all about the bucks, the rest is conversation."

Hollywood seems to have followed up on this Gekko maxim in its attempts to provide some notion of what actually caused the "Great Recession." Of course, giving dramatic life to credit swaps, derivatives, subprime mortgages, and how hedge funds operate is a difficult feat. It was clearly much easier to achieve in fine documentaries like Michael Moore's *Capitalism: A Love Story* (2009) made in his trademark style (where he becomes one of the film's prime subjects) that mixes hard-hitting criticism of capitalism's evils laced with humor, and Charles Ferguson's equally angry but more solemn *Inside Job* (2010) that explores how changes in governmental policies and banking practices helped create the financial crisis.

However, when looking at Hollywood narrative films, what you are given are stories that follow the money, but they rarely offer any real insight into what caused the terrible financial crisis of 2007–2008. It was a crisis that left the banking system on the verge of collapse, millions unemployed, caused hundreds of thousands of home foreclosures, and the entire global economy in shambles, or as one of the characters in these films remarks, "the end of the world."

It was the Great Recession that gave Oliver Stone the opportunity to bring back the character, Gordon Gekko, in his polished *Wall Street: Money Never*

Sleeps (2010). Unfortunately, except for a couple of mentions of the fictional financial firm of Keller-Zabel being overextended in sub-prime mortgages, someone mentioning "moral hazard," and the images of bankers seated in the glistening wood paneled conference room at the Federal Reserve like the Mafioso capos huddled around the conference table in *The Godfather* (1972), there isn't much to go on as to the causes of the Great Recession. What is there is a superficial critique of the Street's predatory practices, and a reference to the Great Recession by a voice-over that repeats the mantra that the definition of madness is repeating the same thing over and over again and expecting different results.

In this film, the charismatic, cynical, arch-manipulator Gekko (Michael Douglas again) returns to the outside world after eight years in prison for corporate malfeasance with barely a penny in his pocket and a cell phone the size of a butternut squash. This is remedied by his publishing a best seller, titled appropriately enough *Is Greed Good?* and lecturing to eager young audiences of aspiring moneymakers whom he casually dismisses as the Ninja generation—"no income, no jobs, no assets." The gist of his talks is that "money is a bitch that never sleeps." His talk offers far from a profound analysis of how the market works, but it's always delivered with flair.

One of those in Gekko's audience is a hotshot, well-heeled broker, Jake Moore (Shia LaBeouf). Jake has a connection to Gekko, since he is living with his estranged daughter Winnie (Carrie Mulligan)—an undeveloped, forgettable character who despises the money culture, writes for a left-leaning blog, and is big on the environment. Gekko is seemingly desperate to reconnect with her. And Jake, who needs Gekko's help to take revenge on Bretton James (Josh Brolin), the film's prime villain, who he blames for the suicide of his aging mentor Louis Zabel (Frank Langella), tries to make peace between Gekko and his daughter.

Unlike Bud Fox (Charlie Sheen) in the original *Wall Street*, who was preoccupied with using any means at his disposal to try to get a piece of the high life, the ambitious Jake may also be enmeshed in the market's ethos, but given the nature of that odious world is almost on the side of the angels. His financial specialty is cheap, alternative energy, but the character is too dull to offer a different moral perspective than Gekko's. He is a man who has little interest in serving the environment or doing good in any shape or form, and is driven as much by the "game" itself as by the money it produces.

Stone's direction as always offers bold strokes with little nuance, but is also propulsive and alive. He uses split screens, accelerated motion, montages, and helicopter shots and strikingly conveys the glow of Manhattan's moneyed world of luxury apartments overlooking the city's jewel-like lights and lavish fund-raising banquets at the Met where the camera floats up to show the lighted candles on the tables making them seem like lily pads floating in a dark sea.

Despite the film being ostensibly critical of the ruthless dealings of Wall Street operators, the latter, especially Gekko, carry all of the film's vitality. (We even begin to root for Gekko at the film's contrived sentimental conclusion.) In a film filled with one-dimensional characters, Gekko is the only one who holds our interest, and his powerful presence ultimately dilutes the film's critique of Wall Street.

For all their discussion of millions and billions of dollars, the characters in *Wall Street: Money Never Sleeps* are practically puritanical compared to the debauched minions of *The Wolf of Wall Street* (2013). In the former, the only indulgence is the scene Jake and Bretton race high-speed motorcycles though the countryside. In contrast, *The Wolf of Wall Street* sets the tone of the film by opening with Jordan Belfort (Leonardo DiCaprio) and his dim-witted cohorts hurling helmet-clad dwarfs at a target in their office.

Some of Martin Scorsese's past films like *Goodfellas* (1990), *Casino* (1994), and *The Departed* (2006), centered on the world of gangsters, guns, and violence. In this true story, *The Wolf of Wall Street* (2013), he replaces them with white-collar criminals who behave like crude, ignorant louts, albeit comic ones with telephones. And their charismatic, master salesman Capo di Tutti Capi is Jordan Belfort—smart, wild, and self-destructive.

In a flashback, we see Jordon's rise, beginning with being mentored by a coked-up broker Mark Hanna (Matthew McConaughey in a virtuoso cameo) who does a thump and grunt exercise while advising him to consume vast amounts of drugs and masturbate to make it on Wall Street. It doesn't take long for Belfort, whose core of associates are outer-borough ethnics striving for their version of the American Dream to start his own pseudo-white shoe, WASP-sounding operation called Stratton-Oakmont. What it is in reality is a "pump and dump" shop, where brokers urge investors to buy worthless penny stocks, driving the price up, and at a certain point selling to make huge profits. Belfort urges his brokers on, telling them he wants them to be "telephone fucking terrorists," engaging in verbally coercing their customers to buy the stocks.

However, the film's emphasis is not on the workings of the market, though Jordon directly talks to the camera informing us that illegality is his company's governing principle, but on consuming every drug imaginable, buying mansions, yachts, and jewelry, and indulging in orgies. Money and its accompanying pleasures are all—and excess and profanity are the rule. Jordan also rips off the working class and has contempt for people who don't strive to become rich. His behavior is without restraint, and along with his right-hand man the fat, infantile, always high Donny Azoff (Jonah Hill), he offers a sales associate $10,000 dollars to shave her head, covers a prostitute with dollar bills, hires a half-naked male marching band, and seems to have prostitutes on call around the clock. In fact, Jordan seems to run the company like the fraternity in *Animal House*, and garners only love and adulation from his employees.

Scorsese means the film to be funny, and though at times tedious in its depiction of Jordon and his cohort's dissipation, some of the scenes are touched with genuine black humor. One crucial scene sees the drugged out Jordan crawling to his Lamborghini to try to get home, he sideswipes a number of cars and totals his own, and without ever being conscious that anything has happened. There is something blackly and bleakly comic about these lower-middle-class guys making so much money that their main goal in life turns out to be getting high.

After being brought down by a solemn, dogged FBI agent (Kyle Chandler) for swindling and money laundering, Jordan gets a reduced sentence for being an informer. After being let out, he goes back to what he knows—giving motivational speeches on salesmanship—without a sign of remorse.

Scorsese doesn't really attempt to illuminate the crisis of 2008. Stratton-Oakmont is too far down the financial food chain from the Goldman Sachses and Morgan Stanleys to be seen as representative of Wall Street. The most problematic are Scorsese's expert zooms, tracking and bird's eye shots, montages, and DiCaprio's seductive, animated performance implicitly glamorize this corrupt and callous world. Scorsese may have seen this film as a black comic critique of the money culture run amuck, but portions of the audience identified with and wanted to emulate the hedonistic behavior of Jordan Belfort and his cohort—the repulsiveness of their actions forgotten in the process.

Belfort's mentor Hanna makes one sharp comment at the film's beginning: "Wall Street is a fake, it creates nothing." It's echoed by Gene McClary (Tommy Lee Jones), a vice president and co-founder of GTX a shipbuilding and transportation firm in TV veteran director John Wells's (*ER, West Wing*) film *The Company Men* (2011). McClary says that "We used to build something here."

However, that has been supplanted by the need, as the CEO of GTX, James Salinger (Craig T. Nelson) says, to keep the share price high so he can get the maximum profit in a looming merger. In pursuit of that, GTX lays off a whole slew of people, among whom are Bobby Walker (Ben Affleck), Phil Woodward (Chris Cooper), and ultimately McClary. The responsibility for its employees is subordinated to the bottom line. As Salinger says, "We work for the stockholders now," and the corporation has become more interested in deal making and the manipulation of stocks and bonds than in shipbuilding.

Hollywood has dealt with the plight of the laid-off middle management executive before in a film like *Up in the Air* (2009), whose opening montage depicted the rage, confusion, and despair of men and women faced with the economic and psychological state that the recession had thrown them into. However, the unemployed are little more than a suggestive device in *Up in the Air*, before it plunges into its real interest—romantic comedy. In contrast, *The Company Men* looks directly at the horrific employment market and psychic pain suffered by men whose comfortable world—replete with six-figure salaries, stock options, and expensively furnished suburban houses—has been shattered.

The film centers on Bobby's plight. The product of a modest childhood, he's become a swaggering, golf-playing, Porsche-driving sales executive, who can't adjust to the fact that he's no longer a top dog. He has a smart supportive wife and a sensitive son, but he's angry and wallows in self-pity. "I'm a thirty-seven-year-old, unemployed loser who can't support his family," he says, but in truth he pays little attention to anyone beside himself.

As a last resort, he does construction work for his salt of the earth brother-in-law Jack Dolan (Kevin Costner). Dolan is a skilled carpenter and a decent man and he and Bobby have an uneasy relationship. High on his prior success, Bobby is condescending toward Jack, and Jack, believing in the dignity and satisfaction of hard work, is dryly ironic about the pretensions of an executive milieu he has little use for.

The film also touches on the indignities of seeking new employment: the hundreds of résumés sent without getting any response; seminars where the unemployed are encouraged to futilely shout, "I will win"; or in the case of the up from the factory floor exec Phil Woodward (Chris Cooper), the advice to color his graying hair, so that he doesn't get turned down for jobs because of his age. It's the sense of failure and mounting debts and bills that drives Phil to suicide.

Of course this being Hollywood, the film ends with a wish fantasy that is supposed to leave us with hope. Bobby and a number of downsized employees are hired back by McClary, who uses part of the outsized bonus he got from his stock options when GTX is bought out, to go back to his beginnings and open a small ship-building outfit.

The Company Men is also about the money. At one point, McClary confronts Salinger saying that because of all the layoffs Salinger has raked in $22 million. Salinger responds by telling McClary that because the merger has gone through his stock options are also worth millions.

One of the more noteworthy of the films that deal with the Great Recession is J. C. Chandor's *Margin Call* (2011). Along with its obsession about money, it also captures the psychology of the people on Wall Street on a night during September 2008. A night when an unnamed 107-year-old financial services firm must deal with, as one character puts it, "the greatest pile of odiferous excrement in the history of capitalism," or it will collapse. Discovered by Eric Dale (Stanley Tucci) on the very day he is fired after 19 years with the firm along with 80 percent of the risk management department. It is revealed when Peter Sullivan (Zachary Quinto), a young whiz of an analyst who survived the cuts, completes Dale's work and discloses it to his bosses Will Emerson (Paul Bettany) and Sam Rogers (Kevin Spacey in the film's strongest performance).

Until that moment, all we know about Emerson and Rogers is that the former chews Nicorette gum compulsively and spent $75,000 of his $2.5 million pay and bonuses on hookers, and that Rogers sheds crocodile tears about his sick dog while the bloodletting occurs in his department.

Nonetheless, Emerson and Rogers turn out to be nebulously decent and sympathetic compared to the revulsion that the film inspires for the upper echelons of the company: Jared Cohen (Simon Baker), the callous corporate hatchet man; Sarah Robertson (Demi Moore), the ice cold head of the risk management department, who had vaguely warned of the impending crisis; and most chilling of all John Tuld (Jeremy Irons), the smooth, elegantly malevolent chairman of the board, who helicopters in to try to solve the crisis.

Tuld, whose name seems a combination of John Thain, the former CEO of Merrill Lynch, and Richard Fuld, the head of Lehman Brothers when it collapsed in 2008, is an executive who claims he understands little about numbers and tells Sullivan: "Speak to me as you would a small child, or a golden retriever." He is told that if the mortgage-backed securities currently on the company's books, which are heavily leveraged, decline in value by an additional 25 percent, the company's losses will be greater than its total assets. Consequently, the answer to the company's problems lies with dumping their subprime derivatives on the market before other firms are aware of their worthlessness. It's a tactic, which according to Rogers, will undermine any credibility that the company has with other firms and totally destroy the market.

Tuld has no hesitation doing this or turning his executives into scapegoats for the problems of the company. His vision is Darwinian, believing the world is divided into winners and losers, and he wants the company to survive no matter the cost.

His soullessness is echoed, albeit in a minor key, by Peter Sullivan's buddy Seth Bregman (Penn Badgley), whose sole obsession seems to be how much each of the other characters earns, and the more sensitive Sullivan, who admits he gave up a career, in Tuld's terms as a "Rocket Scientist," for the money. The self-pitying Sam Rogers, who displays a touch of conscience when the dumping scheme is proposed, surrenders because, as he says, "I need the money." The money is the key, and even Eric Dale laments the fact that he once did productive work and built a bridge that saved commuters thousands of hours of time every year and returns to the company when he is threatened with losing his severance and other benefits.

Margin Call is an unredeemable dark portrait of Wall Street—a world based on a life of acquisition where the investors are treated like suckers. Though some of the executives in the film may have a residue of decency, they all serve a totally soulless and reckless enterprise dedicated to making money.

Chandor skillfully wraps the film in shadows and darkness, using NYC's night streets, bars, and strip joints, to convey a world of suspicion and moral blindness. There are also the almost sinister, alienating moments of shots of empty trading rooms lit only by traders' consoles, and the image of Cohen and Robertson venomously exchanging barbs in an elevator as a cleaning woman silently stands between them. They behave as if she wasn't there, a metaphor for work that cares nothing about human beings or the human consequences of what they do.

The film that provides the most explicit expression of the origins of the 2007–2008 "Great Recession" is Adam McKay's *Anchorman* (2004). *The Big Short* (2015) was based on Michael Lewis's angry and sharp analysis of the causes of the economic catastrophe *The Big Short: Inside the Doomsday Machine* (2010).[12]

The *Big Short*'s portrait of what happened to our economy begins, not with the collapse of venerable financial institutions like Bear Stearns or Lehman Brothers, which precipitated the crash, but back in the 1970s when the Brooklyn-born vice chairman of Salomon Brothers Lewis Ranieri committed the original sin of inventing the financial instrument known as mortgage-backed securities.

It was at that moment that a previously lethargic, even genteel part of banking suddenly became banking on steroids. In fact, where once the bank presidents' underachieving sons and nephews dominated that sphere, it now became the province of young hustlers who were aggressively grasping for end of the year million-dollar bonuses. Or in a famous description it went from "country club to strip club."

Although this bit of background begins *The Big Short*, the film really comes into focus when in 2004–2005 Dr. Michael Burry (Christian Bale in a strong performance), a socially awkward, eccentric, difficult, former neurosurgeon turned hedge fund manager, with a glass eye, a penchant for loud techno rock, and a habit of working in shorts and sandals, crunches the numbers and realizes that these securities are based on mortgages that are doomed to default. He decides, despite the apoplectic rage of his partners, to bet against the banks—gambling that the stocks he buys from them will fail ("going short")—that the housing market will collapse.

Burry's research comes to the attention of Jason Vennett (Ryan Gosling), the film's narrator (addressing the camera directly and breaking the fourth wall), a smooth, contemptuous, unsympathetic manager at Deutsche Bank, who overhears a conversation between Burry and his bosses and doing the numbers decides that Burry is right. He gets nowhere, until he accidentally meets Mark Baum (Steve Carell in a convincing but one-dimensional performance) and his team at Morgan Stanley.

Baum, a perpetually angry fund manager (who is also an integral part of the system that he loudly condemns), is willing to listen to Vennett's pitch. He then decides to do some investigating of his own about the status of the housing market. Baum and his team go to Florida, where they find row upon row of new houses for sale, lap-dancing strippers who own five houses with subprime mortgages, oafish bartenders turned exploitative mortgage brokers selling houses to people without money, and in one instance they are even attacked by an alligator that inhabits an abandoned pool in one of the vacant homes. As a member of the team comments, "It's Chernobyl."

The third plot involves two young, callow ambitious investors, Jamie Shipley (Finn Wittrock) and Charlie Geller (John Magaro), who started a successful hedge fund out of their garage, and who also stumble on Burry's research and want to take make money from the information. They turn for aid to Ben Rickert (Brad Pitt), a retired Wall Street turned New Age guru, currently more interested in colonics than commodity trades. Rickert helps them, but as the film's purported wise man and moralist, startles Shipley and Geller, with the chilling and accurate prediction that after the collapse of the housing bubble there will be unemployment and that for each percentage point the unemployment rate rises, 40,000 people will die.

Still, to the chagrin of Baum, Burry, and others, the housing market doesn't initially collapse. Since the banks are hiding the toxicity of the mortgage securities, the regulating agencies like Standard and Poor and the SEC either do nothing or collude in the sham. It's a world where everybody is in on the con out of self-interest. In fact, the financial markets are seemingly built on nothing more than collusion, corruption, and stupidity. Eventually the bubble does burst and leads to some potent moments in the film—a debate between Baum and a rather pompous and condescending banker. Baum warns that Bear Stearns, one of the financial institutions heavily invested in these securities might be on the verge of collapse, and the banker blindly remarks that he is about to buy more Bear Stearns stock. But suddenly the audience receives news on their cell phones and other digital devices that Bear Stearns is collapsing, and most of the investors flee in panic to dump their stocks. The final moments of the film are equally powerful. One of these has Shipley and Geller wandering through the empty trading floor at the bankrupt Lehman Brothers, which looks like NASA headquarters after a failed rocket launch.

Amidst all the technical talk about subprime mortgages and credit default swaps, McKay's background in comedy and his desire to entertain comes fully into play. He wants to make dry information palatable, so he uses montage, on-screen text, and flashback history lessons. He also includes comic cameos where actress Margaret Robbie in a bubble bath sips champagne and says: "When you hear 'subprime,' think shit." In another, celebrated chef Anthony Bourdain appears comparing mortgage-backed securities to the days-old fish that chef's pour into a concoction they call fish stew. Finally, there is economist Dr. Richard Thaler and actress Selena Gomez at a Las Vegas gaming table explaining credit default swaps by betting on a Black Jack hand as the people around them frantically bet on whether or not they will win. Everybody in the film is betting on winning the big money. The celebs' lectures are patronizing and shallow, but provide relief from the jargon-ridden financial talk that is the film's core.

These moments of humor aside, and except for Rickert's single comment to Shipley and Geller and the angst of a working class man who has lost his Florida house, the film doesn't delve into the economic consequences of what occurred. For most of the film, we are expected to root for not particularly appealing people who are also driven by money and will make billions when the economy collapses and cause untold hardship for the rest of the country. These are characters, who in the main, merely serve the film's theme and narrative rather than have any interior life of their own—the film being stronger in defining the financial world than in dramatizing those who labor in it. McKay ends the film on a bitter note asserting that nothing happened to those who perpetrated the tragedy, nobody is punished, and only one person goes to jail, while many ordinary people are destroyed in its wake. Yes, there have been a few bank reforms, but the system blithely goes on, repeating some of the same destructive tactics and chicanery.

Films like *Margin Call* and *The Big Short* come close to giving a real sense of what it was like to be there when the financial crisis of 2008 occurred. But even in these skillful, knowing works, we get no real sense of what was behind this economic tsunami. Perhaps for any real explanation, we must turn to Moore and Ferguson's documentaries about the crisis or to the novels (*Le Père Goriot, Lost Illusions*) of one of the first great chroniclers of early capitalism, Honoré de Balzac (1799–1850), who succinctly stated that, "Behind every great fortune there is a crime."

In his lengthy journalistic accounts of the Iraq war (2003–2011) and the Afghanistan war (2001–the present), Dexter Filkins, who covered those

conflicts for the *New York Times* and now writes for *The New Yorker*, referred
to them in his title as the "Forever War (2008)."[13] Clearly, that is how those
wars must feel to the American public, which in various polls have over-
whelmingly shown a desire to be free of those foreign entanglements. But
there seems little likelihood at this horrific moment, when ISIS has spread
their terror into the streets of London, Paris, and New York that this will happen. The wars will continue and probably intensify, and refugees will prolifer-
ate without an end point.

Unlike Filkins and the American public opinion polls, our popular culture, especially our films, have not caught up to those feelings in term of
representing those wars. And like the era of the Vietnam War, Hollywood,
perhaps because of the divisive feelings arouse by those wars (see our *How the
War Was Remembered: Hollywood and Vietnam* [1988]),[14] have ventured very
few efforts to depict those wars. However, in recent years, there have been a
few films such as *Zero Dark Thirty* (2012), *Lone Survivor* (2013), and *American Sniper* (2014) that have begun to portray the "Forever War."

The team of Kathryn Bigelow and Mark Boal, who directed and wrote the
Academy Award–winning Iraq war film *Hurt Locker* (2009), produced *Zero
Dark Thirty* (Special Ops speak for 12:30 AM). They begin their film with
an especially chilling moment of a totally dark screen over which we hear
the desperate calls for help of people trapped in the inferno (some making
final cellphone calls to their loved ones) of the World Trade Center towers
on 9/11. The film then moves ahead years to a scene in which a CIA agent,
whose name is Dan (Jason Clarke), is seen torturing a captured Muslim, Amir
(Reda Kateb). Seated in the room is Maya (Jessica Chastain), a CIA rookie
who has come to train at this CIA black site, somewhere in the Middle East.
Uneasy but deeply involved, the red haired, alabaster-skinned, beautiful Maya
sits with arms folded and attention riveted on the scene and ignores Dan's
admonition that "There is no shame if you want to watch from the monitor."

Yet shame is exactly what many critics of the film felt when they denounced
the film's putative support of torture. Dan proceeds to water-board, confines
the sleep-deprived, cowering prisoner to a small box, and taunts him by saying, "I own you, you belong to me."

This kind of film critique, however, only confuses dramatization with
endorsement. As a matter of fact, throughout the film, there are numerous
examples of arguments that torture does not work. And even the hardened,
torturer extraordinaire Dan, who has no reservations about what he does, says
to Maya, "You don't want to be the last one holding the dog collar when the
oversight committee comes."

Clearly, left-leaning documentarian Michael Moore, no apologist for
American policy and tactics in Iraq, saw the film very differently from those

who condemned its seeming collusion with torture: "It will make you hate torture. And it will make you happy you voted for a man (Obama) who stopped all that barbarity." [15] He also quotes Bigelow as calling torture "reprehensible."[16] Though Moore is aware, the average person still may take the film wrong, seeing it as an endorsement of CIA tactics.

But the film, centers on Maya, who is monomaniacal in her relentless quest to capture or kill Osama bin Laden. Unlike other Hollywood thrillers, the film doesn't grant the tough-talking, severe, utterly professional Maya the least bit of a backstory or even the remotest hint of romance—nothing to mute her doggedness. As a matter of fact the only relationship the socially awkward Maya has in the film is a friendship with a fellow female CIA operative Jessica (Jennifer Ehle), whose death in a terrorist attack (a seamlessly constructed, tension-ridden scene) only increases Maya's desire to realize the goal of getting Osama bin Laden.

Since, the film's focus is both on Maya's quest and on the successful assault on bin Laden's hideout—shot from the point of view of the Navy Seals—it would take an audience member who was already skeptical about the CIA to look critically at the film's use of torture. What makes that more difficult is that the final section of the film is a striking set piece where we watch through the Seal's green night vision glasses the unfolding attack (a hand held camera giving us a genuine feel of their entering the compound) and killing of bin Laden. It's a sequence that leaves you sitting anxiously on the edge of your seat, and provides audiences with a real payoff—the death of bin Laden.

This narrative has become the official version of the death of bin Laden. Recently it has been challenged by celebrated investigative reporter Seymour Hersh in an article in the *London Review of Books* (May 21, 2015)[17] and the issues raised by him in a review article that recently appeared in the *New York Times Magazine* (October 18, 2015).[18]

Zero Dark Thirty does not explicitly endorse torture, but it doesn't denounce it either. Still, there is no avoiding being repelled by the powerful images of the CIA's use of torture that open the film. However, Bigelow has made a film whose political perspective is totally subordinated to the primacy of its narrative; action taking precedence over reflection and analysis.

The film's politics on the deepest level may rest with the fact that it directed by a woman (Kathryn Bigelow), produced by a woman (Megan Ellison), distributed by a woman (Amy Pascal, the co-chairman of Sony Pictures), and starring one. The narrative is ultimately about an agency dominated mostly by men, who tend to be dismissive of women, where one driven, uncomfortable woman brings about one of its greatest triumphs.

In contrast to *Zero Dark Thirty* Peter Berg's (*Friday Night Lights*) film *Lone Survivor* (2013) is about another manhunt that goes disastrously and tragically wrong. Based on Marcus Luttrell's book of the same title,[19] Berg's account depicts a raid by Seals in Afghanistan, to capture or kill a Taliban leader, Ahmed Shah. Of the 19 men sent out in the operation, as the title of Luttrell's book tells us, only one survived.

Berg's film is not about politics but about how men deal with battle. At the beginning of the film we are introduced to the four main characters, Matthew "Axe" Avelson (Ben Foster), Danny Dietz (Emile Hirsch), Michael Murphy (Taylor Kitsch), and Marcus Luttrell (Mark Wahlberg), as they banter casually before the mission. They are never really individuated—though Luttrell is depicted as the most morally sensitive of the group—unwilling to kill prisoners who if let go would inform the Taliban. The men are just fearless, committed soldiers that inhabit an all-male universe built on a sense of loyalty—"my brothers."

Once the attacks begin the men demonstrate their courage and professionalism. Surrounded by the Taliban, they keep fighting despite grievous wounds and a forbidding, mountainous terrain. As one by one the team succumbs to their wounds, despite repeated assurances to the question, "Can you still fight?" the film gives off of a sense of tragic inevitability. Despite their bravery, and the film's generally patriotic vision, it emphasizes the suffering of the men as much as their heroism.

It's a film where nonstop action is central, and dialogue is secondary. *Lone Survivor* is an extremely visceral work, with sound effects tracing a bullet's impact on flesh and bone and bullets ricocheting off rocks, blood spurting from wounds, and fluid cutting capturing the Seals falling down a rocky, jagged mountainside.

The film's most sentimental sequence is when a sympathetic Pashtun villager—handsome and noble—finds the severely wounded Luttrell, and protects him from the Taliban. It may have happened that way, but throwing the man's liquid-eyed, watchful, totally sympathetic young son into the mix—he helps save Luttrell from a Taliban killer—is all too much. (Luttrell embraces and even kisses him on the head to offer thanks.) One of the film's final scenes where the American troops and helicopters come to save the day—reminds one of films where the cavalry arrived just in the nick of time to save the settlers from the Indians.

If the film has no overt political point, it does tell us despite obvious technological advantages (though the film criticizes the operation planning involved) the Americans were ill equipped to confront an implacable enemy amidst an alien culture that inhabited a harsh environment. It also repeats what is self-evident, ordinary soldiers fight much less for ideology than because of their bond to their comrades.

One of the biggest grossers of 2014, in addition to receiving six Oscar nominations, Clint Eastwood's controversial *American Sniper* (2014)[20] took a stab at depicting the human costs of war—psychological and physical—while still leaving us cheering its war-loving hero. Eastwood follows a long tradition of American war films that gave us *Sergeant York* (1941), the story of the Tennessean who killed 38 Germans and captured 132 in World War I, and *To Hell and Back* (1955), the story of Medal of Honor winner and future movie star, Audie Murphy, who killed hundreds of Germans in World War II.

Eastwood's central figure and hero is the emotionally low key, tightly wrapped Chris Kyle (Bradley Cooper), the Navy Seal whose 160 confirmed kills over four tours of duty in Iraq made him a "legend" to American troops—the deadliest sniper in U.S. military history.

In the film Kyle is a Texas rodeo cowboy raised by his macho father to love guns, and to be in his father's words a "sheepdog"—a warrior and a hero who can use guns to protect his fellow citizens—instead of one of the nonviolent sheep who need protection from the predatory murderous wolves that must be defeated. These are simplistic categories to define life by, but Eastwood's Kyle is neither a complex thinker nor at all self-reflective, and once in Iraq fully embraces his role as sheepdog.

Kyle goes through an arduous training that shapes men into fearless, indomitable fighting machines. Once "in country" Kyle becomes engaged in urban warfare in Fallujah by lying prone with a rifle on a rooftop providing cover for troops on the ground that are involved in house-to-house fighting. He is unerring in his marksmanship, but he still must decide whether the people he shoots are either terrorists or innocents. He pauses especially when children are involved, but he usually follows orders without hesitation. Kyle has no doubt that he is fighting for his country, his notion of God and for protecting his brother soldiers. He manifests almost no guilt about what he has done, though one knows that among his victims there are innocents as well as genuine terrorists.

Kyle is clearly worn down by the relentless combat he engages in, but is not capable of understanding what he feels. It is left for a fellow soldier Marc Lee (Luke Grimes), to express skepticism about the war, which an ideologically rigid Kyle has no time for, and in response reflexively asks: "Do you want them to attack San Diego or New York?"

But Eastwood still gives Lee's skepticism a significant place in the film. At Lee's funeral his mother reads the last letter that Lee sent home expressing criticism of the war: "Glory is something that some men chase and others find themselves stumbling upon, not expecting it to find them. Either way it is a noble gesture that one finds bestowed upon them. My question is when does glory fade away and become a wrongful crusade, or an unjustified means which consumes one completely?"

However, these are sentiments that Kyle has no room for. And Eastwood himself never raises questions about why we invaded Iraq and destroyed so many lives, including our own, in the process. It is a given in this ahistorical film that the war is a just and necessary one, and the enemy are "savages." In fact, shooting the film from the point of view of Kyle and the other Americans convinces us that the enemy is barely human. In fact, there are no innocent Iraqis depicted in the film (except interpreters)—they are either murderous insurgents or collaborators.

Eastwood nevertheless avoids totally sanitizing Kyle and his fellow soldiers experience in Iraq. He conveys what the war does to Kyle, who on his return to civilian life is totally disoriented and depressed. The sounds and images of war consume him, and he finds it hard getting back to being a father and husband.

Nevertheless, Eastwood's film views Kyle as a hero. His alienation from civilian life is seen only as temporary, and he finds his way back by helping in the rehabilitation of other vets who lost limbs or were emotionally scarred by the war. His return to normality and to being a caring father comes too easily, the film never probing too deeply into Kyle's disorientated state.

Still *American Sniper* does convey that the Iraq war has its horrors and that no one comes out unscathed (Kyle's being shot and killed by a disturbed veteran, who he is trying to help, exemplifies what the war did to many soldiers). However, the dark side of the war that Eastwood touches on is subsumed by his paean to the heroic and intensely patriotic Chris Kyle, and the film's uncritical take on the political basis of the Iraq War. There is no mention in the film of the Bush administration's big lie about the weapons of mass destruction that got us involved, or the fact that Iraq had nothing to do with 9/11. Whatever inner price Kyle suffered in Iraq, what's indelible for Eastwood is the heroism of this warrior with a rifle.

However, Eastwood's film also reminds of the proverb that, "In war all suffer defeat even the victors." And except for the brief victory of the killing of Osama bin Laden in *Zero Dark Thirty*, the "Forever War" films provide little to give us any comfort or insight. Most significantly except for the brief evocation of 9/11, also in *Zero Dark Thirty*, there is very little to tell us about why we have engaged in this continuous struggle. This is hardly uncommon in films that try to portray unpopular wars while those wars are ongoing. But with the "Forever Wars" one wonders if the end will ever come. There are moments that the quagmire seems eternal. Or if as a woman dressed in a burka in Afghanistan once said to Dexter Filkins, "We are stuck here in this cursed place."[21]

It seems such a long time ago since the famous "Beer Summit," of 2009. It was then President Obama sat down with Henry Louis Gates, a major black intellectual and professor at Harvard, and Sergeant James Crowley, of the Cambridge Police Department, after Crowley, had mistakenly arrested Gates for breaking and entering his own home (exemplifying the racially based responses of many white police when encountering blacks in situations they deem suspect). Although it was a toxic incident, it allowed some to fantasize that our racial divide might be resolved with a touch of rational discourse, and perhaps a bit of good will on each side.

Then in 2012, of course, came the murder of Trayvon Martin by George Zimmerman, when even the president, who had long eschewed calling attention to his own race and racial matters admitted that Martin could have been his own son.

Finally, in swift succession came the police killings of Michael Brown in Ferguson, Missouri, of Eric Garner in New York City, and the death of Freddie Gray in Baltimore in 2014, followed by the subsequent rise, after a number of riots, of the "Black Lives Matter" movement.

What was clear that after all the absurd boasting about the advent of a new post-racial society, following the election of Barack Obama, America's original sin, was back in the forefront of our collective consciousness? Indeed it even included a proposed boycott of the 2016 Academy Awards by black actors and directors, who were upset, because no African Americans had been nominated for the leading awards.

The was something ironic about the proposed boycott, because if one looks at the period between 2012 and 2017, awards aside, one sees a succession of films about the African American experience that would certainly hold their own against the best of what had previously been done in American cinema. These include films that dealt historically with the African American experience as well as exploring issues of contemporary African American life, and even events that predated and might even have inspired the "Black Lives Matter" movement.

The first of these and perhaps the most historically rewarding was the Academy Award–winning *12 Years a Slave* (2013), directed by Steve McQueen (*Hunger*, 2008, and *Shame*, 2011). *12 Years a Slave* was adapted from the 1853 memoir of the same title by Solomon Northup,[22] a freeman and violinist who was kidnapped by slavers in Washington D.C. and then sold South. Through all of slavery's horrors and dehumanization, Northup (Chiwetel Ejiofor in a low-keyed, subtle performance), renamed Platt, endures. Indeed in a telling moment illustrative of the slave's dilemma, he and a couple of other black men debate whether to resist or to acquiesce before being sold. Northup chooses, he believes, temporary acquiescence. He would rather survive than fall into despair, for a fellow slave dying is better than being in servitude.

However, he allows his vicious overseer Tibeats (Paul Dano) to torment them, chanting "run nigger run" while they work. Platt driven to the brink by Tibeats's resentment and bullying strikes the overseer, and for this offense is hung from a tree with his toes barely touching the ground to prevent him from choking to death.

No scene evokes the historical powerlessness of the slaves in the face of absolute white power as this moment in the film. As Platt hangs from the tree, McQueen captures the other slaves on the plantation, fearing for their own lives, going about their business as usual, none of them, except one, even acknowledging Platt's horrific predicament.

Finally, released Platt is sold to the volatile, alcoholic, God-invoking slave breaker Edwin Epps (Michael Fassbender). The brutal Epps works his slaves mercilessly, imposes crushing quotas of cotton, whips them for the slightest infraction, has them dance after a day's labor for his own pleasure, and curses them out as "black dogs." He even flaunts his sexual relationship with the beautiful slave Patsey (Lupita Nyong'o)—his "queen"—in front of his unhappy, enraged termagant of a wife (a powerful high-pitched performance from Sarah Paulson), who goads him to punish her. Patsey is so profoundly tormented by her fate as a sexual possession that she asks Platt to kill her—she sees it as a "merciful" act. Instead Platt is later coerced to lash her mercilessly, turning her back into a bleeding sore, when she defies Epps, forcing Platt to become a collaborator in the victimization of his own people.

After a number of futile attempts at contacting someone who might help him, Northup, with the help of a sympathetic, anti-slavery contractor Bass (Brad Pitt), makes contact with people in Saratoga and is finally freed. Pitt, one of the film's producers, who somewhat egocentrically gives himself the role of the understanding, compassionate white man. However, though Bass speechifies about justice and righteousness, the film never loses its way, and becomes a polemic. *12 Years a Slave*'s emotionally arousing conclusion depicts Northup's tear-filled reunion with his wife and by now fully grown children. In the aftermath of this, and what is not shown in the film, is Northup's later career as an abolitionist spokesman both in the United States and abroad.

Despite McQueen's tendency (he came out of the London gallery-and-museum world of short films and videos) to compose stunning images in long shot, and shoot some scenes using striking chiaroscuro, *12 Years a Slave* never seems too aestheticized. It neither romanticizes American slavery as *Gone with the Wind* (1939) in its creation of an antebellum plantation idyll does, or turns it into a source of eroticism as in *Mandingo* (1975). Instead we see the terror and savagery of a world where slaves are never seen as human beings, but as property to be used and abused by their masters according to their every whim and desire. Slavery in the film means men and women being sold like cattle, children, torn from their mothers, and men, women, and children laboring ceaselessly whose only reward was not being whipped. It is a world of white power and privilege built on the backs of slaves.

By centering the film on a respectable, caring, well-spoken freeman like Northup, a man who must hide both his personal history and the rage he feels toward an institution that dehumanizes him, the film forcefully conveys how there wasn't anybody that was black, however advantaged (Northup had been ostensibly accepted in Saratoga, and knew whites who were willing to rescue him), that did not suffer the consequence of America's horrendous racism. It permeated every aspect of the society. In long takes and penetrating tight close ups McQueen's camera focuses on a despairing Northup, whose sorrow is overwhelming, but no more so than the millions of slaves that could not read and write, and would never taste freedom in their lives.

A vivid contrast to Solomon Northup's choosing acquiescence in order to survive is Nate Parker's more conventional, Hollywood style chronicle of Nat Turner's slave rebellion in 1831 Virginia—*Birth of a Nation*. It was a bloody rebellion where 200 blacks and 60 whites died—the most whites killed in any slave uprising in the South.

The film had a highly touted debut at Sundance, and it could have become the kind of film that everybody concerned with African American history felt imperative to see. However, the news that Parker had been involved in a sexual assault case in 1999, for which he was acquitted, and the fact that the victim committed suicide in 2012, cast a pall over the film's reception by theater audiences.

Nevertheless, *Birth of a Nation* provides a forceful and effectively constructed, even more brutal but much less subtle version of *12 Years a Slave*'s evocation of the daily horrors of slavery. What is missing is the creation of almost any other characters besides Turner who are more than one-dimensional and a tendency by the film to heighten a number of scenes, even including angelic choirs on the soundtrack.

Turner as a child is taught to read by the wife of his slave master, who is condescending but relatively kind, given the time, with the proviso that he confines his reading to the Bible. Later as an adult, because of his Biblical knowledge, his drunken master (to save the plantation from its growing debt) rents him out to other plantation owners to preach acquiescence to slavery's brutal exploitation. In the course of serving as a lay preacher Turner witnesses all the terrors of slavery (e.g., force feeding) which are brought home to him personally when his own beloved wife Cherry (Aja Naomi King) and that of his best friend Hark's (Colman Domingo) wife Esther (Gabrielle Union) are raped. It's a commonplace event in a world where black women are seen as mere objects to be used and abused.

These events transform Turner into a full-fledged rebel, and he turns the Bible into the basis for prophetic rebellion. A rebellion, that no matter how brave, was doomed to be suppressed with enormous fury by the white masters, who captured Turner after a few months and visited unspeakable tortures even on his dead body. They even hung the slaves who didn't take part in the rebellion.

Unfortunately at the point the uprising begins, from a sometimes painful, arresting view of the slave world (a slave auction) the film turns into an African American version of Mel Gibson's life of the 13th-century Scottish hero William Wallace in *Braveheart* (1995). It becomes an action film with a martyr/superhero Turner leading his rebels through a trail of blood and gore. Parker has made a labor of love, but his directorial skills aren't as strong as his artistic and political passions.

In a sense Lee Daniels's *The Butler* (2013) begins where *12 Years a Slave* ends. Cecil Gaines (Forest Whitaker) witnesses the rape of his mother (Mariah Carey) and the murder of his father (David Banner) by a drunken white plantation owner (Alex Pettyfer). Touched with guilt the plantation owner's mother (Vanessa Redgrave), who is a racist, takes in Cecil to work as a servant, initiating what would eventually become a three-decade career as a butler in the White House.

Cecil's story was adapted by Lee Daniels (*Precious*, 2009) and his scriptwriter Danny Strong from a 2008 *Washington Post* article by Will Hapgood[23] about Eugene Allen, who worked for 30 years as a butler in the White House. Cecil is a stoical but perceptive observer of history as he alternately serves Presidents Dwight Eisenhower (Robin Williams), John F. Kennedy (James Marsden), Lyndon B. Johnson (Liev Schreiber), Richard Nixon (a profoundly uneasy and politically calculating John Cusack), and Ronald Reagan (Alan Rickman), a star-studded cast all performing generally on target cameos. It's a breezy run through of the presidents' varied personas and their divergent relationships to the civil rights movement.

Cecil's submissiveness—he almost never raises his voice—and commitment to playing it safe (he adheres to the dictum that a butler should be invisible) is vividly contrasted with the political activism of his estranged son Louis (David Oyelowo), by Daniels's fluid crosscutting. Louis is alternately a participant in sit-ins, Freedom Rides, and even for a brief time becomes is a member of the Black Panthers—talking radical cant. Though he is ultimately turned off by their emphasis on guns and violence and drops out. While Cecil and the other black butlers mutely serve at formal, all-white dinners at the White House. Cecil's chain-smoking, heavy-drinking wife Gloria, played with verve by Oprah Winfrey, also has a very different personality than Cecil's. She is as expressive and aggressive as Cecil is emotionally controlled and passive. Still, he is the apotheosis of decency. (He is even sufficiently affected by the civil rights movement that he drops being submissive for a moment, and asks his contemptuous white boss for equal pay and greater opportunities for the black staff.) When Nancy Reagan (Jane Fonda) invites Gloria and Cecil to a White House state dinner, Gloria is exhilarated, but the invitation, which Cecil sees as mainly "for show," doesn't have any effect on Ronald Reagan's right wing racial policies; Reagan continuing to vote against sanctions against the apartheid regime in South Africa.

The Butler is most incisive as a cinematic evocation of W.E.B. Du Bois's seminal insight that African Americans wore "two faces." It also clearly illustrates the black poet Paul Dunbar's lines that African Americans of generations before the civil rights movement, "wear the mask that grins and lies."[24]

The masks that Cecil and the other butlers wore are nonexistent in Ava DuVernay's (*I Will Follow*, 2010) 2014 film *Selma*, which chronicles the struggle of Dr. Martin Luther King Jr. (David Oyelowo) to gain voting rights for African Americans. DuVernay and her scriptwriter Paul Webb portray King as a visionary who is totally focused on gaining equality for his people—a man whose public virtue and those of his associates in the SCLC were beyond question. At the same time it portrays in much less detail his conflicts with his wife Coretta (Carmen Ejogo), who suspects him of infidelity, and his conflicts over political tactics with young radicals of SNCC such as James Foreman (Trai Byers) and John Lewis (Stephan James).

DuVernay avoids portraying King as a man free of self-doubt. One sees this most poignantly when late one evening King calls the singer Mahalia Jackson (Ledisi Young) and asks her to let him hear the voice of the Lord, and she sings him the gospel classic "Precious Lord Take My Hand."

Nonetheless, King is also shown to be an astute political tactician, who has learned from previous defeats of the movement's efforts that only white intransigence and violence can gain the movement the kind of media coverage (i.e., the brutal response of Alabama's racist and demagogic governor, George Wallace) that will produce action on the part of the federal government. And he is also no slouch in standing toe to toe with President Lyndon B. Johnson (Tom Wilkinson), himself no stranger to shrewd political maneuver, to attain his goals. Ultimately, the terrible violence of "Bloody Sunday" (March 7, 1965), when Alabama State Troopers attacked the marchers, and the sympathy it generated throughout the country, resulted in the passage of the Civil Rights Act of 1965.

In her commitment to the heroism of King and the black protest movement, DuVernay seemed to go overboard by diminishing the political significance of

LBJ's commitment to civil rights. He is shown as initially hostile to the efforts of King. However, many historians of the period have denied this. Indeed some of Johnson's former aides have even argued that he encouraged King and they worked together to pass the Civil Rights Act.[25]

Nevertheless, what the film most reminds us of is how charismatic and eloquent King could be. For legal reasons, DuVernay had to reimagine King's oratory, but the soaring words still have King's cadence and moral resonance. If they lose something in authenticity, their authority remains

There is no denying the power of these historical recreations. What were equally weighty and compelling were the films depicting aspects of contemporary African American life, their problems, tragedies, and victories.

Coming two years after the 1965 Voting Rights Act, which was given such dramatic impetus by Dr. King and the Selma marches, was another much quieter but no less important civil rights achievement when the U.S. Supreme Court in *Loving v. Virginia* stuck down miscegenation laws. That decision is the focus of Jeff Nichols's (*Mud*, 2012) film *Loving* (2016).

Loving in its understated way can be as moving as Dr. King's struggles in *Selma*. It portrays the true story of an interracial couple—a black mother and housewife Mildred (Ruth Negga), and a white bricklayer Richard (Joel Edgerton), who comes from poverty, has black friends and seems utterly natural and unself-conscious in a totally black milieu (e.g., racing cars, drinking at a bar).

The film offers no swelling music, melodramatic plot twists, or a big dramatic payoff. Neither the quietly dignified Mildred nor Richard is educated, nor is either of them a civil rights activist. Nor are they particularly articulate. So they make no angry speeches about racism, nor do the ever fully express what they are feeling.

Richard, in fact, barely speaks and can be moody, sullen, and often uneasy with other people. He just simply wants to be able to love his wife and raise his kids in the world he grew up in. And he's tortured by the fact that his masculine dignity is stripped by the state, and he is not allowed to love his wife, whom he gazes at adoringly.

After a number of years of living in Washington, Mildred—the emotionally stronger and more politically conscious of the two (she watches Martin Luther King Jr. on television and realizes that the case allowing them to marry will have larger social implications)—writes to U.S. Attorney General Robert F. Kennedy for help. Kennedy refers her to the American Civil Liberties Union (ACLU), which agrees to take the case. As everything else in this modest, minimalist film, it barely touches on the Supreme Court trial, featuring just a few remarks by the two ACLU lawyers—before delivering the positive verdict—defining marriage as an inherent human right—by telephone to Mildred without ever contriving the predictable catharsis by manipulating our emotional responses.

The film's strength lies in its central performances—Edgerton an Australian, Negga born in Ethiopia—that without much exposition or a backstory powerfully communicate much of what we want to know about their relationship. The Lovings, as they are aptly named, are humble people who are thrown into playing a major historical role, without it changing their personalities or their way of life.

If the film errs it's on the side of being a bit too constrained, and leaving out a few too many important details. At times, it makes it hard to believe that the situation Richard and Mildred face wouldn't have caused some marital tensions, but the marriage is depicted as a serene one—where raw emotions are never expressed. More importantly, the film never fully explains how Richard was able to so easily overcome the prejudices that afflicted so many others growing up in the South. But true to the film's choice of reticence the film never explores what allowed Richard to act as he did. However, though *Loving* may not be either a formally exciting film or does it delve deep psychologically, it contains almost no false notes and stirs one deeply.

Another aspect of these new African American films is the exploration and resurrection of previously ignored elements (usually positive) of African American history. American life. This is the basis of *Hidden Figures* (2016), director Theodore Melfi's debut film, which he also wrote.

Hidden Figures centers around three unsung African American heroines; all of them struggling to fully realize themselves at work in a sexist and segregated Virginia. These women—Katherine Johnson (Taraji P. Henson), Mary Jackson (Janelle Monae), and Dorothy Vaughan (Octavia Spencer)—were exceptional mathematicians and engineers who worked for NASA where they faced discrimination as African Americans and women.

The film begins in 1961 with their working with other women as human computers (this being before digital computers) doing calculations in a separate "colored" building at the Langley Research Center. But the space race with the Soviet Union was at its height and NASA's need for gifted mathematicians and scientists meant that despite the obstacles of segregation and racism their color could ultimately be transcended.

The brilliant Katherine is promoted to a job with the space task force (The only black face in the room), whose crew-cut manager Al Harrison (Kevin Costner) is a decent, low key, work-obsessed man who accepts Katherine's talents.

But Harrison is too distracted to notice the racial indignities Katherine suffers (e.g., no colored bathroom in the building, forcing her to repeatedly run half-mile to find one, and the existence of a separate colored coffee pot), or the competitive tension between her and his favorite Paul Stafford (Jim Parsons) who is threatened by Katherine's talent. When Al does find out about these indignities he does make amends by ending segregated bathrooms and rhetorically decreeing that "At NASA, we all pee the same color."

Each of the three women achieve their own victories as Dorothy becomes a supervisor based on her having the foresight to learn the advanced computer skills that were being introduced by NASA, and Mary overcoming segregation in entering an advanced engineering class at a local university. But far the greatest triumph of all was Katherine's ability to calculate the parameters for John Glenn's heroic safe return from space when all the other engineers and mathematicians at NASA were stumped by the problem.

Hidden Figures is a conventional upbeat film that doesn't get close to the psychic lives of our three heroines. The emphasis is on their talents, courage, shrewdness, and their warm friendship. The three women have sweet, sensitive children, and good marriages, with Katherine, who is a widow finding just the right, loving man, Colonel Jim Johnson (Mahershala Ali), who embraces her strength and independence. They live in a middle class community in Hampton, Virginia (a university town) that seems too picture perfect—church services, neighborhood barbecues—without an existing underside that could undermine this idyllic milieu.

Obviously, this a not a work of social realism, but a Hollywood homage to three gifted African American women who fulfilled their potential at a time when racism still ruled, especially in the South. The only thing Ione can say is that the film is moving despite it being a pure Hollywood product—optimistic, emotionally shallow, and skillfully manipulative. But it succeeds at making one feel good about the triumph of the three women, and, for the moment, the American Dream. That's no small feat in these dismal times.

A portrait of a darker moment in African American history could be seen in Kathryn Bigelow's new film *Detroit* (2017) depicting the 1967 Detroit riot, that follows the pattern of her war films by providing neither an overview nor a backstory for the riot. (Other riots took place that year in Cleveland and Newark.) For example, there is no mention of the city's long history of police abuse and a black unemployment rate that was double the white one.

Bigelow is a director whose films emphasize violent action and immediacy rather than exposition and social and political analysis. Consequently, she centers the film on reconstructing what happened at the Algiers Motel during the night of July 25–26.[26] It's there where one of the film's central characters, a fledgling singing group's lead singer, Larry Reed (Algee Smith), and a close friend end up. There they encounter four black men and two young white women from Ohio. One of the young men had with self-destructive bravado shot a blank with a starter pistol at the Guard and police. It leads to a night of torture and horror, which Bigelow intensifies by shooting in close-up in a tight space. The three policemen who arrive are racists, who quickly line up the men and women against the wall with the white women arousing their particular rage for being with black men. They pistol whip and beat them, and ultimately kill three innocent men. Bigelow is less interested in the psyches of her characters than in the barbarism of the police, who are out of control with the power they wield over black men. The most vicious cop, the sociopathic Krausse (Will Poulter) revels in his capacity to intimidate and arouse fear. Other forces, like the National Guard are for the most part passive and give the policeman free rein. When the riot ends, the three policemen go on trial for murder with predictable results—given that racism stacks the deck—and they are freed.

Bigelow tries to conclude with a glimmer of hope amidst her searing vision of Detroit. She returns to a profoundly depressed Larry who quits singing and finds a place in life leading a church choir. It feels like a contrived Hollywood touch in a film that rarely indulges in such devices. Bigelow has said that she made this film "to generate a conversation," and she generally succeeds, especially in her powerful image of police taking the lives of people who present no threat, regardless of their innocence or guilt, and who ultimately pay no price.

African American history was not the only source of inspiration for African American filmmakers. Their imagination was also stirred by literature. In this latter, no one fit as well as August Wilson (1945–2005), with Miller and Williams some of the premier playwrights of the American theater in the latter half of the 20th century and the early 21st. Wilson was a playwright whose cycle of 10 plays—most set in Pittsburgh's working class Hill District in different decades of the 20th century—was constructed as a poetic saga of black life. It has been compared in its narrative drive, the complexity of his characters, and their humor and tragedy with other imaginative places such as Hardy's Wessex and Faulkner's Yoknapatawpha. His stage is populated with Jitney drivers, preachers, railroad porters, blues singers, trumpet players, and boardinghouse landladies. Few white characters appear. It's in the main an insulated black milieu with its own rituals and traditions and an intergenerational camaraderie and banter among black men that he observed growing up.

Fences, written in 1985, won the first of Wilson's two Pulitzer prizes; the other was for the *Piano Lesson* in 1990. Denzel Washington, who had starred in a Broadway revival of the play in 2010, brought it to the screen. Washington, who both stars and directs the film, partially opens it up with some street scenes. But the film essentially remains a play—where language and performance take precedence over the visual aspects of the work. It is also one of Wilson's most accessible plays—dealing with the dynamics of familial conflict that without the inevitable role of racism in their lives could as well be white.

The focus and center of the film is Troy (Denzel Washington), a sanitation worker. Troy, by turns is avuncular, sadistic, destructive, obscene, and ultimately tragic. Troy is also an illiterate, ex-con who turned his life around and became a star in the Negro baseball leagues, but came along too early to benefit from Jackie Robinson's historic breakthrough.

Troy's wife of 18 years, the dignified, long-suffering Rose (Viola Davis), puts up with his bombast, self-pity, and his playing around with other women. But she is clearly the anchor of the family, as each week Troy meekly hands her his pay envelope and receives his allowance. Rose tries to set limits for Troy, and in a brilliant speech in reply to Troy's lamentation about what he sees as his constricted, too dutiful life, she confronts him with the tearful: "Don't you think I ever wanted other things? Don't you think I had dreams and hopes? What about my life? What about me?"

Troy, who acts with little consciousness of how his behavior impacts on other people in his family, has difficult relationships with his two sons. Troy's jazz musician son Lyons (a too smooth yet sensitive Russell Hornsby) from an earlier relationship is an accomplished moocher, who knows when to come around for a handout on Troy's payday. His younger son Cory (Jovan Adepo) is an accomplished football player, who has hopes for a football scholarship. His conflict with an angry, bullying Troy comes to a head when he forbids Cory from pursuing his dream: "White man ain't gonna let you get nowhere with that football." Troy, who never achieved his baseball dreams, tells him to get a decent job—clearly threatened that his son may achieve something more than he ever did.

Cory doesn't give in and asserts his independence by leaving home to join the marines, though there may be few dreams in the offing for him in the future.

In fact, the only easy relationship Troy has is with his work colleague and buddy Bono (Stephen Henderson) with whom Troy can feel genuine pleasure bantering and telling stories. It's one of the few times in the film Troy stops being hard and controlling.

Fences may not be *Death of a Salesman*—the play and film that tends to speechify a bit too often, and the concluding scenes meander. But in Troy, Wilson with the gifted Washington's assistance has created a larger-than-life figure out of a harsh and difficult ordinary man. He's a character whose talk using Wilson's brilliant colloquial speech can soar to poetic heights. And the film evokes the humor, sadness, and small victories and painful defeats inherent in African American life at a time before the civil rights movement came to the fore.

The film *Moonlight* (2016), which won the Academy Award for best picture in 2017, was also based on a play—Tarell Alvin McCraney's *In Moonlight Black Boys Look Blue*. But it's much more richly imagistic than *Fences*, composed in lush colors, using much less dialogue, and employing emotionally memorable medium close ups that capture Chiron's pain.

Moonlight, written and directed by Barry Jenkins (*Medicine for Melancholy*, 2008), is built around a triptych of episodes depicting three stages in the development of Chiron respectively played by Alex Hibbert, Ashton Sanders, Trevante Rhodes, as a young black child, an adolescent, and a young man in his twenties. Chiron grows up with few options in the poverty-stricken, drug-afflicted neighborhood of Liberty City, Miami.

At first glance when we meet Chiron, he might be mistaken for autistic, as each word he utters is a struggle for him. At school, Chiron is bullied because of his small stature. And things are no better at home with his mother Paula (an incandescent performance by Naomie Harris), who loves Chiron, but slides inevitably from casual crack user to full-fledged addict, and in the process becomes uncontrolled, cruel, and rejecting—a mother from hell. She does achieve some stability and self-knowledge with age, but Jenkins's film doesn't indulge in magical transformations or reconciliations.

It's only when he meets the confident, commanding drug dealer Juan (Mahershala Ali) and his empathetic girlfriend Theresa (Janelle Monae), who becomes his caring surrogate father and mother, we begin to sense that Chiron's silence hides sensitivity and intelligence. In one powerful moment, we see Chiron put things together about Juan and drugs when he says, "My mama does drugs, and you sell drugs." And watch Juan's agonized reaction. In the world that Chiron inhabits, it's the ultimate irony that one of its destructive forces is the only kind refuge, and Jenkins makes it seem believable not contrived.

When Chiron reaches adolescence, the other boys assume that he is gay, and the violent bullying becomes unendurable. He engages in violent retribution with dire consequences for him.

The final episode has an unrecognizable Chiron, a young man fully bulked up and even more sullen after a stint in prison. He's now following the very masculine Juan's path by becoming a drug dealer (he even dresses like him). He is still silent and carries the emotional baggage of a life that is essentially a vale of tears. But a meeting with an old friend Kevin (Andre Holland), whom he has secretly loved, provides him with his first real human connection, and the film ends with a soulful embrace and kiss between them.

Jenkins's film is not *The Wire*—he makes no attempt to explore the inner city ethos and institutions; nor do any whites play a role here. However, his characters do inhabit an all-black world, and there is no question race and class implicitly helps shape their lives.

The film's central subject is the nature of Chiron's identity, and there are no easy answers offered. The conclusion is open-ended—Chiron can go in multiple directions—nothing is prefigured. One thing Jenkins avoids is defining Chiron solely by his sexuality or race. Though in a world where everybody seems to end up in prison, including Kevin, and fathers are usually absent, one's sense of self can't be helped being determined by one's masculinity or lack of. Rejecting that notion of self is turning oneself into a victim. Chiron never expresses his feelings about himself, but he confesses to Kevin, "I cry so much sometimes I might turn to drops." It's a luminous film that is never explicit, but always emotionally resonant.

Jordan Peele's (of Comedy Central's *Key and Peele*) debut film *Get Out* (2017) proves that satire is still alive—so far being 2017's most profitable film and garnering universal critical acclaim. *Get Out* is a hybrid of a horror film and angry satiric takes on white liberalism. The film begins as Chris (Daniel Kaluuya) is invited to the suburban home of his seductive white girlfriend Rose (Allison Williams of *Girls*). He is wary about meeting her parents who don't know he's black, but she says that it will be fine for they are faithful liberals. That feels like a setup, and we have a feeling that everything that follows will be fraught with peril.

Chris's first dealings with Rose's parents make us a bit uneasy. They strain to be warm and liberal, the neurosurgeon father Dean (Bradley Whitford) calling him "my man," proclaiming that he would have voted for Obama a third time, and mentioning what an honor it was when his father lost a potential Olympic competition slot to Jesse Owens. And Missy (Catherine Keener) Rose's hypnotherapist mother insists on trying to hypnotize Chris out of his smoking habit. The parents may be slightly menacing, but a somewhat passive Chris isn't truly alarmed by their behavior. For Peele who both writes and directs smartly, agilely avoiding crude white racist stereotypes, by depicting the parents as patronizing liberals. More disturbing for Chris are the couple's two ever-smiling, robotic black servants, whose speech is oddly formal, and periodically show flashes of aggression.

Chris's racial unease reaches a crescendo with a party in which its all-white guests take part in a bingo game that looks like a slave auction. They also indulge in faux pas such as commenting on black people's genetic makeup. These are white people who envy him for his supposed physical attributes. Little does Chris know how literal their desires are.

The racial satire soon shifts into full-fledged horror whose violence and terror Peele handles with consummate skill, though it dilutes the impact of the racial satire. And it becomes one more well-crafted genre film. Still, if the film's horror elements explain some of the film's commercial success, what one remembers most is the racial pessimism at the heart of *Get Out*.

A different order of satire, devoid of the horror mix is Justin Simien's very smart and bold debut film *Dear White People* (2014). Simien's film loosely based by a series of scandalous black-face parties at all-white fraternities doesn't take place in suburbia but at Winchester University, so Ivy that it is supposed to make attending Harvard seem like slumming.

Winchester is where Samantha ("Sam") White (Tessa Thompson) presides over her campus radio show "Dear White People" where she angrily mocks the condescension toward and stereotyping of blacks that whites indulge in. It is also where she launches her crusade against "randomization": the university's attempt to foster more diversity, by integrating frat houses' culture. For Sam, this anodyne act is seen as subverting black identity and culture removing one of the only places that blacks seemingly feel free to be themselves.

Sam's sharp-tongued, livid posturing aside, Simien's film rejects rage and polemic preferring to view the world of "postracial" America through a lens of perplexed, sometimes dark humor and one-liners.

He constructs a world of varied types that skirt caricature and are almost always more than a representative of a social or political position. There are three other students that play central roles: Coleanda ("Coco") Conners (Teyonah Parris), an ambitious young woman who wears blue contact lenses and flat hair, craves white acceptance, and desires to become a star on reality TV; Troy (Brandon Bell), a big man on campus, Sam's ex-boyfriend, and the weed-smoking son of the school's dean; and finally Lionel Higgins (Tyler James Williams), a wild Afro-haired, timid gay outsider, who loves Altman films, writes for the campus newspaper, and is alienated from every group on the campus.

Simien presents all these types with all their confusion and complex identity issues and offers a wealth of interesting ideas on the subject of racial identity. But the film tends to be messy, for Simien can't always realize his large ambitions. Still he is often on target in his depiction of his characters' contradictions as they struggle to make sense of their lives inhabiting a world of privilege.

The film concludes with a wild frat party that crudely displays every repellent racial stereotype. It goes on too long, and though a final credit sequence makes it clear that it's based on reality, it misfires.

At the other end of the social scale are the people in Benh Zeitlin and Lucy Alibar's *Beasts of the Southern Wild* (2012). The film carries a hint of the anthropological, but is also clearly influenced by the romanticism of Terrence Malick. It is set in a fictional place in Louisiana called "the Bathtub." The Bathtub is a swamp-ridden, barren-looking bayou neighborhood of black and white families living in ramshackle homes and beached wrecked boats, whose lives seemed to revolve mainly around heavy drinking and fishing. Their homes are squalid, and the neighborhood is filled with rubbish and dogs, chickens, and pigs freely wandering about. The people live lives far removed from middle-class norms and behavior. Still, they may be dirty and living on the margins, but they adhere to a serious code of their own: "You don't let anyone down who's in trouble." One also feels the sense of true community among them where race plays no role.

The film focuses on the lives of the too cutely named Hushpuppy (the precocious six-year-old nonprofessional, Quvenzhane Wallis, whose point of view and voice dominates the film) and her angry father Wink (the nonprofessional Dwight Henry). Wink is an irresponsible father. He feeds Hushpuppy a steady diet of chicken, leaves her alone to fend for herself for long stretches of time, hits and shouts at her, but despite it all one can see that there is a fierce love and attachment between them.

Hushpuppy who narrates some of the film is an almost magical child—a bit too self-consciously and pretentiously so. She mourns and fantasizes about the mother who deserted her, communes with the animals, talks about the universe, and has a rich imagination. The film includes magic realist scenes of ferocious primordial beasts called Aurochs who are dislodged from polar icecaps and drift down to wreak havoc on the Gulf Coast. The images may be too literal, but Hushpuppy conjures them up at times to make some sense of the darker aspects of her life.

The community is destroyed by a storm, and, despite protests, everyone is evacuated to a medical center where they are given clean clothes. After the death of Wink, who has heart problems, some of the inhabitants of the Bathtub including Hushpuppy throw off the new clothes given to them by aid workers and march over water proudly back home in a scene reminiscent of Soviet filmmakers choreographing Chekhov's *Three Sisters* striding off to Moscow. In its final image, this quasi-fable embraces the indomitability of an impoverished, mixed-race community; a lovely, utopian fantasy.

Equally fierce in their attachment to their culture and to their origins in South Central Los Angeles are the young black men who became one of the first gangsta rap groups N.W.A. (Niggaz Wit Attitude) in *Straight Outta Compton* (2015), a film directed by F. Gary Gray (*The Italian Job*, 2003). Dr. Dre (Corey Hawkins), Ice Cube (O'Shea Jackson Jr., son of the real Ice Cube), D. J. Yella (Neil Brown Jr.). M. C. Ren (Aldis Hodge), and Easy E (Jason Mitchell) make up the group after Easy E, tired of the constant danger of dealing drugs, decides to finance their venture into rap.

On one level, the film is a rags to riches tale as the group burst onto the music scene from nowhere and is catapulted to fame and fortune including grand houses with pools where bikini-clad young women party with the rappers and their entourage. But it is also a cautionary tale of what big money can do, as the group begins to break apart as a result of squabbles with their shrewd, duplicitous manager, Jerry Heller (Paul Giamatti) around cash and contracts. Given that the street binds N.W.A.'s knowledge of the world, and their obsession is with money and fame, they are easily preyed upon by anybody who can read a contract. The result is that their success begins to be undermined.

But more importantly the film is about the social world—the street culture—out of which the group emerged. Or as Ice Cube put it, "Our art is a reflection of our reality." And that reality is conveyed in the unfiltered rage and obscenity-laced lyrics about volatile inner city life—guns, weed, cars, intimidating, vicious cops, and toxic violence—that became the hallmark of West Coast Rap. (Much of that same self-destructive rage, but without the shaping of an artistic sensibility, determines some of their personal encounters.) Perhaps the moment in the film where that is most clear is when, after being warned not to, the group does its most famous rap "Fuck the Police," and it causes, given the lyrics, a riot. As we write—police have killed more black men—and we can see how little has changed in that dynamic.

The film also depicts some of the seamier sides of the rap world. For example, hovering around the group, and doing his best to turn them against one another, is the thuggish, violent record producer Suge Knight (R. Marcus Taylor), who is surrounded by heavyweight enforcers. There is nothing redeeming about Suge. The group and the film's final moments coincide with the death of Easy E from AIDS—a result of his life choices, but also a genuinely forlorn and moving conclusion.

Nor does the film follow the lives and careers of the N.W.A. rappers after the group dissolved. So nothing is said about the most successful of the rappers, Ice Cube, who parlayed the group's success into a career as an actor (*Boyz 'N the Hood*, 1991) and film producer (*Barber Shop*, 2004, and *Ride Along*, 2014). In addition, there is no mention of Dr. Dre, who became a rap album producer, but was more noted for his brushes with the law, which resulted in a prison sentence in 1995. And while the other members of the group did not disappear into total obscurity, their careers were hardly equivalent to their success with N.W.A. as D. J. Yella became a pornographer, and M. C. Ren turned from rap to the Sunni Muslim faith.

The reality of black life that N.W.A. rapped about could have been a chorus's comments on the life of Oscar Grant III (Michael Jordan). Grant was killed by a police officer January 1, 2009, and it was turned into a quietly powerful, realistic film closely based on the real story, *Fruitvale Station* (2013), directed by Ryan Coogler. The film begins with the actual cell phone video from that fateful night.

Oscar is an ordinary man who at times can be sweet and kind, is trying to be faithful to his often disappointed girlfriend (Melonie Diaz), dotes on their lively, smart little daughter (Ariana Neal), and attempts to be a good son to his strong, nurturing mother (Octavia Spencer). The director adds gratuitously to his virtues by having him sensitively comfort a dog after an accident. But try as he might Oscar has a hot-tempered, self-destructive and feckless side (we quickly learn that he is a "fuck-up"). He is fired from his job working in a supermarket for constant lateness, and in order to pay his bills he deals drugs—an offense that he has already done some hard jail time for. But he suddenly decides to give up dealing drugs and transform his life.

But on that fateful night, Oscar is dissuaded from driving into downtown to celebrate New Year's Eve, and instead ventures with friends and girlfriend out on BART (Bay Area Rapid Transit). The trip, depicted by Coogler, is initially a festival of diversity, as white, black, and Hispanic, gay and straight, drink, dance, sing, and celebrate on board the subway car. But when a fight breaks out, the police are called—they are viewed in the film as either brutal or dangerously inexperienced—which leads to Oscar's angry and deadly confrontation with them.

In a hint of countless demonstrations to come, there were large-scale protests in Oakland over Oscar's death. And eerily prefiguring the future: the police officer that shot Oscar was convicted of involuntary manslaughter because he claimed he thought he was shooting Oscar with a taser instead of a gun. Of course, he received a sentence of a little over a year and was released in 11 months, typical of the minimal or nonexistent punishments that were meted out to police in the killings that followed.

More than just a memorial to Oscar Grant III, *Fruitvale Station* is a stirring reminder of how often these kinds of scenes have been reenacted in this country even before Ferguson, New York City, Baltimore, St. Paul, Baton Rouge, and into the future. The film makes no explicit critique of the nature of American society. But the film strongly suggests that there are too many young black men with potential like Oscar's adrift, and the notion of a post-racial society will take a long time coming. A modicum of economic and social justice and police restraint is all we can hope for. Though in the Trump era, those hopes are probably pollyannaish.

One knows these films, however impressive, are just an early step toward the many works that will follow focusing on both African American history and on the social and psychological reality of black life in present-day America. Some will be polemical, others will have complex political points to make, and still others will deal with more universal themes—friendship, family dynamics, work, and how to shape a meaningful life. Though one should have no expectation that films can in any way cure the ills of our society, what they can do is dramatize the texture of black life—its strengths, imperfections, and clear, justifiable grievances. So, if we ever begin to believe we can make the kind of progress that makes race and racial issues a peripheral rather than primary problem (a color-blind society?), these films may make a difference. More importantly for African Americans, they may help them achieve what Professor Henry Louis Gates spoke of after the Beer Summit: "If we take control of our own stories, we can take control of the narrative."[27]

As Hollywood began to produce more films about the history and contemporary life of African Americans, it also embraced films about LGBTQ life as well. It also depicted heroic women who fought against dystopian societies and took their place in the pantheon of superheroes, and even some films that asserted the power of ordinary women.

Perhaps the most formally striking and emotionally nuanced of the films was Todd Haynes's (Far from Heaven, 2002) Carol (2014) starring Cate Blanchett and Rooney Mara. Adapted from Patricia Highsmith's (The Talented Mr. Ripley) novel The Price of Salt, which she wrote under the pseudonym Claire Morgan (for in the 1950s lesbianism was certainly a taboo subject). It centers on a forbidden yet passionate love affair between Carol Aird (Blanchett), an unhappy mother and a stylish and elegant upper-middle-class suburbanite heading for a divorce from an insensitive, controlling husband, and a doe-eyed Therese Belivet (Mara), an unformed, callow, waif-like young woman, hoping to be a photographer.

Carol and Therese meet in Sinatra's classic 1950s "Strangers in the Night" fashion, exchanging significant glances in the department store where Therese is working during the Christmas rush. When Carol purposely forgets her gloves, Therese returns them, and their affair hesitantly and slowly evolves through passing touches and looks. The film focuses on this simmering love affair that is consummated in a motel in a delicately sensual bedroom scene, on a road trip that ultimately has destructive consequences.

Haynes with his gifted cinematographer Ed Lachman create a rich, cool atmospheric world that uses a muted palette, striking light and shadow, and shots through glass, and other shots where the subject is sometimes obscured by objects within the frame. It's all done to successfully create a world that is an almost intoxicating expression of their passion.

The film also takes great care with Carol's dress—her full-length mink coat, and her almost perfect 1950s coiffeur. Carol's glamorous surface is maintained despite the painful loss of her beloved daughter in a custody battle with her husband that leaves her in despair. (Blanchett is brilliant at creating a character whose commitment to sustaining appearances is central to her being.) Given the period, it's Carol's lesbian affair that opens her to charges of immorality and the loss of custody over her daughter. (One senses that her affair with Therese can be partially viewed in mother/daughter terms.) Without delivering an overt message, the film affirms Carol's declared sexual preference at a time when being gay was usually closeted and there weren't many women who broke from conventional domestic roles.

The film depends more on its images to convey the nature of their relationship than its dialogue. And by the conclusion, Therese is less passive, working at a job she likes, and ready for a more equal relationship with Carol. The film may be a touch too calibrated, but it's a quietly stunning work.

In contrast to Carol and Therese's intense affair, there is the unstated ennui that characterizes Nic (Annette Bening) and Jules's (Julianne Moore) 20 years of lesbian domesticity in *The Kids Are All Right*. Though they still love each other, the marriage seems to have become a bit stale. Nic, a successful doctor, is controlling, easily angered, and judgmental and drinks a bit too much. The smart Jules has always been a bit flakey and insecure—moving from job to job, coming up with many artistic ideas that are never realized—and been mostly a stay-at-home mom. She is now trying to start a new landscape design business. Their two children Joni (Mia Wasikowski) and Lazer (Josh Hutcherson), each a result of the same sperm donor, are bright, articulate, and attractive. It all sounds pretty routine until the children decide to find out who their biological father is.

Enter Paul (Mark Ruffalo at his most natural), the shambling, laid-back owner of an organic restaurant and farm, whom the kids identify as their sperm donor father. They quickly bond with him and Jules goes a step further and has a passionate affair with someone who is looser and more appreciative of her than Nic. Even Nic, suspicious of the charming, immature Paul, begins to soften when they too cutely discover mutual love for the songs of Joni Mitchell. All this good feeling and the fact that Paul is a perfect match for their family comes crashing down when Nic discovers Jules and Paul's affair. Everything then gets somewhat unglued.

Lisa Cholodenko, as she did in an earlier film about New York drug-taking bohemians and artists (*High Art*, 1998), which also depicted lesbian relationships, has a gift for capturing the speech and atmosphere of a particular world. Here the language of upper-middle-class Southern California is perfectly caught. In one scene, Nic angry at her kids for not sending out thank you notes says, "maybe instead of thank you notes, you could send out good vibes." Upon learning that his children's parents are lesbians, Paul says, "I love lesbians."

The film's central characters are mostly three-dimensional and sympathetic, and the warm, amiable Paul is also self-centered, and childishly doesn't think through the consequences of his new familial commitments. The sensitive, inexperienced Joni is an achiever like Nic, but more febrile and emotional than her.

The film doesn't try to convey big truths about human relationships, but is consistently intelligent in conveying their messiness. No one is quite in the wrong here—everyone has their reasons—and as Jules says, "marriage is hard." The film also doesn't romanticize lesbian marriages—the film avoids the polemical and usually the sentimental. The point is that same-sex marriages are just as difficult as heterosexual ones.

As important as the issue of same-sex marriage was in the 21st century, another equally explosive issue that arose almost simultaneously with the Supreme Court's decision to permit same-sex marriage was discrimination against transgender people. This discrimination became national news when a conservative North Carolina governor and legislature adopted a law known as the "bathroom law," which prohibited transgender people from using a bathroom that didn't correspond to the sexuality on their birth certificate. Nationwide condemnation was quick, and North Carolina suffered some negative economic consequences. A number of sports teams cancelled championship series that were to be held in North Carolina, and some major corporations abruptly halted plans to build plants and establish headquarters in the state. Ultimately the law was partially overturned under a new Democratic governor.

Films had been slow to depict anything involving transgender men and women. One can think of *Myra Breckinridge* (1970) and later *Transamerica* (2005), but in each of these films, it was a female actress who became a man (Raquel Welch, Felicity Huffman). However, television had been quick to seize on the issue. There was of course the real-life transformation of the conservative Republican Bruce Jenner into the equally conservative Caitlyn Jenner and a short-lived reality TV show that followed her life. We should include the Emmy-winning, subtle, and intricate cable TV series that explores gender identity, Jill Soloway's *Transparent*.

There could be no doubt that film would follow suit, and it did with the film *The Danish Girl* (2015) directed by Tom Hooper (*The King's Speech*, 2010). This time with a male actor (Eddie Redmayne) playing the role of Einar Wegener/Lilli Elbe—who undergoes the first operation trying to turn a man into a woman.

Einar and his wife Gerda (Alicia Vikander) seem to have an almost perfect life in 1920s Copenhagen. They are deeply in love and compassionate with each other, and they are both dedicated, hardworking painters (Einar of landscapes and Gerda of portraits) who are trying to have a child. One day Einar sits for Gerda in place of a woman friend and puts on the latter's costume, which sets off in him the explosive uncontrollable desire to become a woman. It's a need that has existed in him from boyhood, but hasn't known what to do with it. Given the time and psychiatry's view of homosexuality as an illness, the many doctors he sees offer solutions like radiation, or diagnose him as a schizophrenic and want to institutionalize him. Ultimately he finds a doctor (Sebastian Koch) who is willing to attempt the then experimental surgery (a two part process) of turning Einar into to a woman—it's a risky procedure that results in his death.

Redmayne seems to delight in quirky odd roles such as his Academy Award–winning performance as Stephen Hawking in *The Theory of Everything* (2014). In *The Danish Girl*, his transformation from Einar to Lilli Elbe is almost perfect, though he indulges in too many coy looks and smiles. But a scene in a warehouse full of women's clothes, where he looks in a full-length mirror and hides his genitals, so it appears he has a vagina is almost heartbreaking. But except for his desperation to become a woman, we learn nothing else about his inner life. Similarly, with the feisty, liberated Gerda, convincingly played by Vikander, we gain no notion of what was the source of her long-suffering commitment to Einar, who loses sexual interest in her. We also learn little about them as painters, except that almost every scene's interior is ravishing as are the costumes—possibly a painter's view of the world. However, the film is too self-consciously decorative for its own good.

The Danish Girl is the kind of film where the characters primarily serve a subject of intense current interest and have little inner life of their own outside of Einar's profound problem with his sexual identity and his undertaking an historic operation. Einar's words after his first successful procedure—"I am entirely myself" sums up the film's prime reason for being.

Though LGBTQ issues were at the forefront of cinematic gender struggles, there was still a place for heterosexual feminist images. However, a number of them were not the kind that early second-wave feminists might have had in mind. One of these images came in the form of the almost comic book female rebel and heroine Katniss Everdeen, who stands against the dystopian society Panem in *The Hunger Games* (*Hunger Games*, 2012; *Hunger Games: Catching Fire*, 2013; *Hunger Games: Mocking Jay, Part 1* 2014; *Hunger Games, Mocking Jay Part 2*, 2015).[28] These box office blockbusters featured Jennifer Lawrence as the indomitable Katniss Everdeen (a name taken from Thomas Hardy's *Far from the Madding Crowd*), who begins the series as a victim of the totalitarian regime that rules Panem (the word comes from Panem et Circenses—the Latin for "Bread and Circuses.")

The Hunger Games are the yearly struggle decreed by President Coriolanus Snow, played with sly, purring, insidious complacency by Donald Sutherland, to amuse the people of Panem, and take their minds off their impoverished lives and lack of basic rights. Complete with pregame ceremonies and beauty pageant–style interviews, the combat (manipulated by the state with all sorts of high-tech effects) is the ultimate in reality television. The killing ritual is shown throughout the country as two young people from each of the country's 12 districts must fight to death until only one survives.

Of course with her almost magical bow and arrow and enduring a lot of tedious action film obstacles, she is a winner. A more striking aspect of the film is District 12, which Katniss hails from and looks like a movie version of the FSA photographs (Dorothea Lange, Walker Evans) of 1930s poverty-ridden rural America. Over time, as the films follow Suzanne Collins's science fiction, young adult trilogy, Katniss changes from a 16-year-old girl cowed by the affluent, decadent society of the capital city of Panem to a poster girl for the rebellion against it, and then something of a Joan of Arc for the rebel forces.

The film has more than a touch of camp, with Stanley Tucci as the obsequious, flamboyant host of the Hunger Games, Caesar Flickerman, the late Philip Seymour Hoffman as the Head Gamemaker Plutarch Heavensbee, and Elizabeth Banks as the upbeat District 12 escort Effie Trinket, who wears many different colored wigs. Some of the characters are flashily costumed, and the Capitol is conceived in futuristic terms.

Still, the central character is Katniss, who is resourceful, courageous, self-contained, tender, and loving. She is a feminist heroine and role model any young girl could idealize. Katniss even has a duo of pallid suitors Peeta Malick (Josh Hutcherson), and Gale Hawthorne (Liam Hemsworth), but except for an occasional kiss there is little emotional substance to these relationships.

The most serious problem with the film is that its politics are subsumed in a girl's adventure narrative. Except for being against the fascistic regime of President Snow, and some images that hint at the wars in Iraq and Afghanistan, the rebels who overthrow President Snow's regime seem to have no alternative vision. As a result, we are made to believe that if President Snow goes, truth, beauty, and equality will reign. But the film does stress female empowerment by making the three most powerful leaders of the rebellion female—Katniss, self-proclaimed "president" of the rebels Coin (Julianne Moore), and Commander Paylor (Patina Miller). I suppose one could say that the film, for all its slickness and shallowness, can be seen as successfully projecting a version of pop feminism—a young brave women, armed with a bow and arrow who can triumph over adversity.

Anyone desiring a less-mortal, more-fantastic comic book heroine had only to turn to the Amazonian *Wonder Woman* (2017).[29] The creation of William Moulton Marston who invented her in 1941, Wonder Woman joined Superman (1938) and Batman (1939) in the so-called Justice League and the pantheon of DC Comics' superheroes. Marston drew a great deal of inspiration for his character from early feminists, and especially from birth control pioneer Margaret Sanger. The Wonder Woman comic has never been out of print, and she even enjoyed a short-lived life as a TV series (1977–1979), starring Lynda Carter.

Directed by Patty Jenkins (*Monster*, 2003), the film's best moments take place during Princess Diana/Wonder Woman (Gal Gadot) years on the hidden island of Themyscira, a man-free world populated by Amazons. This serene paradise, which looks like the setting for one of Hollywood's sword and sandal epics, is ruled by Diana's mother Queen Hippolyta (Connie Nielsen), who tries to protect her from the violence of the world. But her warrior aunt, Antiope (Robin Wright), understands that there is no escaping the world and trains her to become a fighting machine. It may be merely a comic book fairy tale, but it conjures up a sweet, pacific alternative world to the violent patriarchal environment we live with every day.

But the idyll is ended with the intrusion of German troops fighting "the War to End all Wars" (World War I) pursuing her future love interest and British spy Steve Trevor (Chris Pine). Steve convinces Diana that she must join the fight against the Germans. But Diana, who was raised to believe Ares (David Thewlis), the God of War, is the nemesis of peace who wants to destroy mankind, joins Steve to terminate him rather than the Germans. The lovely, caring, well-balanced Wonder Woman is armed with a shield, sword, her Golden Lasso of Truth and bracelets that can repel bullets, and after an endlessly dreary titanic one-on-one battle, she succeeds in destroying Ares. However, she slowly comes to the realization that she was raised with the false belief that destroying him would bring peace to the world. The film sees the world's murderousness as the product of the choices made by many individuals and states and no mythic figure is powerful to bring it about.

It's a dark view of human nature, but far from the film's central theme. What add to the film's appeal are clever moments where the innocent, vulnerable Wonder Woman learns the ways of modern life—like the idea of men and women sleeping together means more than just sleeping, or her surprise that women are not expected to participate in high-level political meetings.

These moments are accompanied by witty banter nicely executed by Pine and Gadot. But it's all subordinated to the film's exhausting action/adventure narrative including saving a French town from the Germans (though the scene where an unconquerable Wonder Woman crosses "No Man's Land" fighting off a hail of bullets is stirring) and defeating the arch villains fascistic General Ludendorff (Danny Huston) and a diabolical, humanity-hating scientist, Doctor Maru (Elena Anaya). There are too many special effects and explosions that are deafening and ennui inducing—the way of big budget superhero films.

This version of *Wonder Woman* has drawn praise from some feminists, because in their eyes it shows a powerful and openhearted woman confronting male patriarchy and brutality, and because it has taken a long time for a woman superhero to take her place beside the likes of Superman, Batman, Spiderman, Iron Man et al. And the film's box office has been huge (a sequel is already planned), and the possibility of little girls buying lots of Wonder Woman lunch boxes and backpacks has no doubt great commercial potential. Still, it's clear that if the Golden Lasso of Truth were applied to its producers they would admit that profit rather than promoting feminism was their prime aim. I assume that much of its audience was drawn to the film not for its sexual politics or vision of human nature, but for a beautiful woman in a sexy costume, who can destroy the forces of evil.

Two other films centering on less heroic but strong women characters were the independent, slick *Equity* (2015) and *Joy* (2015). *Equity*, a film directed and written by women, also focuses on Wall Street women at work (a rarity). A tough, abrasive, driven investment banker Naomi (*Breaking Bad*'s Anna Gunn) operates in a world where cutthroat competition, manipulation, and betrayal are the rule. Women may be central here, but they are as flawed as the men on Wall Street. It is a small, unsentimental, slightly schematic film that works well within the parameters it sets for itself.

Joy, a loosely adapted biopic, directed without a hint of nuance by writer/director David O. Russell (*American Hustle*), may have a bigger budget and stars (Jennifer Lawrence and Robert De Niro), but it doesn't work as well. The central figure Joy Mangano (Lawrence) is a stubborn, resolute, lower-middle-class mother and shrewd businesswoman who struggles against adversity to realize the American Dream. She becomes the founder of a million-dollar family business (though her screwball comedy–style family is of little help) that introduces the idea of a more effective form of mop. The comedy is broad and often unfunny, though there are scenes where Joy appears on the QVC—a home shopping network—that are humorous and enjoyable. *Joy* is a basically a feel-good parable about the triumph of a smart, powerful ordinary woman—more the Capracorn of Frank Capra than feminism.

One can see that during the second decade of the 21st century, the sources of social change were depicted in films dealing with the African American community, the world of LGBTQ, and the roles of women. However, the most dynamic sources of change in the lives of people on a day-to-day basis in this century probably could be discovered in the world of technology, primarily in digital technology and one of its major sectors—social media.

The social media have been singled out for the significant role they played in political events like the "Arab Spring," where Tahrir square and the overthrow of Egyptian president Hosni Mubarak probably could not have occurred without the use of Facebook and Twitter. But social media have also had their dark side: cyberbullying; the increasing isolation of many teenagers whose lives are totally obsessed with social media; as a catalyst for racism and hate; and even affecting its users capacity to think independently. Two strong films depicting the titans of that revolution in communication and information—Mark Zuckerberg (Facebook) and Steve Jobs (iMacs, smartphones, iPads)—came out during that period.

The Social Network (2010) was directed by David Fincher (*Fight Club*, 1999, and *Zodiac*, 2007) and smartly and entertainingly written by Aaron Sorkin (*Moneyball*, 2011) from the nonfiction book *The Accidental Billionaire* by Ben Mezrich. It's all about how Mark Zuckerberg created Facebook and all the personal and legal conflicts that were an integral part of the process.

The very first scene of the film establishes the character of a thoroughly unappealing, hoodie wearing Zuckerberg (Jesse Eisenberg provides a pitch-perfect performance). He is cold, condescending, and contemptuous and talks compulsively to his then girlfriend, Erica Albright (Rooney Mara), about Harvard's elite final clubs and his intense desire to be accepted by them. When Erica can't bear his repellently insensitive behavior any longer, she calls him an "asshole" and leaves. In response, an angry, alcohol-fueled Zuckerberg posts a vicious, vengeful blog attacking her and creates Facemash, a misogynistic site that invites Harvard men to rate campus girls. It may have been technologically ingenious, but it was an ugly act of misogyny, caused by both his status anxiety and being traumatically dumped by the one woman he cares about. At least in Fincher and Sorkin's view, Facebook had a very abject and mean beginning.

A great deal of the rest of the film turns to scenes of legal depositions filed against Zuckerberg, though there are flashbacks to what led up to this situation. The scenes of legal wrangling could have been tedious, but in Fincher's hands the rapid pacing makes them come alive. The first of the legal suits comes from the privileged, athletic, handsome Winklevoss twins (both played by Arnie Hammer), who claim that Zuckerberg stole their idea. Zuckerberg's encounter with them exemplifies the conflict between the complacently privileged and someone who depends totally on how smart and sharp he is. (What's interesting is that though all of them are elite Harvard men, none shows much intellectual interest in anything outside making money and asocial technical skills.) Indeed there is a priceless moment when the Winklevoss twins take their case to Harvard president, and previously Clinton's secretary of the treasury, Larry Summers (Douglas Urbanski). The Winklevosses feel that as gentleman Harvard should back them up. What they hadn't counted on was Summers, who is an avatar of arrogance, famed for not suffering fools gladly, curtly dismissing them and their case.

While neither Zuckerberg nor the Winklevoss twins arouse our sympathy, the film has no such ambivalence regarding Zuckerberg and his relationship with Eduardo Saverin (Andrew Garfield). He is perhaps the isolated Zuckerberg's one close friend and the earliest financial backer of what was then called, "The Facebook." In all respects, the less-driven, pleasant Saverin (an uninteresting character) is a bit of a naive who expects his friend Mark to protect his financial interest in Facebook, even neglecting to bring a lawyer along when Facebook is reorganized financially and he finds his stake in the company reduced significantly. The ease with which Zuckerberg callously throws over Saverin is indicative of how quickly he has succumbed to the potential celebrity that Facebook has created and his lack of real concern for anyone else in his life.

Part of that lure comes in the form of a laid-back Sean Parker (Eduardo can't abide him)—who cofounded the file-sharing computer service Napster—played with cool, overweening confidence by Justin Timberlake. Fincher depicts him conveying such demonic seductiveness that you can almost feel the flames licking at his heels. (In one scene, he says to Mark that, "A million dollars isn't cool. You know what's cool? A billion dollars.") Unfortunately, Parker has an Achilles heel, and his self-destructive penchant for drugs and young girls is a bridge too far for Mark and Facebook.

One weakness of the film is that after initial Harvard scenes, Zuckerberg becomes increasingly remote. Except for sarcastic and snide eruptions at his depositions, we just don't get enough of who he is.

In fact, most of what we see is Mark at work, since nothing else seems to give him much pleasure. Even when Facebook passes 1 million members, and while everyone around him celebrates, he seems only mildly excited. On a human level, he seems to have more than a touch of Asperger's.

In addition, though Zuckerberg created the world's most significant source of personal information, the film is less interested in Facebook's significance than in the personal dynamics of its founders. The ultimate irony is though Facebook is committed to a virtual community that connects humanly, the asocial Zuckerberg is seen at the end obsessively trying to "friend" Erica—the woman who unceremoniously rejected him. One can assume that this may not be the whole truth about Zuckerberg, but even if some of it is fictional, it's a generally convincing portrait.

One might say that a companion to Zuckerberg's mixture of visionary brilliance and asocial behavior was Steve Jobs. The screenplays for both films were written by Aaron Sorkin. For *Steve Jobs* (2015), directed by Danny Boyle (*Slumdog Millionaire*, 2008), Sorkin adopted his screenplay from Walter Isaacson's authorized biography of this seminal figure in the history of digital technology.

Sorkin built his screenplay around three important moments in the life of Jobs (Michael Fassbender): 1986, when the first Apple computer is introduced, 1989, when after being forced out of Apple, his new company produces the NeXT computer, and 1990 after his return to Apple, he intro- duces the iMac.

All of the action in the film takes place backstage before Jobs launches these new technologies to an overflow crowd of adulating fans. But the real action centers on Jobs's often charged encounters with the central people in his life—all of it handled in the Sorkin-style, with the characters talking fast and moving about the room. These include his neurotic former partner Chri- sann Brennan (Katherine Waterson), whose life is a mess (she's on welfare), and her daughter Lisa (played at different stages by three different actresses), whom he has never acknowledged as his child despite DNA evidence to the contrary, his collaborator on the original Apple computer in the garage in Los Altos, CA, Steve Wozniak (Seth Rogen), his marketing executive and his only confidante, a protectively maternal Joanna Hoffman (Kate Winslet), and the executive who replaced him at Apple for a time, John Sculley (Jeff Daniels).

We are given an explanation for Jobs's behavior toward his daughter, which involves his own abandonment by his biological parents, his subse- quent adoption, and the detachment of his biological Syrian father. Despite his rejection of his daughter, she is one of the few people he displays any lov- ing feelings toward (she appears in all three sequences)—even calling the first prototype of the Apple computer, Lisa.

The others around Jobs, who seemingly can speak truth to power are Hoff- man, who refers to herself as his "work wife," played with great calm and sen- sitivity by Winslet, Sculley, the one-time father figure who ultimately fires him, and Wozniak—the tech-savvy cofounder of Apple, a much less aggres- sive man than Jobs, who tends to bulldoze him. Wozniak, who never felt he was fully recognized by Jobs, is particularly upset with Jobs when he refuses to acknowledge the work of the engineering department in the development of the various Apple products. He responds to Jobs with the telling line, "You can be decent and gifted at the same time. It's not binary."

Jobs, who was a master of closed systems, streamlined construction, and conceptual simplicity—an artist for the computer age—is also, as Sorkin por- trays him, a patronizing control freak and a colossus of insensitivity. He is also someone who sees himself as an Einstein of the computer age. However, he does have one moment in the film that he movingly confesses, "I'm poorly made" to his daughter.

While the film does give us a sense of the complexities of Jobs's generally unlikable personality, it does little to give us any insight into the creation of the digital industry and culture. For instance, by focusing on the triptych of scenes before the introduction of various digital products, we get nothing of the kind of high-tech culture that existed in California surrounding the making of the first Apple computer, or the intense competition between Apple, Dell, IBM, and Microsoft for dominance in the individual computer market. After seeing *Steve Jobs*, one may wonder how Apple, which is the most highly valued company in America ($700 billion), actually achieved that status. Though how dramatic a film that would be is another question.

It would be good for us to think about what these advances in social media have done for us and to us. For this we might look for guidance back to the 19th century and the introduction of the telegraph, the first major new form of communication in millennia, which its inventor Samuel F.B. Morse introduced with the bombastic message, "What hath God wrought."

Another more skeptical perspective came from Henry David Thoreau who wrote, "We are in great haste to construct a magnetic telegraph from Maine to Texas, but Maine and Texas it may be have nothing to communicate. . . . We are eager to tunnel under the Atlantic to bring the old world some weeks nearer to the new; but perchance the first news that will leak through into the broad flapping American ear will be that Princess Adelaide has the whooping cough."[30]

NOTES

1. Mark Halperin and John Heileman, *Double Down: Game Change 2012* (New York: Penguin Press, 2013).

2. Jann Wenner, "Barack Obama: Ready for the Fight," *Rolling Stone* (April 25, 2012).

3. Richard Engel, *And Then All Hell Broke Loose* (New York: Simon and Schuster, 2016).

4. Jonathan Chait, *Audacity: How Barack Obama Defied His Critics and Created a Legacy* (New York: Custom House, 2017).

5. Mark Lilla, "The End of Identity Liberalism," *New York Times* (November 18, 2016).

6. http://Boxofficemojo.com.

7. Richard Verrier, "China Is on Track to Surpass U.S. as World's Largest Movie Market by 2017," *Los Angeles Times* (November 5, 2015), p. 2.

8. Manohla Dargis, "In Hollywood It's a Men's, Men's, Men's World," *New York Times* (December 24, 2014).

9. Eric Foner, *The Fiery Trial: Abraham Lincoln and American Slavery* (New York: W.W. Norton, 2010).

10. James Oakes, *The Radical and The Republican: Frederick Douglass, Abraham Lincoln, and the Triumph of Anti-Slavery Politics* (New York: W.W. Norton, 2007).

11. Robin Blackburn, *An Unfinished Revolution: Karl Marx and Abraham Lincoln* (London: Verso, 2011).

12. Michael Lewis, *The Big Short: Inside the Doomsday Machine* (New York: W.W. Norton, 2010).

13. Dexter Filkins, *The Forever War* (New York: Vintage, 2009).

14. Albert Auster and Leonard Quart, *How the War Was Remembered: Hollywood and Vietnam* (New York: Praeger, 1988).

15. Michael Moore, "In Defense of Zero Dark Thirty," *Facebook* (January 24, 2013).

16. Ibid.

17. Seymour Hersh, "The Killing of Osama Bin Laden," *London Review of Books* (May 21, 2015), pp. 3–12.

18. Jonathan Mahler, "What Do We Really Know about Osama Bin Laden's Death," *New York Times* (October 18, 2015), MM2.

19. Marcus Luttrell with Patrick Robinson, *Lone Survivor: The Eyewitness Account of Operation Red Wings and the Lost Heroes of Seal Team 10* (New York: Back Bay Books, 2007).

20. Chris Kyle and Scott McEwen, *American Sniper: The Autobiography of the Most Lethal Sniper in U.S. Military History* (New York: William Morrow and Co., 2012).

21. Filkins, *The Forever War*, p. 43.

22. Solomon Northup, *12 Years a Slave* (Auburn, NY: Derby and Miller, 1853).

23. Will Haygood, "A Butler Well Served by This Election," *Washington Post* (November 7, 2008).

24. Joanne M. Braxton, ed., *The Collected Poetry of Paul Laurence Dunbar* (Charlottesville: University of Virginia Press, 1993).

25. Alicia Brooks, "Controversy Grows over LBJ Clash with Martin Luther King over Civil Rights," *The Wrap* (January 2, 2015).

26. John Hersey, *The Algiers Motel Incident* (New York: Knopf, 1968).

27. Henry Louis Gates, *Finding Your Roots: The Official Companion to the PBS Series* (Durham: University of North Carolina Press, 2014).

28. Suzanne Collins, *The Hunger Games; The Hunger Games: Catching Fire; The Hunger Games: Mockingjay* (New York: Scholastic Press, 2008, 2009, 2010).

29. Jill Lepore, *The Secret History of Wonder Woman* (New York: Vintage, 2015).

30. Henry David Thoreau, *Walden: A Life in the Woods* (Boston: Ticknor and Fields, 1854), p. 67.

SELECTED BIBLIOGRAPHY

Acheson, Dean. *Present at the Creation.* New York: W. W. Norton, 1969.

Adler, Renata G. *A Year in the Dark.* New York: Berkley, 1969.

Agee, James. *Agee on Film: Reviews and Comments.* Boston: Beacon Press, 1966.

Alpert, Hollis, and Andrew Sarris, editors. *Film 68/69: An Anthology by the National Society of Film Critics.* New York: Simon and Schuster, 1969.

Altman, Rick, editor. *Genre: The Musical.* London: Routledge & Kegan Paul, 1981.

Ambrose, Stephen. *Rise to Globalism: American Foreign Policy 1938–1970.* Baltimore, MD: Penguin, 1971.

Auster, Albert, and Leonard Quart. *How the War Was Remembered: Hollywood and Vietnam.* New York: Praeger, 1988.

Balz, Dan, and Haynes Johnson. *The Battle for America, 2008: The Story of an Extraordinary Election.* New York: Viking, 2008.

Barbour, Alan G. *John Wayne.* New York: Pyramid, 1974.

Barnouw, Eric. *Tube of Plenty: The Evolution of American Television.* New York: Oxford University Press, 1977.

Bart, Peter. *Who Killed Hollywood? . . . and Put the Tarnish on Tinseltown.* Los Angeles: Renaissance Books, 1999, pp. 64–65.

Beschloss, Michael, and Strobe Talbott. *At the Highest Levels: The Inside Story of the End of the Cold War.* New York: Little, Brown, 1994.

Blackburn, Robin. *An Unfinished Revolution: Karl Marx and Abraham Lincoln.* London: Verso, 2011.

Bogle, Donald. *Toms, Coons, Mulattoes, Mammies and Bucks.* New York: Bantam, 1973.

Braxton, Joanne M., editor. *The Collected Poetry of Paul Laurence Dunbar.* Charlottesville: University of Virginia Press, 1993.

Brodie, Fawn. *Richard Nixon: The Shaping of His Character.* Cambridge, MA: Harvard University Press, 1983.

Bywater, Tim, and Thomas Sobchack. *Film Criticism: Major Critical Approaches to Narrative Film*. White Plains, NY: Longman, 1989.

Cannon, Lou. *Ronald Reagan*. New York: G. P. Putnam's Sons, 1982.

Capra, Frank. *The Name above the Title*. New York: Bantam, 1972.

Chait, Jonathan. *Audacity: How Barack Obama Defied His Critics and Created a Legacy*. New York: Custom House, 2017.

Christensen, Terry. *Reel Politics: American Movies from Birth of a Nation to Platoon*. New York: Basil Blackwell, 1987.

Ciment, Michel. *Kazan on Kazan*. New York: Viking, 1973.

Collins, Suzanne. *The Hunger Games*. New York: Scholastic Press, 2008.

Collins, Suzanne. *The Hunger Games: Catching Fire*. New York: Scholastic Press, 2009.

Collins, Suzanne. *The Hunger Games: Mocking Jay*. New York: Scholastic Press, 2010.

Cooke, Alistair. *A Generation on Trial*. Baltimore, MD: Penguin, 1952.

Cooke, Pam, editor. *The Cinema Book*. New York: Pantheon, 1985.

Davies, Philip, and Brian Neve, editors. *Cinema, Politics, and Society in America*. Manchester, UK: Manchester University Press, 1981.

Deming, Barbara. *Running Away from Myself: A Dream Portrait of America Drawn from the Films of the Forties*. New York: Grossman Publishers, 1969.

Dickstein, Morris. *Gates of Eden: American Culture in the Sixties*. New York: Basic Books, 1977.

Engel, Richard. *And Then All Hell Broke Loose*. New York: Simon and Schuster, 2016.

Engelman, Ralph. *Friendlyvision: Fred Friendly and the Rise and Fall of Television Journalism*. New York: Columbia University Press, 2009.

Ferguson, Thomas, and Joel Rogers. *Right Turn: The Decline of the Democrats and the Future of American Politics*. New York: Hill and Wang, 1986.

Fiedler, Leslie. *Love and Death in the American Novel*. New York: Dell, 1967.

Filkins, Dexter. *The Forever War*. New York: Vintage, 2009.

Finkelstein, Norman. *The Holocaust Industry: Reflections on the Exploitation of Jewish Suffering*. New York: Verso, 2000.

Fitzgerald, Frances. *Fire in the Lake*. New York: Vintage, 1973.

Fitzgerald, F. Scott. *The Crack-Up*. New York: New Directions Paperback, 1993.

Foner, Eric. *The Fiery Trial: Abraham Lincoln and American Slavery*. New York: W. W. Norton, 2010.

Ford, Gerald R. *A Time to Heal*. New York: Berkley, 1980.

Fordin, Hugh. *The World of Entertainment: Hollywood's Greatest Musicals*. Garden City, NJ: Doubleday, 1975.

French, Brandon. *On the Verge of Revolt: Women in American Films of the Fifties*. New York: Frederick Unger, 1978.

French, Phillip. *Westerns*. New York: Oxford University Press, 1977.

Friedman, Thomas. *The Lexus and the Olive Tree*. New York: Anchor Books, 2000.

Fukuyama, Francis. *The End of History and the Last Man*. New York: The Free Press, 1992.

Gabler, Neal. *An Empire of Their Own: How the Jews Invented Hollywood*. New York: Crown, 1988.

Garnham, Nicholas. *Samuel Fuller*. New York: Viking, 1971.

Gates, Henry Louis. *Finding Your Roots: The Official Companion to the PBS Series*. Durham: University of North Carolina Press, 2014.

Gillett, Charlie. *The Sound of the City: The Rise of Rock and Roll*, revised edition. New York: Pantheon, 1984.

Goldman, Eric F. *The Crucial Decade—and After, America 1945–1960*. New York: Vintage, 1960.

Goodman, Walter. *The Committee: The Extraordinary Career of the House Committee on Un-American Activities*. Baltimore, MD: Penguin, 1969.

Goulden, Joseph G. *The Best Years, 1945–1950*. New York: Atheneum, 1976.

Gow, Gordon. *Hollywood in the Fifties*. New York: A. S. Barnes, 1971.

Hacker, Andrew. *Two Nations: Black and White, Separate, Hostile, Unequal*. New York: Charles Scribner's Sons, 1992.

Halberstam, David. *The Best and the Brightest*. New York: Fawcett, 1973.

Hall, Stuart, and Paddy Whannel. *The Popular Arts*. New York: Pantheon, 1965.

Halliday, Jon. *Sirk on Sirk*. New York: Dell, 1980.

Halperin, Mark, and John Heinemann. *Double Down: Game Change 2012*. New York: Penguin, 2013.

Haskell, Molly. *From Reverence to Rape: The Treatment of Women in the Movies*. Baltimore, MD: Penguin, 1974.

Herndon, Venable. *James Dean: A Short Life*. New York: Signet, 1975.

Hersey, John. *The Algiers Motel Incident*. New York: Alfred A. Knopf, 1968.

Hetzberg, Hendrik. *Obamanos! The Birth of a New Political Era*. New York: Penguin, 2009.

Higham, Charles, and Joel Greenberg. *Hollywood in the Forties*. New York: Paperback Library, 1970.

Hill, John, and Pamela Church Gibson, editors. *The Oxford Guide to Film Studies*. New York: Oxford University Press, 1998.

Hobsbawm, Eric. *The Age of Extremes: A History of the World, 1914–1991*. New York: Vintage Books, 1996.

Hodgson, Godfrey. *America in Our Time: From World War II to Nixon, What Happened and Why*. New York: Vintage, 1978.

Jacobs, Diane. *Hollywood Renaissance: The New Generation of Filmmakers and Their Works*. New York: Delta, 1980.

Jowett, Garth. *Film: The Democratic Art*. Boston: Little, Brown, 1976.

Kael, Pauline. *Going Steady*. New York: Bantam, 1971.

Kael, Pauline. *Kiss, Kiss, Bang, Bang*. New York: Bantam, 1969.

Kagan, Norman. *The Cinema of Stanley Kubrick*. New York: Grove Press, 1975.

Kagan, Norman. *The War Film*. New York: Pyramid Publications, 1974.

Kaminsky, Stuart M. *Don Siegel: Director*. New York: Curtis Books, 1974.

Kass, Judith. *Robert Altman: American Innovator*. New York: Popular Library, 1978.

Kearns, Doris. *Lyndon B. Johnson and the American Dream*. New York: Signet, 1976.

Keegan, John. *The Second World War*. New York: Penguin, 1990.

Kracauer, Siegfried. *From Caligari to Hitler: A Psychological History of the German Film*, 3rd edition. Princeton, NJ: Princeton University Press, 1970.

Lang, Godfrey Berel. *Act and Idea in the Nazi Genocide*. Chicago: University of Chicago Press, 1990.

Langer, William L. *Political and Social Upheaval, 1832–1852*. New York: Harper and Row, 1969.

Lasch, Christopher. *The Culture of Narcissism*. New York: Warner Books, 1979.

Latrell, Marcus, and Patrick Robinson. *Lone Survivor: The Eyewitness Account of Operator Red Wings and the Lost Heroes of Seal Team 10*. New York: Back Bay Books, 2007.

Lawrence, D. H. *Studies in Classic American Literature*. New York: Doubleday, 1951.

Lepore, Jill. *The Secret History of Wonder Woman*. New York: Vintage, 2015.

Lewis, Michael. *The Big Short: Inside the Doomsday Machine*. New York: W. W. Norton, 2010.

Mailer, Norman. *Armies of the Night*. New York: Signet, 1968.

Mast, Gerald, and Marshall Cohen, editors. *Film Theory and Criticism*. New York: Oxford University Press, 1974.

Monaco, James. *American Film Now: The People, the Power, the Money, the Movies*. New York: Oxford University Press, 1979.

Morgenstern, Joseph, and Stefan Kanfer, editors. *Film 69/70: An Anthology by the National Society of Film Critics*. New York: Simon and Schuster, 1970.

Morris, Benny. *Righteous Victims: A History of the Zionist-Arab Conflict, 1881–2001*. New York: Vintage, 2001.

Navasky, Victor S. *Naming Names*. New York: Viking, 1980.

Northup, Solomon. *12 Years a Slave*. Auburn, NY: Derby and Miller, 1853.

Oakes, James. *The Radical and the Republican: Frederick Douglass, Abraham Lincoln, and the Triumph of Anti-Slavery Politics*. New York: W. W. Norton, 2007.

Obama, Barack. *Dreams from My Father: A Story of Race and Inheritance*. New York: Three Rivers Press, 1995.

O'Connor, John E., and Martin A. Jackson, editors. *American History/American Film: Interpreting the Hollywood Image*. New York: Frederick Unger, 1979.

O'Neill, William L. *Coming Apart: An Informal History of America in the 1960s*. New York: Quadrangle, 1971.

Pierson, John. *Spike, Mike, Slackers, and Dykes: A Guided Tour across a Decade of American Independent Cinema*. New York: Hyperion, 1997.

Poitier, Sidney. *This Life*. New York: Ballantine, 1980.

Power, Samantha. *A Problem from Hell: America and the Age of Genocide*. New York: Basic Books, 2002.

Pratley, Gerald. *The Cinema of John Frankenheimer*. Cranbury, NJ: A. S. Barnes, 1969.

Quart, Barbara Koenig. *Women Directors: The Emergence of a New Cinema*. New York: Praeger, 1988.

Remnick, David. *The Bridge: The Life and Rise of Barack Obama*. New York: Alfred A. Knopf, 2010.

Rich, Frank. *The Greatest Story Ever Told: The Decline and Fall of Truth in Bush's America*. New York: Penguin, 2006.

Ricks, Thomas E. *Fiasco: The American Military Adventure in Iraq*. New York: Penguin, 2006.

Robinson, Randall. *The Debt: What America Owes Blacks*. New York: Dutton, 2000.

Roffman, Peter, and Jim Purdy. *The Hollywood Social Problem Film*. Bloomington: Indiana University Press, 1981.

Rosenfelt, Deborah Silverton, editor. *Salt of the Earth*. Old Westbury, NY: Feminist Press, 1978.

Rosenstone, Robert A. *Romantic Revolutionary: A Biography of John Reed*. New York: Alfred A. Knopf, 1975.

Rovere, Richard. *Senator Joseph McCarthy*, revised edition. New York: Harper and Row, 1973.

Russo, Vito. *The Celluloid Closet: Homosexuality in the Movies*. New York: Harper and Row, 1987.

Ryan, Michael, and Douglas Kellner. *Camera Politica: The Politics and Ideology of Contemporary Hollywood Film*. Bloomington: Indiana University Press, 1988.

Sale, Kirkpatrick. *SDS*. New York: Vintage, 1974.

Sayre, Nora. *Running Time: Films of the Cold War*. New York: Dial Press, 1982.

Schatz, Thomas. *The Genius of the System: Hollywood Filmmaking in the Studio Era*. New York: Pantheon, 1988.

Schell, Jonathan. *The Time of Illusion*. New York: Alfred A. Knopf, 1976.

Siegel, Frederick F. *Troubled Journey: From Pearl Harbor to Ronald Reagan*. New York: Hill and Wang, 1984.

Sklar, Robert. *Movie-Made America: A Cultural History of American Movies*. New York: Vintage, 1975.

Sontag, Susan. *Against Interpretation*. New York: Dell, 1969.

Spoto, Donald. *Stanley Kramer: Filmmaker*. New York: G. P. Putnam's Sons, 1978.

Stephanopoulos, George. *All Too Human: A Political Education*. New York: Little, Brown, 1999.

Summers, Anthony. *Not in Your Lifetime: The Definitive Book on the JFK Assassination*. New York: McGraw-Hill, 1998.

Thernstrom, Stephan, and Abigail Thernstrom. *America in Black and White: One Nation Indivisible*. New York: Touchstone, 1997.

Thoreau, Henry David. *Walden: A Life in the Woods*. Boston: Ticknor and Fields, 1854.

Toobin, Jeffrey. *A Vast Conspiracy: The Real Story Behind the Sex Scandal That Nearly Brought Down a President*. New York: Touchstone, 1999.

Trilling, Diana. *We Must March, My Darlings*. New York: Harcourt Brace Jovanovich, 1977.

Unger, Irwin. *These United States: The Questions of Our Past, Vol. 2, Since 1865*. Englewood Cliffs, NJ: Prentice Hall, 1989.

Walker, Martin. *The President We Deserve: Bill Clinton: His Rise, Falls, and Comeback*. New York: Crown, 1996.

Warshow, Robert. *The Immediate Experience*. Garden City, NY: Anchor, 1964.

White, Edmund. *The Beautiful Room Is Empty*. New York: Ballantine, 1988.

Wilentz, Sean. *The Age of Reagan: A History, 1974–2008*. New York: HarperCollins, 2008.

Williams, Raymond. *Communications*, 3rd edition. London: Pelican, 1976.

Wills, Garry. *Reagan's America: With a New Chapter on the Legacy of the Reagan Era*. New York: Penguin, 1987.

Wilson, William Julius. *The Truly Disadvantaged: The Inner City, The Underclass, and Public Policy*. Chicago: University of Chicago Press, 1987.

Wood, Michael. *America in the Movies: or, "Santa Maria, It Had Slipped My Mind!"* New York: Basic Books, 1975.

Wood, Robin. *Arthur Penn*. New York: Praeger, 1969.

Wooten, James. *Dasher*. New York: Signet, 1978.

Wright, Lawrence. *The Looming Tower: Al-Qaeda and the Road to 9/11*. New York: Alfred A. Knopf, 2006.

Yeats, W.B. *The Collected Poems of W.B. Yeats*. New York: Macmillan, 1956.

INDEX